Volume I

THE MANAGING
OF ORGANIZATIONS

VOLUME I

The
MANAGING *of*
ORGANIZATIONS

THE ADMINISTRATIVE STRUGGLE

BERTRAM M. GROSS

The Free Press of Glencoe
Collier-Macmillan Limited, London

PREFACE

THE MOST PLEASANT of all debts are those stemming from the challenges, opportunities, and ideas that an author receives from others. He is expected merely to acknowledge—rather than repay—them.

First of all, I am indebted to the many organizations—public and private, local, national, foreign, and international—with which I have worked during the past quarter century. More concretely, I am indebted to the many people—friends, rivals, and neutrals—who served as my associates, superiors, and subordinates. Their mysterious ways have constantly confronted me with the challenge of trying to understand the behavior of people in organizations. My continuing experience with them has provided the opportunity of interrelating practice and theory with respect to the managing of organizations.

When, as a young civil servant, I first entered the United States Housing Authority under Franklin D. Roosevelt's New Deal, it was a puzzling experience. I soon found myself asking, "What's going on here? How do the people in charge get anything done?" A little later, during World War II, this line of questioning became more insistent. It became a central theme of the questions I asked when, as staff director of the U.S. Senate Military Affairs Subcommittee dealing with war mobilization and postwar planning, I interrogated civilian and military officials. It entered into my daily efforts to get things done in Congress—from the conduct of a hearing to the drafting of a bill and the enactment of a law. Yet the

10712

questions concerning *is* could rarely be separated from questions *should be:* "How can its performance be improved? How can it be better administered?" The Senators with whom I worked insisted upon answers to this kind of question with respect to the executive agencies of the federal government. Some of my answers were incorporated in the organizational and administrative provisions of legislation which I drafted or helped to draft: the Contract Settlement Act of 1943, the Surplus Property Act of 1944, the War Mobilization and Reconversion Act of 1944, and the Employment Act of 1946. Further, many members of Congress were asking themselves such questions about Congress itself. Inspired by Roland Young's *This Is Congress*, I submitted a concurrent resolution to Senator Maloney (Conn.) proposing a Joint Committee on the Reorganization of Congress. The more immediate results were a comprehensive study by the Maloney-Monroney Committee, with the able assistance of George Galloway, and the passage of the Legislative Reorganization Act of 1946. Somewhat later I dealt with the same subject —albeit with restrained skepticism concerning reforms in the formal structure of the Congress—in my *The Legislative Struggle: A Study in Social Combat.*

The two questions of "what really is?" and "what should be?" arose in still more challenging forms during my administrative struggles in the Fair Deal of President Harry S Truman. As executive secretary of the President's Council of Economic Advisers (the quasi-planning agency set up under the Employment Act), I faced the problems of large-scale administration from the vantage point of the White House. The two questions were inextricably intertwined with the effort to establish a new agency and to assist the President in the reconversion from war to peace, in the mobilization for the Korean War and in the economics of "cold war." At an "Intermediate" level I faced the same questions as Chairman of the National Capital Regional Planning Commission. At a "lower" level I faced them as county planning commissioner in Arlington, Virginia. These questions became still more disturbing when I left the comparative tranquility of the administrative struggle in my native country. For a brief period I served as a consultant to the United Nations on its economic reconstruction work with the government of South Korea. For a much longer period I was associated with the government of Israel as an adviser to the Prime Minister's Office, the Ministry of Finance, and the Department of Labor. In each of these situations my associates and I found ourselves sharply criticized by local officials who said, "Your ideas may be appropriate where you come from, but *conditions are different here.*" Some of us began to feel rather strongly that ideas of "is" and "should be" from the United States of America cannot be automatically applied to other countries, economies, and cultures.

I have also felt the "culture shock" associated with crossing the frontiers between public and other forms of administration. As business consultant, I have wrestled with balance sheets and accountants, equipment costs and engineers, marketing strategies and sales managers. As Research Director of a major political party during a presidential election year and a campaigner in various state and local elections, I have seen at first hand, and suffered from, the crudities of American party organization and administration.

Underlying this inordinate occupational mobility there has been an ever increasing concentration on trying to discover the *common elements* in the administration of different types of organizations. This concentration was intensified upon formally entering academic life. Here I was asked to help develop new programs of instruction in public and business administration. Here an endless stream of students, both youngsters and experienced managers, awaited words of wisdom from their teacher. At the same time I came to feel no less deeply the need for understanding the *differences* between administration in different types of organizations and parts of the world. Similarity is a far cry from identity. Great universal generalizations are delightful to concoct (and more useful than generally recognized), but their application to any particular organization calls for attention to many new variables. Could we not develop a method of thinking which can bring such variables into the picture and provide rational as well as institutional instruments for encompassing both the variety and the unity of administrative experience?

And then a strange thing occurred. At two turning points in my life I found myself fleeing administrative responsibility in order to think and write about administration. This happened when I left government service and entered full-time academic life. It happened again when I resigned from the onerous burdens of organizing a business administration department. It might be said that these change-overs merely expressed a desire to engage in thought instead of action. But directed thought and research are also forms of activity. A deeper explanation would indicate that my growing passion for the dissection of administration was tied up with a distaste for administration. It reflected a desire to escape organizational life and carve out a larger measure of independence from superiors and subordinates, policy papers and budgets, recruitment woes and conferences. In the classroom, the library, and my study, like those of my colleagues who were not sucked too far into the quicksands of academic administration, I breathed the free air which earlier Americans could most easily find by staking out a farm on virgin soil or opening up a small shop where chain stores had not yet appeared. But in a world dominated more and more by large-scale organizations such escape is not easily found. What is and can be the place of individuals in a society increasingly dominated by large-scale organizations? This question also I felt impelled to explore in my effort to develop a practice-oriented general theory of administration.

I am also indebted to those timid or fearful souls who have bluntly warned me that "it can't be done" or that, if done, it might be worthless. "Stolen waters are sweet," writes Solomon (Proverbs 9:17). The old lecher's implication is that people usually yearn for what they are told they cannot get. My own version, as illustrated in this book, is that one's fingers itch the most to reach for that which is held to be beyond one's grasp. Thus, I have always felt goaded into greater efforts by the discouragement voiced by administrative colleagues who shrink from theory or academic colleagues who pale at the thought of venturing across the sacred boundaries dividing the academic disciplines. A similar form of inspiration has been provided by those writers who, in purveying popular fallacies of administration, have belabored the obvious, embroidered the picayune and oversimplified the complex. By unwittingly convincing many others that it can't be done, they have thereby rendered the entire undertaking more challenging.

My debt is greater, naturally, to those who have unwittingly helped me do it. These include those many people, alive and dead, whom I have categorized in the text as the ancestors and pioneers of administrative thought, the developers of special administrative fields, and the contributors from other disciplines. Any full listing would include such strange bedfellows as Aristotle and Argyris, Bentley and Blau, Kautilya and Kohler, Machiavelli and Maslow, Plato and Perry, Simmel and Sayre, Weber and Wiener. A more uniform list would start with those who pioneered the "new beginnings" in modern administrative thought: Mary Follett, Elton Mayo, Fritz Roethlisberger, Chester Barnard, and Herbert Simon. It would then go on to include the scores of less-publicized pioneers who have made empirical studies of administrative and organizational behavior.

I am still more indebted to those who have knowingly helped me. Of these, perhaps the most active and encouraging have been a set of remarkable Deans of remarkable institutions. The last year of work on the manuscript was performed at Harvard on invitation from Stanley F. Teele, Dean of the Harvard Graduate School of Business Administration. Although the nominal purpose of my visit was to give the annual Leatherbee Lectures on management, it was Dean Teele's express purpose that I work on administrative theory at an institution where theory had been traditionally looked at skeptically. I did this while sitting in the very office that years earlier had been occupied by Professor Charles I. Gragg, who—together with Teele—had worked in Washington during World War II and had been my mentor on the high policy issues of wartime planning. Another full year on the project was provided by Harlan Cleveland, then Dean of the Maxwell School of Citizenship and Public Affairs, Syracuse University. Under Dean Cleveland's prodding I conducted an all-University interdisciplinary seminar on administrative theory, at which time many of the ideas in this book took shape in the heat of sustained debate. During the last two years of his extremely active life and almost up to the very time of his death in 1963, I received the benefit of detailed suggestions and often caustic comments from Paul H. Appleby, Harlan Cleveland's predecessor as Dean of the Maxwell School. From 1956, when I drafted the first outline of this book, to the very end I have sustained encouragement and uninhibited criticism from Stephen K. Bailey, now the present Dean of the Maxwell School. Many of the ideas in the book —more than I could readily identify—represent an effort to express the wisdom of Appleby, Bailey, and Cleveland. The spirit of the book, I hope, expresses something of the combined pragmatism and humanism which I tried to learn during the war from Stanley F. Teele and Charles I. Gragg.

A tremendous list of specific debts is owed to a long list of hardy souls who have given me the benefit of their reactions to specific chapters. Among political scientists this list includes Benjamin Akzin, Guthrie Birkhead, Paul David, Yehezkel Dror, David Easton, Milton Esman, Ralph Goldman, Emanuel Gutmann, James Heaphey, Robert T. Holt, Max Kampelman, Joseph LaPalombara, Val R. Lorwin, Arthur MacMahon, Roscoe Martin, the late Sigmund Neuman, Don Price, and William A. Robson. My most active commentator from the business administration field has been Edmund P. Learned; others consulted on specific chapters are Kenneth Andrews, E. Wight Bakke, Raymond A. Bauer, Charles Glover, Paul R. Lawrence, George F. F. Lombard, Charles Orth, and Renato Taguiri. Among economists I am indebted to Moses Abramovitz, Sidney Alexander, Joseph Berliner, Jesse Burkhead, Simon Kuznetz, and Wassily Leontief; among sociologists, to Albert K. Cohen, Alvin W. Gouldner, Paul Meadows, and Robin M. Williams, Jr.; among psychologists and psychiatrists to Floyd H. Allport, Charlotte Babcock, Kenneth M. Colby, Lawrence Kohlberg, James Mann, Abraham H. Maslow, Milton Rokeach, Yonci Schossberger, Thomas S. Szasz, and Eric Trist; among anthropologists to Charles Hughes, McKim Marriott, and Victor Turner; in jurisprudence to Layman E. Allen and John N. Hazard; among philosophers to Sidney Hook and Michael Polanyi; and among military men to Generals Moshe Dayan and Dan Tolkowski. In educational administration, which I have recently used as a testing ground for many of the ideas in this book, I have been particularly fortunate. In preparing my recent "The Administration of Public Schools,"* I have had the benefit of detailed comments from educational administrators—E. Gil Boyer, Jack Culbertson, Finis Engleman, Clayton D. Hutchins, Sam M. Lambert, Lorne Woolatt, and J. Wayne Wrightstone—as well as various professors and researchers—Eric F. Gardner, Daniel Griffiths, Thomas James, Richard C. Lonsdale, William P. McClure, Virgil Rogers, Roger C. Stewart, and Sidney G. Tickton. I have benefited from the editorial advice of Martin Kessler, who as editor at The Free Press has helped me to clarify many questions of substance as well as of form.

Still more intensive and continuous assistance has been received from those members of my immediate family who saw most of the following chapters in their various stages of slow evolution: Nora Gross, Larry Gross, and David Gross. In addition, Nora Gross and Larry Gross between them did most of the work in preparing the abstracts in the bibliographical appendix "Research Studies of Organizational Behavior," as well as the much larger set of abstracts from which this limited number has been selected. Larry Gross and Brian Stewart worked with me in developing full-color graphic illustrations to express many of the most abstract ideas in the book. This exercise in other media of communication has often helped clarify the ideas herein presented in words alone.

A number of organizations have helped by providing such indispensable inputs as salary, grants, time, space, and intellectual stimulation. If strongly pressed on the point, I might be willing to accept this as an illustration of irrationality in the administration of the Maxwell Graduate School at Syracuse, the Harvard Graduate School of Business Administration, the Center for Advanced Research in the Behavioral Sciences, and the Social Science Research Council. But upon entering the academic world I carefully limited my approach to *all* organizations by firmly resolving *not* to deal specifically—not even at the distance of the proverbial ten-foot pole—with the administration of educational and research organizations with which I myself have been connected. I can only note—in light of my own analysis of the evaluation process—the difficulty that any evaluator would have in drawing the line between their irrationality and mine.

I must also acknowledge my debt to the many students who have served as captive audience and guinea pigs. "From all my students," runs an old rabbinical saying, "I have learned." From my students with long

* Chapter 2 in Jesse Burkhead, *Public School Finance: Economics and Politics.* Syracuse: Syracuse University Press, 1964, p. 23-49.

administrative experience I have gained invaluable insights into the administrative life of many organizations. From my inexperienced students
I have learned how much easier it is to tell things that one does not know.
From them, too, I have gained insights into the belief-disbelief systems
that grow up in people's minds concerning organizational and administrative behavior. From both I have obtained criticism, suggestions, help, and
encouragement. Finally, in observing some of them in action, I have
strengthened my hope that with the dedication of both mature and youth-
ful energies to the ongoing progress of administrative thought, the time
may not be too far off when this book will have become hopelessly
out-of-date.

Bertram M. Gross

SYRACUSE, NEW YORK
June 1964

CONTENTS

Part IV. The People

OUTLINE OF VOLUME II

Part V. The Purposes

Part VI. The Future

A Bibliographical Report

VOLUME I

VOLUME II

Part V. THE PURPOSES

A BIBLIOGRAPHICAL REPORT

*T*o NORA, DAVID, LARRY, SAMUEL, THEODORE, AND
SHULAMIT

Chapter 1

AN ACTION-THEORY MARRIAGE

*T*HE STAGE is the entire planet. The plot and the settings are as diverse as life itself.

In New York, Moscow, Bombay, and Buenos Aires hundreds of men are engaged in getting thousands of others to run the machines that wrest materials from the earth, transport them near and far, and produce food, clothing, medicines, building materials, books, and other machines. In Berlin, Budapest, Shanghai, Cairo, and Jerusalem thousands more are employed in collecting taxes, and many more in spending money. In Accra, Manila, and La Paz critical minds find an Achilles' heel in ambitious plans for economic development: the shortage of managerial personnel. Steps are discussed to import or train the men who are needed.

In Paris, an automobile company pays out unexpected dividends to its stockholders. "The new management really knows its business," runs the comment on the Bourse. In London, the chief of a government corporation with a growing deficit announces his resignation. "He was a brilliant engineer," members of the Board of Directors tell each other, "but a wretched administrator." In Little Rock, Novosobirsk, and Barcelona the field representatives of national organizations exchange the standard jokes on "central office idiots." In even more standardized fashion they quietly interpret or sabotage the latest directives from headquarters. In thousands of places throughout the world foremen argue with workers' committees. Unit chiefs debate with workers on procedures

1

and work methods. Advisers complain that their proposals for reorganization are ignored.

In scores of secret offices anonymous administrators work busily in organizing the super-secret work of the scientists and technicians who conduct the calculations and experiments which will enable a still larger group of people to prepare and perhaps deliver the latest missiles, gases, rays and whatnots that may yet destroy the stage itself.

All these activities differ from each other in innumerable ways. Many of them compete or even directly conflict with each other. Many are so far apart in objectives, methods and language that they might as well take place in different worlds. Yet they have two things in common: all involve people in organized groups or institutions and all involve the administration or management of organizations.[1]

The participants in these activities include presidents of corporations, governments, universities, and trade unions; generals, bishops, and kings; chairmen of government boards, councils, and executive committees; and the heads of ministries, agencies, banks, cooperatives, and cartels. Less conspicuous but of no less significance are the thousands upon thousands of officials who grease the wheels and control many parts of the administrative mechanism. Whether they will it or not, doctors, engineers lawyers, economists, statisticians, and physicists are drawn into the whirl of administrative activity. This even happens to many of the growing number of experts in administration itself. Most people, in fact, spend a large part of their waking hours as participants in the activities of administered organizations. For this aspect of human life has become increasingly important with the onward sweep throughout the world of an administrative (also referred to as "organizational," "managerial" or "bureaucratic") revolution which is enlarging the role of large and complex organizations in all societies.

The governance of organizations is an ancient human skill. No matter what our criteria, we find that many practitioners have raised it from a skill to an art. We find that others have gone still further and attained the level of administrative wisdom. Some have even provided examples that administration "is not only the faculty upon which social stability rests but it is possibly the highest faculty of the human mind" (Adams, 1913, p. 206.*

---

1. The terms *administration* and *management* are here used as synonyms. The reasons for this usage—together with a full consideration of the terms *organization* and *institution*—are given in "The Management of Organizations" (Chapt. 10).

* The "General Bibliography" contains the full citation for all documents referred to in the text. As explained on page 25, italicized references refer to books or articles covered by the bibliographical report in Volume II, "Research Studies in Organizational Behavior."

At the same time we see—perhaps more than in any other field—a persistent unevenness. In one and the same person we find skill associated with clumsiness, wisdom with shallowness. We see vast numbers of administrators who never rise above—or even up to—a level of deadly mediocrity. Above all, we find no simple relation between administrative skill and the purposes for which it is used. We see well-meaning organizations abominably administered and well-administered organizations spewing forth abominations. Within the same organization we see men and women rising higher than the angels and falling lower than the beasts.

If we look a little more closely, we can also see a new and immature area of human knowledge. We see a widening trend in many societies toward the ever more serious study of organizations and their administration. This trend brings together—with a certain degree of friction—experts from many disciplines. With still more friction it brings together the Men of Action and the Men of Academia. This book is part of that trend.

One of the purposes in writing this book has been to summarize and consolidate the progress that has been made in trying to understand the administration of organizations. From the viewpoint of man's previous history, this progress is tremendous. But from the viewpoint of what remains to be learned, we have barely started. Another purpose of the book, therefore, is to present a set of ideas that may stimulate others to move forward on the long road of creative action, theory, and research.

The major purpose of this introductory chapter is to provide a general perspective on the book and its subject matter. This can best be done by

- indicating the vital nature of the questions asked by those seeking to understand more about the administration of organizations;
- pointing out the seriousness of the obstacles to such understanding;
- identifying the limited aids to understanding that can be provided by theory and research;
- explaining the strategy I have used in presenting such aids to understanding; and
- discussing the methods I have used in finding and organizing my materials.

A. *The Vital Questions*

THERE ARE few questions more perplexing probably than those concerning the administration of organizations.

These questions arise not only in the minds of private and public administrators. They are asked even more frequently by the larger number of people subordinate to administrators or even inconvenienced by them. They are asked by aspirants to administrative posts. They are asked by all those who attempt to study and understand the behavior of people in organizations.

This does not mean that such questions are clearly identified. They may be asked by people with no concept of either an organization or its administration. They are asked in a variety of colloquial, technical, and academic terms that mask their relevance to the administration of organizations. Even when clearly stated, they are usually intertwined with nonadministrative questions.

This gives rise to a strange "nothing-everything" phenomenon. At times there seem to be no truly important questions concerning administration; the subject dwindles to nothing. At other times all-important questions relate to administration; the subject expands to include everything.

There is good reason for both viewpoints. Administration is merely an aspect of organizational activity. It is nothing by itself; it must always be seen with specific reference to just what it is that an organization is doing. Yet it is an essential—or at least unavoidable—aspect of all organizational activity and therefore of human society. Without it man's organizations would fall apart, his larger purposes would be will-of-the-wisps, his greatest hopes would be empty dreams.

1. WHAT WAS, IS, AND MIGHT BE?

The newcomer in any organization is apt to find himself faced with a big, booming, buzzing confusion. Even after he learns his own role, he may well ask, "What's going on here? How do things really work? How does anything ever get done?"

As he acquires experience, he learns partial answers to these questions in the form of what Michael Polanyi calls "tacit knowledge" (1958, p. 49 –65).[2] He knows how things get done in his immediate environment and uses this knowledge in doing things himself and getting other people to do things with him or for him. But an interest in better performance, intellectual curiosity, or both may impel him to ask more difficult questions. He seeks an understanding of the past to throw light upon the present. By looking at past and present, he tries to answer such questions as "What might happen in the future if I should do such-and-such?"

2. Polanyi's path-breaking *Personal Knowledge* on the philosophy of science is one of the few such books written as a long-term serious venture by a scientist of vast experience. To a considerable extent it represents the transformation of tacit knowledge gained by the author into systematically recorded knowledge.

If he rises to positions of higher responsibility in an organization, these questions concerning what has been, is, and might be are applied to a wider range of experience. They are asked concerning many different kinds of units at different hierarchic levels within an organization. They relate to a variety of external organizations: government agencies, business enterprises, associations, federations, and many others. They may even deal with organizations in other countries and very different cultures.

Experienced administrators develop amazing skills in answering these questions quickly. They learn how to ask questions, appraise the relevance of information, make judgments, and adjust judgments to changing circumstances. For this purpose they use rough-and-ready concepts, unstated premises, rules of thumb, and liberal doses of intuition.

But the more questions they may handle in this fashion, the more remain to be answered. Knowledge in the sense of personal acquaintance with (as expressed in the French *connâitre*) is quite different from knowledge in the sense of recorded and communicable facts and generalizations (as expressed more closely in the French *savoir*).[3] Although the tacit component of knowledge can never be fully expressed in words and other symbols, it can never become highly developed unless a significant part of it is so expressed. Unless this is done with some degree of precision and consistency, communication with others is haphazard and fragmentary. And organizational life constantly demands communication on such matters, particularly among and from administrators.

Thus even the most rough-and-ready administrators often become theorists despite themselves. They grab some simple set of principles, fully or partially expressed, and hang on for dear life. These crude theories help them grope their way through the vast jungle of information and misinformation about the past and the present. They help them make useful predictions about the future. And somehow or other things do get done.

But the *was, is,* and *might be* questions are so persistent and so challenging that many administrators feel the need for something more substantial. The more simple-minded try to use social science the way a drunk uses a lamp post—for support, not illumination (*Leighton,* p. 128). Or else they seek formulae that will produce prefabricated answers. Those with a little background in some substantive field of science or technology often seek the same degree of certainty in administrative thought. When they cannot find it, they complain that "the professors don't know what's

3. This discussion is based not only upon Polanyi's *Personal Knowledge,* but also upon the ideas developed in James, *The Principles of Psychology,* Vol. I, p. 221; Mayo, *The Social Problems of an Industrial Civilization,* p. 15-19; and Miller, Galenter, and Pribram, *Plans and the Structure of Behavior,* p. 81-93.

going on," "the textbooks are impractical," or "that may be all right in theory, but not in practice." Through this lament the men of action do more than proclaim their own superiority. They also suggest that they would be happier if professors "knew the score," textbooks provided more useful knowledge, and theory came into closer contact with reality.

The search for better answers is dramatically underscored by the rising popularity of "management training" and "executive development." These activities are based on the idea that responsible managers, although possibly "born administrators" and already clothed in the trappings of authority, may still have something to learn about management. Although this idea is always more readily accepted *vis-à-vis* one's subordinates, the important development of the last decade is that more and more frequently it is the King himself who declares "The King has no clothes."

The same uneasiness haunts the halls of academia. In universities and colleges throughout the world, teachers and students have the feeling that the ideas taught have too little relation to the questions of *was, is,* and *might be* in the wide world of organizational action. The same body of administrative thought damned by practical men as too theoretical and academic is looked down on by academic leaders as too practical. Many great institutions of splendid achievement disdain to enter a field which they regard as vocational instead of theoretical or scientific.

In greater part, perhaps, this feeling of uneasiness stems from self-criticism. The latecomers are dissatisfied with the patterns that they may have slavishly copied from others. The pioneers and the patternmakers are themselves seriously pondering new approaches—more practical and more theoretical—to *was, is,* and *might be* questions.

This sense of dissatisfaction reaches its peak when the teachers decide that they have little to teach and that their only contribution is to help students talk to each other about problems or case studies. The use of case studies and nondirected discussion springs to some extent from well-founded theory on the nature of the learning process. It also represents a jaundiced estimate of the present level of organized knowledge concerning administration. It expresses righteous refusal to bluff students by presenting them with empty principles or by drilling them in techniques of limited managerial use.

Despite these dissatisfactions, a growing number of serious thinkers from better-established disciplines have entered the management field. At first it was mainly political scientists, lawyers, and sociologists. Then came the psychologists, psychiatrists, anthropologists, and historians. More recently, the mathematicians and the economists have joined the undertaking. The result has been an unbelievable outpouring of books and articles, backed up by a growing body of research relating to organizations and their administration. The volume of relevant documents is already so great that anyone who tried to keep up with current writing on the subject would be drowned in a flood of paper.

2. WHAT SHOULD HAVE BEEN AND SHOULD BE?

Far more pressing than the *was, is,* and *might be* questions are those phrased in terms of *should have been* and *should be.*

All men and women sit in judgment of the activities of organizations and their administrators. Finding fault is a popular sport—particularly when directed at superiors or rivals. It is a form of self-expression, of personal relief from tension, and also a form of influence. Giving credit, albeit somewhat less popular, serves the same functions. In either case the evaluators may be more interested in what *should have been* than in what *was.*

Many men and women—administrators above all—are exceedingly active in trying to shape the future. They ask not only *what might be* but *what should be?*

In their simplest form these questions relate to the operations of a single unit of a single organization. What should its goals be? What should be done to help it achieve these goals more effectively?

In more complex form these questions relate to aggregations of organizations. How should scientific research, industry, transportation, trade, or banking be organized and administered? What is the best structure for agriculture—particularly in a country where there is a vigorous demand for land redistribution? How should trade unions be organized and collective bargaining handled? How should trade associations and national federations be organized? How should cooperatives be managed? How should the various agencies of government be related to one another and administered? What should be done, if anything, to strengthen various international organizations?

The *should* questions become still more perplexing when we turn from these huge aggregations and focus upon the individual in the era of the administrative revolution. What should a person—be he among the administrators or the administered—expect from organizational activity? What should be done, if anything, to help people escape the tyranny of organizations without becoming anonymous specks in a purposeless cloud of dust?

These *should be* questions are so overwhelmingly important that people are often impelled to seek answers in bland abstraction from the more mundane consideration of what *has been, is,* and *might be.* Thus much of administrative thought has been prescriptive and normative before attempting to be descriptive and analytical. This has been most obvious in the sphere of government organizations, where discussions of public administration often center around alternative approaches to philosophy and ethics. It is less obvious in the sphere of business administration. But even here we find a central role (although less frequently expressed) for various conceptions of the good life and the good society. The most practical-minded businessman may be a moralist or philosopher despite himself. He may be so passionately dedicated to a few *should be* conceptions that he has lost all sense of orientation to what really *has been, is,* or *might be.*

On the other hand, there are those who seek wherever possible to transform questions of desirability into questions of fact and probability. Consider the statement that "the administrator of this organization should take Action A instead of Action B." An analysis of facts relating to similar circumstances can lead to a restatement as follows: "If under such-and-such circumstances the administrator takes Action A instead of B, there is a much greater likelihood that his organization will achieve goal C." But what about C? Why should C be a goal? The reply: "If C, then a greater likelihood of achieving goal D."

So far so good. But the transformation cannot be extended *ad infinitum.* Somewhere between D and Z will come a point where an "ultimate value" may be found.

At this point some administrative theorists try to simplify their intellectual problems by drawing a sharp dividing line. "Here," they proclaim, "is where administrative thought stops and ethics begins. Administrative thought must limit itself solely to means. It cannot deal with ends."

This self-denying ordinance has some practical value for theorists. It allows them to sweep under the carpet some of the most puzzling of all organizational and administrative questions. It allows them to concentrate upon the more definitive handling of limited questions. It affords them the luxury of leaving unclear and unstated the specific aims toward which they themselves are motivated.

It also restricts the value of administrative theory to practical men. It introduces the fatally unrealistic conception of a clear and unmistakable separation between means and ends. It is usually based upon the still more unreal myth of some single ultimate end, as contrasted with the real world in which administrators are constantly making adjustments between a variety of highly desired ends.

Hence those who feel the need for a more realistic and more scientific orientation toward the vital questions of *was, is,* and *might be* find themselves increasingly obligated to face up to the still deeper questions of *should have been* and *should be.*

B. *The Obstacles to Understanding*

THERE IS NOTHING EASY about any effort to understand the world or any part of it. It is difficult even to ask the right questions. Final answers are impossible.

In the natural sciences the obstacles to understanding are difficult enough. As scientists and philosophers have repeatedly pointed out, the very act of observing has itself an effect on what is being observed. Although the observer may seek certainty, he must often be satisfied with probability. He is sure to find certainty and precision only when he puts them there in the first place through the assumptions he uses. These assumptions, in turn, are continually being replaced by new ones more useful in explaining larger arrays of phenomena. The new explanations invariably give rise to previously undreamed-of questions. The paradox of scientific progress is that it always opens up new areas of ignorance and greater challenges to future discovery.

The social scientist faces all these difficulties and many more. First of all, the people he observes observe him and react to him. The social scientist must always assume that the people he observes are in some way trying to influence the observational process. This may even take the form of deliberate efforts to deceive or exploit the observer. Second, the observer's values and biases can rarely, if ever, be disentangled from the recorded observations. At the very least the objects of observation are sensitive to—and influenced by—the observer's values and acts. Third, careful measurement is far more difficult in the social than in the physical sciences—and even where feasible, it may often be far less relevant. Nor are controlled experiments possible on any significant scale. The laboratory of the social scientist is society itself. What happens there is usually far beyond his puny power to control. Finally, the social scientist deals with more complex systems. The number of variables and of interrelationships between them is far greater than the relatively simple aspects of the world which physical scientists try to understand.

Yet when we try to understand the administration of organizations, we face still greater obstacles. Here we are confronted with higher degrees of complexity, deeply-rooted myths and taboos that thwart understanding, and an inevitable insularity on the part of all observers.

1. COMPLEXITY

In most of the social sciences theorists and researchers usually cope with complexity by acts of self-limitation. Political scientists tend to look at governments, economists at economies, psychologists at individuals, sociologists and anthropologists groups and societies. When their paths cross, the division of intellectual labor is preserved by using different concepts. In either case the object of study is simplified by excluding from the universe of discourse or attention all except certain aspects of human behavior and certain conceptual tools for its analysis.

The urge for deeper understanding, however, often leads social scientists to abjure these oversimplifications and more boldly to face human behavior in all its baffling complexity. In certain fields this seems to be required by the very nature of the subject matter. Historians are expected somehow or other to deal with the seamless web of the past, and the past includes every conceivable type of phenomena. The "policy scientists" —a term which refers to a small minority of pathfinders—orient themselves toward significant problems of the future. For this purpose they too must try to exploit all conceivable conceptual tools.

Administration is another of these fields. But here we cannot simplify matters by concentrating on the past or on the future. We must concern ourselves with both. We must behave like historian-policy scientists. In so doing we must look at the behavior of organizations and their administrators from many viewpoints, since we are dealing with life as a whole rather than an artificial or imaginary slice of life. Almost everything we look at is something that can be called a government or an economy (if only in a microscopic sense) and is composed of individuals and groups within a certain culture. We must therefore go very far in exploiting the aids to understanding that have been developed by political scientists, economists, psychologists, sociologists, anthropologists, and others.

In the effort to understand administration anyone can make his task simpler by concentrating on certain types of organizations or on certain aspects of administration. In fact, such concentration of effort is essential to the subdivision of intellectual labor. In the study of administration, as in anything else, if everyone tried to do everything, nothing would ever get done. But the deeper one goes at any one point, the more he will find an extremely large number of complex and interrelating variables. Not for him the luxury of *ceteris paribus* assumptions that allow him to "freeze" all variables except the one he is watching. Every situation is unique and to grapple with it he must help identify the *ceteris* rather than blithely ignore them. Administrative analysis, above all, is action-oriented. If his theoretical model is not close to reality he cannot, in good conscience, ignore the problem of building the bridges that connect it with reality.

The closer he gets to reality, however, the more it changes. Organizations change, people change, and circumstances change. Purposes change and methods change. There are even unanticipated changes in the rate of change. Under these circumstances one of the few things that is always certain is an important element of uncertainty. The better the resolution of any problem the more certain that it will give rise to new problems.

2. MYTHS AND TABOOS

It has become common practice to explode the fallacies, the folklore, or the proverbs which many people accept as a substitute for knowledge about administration. But as any logician can demonstrate, fallacies are ordinary obstacles to understanding. And as any expert can testify, they are found in every field of human thought.

Man's efforts to think rationally about administration, however, are impeded not only by fallacies but also by deeply-rooted myths and taboos. These cannot be readily dispelled by logic or demonstration.

One of the reasons for this is that myths and taboos are often born in the womb of organizational necessity. They are sired by administrators who see in them a way of enhancing their power, resolving or living with internal conflicts, or adjusting to a difficult environment.

Some of these myths serve as filters through which many of us look at either single organizations or social organization in its broader aspects. Among these are the myths of ultimate authority and central omnipotence; these receive major attention in Chapter 3. Others are more narrow in focus—such as the myths of number magic and of impersonality and rationality in large-scale organizations.

The taboos serve as barriers to keep people from looking at certain things at all. Taboos on certain words and their referents often make it difficult to deal openly with such subjects as the use of power, pressure, propaganda, manipulation, or double bookkeeping—particularly by or- ganizations and administrators enjoying high status in society. Other taboos surround any effort to deal scientifically with the referents of such "hurrah" words as democracy, freedom, justice, enterprise, and responsibility and such "boo" words as dictatorship, control, bureaucracy, frustration, and deviation. Above all, we all tend to surround with a fence of taboos anything we really hold dear—whether it be a form of social organization to which we feel ideologically committed, a way of organiza- tion life to which we are accustomed, or our own self-image of how we would act, or have acted, as administrators.

A person's status as a scientist does not automatically free him from the grip of myth and taboo. What he can readily see if he looks at another society (particularly a primitive one) he may never be able to detect in his own environment. Nor does organizational and administrative experience do the trick. It may merely exchange one set of intellectual obstacles for another. Many experienced administrators will themselves become the most blinded by the myths and taboos that they have helped to propagate. The wiser administrators usually know better. But here, unfortunately, there is too much truth in the old adage that "those who know don't tell."

3. INSULARITY

Additional obstacles are provided by insularity in many forms.

One form of insularity is the culture-bound nature of most serious studies in the field. It is only natural for social scientists to focus their attention upon the phenomena near at hand in their own society. It is still more natural for the values and customs of their own society to affect their perception of other societies. Thus theorists and experts from the U.S.A. and Western Europe—where systematic administrative thought has thus far developed most intensively—have often blithely assumed the immediate relevance of their knowledge to countries of Asia, Africa, and Latin America. With the emergence of large-scale technical assistance programs in public and business administration, however, the naïveté of expecting saltwater fish to understand all the problems of freshwater fish has been revealed. The experts of the U.S.A. and Western Europe have begun to see that just as fish who have spent all their life in a big ocean cannot be good judges of the salinity of water, they themselves still have a long way to go in understanding their own environment.

A second form of insularity is the narrow and constricting environment in which most administrators learn about administration. The average administrator spends most of his life on a handful of islands on a vast, mysterious ocean. Even those who are most capable of learning from experience (and experience itself does not automatically produce this capability) are usually limited by a relatively small variety of experiences. This is particularly true of administrators who stay in one organization for most of their adult lives, for businessmen in general and for small businessmen in particular. It may be less true of the managers of large business enterprises and public administrators who deal with varied segments of their society. Even in these cases intensive experience with one sector may be counter-balanced by comparative ignorance of another sector. Both tacit and organized knowledge of administration tends to be parochial.

A third form is the intellectual insularity of social scientists. Many of those who presume to study administration cut themselves off from the knowledge that can be obtained only through some sort of personal experience. They study the deep waters of organizational and administrative life by looking at them from afar. They then "go into the field," fill out questionnaires, run cards through calculating machines and come out with the tentative and cautiously phrased hypothesis that water may be wet. . . .

Moreover, the growing specialization of scientific activity produces a special kind of insularity. C. P. Snow barely touched on this in his superficially stated lament that "the intellectual life of the whole of western society is increasingly being split into two polar groups . . . literary intellectuals at one pole—at the other scientists . . ." (1959, p. 4). He completely ignored the growing gap which separates each field and subfield of science from all the others.

To understand the predicament of social scientists we may regard the universe of human behavior as a vast jigsaw puzzle composed of thousands of multicolored pieces.[4] Because the puzzle is so large, some subdivision of labor is needed among those who try to piece it together. So the labor is divided—with some concentrating on pieces of a certain size, some on pieces of certain colors. The system works when the pieces are put together in sight of all the others and people can exchange information on the pieces they hold and others hold. Only in this way can one person capitalize on the progress of others or know what next steps are required.

But this does not happen so frequently or so easily. The task of examining single pieces is so difficult that not many have time to look at what is being done by those working on different sizes, shapes, or colors. Nor is this easy to do. The specialized tasks call for specialized terminologies. Thus each group invents new terms of its own or uses old words in new ways. They find themselves using different words to talk about the same things and the same words to talk about different things. The edifice in which they work, therefore, becomes more and more like the tower of Babel. The flood of published documents in all fields leads many people to give up the effort to keep up with anything outside of their own subspecialities.

4. I am indebted for this metaphor to Michael Polanyi's *Logic of Liberty*, p. 35. However, Polanyi assumes—as I cannot assume—a full flow of information. On the basis of this assumption he concludes that "a series of independent initiatives are organized to a joint achievement by mutually adjusting themselves at every successive stage to the situation created by all the others who are acting likewise."

c. *Aids to Understanding*

DESPITE THE OBSTACLES described above, administrative thought can already aid in the handling of the vital questions of *was, is,* and *might be,* and of *should have been* and *should be.*

This aid can appear in the form of:

> ⟊ a language of administration,
> ⟊ generalizations at various levels, and
> ⟊ an identification of major values.

In this book I have tried to provide each of these aids to understanding. I have done this by synthesizing major ideas developed by others and adding certain ideas of my own. The aim is not to present final answers but to stimulate closer cooperation on these matters between men of action and social scientists and among social scientists themselves. Only thus can a more mature body of administrative knowledge come into being.

But even the maturation of administrative knowledge would not yield automatic answers to the extremely complex questions that will always plague private and public organizations. Theory and research can supply nothing more than intellectual tools. These tools can never take the place of the abilities and values of those who may want to use them or of the power that such users can organize to transform human purposes into living reality.

1. A LANGUAGE OF ADMINISTRATION

The need for a rich and vigorously growing language of administration is by no means limited to theorists and researchers. It is a practical problem facing all administrators.

Every organization has its own language of administrative action. In larger and older organizations these languages become part of the spirit of the place and perform a morale-sustaining function. They are picked up slowly by newly initiated insiders and are never fully understood by outsiders. In smaller and younger organizations they tend to reflect the idiosyncrasies and folklore of an economic sector, a geographic area, or an entire culture.

When people from different organizations get together to discuss common problems, communication between them is impossible unless they have a common language adequate to deal with the complexities of the problems they face. A similar impasse often occurs among the administrators of federations and international "peak associations." It also occurs within single organizations wherever the common language of administration is not sufficiently sophisticated or widely enough shared to span the widely divergent approaches of people from highly specialized units within the organization.

But it would be a mistake to think of language as only a means of communication, as a means of expressing ideas already well formulated. Language is much closer to the very substance of idea. Its more mature development always means that we have more to communicate. Thus the maturation of the language of administration will mean not only that administrators will be better able to share their experiences, but that they will be able to experience administrative action more richly, and organize their experience more consciously, and benefit more deeply from the lessons that can be provided in the school of experience. For theorists and researchers, on the other hand, the maturing language of administration will provide the basic concepts without which facts cannot be classified and generalizations cannot be shaped.

In moving toward a general language of organization and administration I have tried to use a vocabulary that is "both small enough and simple enough to be learned, precise enough to communicate, and large enough so that all of the important ideas that are contending can be comfortably and easily described" (Kahn, p. 5). In so doing I present many terms and concepts that until now have been regarded as the special property of business, military, or public administration or of one or another discipline or profession. The reader will thus find liberal use of such terms as aspiration level, bureaucracy, clientele, goods and services, input, output, polyarchy, power, pressure, products (both end and intermediate), product mix, propaganda, and rule. This will be disconcerting to those who regard some of these terms—such as bureaucracy, double bookkeeping, power, and pressure as "nasty words" with derogatory connotations. I have therefore used specific definitions in the effort to convert their nastiness to neutrality.

My usage may also prove initially confusing to some specialists who will find that my use of "their" term differs from their own use. Thus "end product" as herein used is not the same as "end product" in national economic accounting. Here, as in other cases, I have had to adapt technical terms to the special requirements of organization theory. My approach is to specify the usage I am employing, often after a full identification of alternative usages.

This approach is carried furthest in my presentation of a language of organizational purpose, which in my judgment must become the most important element in a general language of organization and administration. Here I provide an arbitrary division of labor between the words purpose, objective, goal, target, and norm, and have related these terms to needs, interests, drives, and motives. I give concentrated attention to the formulation of concepts relevant to the key categories of organizational purpose: the satisfaction of human interests, the production of goods and services, efficiency in the use of scarce resources, investment in organizational viability, resource mobilization, observance of codes, and technical and administrative rationality. Through the incorporation of accepted technical terms and the largest possible reliance on ordinary language I have been able to get along with no neologisms other than "commergence" for belonging or togetherness without pejorative connotations (Chapt. 14), "purpose surrogate" for an indirect measure of purposes, and "teletics" for the study of human purposes (both in Chapt. 19).

In presenting a presumably consistent set of terms, I am not suggesting that they are the "right" ones. To do so would be to indulge in word magic. Anyone has the right to use words, and other symbols, as he chooses. For purposes of sustained communication his symbols, apart from consistency in use, need only be useful and clear.

Utility, however, is a relative matter. "All definitions are essentially *ad hoc*. They are relevant to some purpose or situation, and consequently are applicable only over a restricted field or universe of discourse" (Ogden and Richards, 1946, p. 111). Here the universe of discourse is organization and administration. I am not suggesting that the terms I use here can be automatically transferred, without adaptation, to other spheres. Moreover, even with *ad hoc* definitions, there can be no "one best way." A frozen language is a dead language. The best test of the language herein offered will not be found in the degree of adoption but in its contribution to the continuing process of linguistic adaptation and growth in this field.

Clarity also is relative. Words merely "symbolize people's thoughts (or references) about things rather than things (or referents) directly" (*op. cit.*, p. 11).[5] The thoughts themselves, with their overtones of feeling and attitude, can probably never be fully expressed in any single set of terms. We grope for words to tell what we know, as Polanyi has pointed out, and our words hang together by these roots. "The true artists of speech remain always conscious of the metaphorical character of language. They go on correcting and supplementing one metaphor by

5. Here Ogden and Richards add: "But just as we say that the gardener mows the lawn when we know that is the lawn-mower which actually does the cutting, so, though we know that the direct relation of symbols is with thought, we also say that symbols record events and communicate facts. . . ."

another, allowing their words to contradict each other and attending only to the unity and certainty of their thought" (Polanyi, 1958, p. 102). Even if we eliminate metaphors, we can often express ourselves properly only by "successive definition"—by restating the same thought a number of times in different terms. Whenever someone goes too far in using identical and presumably consistent terms, there is reason to suspect that behind the words may lie deeply hidden ambiguities or, as in the case of the student who has learned his lesson by rote, an utter absence of thought.

2. GENERALIZATIONS AT VARIOUS LEVELS

Generalizations serve two purposes. In the jargon of medical doctors these may be termed "diagnosis" and "therapy." In military circles the same ideas are expressed by "evaluation of the situation" and "formulation of strategy and tactics."

In medical practice a good diagnosis is much more than merely providing a name for something that ails a patient. It applies to the patient's ailment some generalizations concerning how he got that way and what is likely to happen. Similarly administrative theory can do more than merely provide names. Its generalizations can help administrators and researchers in identifying the many aspects of problems and situations. It can help in the interpretation of situations by suggesting possible relations between various events. It can help in preparing an evaluation of what might happen in the future, if no special steps are taken.

Generalizations are equally valuable in developing the strategy and tactics of therapeutic action. They can contribute to an administrator's awareness of various ways of doing things, thereby broadening his perspective and freeing him from the chains of habit and routine. They can help in predicting the possible consequences of such alternatives, thereby aiding in the difficult process of choosing between them. They can be particularly helpful in the imaginative creation of new and previously unsuspected alternatives.

Whether generalizations are used for diagnosis or therapy, they also serve some extremely useful psychological functions. They provide the administrator and/or researcher with the indispensable "selector mechanisms" without which they are apt to be drowned in a flood of irrelevant or misleading information. By making him more aware of the universal aspects of even his most unique problems, they can free him from the overpowering onus of guilt which is apt to develop from the very natural feeling that he alone is in such a terrible predicament. They can provide a rational justification for action that he intuitively knows is correct but could not otherwise defend in communicable terms.

Generalizations, of course, can be made at many levels. At the lowest, we find singular generalizations. In the terms used by David Easton, these are "statements of observed uniformities between two isolated and easily identified variables." In the language of Robert Merton, these are "minor working hypotheses evolved . . . during the day-by-day routines of research."

At a somewhat higher level stands synthetic or narrow-gauge theory. For Easton, this is "a set of interrelated propositions that are designed to synthesize the data in an organized body of singular generalizations." This is similar to Merton's "theories of the middle range . . . special theories applicable to limited ranges of data."

A still higher level of generalization is provided by broad-gauge or systematic theory. For Easton this is "the conceptual framework within which a whole discipline is cast . . . those theories and assumptions which an investigator uses in undertaking an analysis within a given field." This is very close to what Merton refers to as a "master conceptual scheme" for deriving or consolidating all subsidiary theories.

These distinctions are often made in order to indicate that level of abstraction which, in the judgment of the author, needs major emphasis. Thus Easton attacks "hyperfactualism" and calls for more broad-gauge, systematic theory. Merton favors middle-range theory. By his sharp attacks on abstracted empiricism and grand theory, C. Wright Mills stakes out his own position along with Merton as a "middle of the roader."[6] A good case can indeed be made for the middle of the road. Theorists can easily go to the one extreme of getting lost in an unconnected mass of minor generalizations or the other extreme of vanishing in the cosmic distances of intellectual space.

In this book I have run up and down the ladder of abstraction. Some of the material in the following chapters consists of singular generalizations, some of synthetic theory, and some of broad-gauge theory. The greatest emphasis, perhaps, is upon broad-gauge theory. I would not want, however, to use Easton's term of systematic theory. While I have concentrated upon developing a broad conceptual framework I have deliberately tried not to oversystematize it. At this stage in the development of a subject there is greater merit in "dynamic openness" than in "premature closure" (Kaplan, p. 68-71).

The generalizations I have used may also be ranked in terms of the level of confidence expressed in them. This is the "fiduciary element of

6. The references referred to in the above paragraphs can be found in Easton, *The Political System*, p. 51-63; Merton, *Social Theory and Social Structure*, Chapt. 2, "The Bearing of Sociological Theory in Empirical Research"; and Mills, *The Sociological Imagination*, Chapts. 2 and 3.

an affirmation," which, according to Polanyi (1958, p. 29), enters openly or covertly into all assertions. At the lower levels of confidence such a generalization is merely an hypothesis. At the other extreme there are those generalizations which are regarded as necessary starting points and can therefore be called "axioms." In between there is a host of "principles," some analytic and descriptive, some prescriptive. In either case their truth can be verified by checking observable phenomena. Or else their validity can be demonstrated by deductions from axioms and empirically-supported principles.

3. A SUBSTANTIVE HANDLING OF VALUES

If social scientists were able to limit themselves to statements of fact, there might be little need for them to deal with values. Similarly, there would be little chance of dealing with values separately if it were completely impossible to formulate value-free statements or conclusions. The worlds of fact and value would be so indissolubly fused that any attempt to separate them would be wasted effort.

As Ernest Nagel (1961, p. 485-502) has cogently argued, neither of these extreme positions is a useful guide in the social sciences. On the one hand, social scientists must inevitably deal with many value judgments that cannot be reduced to purely factual or probabilistic terms. On the other hand, there are many statements about means-ends relations that (despite the values that might be placed on some means) may be value-free.

A major role of theory in the social sciences, therefore, is to help in the difficult process of distinguishing between the two kinds of statements. The effort to do this is difficult and drawn-out. "For the most part," as Nagel says, "we are unaware of many assumptions that enter into our analyses and actions, so that despite resolute efforts to make our preconceptions explicit some decisive ones may not even occur to us. But in any event, the difficulties generated for scientific inquiry by unconscious bias and tacit value orientations are rarely overcome by devout resolutions to eliminate bias. They are usually overcome, often only gradually, through the self-corrective mechanisms of science as a social enterprise. For modern science . . . progressively diminishes the effects of bias by retaining only those proposed conclusions of its inquiries that survive critical examination by an indefinitely large community of students, whatever be their value preferences or doctrinal commitments" (p. 489).

Administrative theory can assist in this process only if it specifically identifies various kinds of means and various kinds of ends and various types of means-end relations. It is not enough to speak of values in hushed terms as though they were gods or the spirits of the departed.

In this book, therefore, I have given considerable attention to the process of evaluation. I have tried to set forth in factual terms the various categories of criteria that are used in evaluating organizational and administrative performance. To do this I have had to identify the basic interests of human beings and the varying ways in which these interests are revealed in their nonpurposeful, purposeful, and evaluating behavior. In making this effort I have openly set forth a set of personal moral commitments. By so doing I think I can be most helpful to administrators and theorists in their constant checking back and forth between *was, is,* and *might be,* on the one hand, and *should have been* and *should be,* on the other.

D. *An Action-Theory Strategy*

THIS BOOK strives to achieve an action-theory marriage. It tries to deal with the major questions asked by both administrators and scholars concerning the governance of organizations. It tries to give some feeling for the art and wisdom of seasoned administrators. It tries to record the major aspects of such art and wisdom. It stresses the primacy of administrative action as both a source of theory and a test of theory's utility.

In making this effort I have felt it essential to look at a much broader sphere of action than that of individual organizations at any one place in time. I have felt it essential to look also at the broad historical processes of social action and their interrelation with administrative theory in its various forms. This has meant probing back into the distant past. It has meant peering forward into the misty future.

1. THE PAST AND THE PRESENT

Parts One and Two analyze the present against the background of historical trends.

Action is the theme of Part One, "The Administrative Revolution." It describes the historical sweep of the administration revolution through major parts of the world. Refuting the energetically propagated myths of "ultimate authority" and "central omnipotence," it presents a flexible model for the distribution of authority within organizations. It identifies the major threats that the administrative revolution has created with respect to the place of the individual in society, the nature of social organization, and man's survival on the planet.

Theory is the theme of Part Two, "The Development of Administrative Thought." It approaches administrative thought as both an outgrowth of the administrative revolution and a factor in accelerating its onward sweep. It identifies many of the early, scattered and undifferentiated ideas on administration embedded in the political philosophy of previous centuries. It summarizes the basic views of the outstanding "pioneers" in administrative thought: Henri Fayol, Frederick Taylor, Max Weber, Luther Gulick, Lyndall Urwick, Mary Follett, Elton Mayo, Fritz Roethlisberger, Chester Barnard, and Herbert Simon. It discusses the contributions to administrative thought from the various disciplines and surveys the rising flood of publications dealing directly with the major aspects of administration.

2. THE UNDERLYING CONSENSUS

Despite the growing variety of administrative thought and research, a surprising degree of underlying consensus can be found on basic aspects of administration. Much of this consensus, however, is hidden by terminological ambiguity and substantive disagreements on other matters.

Part Three, "The Emerging Integration," maps out this consensus in general terms. In Chapter 10 the question "What is administration?" is answered by indicating what the term usually refers to in modern administrative thought and by setting forth certain broad areas of agreement on the common characteristics of all administration and on its varying characteristics in different organizations, at different levels and in different environments. Special chapters then deal with the "conflict-cooperation nexus" and the relationships between power, authority and responsibility. Part Three ends by discussing a number of traditional oversimplifications which, although still looming large in the belief-disbelief systems of many people, are being torpedoed by modern administrative thought.

3. THE DEEPER PENETRATION

The next two parts represent a penetration of the subject which, while built upon the emerging consensus, goes far beyond it.

Part Four, "The People," deals with the actors in the administrative drama: people-in-organizations-in-environments. It starts by looking at the interests and motivations of human beings, apart from any particular roles they may play in organizations. It deals separately with the formal and informal aspects of organizations. It analyzes both the broad social environment of organizations and their immediate environment.

Part Five, "The Purposes," deals in detail with the major dimensions of organizational performance:

- the satisfaction of interests
- the output of services or goods
- efficiency or profitability
- investment in organizational viability
- mobilization of resources
- observance of codes, and
- rationality.

Chapter 19, "The Matrix of Purposes," outlines these dimensions in summary form and discusses them in the context of purposefulness in organizations. The following ten chapters discuss each of these in detail, with both output and rationality the subject of two or more chapters. The last section of Chapter 29 demonstrates how these same concepts are used in formulating the criteria of evaluation. This same chapter deals with the "decision-making struggle." Indeed, all the chapters in Parts Four and Five deal with administrative decision-making—but in terms of the concrete issues faced by administrators rather than of substanceless abstractions.

4. THE FUTURE

Part Six, "The Future," returns to the threat discussed in Part One. In the light of the preceding analyses of organizations and their management, it attempts to point out some of the potentialities for human progress within the administered society. It suggests that the threats created by the administrative revolutions are in part counterbalanced by the opportunities for democratic and professional administration, organizational, individualism, and international organization. It outlines the possibility that multidimensional administrative theory and research, based upon a closer knit marriage between action and research, may progress much further on the long road from an emerging to a mature science. It explores the potentialities of administrative education as an aid in the process whereby people acquire the knowledge, abilities, and interests needed for more successful administration.

E. *The Methods*

THE MOST POPULAR METHOD of writing a book about administration is to rewrite the books written by others on the same subject during the previous decade. This method yields scores of new books every year, with little that is original beyond the re-editing and rearrangement of the same old stuff.

It would be presumptuous to say that I too have not used this method —at least in part. In fact, I have carried it to its logical extreme by exploiting all past writings that I could find on related subjects over many decades. Among other things, this has led me to a large body of empirical data which no one had previously tried to exploit. The process of exploitation, in turn, has required efforts at synthesis which have drawn heavily upon personal experience.

1. THE EVIDENCE SUPPLIED BY OTHERS

The essence of any attempt to study phenomena seriously is direct observation. Not just any observation. Rather, observation which is carefully directed, refined by the use of precise concepts, systematically recorded, systematically repeated, replicable by other observers, and enlivened by the imaginative formulation of hypotheses that try to explain the phenomena. From such observation comes the evidence that bears on the utility of a concept and the validity of a generalization.

In the late 1930's, when Chester Barnard wrote *The Functions of the Executive*, he had little more material and information to turn to (apart from personal experience) than the Hawthorne experiments and various then-new theorists in psychology and sociology (those theories themselves based upon but a sparse amount of carefully observed data).

Today, however, the situation is quite different. The observational basis for administrative and organizational theory is much stronger. What was then but a minor trickle of empirical research has swollen into a significant stream. Between 1940 and 1960, for example, at least four hundred articles and 200 books have been based largely, if not entirely, upon the empirical study of specific organizations. Although there is considerable discontinuity in the facets observed, this represents a rich fund of data and hypotheses. Nor does this include the less rigorous— but not to be neglected—observational data in case studies prepared for instructional purposes, in historical studies and in biographies and memoirs. All in all, the empirical study of organizational and administrative behavior has reached a stage where the records have already outrun the ability of most students of the subject to keep up with them. My own contribution here, rather than adding another empirical study to the growing accumulation, is more in the nature of review and consolidation of the specific studies done by others. The authors of such studies usually indicate that their purpose is to provide bricks for anyone interested in building the structure of more general theory. One of my purposes has been to use all such bricks that seem capable of helping support the weight of generalizations.

I have also had the benefit, as Barnard did not have, of the impressive forward thrust that has occurred during the last twenty-five years in the social sciences. Economics, political science, sociology, anthropology, and psychology have all moved forward at a rapid pace. Together with such newer points of focus as operations research, cybernetics, information theory, and general systems theory, they have provided theoretical, methodological, and factual aids to the study of administration.

Yet I have carefully refrained from attempting a thorough verification of the total body of these generalizations. Verification is a painstaking task that can better be handled one item at a time by those who concentrate on small sections of a subject. It is not appropriate to the task of presenting a general theory and a comprehensive survey.

Nor do I present all my generalizations in "operational terms"—that is, in terms immediately and automatically susceptible to measurement. In this sense many of the generalizations may therefore be regarded as more suggestive than definitive. This qualification is particularly important in any study that presumes to range over a wide array of subjects customarily dealt with by specialists. From the viewpoint of almost every specialist group there will be serious flaws in all of my generalizations touching upon their restricted areas. In some cases, I am sure, they will find outright errors and inconsistencies. But these are minor flaws that can readily be corrected. The more serious flaw is the built-in superficiality which is unavoidable when one refuses to dig down all the way in a small area. To some extent this is the unavoidable price that one must pay for a comprehensive viewpoint that attempts to avoid the Scylla of ignoring the wisdom in relevant disciplines and the Charybdis of getting mired down and lost forever in the endless depths of any one of them.

2. DOCUMENTATION AND INFORMATION RETRIEVAL

Because of the comprehensive scope of the book and the large amount of data drawn upon, I have adopted the strategy of building up a general body of documentation rather than attempting an intensive documentation of separate points.

The general documentation is found in three places.

The first is the survey of administrative thought presented in the five chapters of Part Two. Having thus summarized the views of other writers within one setting, I have not provided bibliographical surveys for each chapter or for each important subject. Nor have I attempted to survey all the most relevant views of others even on such crucial subjects as power, authority, responsibility, interests, purposes, structure, and process. Although documentation services of this type are sorely needed, it could not be a function of this book to provide them. As suggested in the discussion of information retrieval in the last chapter, it is to be hoped that they will someday be provided on a continuing and professional basis for both practitioners and academics.

The second is the bibliographical report, "Research Studies in Organizational Behavior." Although this selective bibliography includes only about a fourth of the available empirical studies, it highlights one of the great achievements of modern behavioral studies: the building up of a growing body of empirical data. The abstracts serve to indicate the various aspects of organization and administration dealt with, thereby tying the documents cited a little more closely to the structure of the book. They will also partly compensate for the skimpy nature of the references I have made to the tremendous amount of illustrative material now available.

The third is the "General Bibliography." This lists in traditional fashion all the other books, articles, and reports cited in the text.

Since there are two bibliographies, there are two forms of reference to them. References to the "Research Studies in Organizational Behavior" appear in italics, references to the "General Bibliography" in ordinary print. Thus *Argyris* (1953) refers to his *Executive Leadership*, which appears among the research studies, while Argyris (1957) refers to *Personality and Organization*, which appears in the "General Bibliography." At times, of course, the distinction between empirical studies and other documents is not very clear.

Having provided this rather high degree of general documentation, I have assiduously avoided the temptation of using footnotes for the purpose of marshalling "authorities" to support my views. The footnotes have been reserved for (a) expressing occasional "asides" (including comments on quoted sources) that depart somewhat from the continuity of the text, (b) providing more specific references than can be provided by text and bibliography alone to the sources of quotations, illustrations, and ideas borrowed from others, and (c) referring to related materials in other chapters.

3. THE ANALYSIS OF PERSONAL EXPERIENCE

In addition to the evidence obtained from others, personal observation in a variety of organizations and a number of countries have gone into the making of this book.

Most of these observations have been recorded in memory only. The flow of action has usually been too quick to allow for anything else. In piecing together my evidence I shall therefore rely upon a large amount of nondocumented personal observations and introspective analyses of my own failures and successes "recollected in tranquillity." This firsthand experience is supplemented by secondhand experiences gleaned from a multitude of discussions with other participants in organizational and administrative life. The last kind of evidence may not mean much to those with little experience of their own. For those with significant experience in organizational and administrative activity, it will often "ring a bell." It may just as often inspire counterobservations and alternative generalizations based on a different background of personal experience.

If the reader has reservations concerning evidence obtained from personal experience, so have I. Among the things I have learned from experience are the reasons why "those who know don't tell." One motive for not telling, of course, is a gentlemanly concern for those who might be injured by the telling (and I shall studiously refrain from disclosing information that could damage any specific individuals or organization). Another is to magnify one's reputation for wisdom by maintaining an impressive silence.

A more important reason is that telling is so terribly hard. It is much easier to speak of things that one does not know than to put "tacit knowledge" into intelligible words. Nor is it easy to acquire enough knowledge, tacit or otherwise, about any one organization in which one has been active. I could never "tell all" about my own organizational and administrative experience because I never succeeded in knowing all. Personal knowledge of administration is always partial.

Yet knowledge based upon personal experience has much to commend it. It provides clues that could never be obtained by looking on from the outside. The physicist, poor fellow, will never learn what it is like to be one of the electrons or mesons in the atoms he studies. This is the price he pays for the advantage of nature's not being against him. But the administrative practioner or theorist—so long as he follows the example of Antaeus and keeps his feet on the ground of personal experience—can always know what it is like to be among the administrators or the administered.

When administrative thought (and the various disciplines that nurture it) becomes more mature, there will of course be a much greater role for systematic, recorded and replicable observation. But this will not eliminate the analysis of personal experience. I suspect that it will merely provide a foundation for raising such analysis to still higher and more fruitful levels.

4. BALANCING THE QUALITATIVE AND THE QUANTITATIVE

One of the most striking things about modern social science is the great factional conflict between the "quantifiers" and the "imponderabilists."

The quantifiers know that any highly developed science requires precise observations. They maintain that until we can measure, we cannot really understand. They point out that many abstract concepts can never be elegantly formulated until put to use in the measurement process. Moreover, ordinary language may be too crude to handle the complex interrelations of many variables. They have therefore concentrated on rigorous efforts to measure various aspects of human behavior. They have applied the notational forms of modern mathematics to social phenomena. This often leads them into dealing with relatively unimportant aspects of administration. At times it leads to the most misleading forms of number magic, as pointed out in the final section of "The Matrix of Purposes" (Chapt. 19).

Their opponents know that many of the most important things in human life cannot be measured. They protest against misplaced or premature quantification. They would rather be vaguely right than precisely wrong. They honor the role of insight and intuition. This often leads them into dealing with the most important aspects of administration in a fashion more literary than scientific.

As for myself, I have one foot planted firmly in each camp. This is more than a matter of mere compromise; it is rather an effort at integration. Neither approach is by itself sufficient. Each has a lot to contribute, partly in its own terms and partly by way of correcting the excesses of the other.

I put more weight, however, on the foot in the qualitative camp. In every discipline there is probably a period of painful evolution from the predominantly-qualitative to the use of greater quantification. In administrative theory I believe we are still at a very early stage. Above all, genuine progress in quantification—as distinct from razzle-dazzle to impress *hoi polloi*—must rest on units within categories (which can also be referred to as sets, classes, or groups) having certain identifiable boundaries. Ordinal measurement rests on establishing relationships between such cate-

gories. The identification and definition of these boundaries and relationships are largely tasks in the formation of qualitative concepts.

By placing major emphasis upon these qualitative foundations, therefore, it has been my aim to promote a stronger foundation for quantification and a framework more suitable for bringing the qualitative and
quantitative approaches together in a fruitful balance.

Part I

THE ADMINISTRATIVE REVOLUTION

Chapter 2

THE RISE OF
THE ADMINISTERED SOCIETY

*T*HE TERMS "managerial revolution" and "organizational revolution" (which appear in the titles of books by James Burnham and Kenneth Boulding, respectively) are now widely used to describe a major social change that has taken place in many countries during the nineteenth and twentieth centuries. If no "The Bureaucratic Revolution" has yet appeared, some book with this title is bound to be published in the not-too-distant future. These terms all have the great merit of indicating that the industrial revolution is not something that can be fully understood in terms of scientific and technological change alone. They direct attention to the fact that science and technology have been able to change the face of the world only through the use of administered organizations.

Although any of these terms will do, I prefer the concept of the "administrative revolution." This term recognizes the dynamic role of administrators in the guidance of organizations without making the mistake of equating all administrators with bureaucrats. It also helps distinguish my point of view from the oversimplified and extreme doctrine expounded by Burnham in *The Managerial Revolution*.[1]

No matter what term is used, we should not think that organizations,

---

1. See critique of Burnham's views in the section on "The Myths of Central Omnipotence" in "The Dispersion of Power in Organizations" (Chapt. 3).

bureaucrats, managers, and administrators are new phenomena in the world. To understand the nature of the administrative revolution, we must keep in mind that administration is an ancient activity and must specifically identify those changes which comprise the administrative "revolution" that has occurred more recently.

A. *An Ancient Activity*

A FREQUENT WAY to suggest the venerable character of administration is to quote such ancient administrative wisdom as Jethro's famous advice to Moses on how to "judge the people" or the Confucian or Platonic ideas on how to govern a state.

Yet such references belong to the history of administrative thought, not of administration itself. Administrative thought—in the sense of specialized, concentrated, continuous, and recorded observation and speculation—is distinctly a modern development. If one confuses it with administrative activity, one runs the risk of seriously underestimating the vast scope of administrative activity throughout the ages. No one could be so foolish as to assume that the bloodstream played no role in the human body before Harvey's "discovery" of the circulation of the blood. It would be just as ridiculous to suppose that the words of Jethro, Confucius, or Plato tell us much about administration among the Hebrew tribes, in the Chinese states in the fifth and sixth centuries B.C., or in the Greek city states after Pericles. For information on these matters we must turn to the historians.

The historians open a vast treasure house of information and hypotheses concerning administrative activity in the distant past. This knowledge is enriched by the findings of social anthropologists concerning primitive societies still in existence, findings that are extremely suggestive with respect to earlier primitive societies which left few records behind them. An examination of this rich and expanding field of human knowledge reveals two aspects of the subject which are pertinent at this point: the antiquity of administrative activity and its close relationship with the general processes of historical change.

1. ITS EARLY EVOLUTION

There was a time when political philosophers wrote about an ancient age in which men and women ran about as isolated entities in a "state of nature." Later, the story goes, they decided they should come together in some form of community in order to protect property, assure peace, or guarantee natural rights.

As fiction, this explanation of social organization had some uses for Hobbes, Locke, and Rousseau and their contemporaries. As an explanation of historical development, it is nonsense. Men and women, we now know, have always been social animals. First of all, human beings always come together in some form of family group. In this respect, they are like all other animals who engage in sexual activity throughout the year and whose offspring need long periods of care. Among human animals, however, the division of labor within the family is more developed and coordination through superior-subordinate relationships invariably develops (Chapple and Coon, 1947, p. 277-298).

Second, even when the pastoral or agricultural family unit continues to be the major unit of economic production, "extended family organizations" such as clans and tribes play an important role. They settle internal conflicts, organize military aggression and defense, provide general economic services with respect to land and water and handle the magic and religious techniques for dealing with serious crises faced by individuals, families, and the community as a whole. Here the division of labor is still more highly developed, the levels of subordination more numerous, and the role of various tribal leaders more formalized. We see the beginnings of administration and the first appearance of formal administrators. This is particularly apparent in the organization of fighting forces and in the development of means whereby the victor may maintain control over the vanquished.[2]

Third, more separate and more clearly differentiated types of organizations came into being: special agencies of civilian and military government, churches, economic enterprises and various professional and political associations. For long periods of history many of these organizations were closely linked together—as with the combination of sovereign, high priest (or even god) and chief warrior in one monarch. One of the strongest links was kinship, which made itself felt in political and religious dynasties and family-controlled enterprises. These links gradually became more tenuous. The process of differentiation continued. A greater and greater variety of formal organizations, each with its own set of administrators,

2. For a valuable review of the growth of political organizations in certain primitive societies of Africa, see *African Political Systems,* edited by Fortes and Evans-Pritchard. A broader approach, including the development of religious institutions as well, is provided in Parkinson, *The Evolution of Political Thought.* The title of this book, however, is somewhat misleading. Parkinson's major emphasis is on the evolution of different types of political organization, with subordinate attention to the political theories written to explain or justify them.

came into being. This process was hastened by the development of writing, systems of measurement, standardized units of currency, advanced handicrafts and metallurgical techniques. The list of those specially skilled expanded to include not only national leaders and their councillors, prophets, priests and warriors but also scribes, calculators, master craftsmen and traders.

Finally, at many different stages of ancient history large-size organizations—with great numbers of fulltime personnel and complex administrative hierarchies—came into being. The armies of ancient Babylonia, Persia, Rome, and Byzantium were huge affairs. The God-Kings of ancient Egypt built government agencies which administered an entire economy. The administrative structure of the Chinese and Roman Empires—and sometime later of the Roman Catholic Church—reached vast proportions.

2. *ADMINISTRATION AND HISTORICAL CHANGE*

In any process as dynamic as administration, change is the eternal law. Organizations come into being and vanish. Leaders rise and fall. Some retire voluntarily, others under compulsion of death or removal. These changes are often merely in personnel or external forms: the tune and the words are the same, only the voices are different. In this sense *le plus çe change, le plus le procès administratif c'est la même chose.* But in a broader sense administrative change is closely associated with basic changes in the fabric of society. As shown in the preceding section, certain changes in organization and administration were part and parcel of the revolutionary transition from clans and tribes to city-states and empires. Illustrations from later periods bear out the same principle. The growth of the feudal system in the Carolingian Empire after Charlemagne was associated with basic changes in administrative structure and relationships. The development of the modern nation-state was associated with an expanded system of government administration. The development of Western capitalism was rooted in such new organizational forms as joint stock companies and the factory method of industrial manufacturing. The development of modern economies—in both "advanced" and "underdeveloped" countries—is largely a process of change not only in technology but also in the organization and administration of economic activity.

The nature of this close relationship can be stated very simply. Whenever people want to accomplish a difficult social task, they must strengthen existing organizations or build new ones. But organizations do not run themselves. They must be administered. If people want to undertake still more difficult tasks, they must build larger or stronger organizations. This leads to still more administration.

Thus, in examining the history of bureaucracy, Max Weber finds that the "proper soil for the bureaucratization of administration" has always been the qualitative and quantitative development of administrative tasks. "In Egypt, the oldest country of bureaucratic state administration, the public and collective regulation of waterways for the whole country and from the top could not be avoided because of technical economic factors. This regulation created the mechanism of scribes and officials. Once established, this mechanism, even in early times, found its second realm of business in the extraordinary construction activities which were organized militarily." He maintains that the failure of the Crusades and the collapse of the great Negro Empires of Africa were associated with the absence of a large administrative apparatus to back them up (Gerth and Mills, p. 204-214).[3]

The reason for this relationship is also rather simple. A large task cannot be undertaken without the use of power. A larger task calls for still more power. Individuals by themselves are relatively weak. They are somewhat stronger if they cooperate informally. They are much stronger if brought together into a formal organization. Thus organization and administration are prerequisites for the development of significant and social power, as well as for its maintenance or enlargement. Every organization is a system of power. Every administrator is a wielder of power.

True, resources are also a factor in the power equation. These include physical resources (such as land, materials, equipment, tools, and machinery), human resources (people with various abilities, values, and inclinations), and monetary claims that can be used in obtaining the services of either. Yet physical resources by themselves are not social power. They are merely a potential which can be exploited only by people. People in turn (that is, human resources) can exploit physical resources in a significant way only through administered organizations. Thus the basic equation is $P = A \cdot R$. Power comes from the administration of resources.[4]

Special attention must be paid to the dynamic role of discovery and

3. Weber also spells out two other contributing but not essential factors. The first is a money economy, which makes it easier to keep an officeholder dependent upon an organization and to detach him from any proprietary rights in his position. The second is the abolition of slavery. People can be tied to their tasks more securely by money salaries than by legal enslavement. Weber concedes that many bureaucracies have developed in the absence of these two factors, but holds that their absence tends to subvert bureaucratic forms.

4. This theme is developed in greater detail in "The Power-Authority-Responsibility Triangle" (Chapt. 12).

invention, of the development of new techniques of doing things. This enters into the power equation on the side of human resources. Technology is fundamentally the ability of identifiable human beings to get certain things done with the use of various physical or mental tools. It implies some degree of progress toward the triumph of reason over magic.

But technological change is also intimately connected with administrative change. First of all, many new techniques cannot be put to use without changes in organizational forms and administrative systems. This is particularly true with all technical advances that require a division of labor among specialists who cannot by themselves complete the production of certain goods or services. The unification of what has been divided calls for organizational changes. This is what Marx and Engels had in mind when they maintained that "the feudal organization of agriculture and manufacturing industry . . . became no longer compatible with the already developed productive forces; they became so many fetters. They had to burst asunder: they were burst asunder" (*Communist Manifesto*, p. 326). The same might be said concerning the fate of older systems of military organizations with the introduction of new techniques of destruction.

Second, the discovery and invention of new methods of administration is itself a part of technological development. Thus Weber regards the Western development of rational structures of administration in terms of formal rules as one of the most important reasons why capitalism developed in the West earlier than in the Orient (*The Protestant Ethic and the Spirit of Capitalism*, p. 25; *General Economic History*, p. 338-351). Others have pointed out that administration is itself an integral part of the process of exploiting technical knowledge. Drucker maintains that "mass production does not rest on the assembly line, the conveyor belt, or any other gadget or technique: its basis is rather a conscious, deliberate and planned order of relations between man and man and man and technical process . . . (1946, p. 25). It is in this sense that Barnard refers to organization as "the chief instrument of economic development" (1938, p. 285). Thus only part of the story is told in the dramatic finding that older forms of organization "were burst asunder" by new techniques of administration. The truth is that people "burst them asunder" by devising new forms of organization and styles of administration.

The process of social change, however, is too complex to be explained only in terms of the effort to develop the power to accomplish new tasks. A task exists only if people see it as such, only if they have the will to undertake it. When people prefer leisure and contemplation and shudder at the idea of conquering the territory of others, they are unlikely to be interested in building a huge army or empire. If their major purpose in life is to achieve a state of Nirvana or to obtain a guarantee of entering the City of God after death, they will be much less interested in large-scale economic undertakings to expand their worldly possessions. Thus, religious ideals may exercise a profound effect upon people's interests in large-scale organizations. According to Weber, for example, a contributing factor to the growth of large-scale modern capitalism was the "Protestant ethic" which legitimatized the transfer to secular affairs of the religious devotion previously dedicated to other-worldly considerations.[5]

Yet these qualifications merely relate to whether or not people are interested in the power to take on larger tasks. The proposition still stands that whenever people have been so motivated, they have been able to obtain additional social power only through changes in the administration of resources. These changes have been at the very heart of almost all major changes in the structure of societies.

It should be added that cultural ideals and values must also be regarded as instruments in the hands of those who develop organizational power. People are not brought together into organizations by mechanical means alone, as when one uses mortar and the force of gravity to convert stones into a wall. People are cemented together only by common interests and values, whether these be as modest as the simple desire to survive or as ambitious as the aspiration to create a Heaven on earth. Only by exploiting or developing such interests and values can leaders and administrators transmute the divergent purposes of individuals into the purposes of organizations.

B. *The Revolutionary Changes*

PERHAPS the most revolutionary change in modern civilization started with the so-called Industrial Revolution which got underway in the Western World in the mid-eighteenth century. In its more obvious aspect, the "factory system," this revolution began in manufacturing. Yet it quickly spread to agriculture, transportation, finance and, despite recurring lags, to construction, distribution, and public services. It is

5. *The Protestant Ethic and the Spirit of Capitalism*, p. 155-183. Weber also relates the growth of rational capitalist bureaucracy to "that great historical process in the development of religions, the elimination of magic from the world, which had begun with the Hebrew prophets" (*Ibid.*, p. 105). The perceptiveness of this observation is impaired by Weber's ignoring of the large amounts of magic or quasi-magic still used in both modern religion and modern bureaucracy.

now spreading to the "underdeveloped" countries of Asia, Africa, and South America, which by any definition still comprise from 65 to 75 per cent of the world's population. Nor is the process completed in even the most "advanced" countries of North America and Europe. The onward pace of modern technology is so rapid that the technological advances of the past two centuries may soon prove to be merely a small dash of surf preceding a massive wave.

One may view the Industrial Revolution from many aspects. One may stress the sharp rise, although at varying rates, in living standards, literacy, and life expectancy. One may note the expansion of large urban areas and the contraction of agricultural populations. One may focus upon the abolition of chattel slavery in most parts of the world and the rise in political liberties in many parts. One may point to political and economic imperialism, new forms of organized oppression and a series of wars unprecedented in territorial coverage and destructiveness.

But if one concentrates upon the underlying social aspects of this revolution one finds that one of the most fundamental changes has been in administrative technology which has made it possible to exploit new mechanical techniques. This administrative revolution has been characterized by more organization, larger-scale organization, more bureaucracy, and more administrators.

1. MORE ORGANIZATION

One need not assume that the classical economists' world of perfect competition ever existed to concede that in past periods of history a larger role in economic life was occupied by informal groups and single individuals. But with the advent of the administrative revolution both of these have yielded ground to formal organizations. The family's role in direct economic production has declined. Informal groupings of artisans and craftsmen have been largely displaced by factories, trade unions and trade associations. The strictly individual entrepreneur is a peripheral person. He is found mainly in small-scale retail trade and among those artists, writers and thinkers who somehow or other manage to survive without membership in an orchestra, theatrical company, publishing concern, or university. Even in these fields, as in all others, it is increasingly difficult to obtain the facilities for important achievement without participating in an organization capable of bringing together a larger amount of resources than an individual can usually amass by himself. Where nominal independence is achieved, moreover, the lonely entrepreneur is often little more than a subservient satellite to the large organizations which supply him with goods and services or, as in the case of the artist, market his wares.

The Rich Capitalist, the Speculator, the Big Investor—these individuals are also beginning to fade in significance. Individual ownership of wealth and individual investment are being transformed into collective activities. Capital—even in the United States of America, the last stronghold of the myth of individual enterprise—is being socialized. The word "private" in "private property" has come to mean "nonstate" instead of "individual." Most private property in the means of production and distribution is owned not by individuals but by corporations. The ownership of corporations, in turn, is moving increasingly into collectivist—even though nonstate—hands. In the critical sphere of corporate investment, as stressed by Adolph Berle, individual initiative amounts to less and less. Thus, during the period from 1947 to 1956, 60 per cent of the capital investment of U.S. corporations came from internal sources, retained earnings and depreciation allowances; another 10 to 15 per cent was handled by pension trusts, mutual funds, and insurance companies; another 20 per cent was borrowed from banks; little more than 5 per cent could possibly represent truly individual investment. Berle concludes that even outside the sphere of government action, most of American society is "no more private than a seat in a subway train" and that more than two-thirds of enterprise is "possible only because it is collectivist" (*Power Without Property*, p. 27-58).

But organization and administrative activity are by no means limited to economic enterprises. De Tocqueville's observation concerning the growth of associations in the United States during the early nineteenth century is today applicable on a worldwide scale:

> Americans of all ages, all conditions, and all dispositions, constantly form associations. They have not only commercial and manufacturing companies in which all take part, but associations of a thousand other kinds—religious, moral, serious, futile, extensive or restricted, enormous or diminutive. The Americans make associations to give entertainments, to found establishments for education, to build inns, to construct churches, to diffuse books, to send missionaries to the Antipodes; and in this manner they found hospitals, prisons and schools (1947, p. 319).

To bring this description up-to-date for America is not difficult. We need merely refer to the development of trade unions representing workers, trade associations representing large numbers of single economic enterprises, the federations of trade unions and trade associations, professional associations, and political parties. In all these groups people have set themselves certain objectives—such as raising wages or prices, enforcing professional codes, removing others from office or staying in power themselves—which can be achieved only through the use of the power provided by formal organizations. Above all, we should have to add the network of scientific organizations which provide the basis for modern technology and science-based industries—the scientific academies, institutes, laboratories and university departments without which scientists could not gain access to essential information, equipment, and other resources.

With certain variations the same picture is applicable to countries just embarking on the process of industrialization. The period of "take-off" from an agricultural to an industrial economy is one of the continuing emergence of new organizations. This is true not only of government agencies and business enterprises but also of a great variety of groups representing various local, religious, sectional, cultural, or political interests. In the earlier stages the civilian and military institutions of government may be dominant, with only a minor role played by nonassociational and anomic interests (Almond and Coleman, 1960). But as economic growth gets underway, as in India, it tends to be accompanied by "a growing mobilization of groups exerting pressure on government" (Weiner, 1962, p. 238).

Under dictatorial or totalitarian regimes, the same tendency is not only evidenced; it is carried to an extreme. Here efforts are made to organize more and more aspects of human life. In the more extreme cases drastic steps are taken to prevent or suppress the growth of any organization that might serve as a basis for attack upon the dictators or as a competitor for popular loyalties. Spies and party agents are used extensively in an effort to weld all permitted organizations together into one big cluster of organizations.

2. MORE LARGE-SCALE ORGANIZATION

While there were occasional organizational giants in previous historical periods, the administrative revolution has ushered in an era of giants.

The size of organizations can be measured by their assets, their use of manpower and other resources, or their output of goods or services. By any of these measuring rods, a vast and ever increasing portion of human activity is now handled by large-scale administrative organizations.

Historically, the largest organizations have often been found in the military field. In modern warfare, the sheer size of the administrative operation staggers the imagination. During the first four weeks alone of the Second Front against Hitler in 1944, for example, the Allied Forces moved about 1,000,000 men, 567,000 tons of supplies, 172,000 vehicles across the British Channel to the Normandy Coast (Eisenhower, p. 305). Such an unprecedented large operation was possible only because it was preceded by sustained aerial bombardment and a centrally planned buildup which mobilized the support of many thousands of industrial, agricultural, mining and transportation organizations throughout the anti-Axis coalition.

Any future war, it is true, may see a displacement of man-operated airplanes and frontline fighting men by long-range missiles carrying atomic explosives, chemicals, and germs. But the development and operation of the new missile systems and the defenses against them are themselves large-scale activities of an unprecedented nature. They require not only huge central investments and staffs but also the administration of a wide network of relationships with vast sectors of industry and transportation. The entire military system requires elaborate integration with the structure of government as a whole.

An equally impressive growth can be found in the size of civilian agencies of government. This growth is based on the vast expansion of services provided by such organizations. In part, this expansion is attributable to the growth of the territorial areas services by government and the expansion of population within such territories. In still larger part, it is related to the increasing variety of governmental services. In the early nineteenth century the traditional functions of government were those performed by chiefs of state (whether kings, emperors, consuls or presidents), legislative assemblies, courts and a handful of executive departments. These latter usually carried out activities in four basic areas: foreign affairs, defense, justice and finance. Everything else was usually lumped together into a "catch all" ministry or department of the interior or home affairs. In the course of time new governmental activities were initiated or old ones enlarged to the point where new ministries were needed. The most widespread were those in the fields of postal services, education, public works, agriculture, commerce, industry, transport, communication, labor, social insurance, health, and, where the situation warranted, religion or colonies. Most governments also set up offices to regulate private enterprises, either on an across-the-board basis (as in the U.S. Federal Trade Commission) or in specific sectors (as in the U.S. Maritime Commission). The most popular fields for regulation have been utilities, transportation and banking. Across-the-board regulation has also developed in connection with matters relating to public health, public safety, national defense and wages and working conditions.

Thus, even where territorial expanse and population may dwindle, the expansion of government services itself calls for larger government organizations. Between 1935 and 1954, for example, the number of officials in the British Colonial Office grew from 372 to 1,661. During this same period, as successive British colonies achieved self-government, the territory and population served by the Colonial Office shrank considerably. In a delightful satire on bureaucratic behavior in government agencies, C. Northcote Parkinson charges that this increase stemmed entirely from the bureaucratic tendency to multiply subordinates and make work for each other. His famous "Parkinson's Law" holds that there is "little or no relationship between the work to be done and the size of the staff to which it may be assigned" (*Parkinson's Law*, p. 4-15). This point of view is sustained by rigorously ignoring the vast increase in services provided by the Colonial Office during the Welfare State period after the end of World War II, including those services connected with colonial liberation itself. By closing his eyes to the growth of services as the key factor in the growth of government organizations, Parkinson thereby failed to exploit the satirical possibilities involved in the distinctive contribution to growth of many bureaucrats: namely, the invention, propagation and popularization of new and expanded services as a way of accelerating the pace of organizational growth.

The expansion of government services is also accelerated by a steady and continuous entry of government into economic operations. The victory of the communist regimes in Russia, Eastern Europe, and China has resulted in the extension of government enterprise to cover the bulk of economic activities in these countries. In other major areas of the world outside the communist orbit, programs of partial socialism are continually extending government activity to cover major public utilities that were previously subject to regulation only, "natural monopolies" and basic industries. Since smaller enterprises are usually much more difficult for government to handle, the policy of government in both the communist and the noncommunist countries is to concentrate government economic activities in any field in one or a few giant organizations.

A new dimension of government activity has been provided by the proliferation of transnational government agencies. For centuries various national governments had linked themselves by treaties and agreements into various federations or confederations, usually for purposes of offensive or defensive warfare. Sometimes they were the steppingstones to empire. In the nineteenth century, with the creation of the international telegraph and postal organizations, a new type of transnational agency came into being. Subsequently, other agencies were established under the auspices of the League of Nations and its successor, the United Nations. Today, the United Nations itself is an international organization made up of more than a hundred separate nations and including more than a dozen, large-scale special agencies operating on a worldwide scale. The growth of the United Nations network has been paralleled by an upsurge of more than two score regional organizations. Among the most prominent have been the North Atlantic Treaty Organization, the Organization for Economic Cooperation and Development, the European Economic Community, the Organization of American States and the Council for Mutual Economic Assistance (consisting of the U.S.S.R. and the communist nations of eastern Europe). To these must be added the British Commonwealth and the French Community, which have been steppingstones from empire to voluntary confederation.

Economic activities by nongovernment institutions have also contributed to the trend toward larger and larger organizations. Thus in the United States of America the typical "small" company in construction, bituminous coal mining, wholesaling, or trucking is one which, from the viewpoint of capitalization or employment, would have been regarded as a giant a hundred years ago and would still be regarded as large in Costa Rica, Uganda, or Indonesia. The secret of survival for a small company is to grow larger. This, of course, is what most small businesses try to do and is the *raison d'être* of most "small business" associations. The effort to grow larger leads to both "vertical" and "horizontal" integration. The former may extend an organization's scope to cover the extraction of raw materials, various stages of processing, and distribution to the ultimate consumers. The latter combines it with former competitors. The result has been a substantial degree of concentration of economic activity in the hands of organizations each employing tens of thousands of people. In the United States "a relatively small number of large firms own a relatively large per cent of total assets and account for a relatively large percent of economic activity (however measured) in manufacture and in the total area of corporate enterprise" (Mason, 1957, p. 31). A review of the statistical literature on the subject suggests that in Canada and in Britain the degree of industrial concentration is even higher than in the United States (*Ibid.*, p. 37-38).

In all economies the degree of concentration varies from one sector to another. It is usually somewhat lower in wholesale and retail distribution, service activities, agriculture and professional self-employment. In other fields, however, the process of concentration leads to complete monopoly or quasi-monopoly with competition possible only with organizations producing substitute goods or services. In the United States of America complete monopolies of this type are found mainly in the fields of such "public utilities" as electricity, water, telephone services and local transportation services. In small countries and less developed economies the size of the market is regarded as too small to warrant the operation of more than one firm. Many newly developing economies may, in fact, vault over earlier stages of technological development and enter such fields as iron and steel, textiles or chemicals with one or two giant plants built in accordance with the latest technological considerations and unhampered by the competition of smaller, old-fashioned competitors.

Statistics on the size of enterprises, however, underestimate the extent of horizontal and vertical integration. Many organizations consist not of single enterprises but of clusters held together by holding companies, interlocking directorates and cartels. Moreover, many thousands of smaller companies are independent in name only. They operate in fact as controlled satellites of a giant supplier (as in the case of gasoline and automobile distributors) or of a giant buyer (as in the case of factories producing products exclusively for department stores, chain stores or mail order houses).

Along with Big Government and Big Business, bigness has grown in almost every significant field of organized activity. Big Labor and Big Agriculture are major players on almost every national stage. So are Big Science, Big Education, and—although this is less new—Big Religion. At times the growth in one of these areas is bewailed as something forced into being by giantism in other areas. Thus Big Labor is said to be the product of Big Business or Big Government the inevitable result of the two other "Bigs." Although there is undoubtedly a reciprocal effect of one upon the other, little is to be gained by trying to calculate whether the chicken antedated the egg or vice versa. Big Government, Business, Labor, Agriculture, Science, Education, and Religion are also part and parcel of the onsweeping wave of the administrative revolution.

3. MORE BUREAUCRACY

In colloquial usage the term "bureaucracy" usually refers to the red tape, inefficiency, or inflexibility of government officials with whom one has had trouble. In social science parlance "bureaucracy" is increasingly used to refer to certain aspects of administered organizations, both public and private. Three aspects deserve special attention: the detailed subdivision of the labor of many people, hierarchical relationships which are supposed to mesh together the individuals and groups whose work has been divided and general rules to govern the actions of both individuals and groups.[6] In this sense of the term the modern administrative revolution is characterized by a vast increase in bureaucracy.

6. The literature of bureaucracy is full of many definitions of bureaucratic organization. The best known is that of Max Weber, which is summarized in Chapt. 6.

Of the three basic aspects of bureaucracy, the growing subdivision of labor has ramifications far beyond individual organizations. Its results are evident in the distribution of the labor force and in the growing specialization in training, education and science. At the level of manual and clerical labor, specialization has developed for almost every aspect of every industrial and clerical process. This has been paralleled by increasing specialization among engineers, architects, physicists, chemists, doctors, lawyers, economists and other members of the "technocracy" or "liberal professions." Each of these fields has a growing number of professional subspecialties and professional associations.

Further differentiation has taken place in the functions of general managers and administrators. Instead of one man who used to run everything we now find boards of directors with executive committees, and subcommittees, management committees, assistant managers, deputy managers, vice presidents, private secretaries, special advisers, and general staffs. At a somewhat lower level, we find a growing variety of accountants, budgeteers, personnel managers, production managers, method analysts, marketing specialists, and public relations and advertising experts. Specialization has also developed within the field of general administration itself. Thus we can find special experts and expertise—once again with professional associations—among top business executives, army officers, government officials, hospital directors and university presidents.

The more organizational activity is divided the more is done to unite the parts through hierarchical coordination. This involves formal distinction between superiors and subordinates on the basis of "chains of command." Every "high-level" administrator exercises certain defined authority over a number of "lower-level" administrators. Each of these, in turn, is the superior of others. In this way, the points of administrative authority fan downwards from the "top" of an organization to form the traditional "pyramid" of hierarchical authority. These chains of hierarchical authority provide the framework for determining the wages paid to different people, determine their status in the organization (and often in society as well) and define the normal paths of personal advancement.

The rational operation of a hierarchy demands the crystallization of an increasing number of general rules. At the very least, these must prescribe the subdivision of labor and the hierarchical relationships themselves. They are usually quickly extended to deal with terms of employment and major problems of relationships with outside organizations and individuals. In more mature organizations, they reach out to cover general policies and detailed procedures and methods of operation. Although many rules are informal and unwritten, the tendency in a bureaucratized organization is to formalize a growing proportion of them, moving from specific orders and directives to general regulations and, finally, to codified manuals. Such rules always tend to produce amendments and exceptions; thus the process of rule-making often proceeds at a geometrical rate. New expertise develops in the making and interpretation of rules and exceptions and in the juggling of precedents. In the case of government agencies, the rules and regulations which deal with the rights or obligations of the clients of these organizations may have the full effect of statutory or judicial law. In many countries, in fact, this accumulation of "administrative law" has much more of an effect upon the citizenry than the laws written directly by legislatures and judges. The legislatures and judges in turn, often enter the picture once again by prescribing additional regulations governing the way in which government agencies handle the rights and obligations of citizens.

4. MORE ADMINISTRATORS

The administrative revolution has unquestionably produced a larger absolute number of administrators. This has been the inevitable result of the extension of organization and the subdivision of administrative functions. But since organizations have also grown in size, one may very properly ask whether the number of administrators has grown proportionally or disproportionally with the expansion of organizational membership.

For a definitive answer to this question one naturally looks to census documents or sample surveys. But such statistics are usually based upon the concept of "occupations." Thus every individual is arbitrarily placed into one occupational group or another. In the U.S. census one of these occupational categories is "managers, officials, proprietors, excluding farmers." This category excludes not only farmers but also many higher-level administrators who are classified as professionals and a large number of lower-level supervisors who are merged among the various industrial or clerical occupations.[7] Hence the only information available is extremely rough and probably tends toward a considerable understatement of the actual number of administrators.

Nevertheless, the U.S. Bureau of the Census shows a steady, albeit slow, upward trend *(Historical Statistics; Statistical Abstract):*

7. This category, with all its weaknesses from our point of view, is similar to the major group "administrative, executive and managerial workers" in the *International Standard Classification of Occupations* at the International Labor Office.

	1900	1910	1920	1930	1940	1950	1960*	1963*
A. Economically active (in millions)	29.0	37.3	42.2	48.7	51.7	59.0	66.6	67.1
B. Managers, officials and proprietors, excluding farm (in millions)	1.7	2.5	2.8	3.6	3.8	5.1	7.1	7.3
C. B as per cent of A	6	7	7	7	7	9	11	11

* These columns given in terms of "employed persons" rather than the "economically active."

Here the upward tendency is not striking. What is most striking is the high probability of serious understatement of the number of "managers, officials, and proprietors, excluding farm." One of the few careful field studies on the subject, based on 82 Midwestern business firms in the U.S.A., shows 13.3 per cent of all employees with managerial responsibilities *(Loken and Thake,* 1952). Still higher percentages are revealed in a survey of managerial personnel in California school districts *(Terrien and Mills,* 1954).

If we turn to the farm population, which has been steadily dwindling, we find what are perhaps the only definitive data on the absolute and relative increase in administrators. From 1900 to 1950, the Census Bureau shows that the total number of farm managers more than tripled, while the total number of owners, tenants and managers declined by one-fourth. During the same period the total number of farm foremen more than doubled, while the total number of farm laborers and foremen was halved *(Historical Statistics).*

Much shakier indicators are provided by data on the rapidly increasing proportion of employees receiving salaries instead of wages or of indirect employees in industry as against those engaged in direct production. In analyzing such data some authors have used the shorthand term "administrative employees" as a way of referring to salaried or indirect employees. We must guard against being confused by this special use of the term, which is quite different from the usage in this book or in the growing literature on the administration of organizations. In any case, in a number of important countries the ratios of salaried to non-salaried employees have risen as follows during roughly comparable historical periods (Bendix 1956, p. 211-226).

Nevertheless, there may well be an indirect connection between the number of administrators and the general transformations that are taking place in the labor force of every country: the shifts from manual to mental labor, from less to more specialization and from less to more professionalization. The growing specialization requires more administrative work to keep things together. This probably disperses administrative responsibilities among ever growing numbers of technical and professional employees. Paradoxically, it is this very subdivision and dispersion which themselves compound the difficulty of collecting reliable general statistics on the number of administrators. Yet there is reason to believe that if accurate data could be obtained they would probably show a much higher number of administrators than indicated by the information presently available and a sharper increase in the proportion of administrators to the total labor force.

Country		*Rise in Ratio of Salaried to Nonsalaried Industrial Employees*
United States	(1899-1947)	7.7% to 21.6%
France	(1901-1936)	11.8% to 14.6%
Great Britain	(1907-1948)	8.6% to 20.0%
Germany	(1895-1933)	4.8% to 14.0%
Sweden	(1915-1950)	6.6% to 21.0%

Chapter 3

THE DISPERSION OF POWER
IN ORGANIZATIONS

*A*S THE ADMINISTRATIVE REVOLUTION has swept across the world, large-scale organizations have created new and unprecedented aggregations of power. Many of these organizations may give outsiders the impression that they operate in automatic subordination to external controllers who enjoy "ultimate authority." Many give the impression that if one looks inside, one will find a monolithic unity, with all parts operating in smooth coordination and in automatic response to its top commanders. This is the stuff that many dreams (and nightmares) are made of. . . .

In actual fact every organization involves a certain amount of internal dispersion of power. As organizations become larger, the degree of dispersion becomes larger. The more powerful an organization becomes, the more its total power tends to result from cooperation between sub-organizations which to some degree generate their own sources of power and enjoy some degree of independent action. With continued growth of an organization, this degree of dispersion may result in a breakdown of organizational activity, or, if effective administrative measures are taken, may be harnessed in the service of more successful performance.

In this chapter I shall illustrate these tendencies by presenting a general model of the dispersion of intraorganizational power. This model, and the evidence adduced to support it, will then be used as a jumping-off place for an irreverent analysis of various myths of ultimate authority and central omnipotence.

A. *The Centers of Organizational Power*

IN A SCHEMATIC WAY we can easily identify three formally established centers of power within organizations: the members of directorates, the top executives, and the bureaucrats. Moreover, in some organizations elected trade union leaders arise as an organized opposition from within. When this happens, these leaders comprise a fourth center of power.

In some organizations, of course, one or more of these four centers will be underdeveloped, or even missing. In very small organizations there will be very little distinction between directorates and top executives, and very little bureaucracy. Even in medium-sized organizations it may be hard to distinguish between top executives and senior bureaucrats. In some organizations the employees may not be organized into trade unions, or else the trade union leaders may in fact turn out to be undercover representatives of the top managers or the bureaucrats. In all organizations, moreover, there is a tendency for the relations between the various centers of power to vary from one issue to another and to fluctuate with changing conditions. Yet without tracking down the specific power constellations formed by the relations between these four groups, it is impossible to learn how any large organization is really run.[1]

Let it be emphasized that our analysis bears directly only upon the constellation of power *within* organizations. We are not dealing with the very important influences which are exerted *upon* organizations from the outside, usually by other organizations. Nor are we dealing with the more dramatic constellations of power that may be formed by relations *among* organizations.[2] In fact, the interorganizational relations which determine the power structure of any nation, society or civilization cannot be understood merely by looking at organizations as a whole. To know how atoms combine into molecules, we must penetrate inside

1. The relation between these four groups and the formal organizational structure as a whole (including the multiple roles that may be played by individuals in two or more groups) is discussed in "People-in-Organizations: Formal Aspects" (Chapt. 15).

2. This subject is discussed in the section "The Power Structure" in "The General Environment" (Chapt. 18).

the atom. To understand the behavior of organizations and their administrators, we must study the constellation of *intra*organization forces.

1. THE MEMBERS OF DIRECTORATES

Since any representative assembly is usually too diffuse or discontinuous a body to direct the operations of an organization, a small directorate is usually established for this purpose. The clearest-cut example is the cabinet in a parliamentary system of government, where the cabinet serves in effect as the executive committee of the legislative assembly (even though in certain countries and under certain conditions it may contain a few members who do not serve in the legislative assembly). Under presidential systems of government, the directorate of a legislative body is usually found in a small policy committee, steering committee or rules committee. Here, however, none of these legislative committees serve as a directorate with respect to the operations of the various government departments and ministries. This function is exercised by the president and his most immediate advisers and associate. At the level of the individual agencies of government, the directorate may be formally established as a board or a single person.

A similar situation is found in all but the smallest nongovernmental organizations. Even though the boards of directors of corporations rarely include more than twenty people, such bodies cannot be relied upon to give continuous direction.[3] "To make possible emergency decisions between regular meetings, it is common practice to appoint a standing committee of a few board members, usually called the 'executive committee' or 'finance committee.' In effect, this committee is given blanket power to make decisions of a specified character during the interval between meetings. The board agrees in advance to approve such decisions of its sub-committee" (Petersen and Plowman, 1953, p. 147). In German business corporations, stockholders are represented by a separate supervisory board *(Aufsichsrat)*. This leaves the executive committee *(Vorstand)* responsible for the management of the firm (Harbison and Myers, 1959, p. 268). In the case of associations, the governing boards of associations are usually much larger than those of business corporations and meet much less frequently. As a result, the need is even greater for the appointment of a small executive committee.

3. A 1935 analysis of 155 large American corporations indicated that the size of boards of directors range from 6 to 35 members. The average was 13 men per board (Gordon, p. 117).

Yet the actual membership of the directorates may be something other than that which is formally prescribed and readily visible to the gaze of outsiders. In a parliamentary system of government (particularly in the case of a coalition government), the real directorates may be not the formal cabinet but a small group of cabinet members associated with political leaders who hold no cabinet post. Nor should it be thought that under the presidential system, the directorate is identical with the president's cabinet. A president usually "sets up circles of his own, picking this selected group for one purpose and that group for another, playing one off against the other, never allowing anyone else to capture too much power. It is this shadowy set of groups that is often called the kitchen cabinet, a colorful phrase indicating that the members of the formal cabinet are frequently over-shadowed in importance by people who are much closer to the President" (*Gross*, 1953, p. 101).[4]

Similarly, the head of a government agency (whether he be called Minister, Secretary, or Director) usually operates as the leader of a small directorate or kitchen cabinet. The other members may be political associates whom he has brought with him upon entering office, personal assistants, one or two top executives or top bureaucrats who have risen to the "inner circle" and even a close associate entirely outside the agency.

In nongovernmental organizations, similarly, the inner executive committees are much less conspicuous than the governing boards as a whole. People who are not formally members of such executive committees may, in fact, be coopted to serve as members of the real-life directorates.

A distinctive characteristic of the members of top directorates is their breadth of interest. They are but rarely fully rooted in, fully dependent upon or fully devoted to the organizations which they direct. Thus, the members of a parliamentary cabinet may be characterized by at least a fourfold division of interests. They may be rooted not only (a) within the cabinet and (b) with the agency whose portfolio they hold, but also (c) in the representative assembly and (d) in the various organizations which have supported their election to the representative assembly. The members of a corporation's executive committee are usually not only stockholders in the corporation, they almost invariably hold stock in other corporations also. They often serve as directors of other corporations. A similar situation exists with respect to almost all associa-

4. This formulation may have been overinfluenced by the author's familiarity with the practices of Presidents Franklin D. Roosevelt and Harry S Truman. President Eisenhower seems to have gone further than his immediate predecessors in establishing a single informal circle of associates, instead of playing individuals and groups off against each other.

tions with the exception of trade unions and churches (in the two latter cases members of top directorates are usually top managers of the organizations). Nor is this phenomenon in any way accidental. It derives from the fact that the top direction of many an organization calls for the interweaving of its interests with those of other organizations in the same society. This is particularly true of the members of governmental directorates, who are personally vulnerable to attack, and perhaps removal from office, by neglected or offended interests. It is also true of those members of business directorates who—under the threat of nationalization, more restrictive governmental controls or trade union attack— become "business statesmen" and assume the role of "trustees" of consumer, labor, and national interests.

Another characteristic of the members of the directorates is their inability to keep in close touch with the operations of the organization. Their very breadth of interest precludes them from giving concentrated attention to what is going on. They have neither the time nor the expertise to cope with the complexities of organizational problems and behavior. As a result, they are highly dependent upon information provided them by top executives and bureaucrats. This frequently gives the impression that on many matters, the top executives and bureaucrats can lead them by the nose, an impression that can often be readily corroborated.

In corporations, this problem can be ameliorated in part by the appointment of professional directors who devote all their time to their directorship functions.[5] In both associations and corporations, it can be dealt with by the cooption of top executives as members of directorates. Yet by and large this problem is too large to be solved by changes in the composition, structure, or operations of the directorates. The vacuum cannot be done away with. It can only be filled by the more concentrated, professional and specialized activities of top executives and bureaucrats.

2. THE TOP EXECUTIVES

The top executives are the highest ranking officers among the full-time and "permanent" personnel of an organization. In corporations and associations they are the presidents and vice-presidents, treasurers and the heads of certain divisions. In government they are the permanent undersecretaries, the bureau chiefs who are not changed with political

5. Although the appointment of professional directors is usually opposed by many board members and most top executives, Koontz and O'Donnell (p. 273) believe that the professional director can be expected to play an increasingly large role in corporate life.

shifts, their chief assistants and, as in the British Civil Service, the higher members of the "administrative class."

The first distinguishing characteristic of the top executives is that they are occupationally oriented toward, and rooted in, the organization as a whole. This concentration of interest distinguishes them from the members of directorates. It provides them with the opportunity for continuity which is essential to expertise.

Their second characteristic is their interest in broad coordination. It is this which distinguishes them from the bureaucrats, whose basic activity is the provision of highly specialized services. The special service of the top executive is to coordinate the specialists.

While the top executive may have started life as a bureaucrat and have risen to eminence within the organization as a specialized expert, his basic calling or profession is administration. It is in this sense that he is often called a professional administrator, a professional manager or a professional executive. Yet this does not mean that he is a "professional" in the full sense of the term. Law, medicine and other recognized "professions" are based on the principles of systematic training, special requirements for admission and a professional code of ethics. Although there are tendencies in these directions in the field of administration, full professionalization has not been reached.[6]

It would be an oversimplification, however, to see the top executives merely as men who operate between the directorates and the bureaucrats. Their horizon must be much wider. They also stand astride the cross-currents of external forces which buffet the organization. In fact, their ability to coordinate the bureaucrats beneath them and to prepare plans which will obtain the support of the top directorates above them will depend to a large degree upon their skill in mediating and balancing the outside interests which impinge upon their organizations. Thus they also tend to become experts in the broad array of outside organizations and powerful individuals whose support is to be won or whose opposition is to be weakened.

3. THE BUREAUCRATS

"The bureaucrats" is a term used to cover a large number of people and groups with different interests and varying degrees of authority and power. They are divided horizontally by intra-organizational divisions

6. The requirements for more mature professionalization are discussed in "A New Profession in the Making" in "The Challenge of the Administered Society" (Chapt. 30).

of labor. They are further divided by varying levels of authority and responsibility. The professionals—lawyers, engineers, natural scientists, doctors, economists, and so forth—are divided by the hallowed boundaries of their established disciplines. Each of these divisions and subdivisions sets up monopolies and quasi-monopolies of knowledge. Within certain boundaries this knowledge is quickly transmuted into power.

Wherever he is located in the hierarchy and no matter how rapidly he may rise, the bureaucrat usually manages to stay a long time in the organization. The longer he stays, the more he knows and the more important his additional knowledge becomes. Thus his power tends to reinforce itself. It is this combination of knowledge plus tenure that led Weber to the conclusion that "the trained permanent official is more likely to get his own way in the long run than his nominal superior, the Cabinet Minister who is not a specialist" *(The Theory of Economic and Social Organization,* p. 338-339).

A similar comment could also be made concerning the relationship between the trained bureaucratic subordinate and his nominal superior, the permanent top executive. An American historian, who had a splendid opportunity to observe American government during World War II, makes a similar observation: "Matters of routine organization are of primary importance. And if you ever want to run the United States of America, never mind about the top jobs; take over the spots at the operating level and you will really have your hands on the controls . . . in any government organization, the operating man is likely to find himself in possession of an effective veto power over the policy man" (Catton, p. 232-233).

Weber made the mistake, however, of assuming that "the capitalist entrepreneur is in our society the only type who has been able to maintain at least relative immunity from subjection to the control of rational bureaucratic knowledge" *(op. cit.,* p. 339). But even at the time when Weber was writing at the end of the second decade of the twentieth century, the capitalist entrepreneur was vanishing. By the middle of the twentieth century, the expert, specialist and technician had already achieved positions of power in business organizations no less than those enjoyed by their fellow-bureaucrats in government bodies. Here, too, the power of the bureaucrats has become a factor capable of standing alongside that of the top executives and the members of directorates.

The "relative immunity" of which Weber spoke is now enjoyed only by the smallest of government and business organizations and by those associations and federations with small staffs and limited functions.

4. THE WORKERS' REPRESENTATIVES

The last century has seen the rapid growth of employee organizations in the form of trade unions. Also, some professional societies engage in quasi-trade union activities.

The basic explanation of the growth of trade unions is that the individual worker is not strong enough to achieve certain objectives by himself. Here also, as in all other fields, organization is the prerequisite of power. The formation of a union group within an organization is a means of countering the power of the administered against the power of the administrators. It also expresses the innate resentment of the administered against the subordination relationships established in any hierarchy. It provides a potential ladder for advancement on the part of the union leaders outside of the closely policed hierarchic ladder of advancement within the organization.

Unlike other powerholders in corporations and government agencies, executives and the bureaucrats, the trade union leaders exercise no authority formally stemming from the ultimate authority of stockholders or voters. From the viewpoint of the organizations in which they spring up, their power is nonlegitimate. It is rooted in the simple ability of the employees of any organization to bring the organization's work to a halt by going on strike or initiating a slowdown. This power is particularly strong in times of a labor shortage and in areas with democratic traditions. It is nourished by the support that can be obtained from other unions, other groups in society and government agencies. It is legitimized by management recognition and by the use of voting procedures in the selection of trade union leaders and the ratification of basic union decisions.

In the early stages of a trade union movement the interests of its leaders are mainly directed toward the security of the organization itself and the improvement of wages and working conditions. However, as the position of the trade union becomes more secure, the sphere of its activities usually broadens. Its interest progressively moves into such fields as social benefits, hiring and firing, promotions, training, work methods and processes, and general grievances on the part of the workers. Thus, the dynamics of the trade union movement bring trade union leaders inevitably into fields previously regarded as the "traditional prerogatives of management." Yet no matter how vehement the protests of directorates, top managers and bureaucrats may be, the trade union leaders usually succeed in amassing sufficient power to invade these fields and stay put.

The posture of trade union leaders is very similar to that of the leaders of a minority political party which can never hope to displace the majority party. The trade union leaders are "an opposition which can never become the government."[7] Since they are destined to be leaders of an eternal opposition, the hope of winning formal control cannot serve as a factor in enhancing their sense of responsibility toward the future of the organization. In fact, the tendency toward "irresponsibility," that is, toward emphasizing demands that could jeopardize the operation of the organization as a whole, is always evident. It is aggravated by the fact that, unlike the usual minority political party, a trade union may represent the majority of its electorate without winning power. This creates a need for continual victories, a need made more intense by rosier promises easily made by rival contenders for union leadership. The more "responsible" a union leader becomes (in the sense of taking into account the needs of the organization as a whole), the more he runs the risk of being rejected by his followers.

On the other hand, the perspective of the trade union leaders may sometimes be much broader than that of the top executive and the bureaucrats. Like the members of the directorates, the trade union leaders often develop much broader interests outside the organization. They may take part in union activities covering the entire craft, locality, industry or nation. They may serve as leaders in a political movement which aspires to, or has already achieved, a considerable degree of political power. They may be interested not only in elections within the organization but in national elections as well.

When we withdraw our attention from the organization within which trade union leaders function as the representatives of employees and look at a trade union itself, the picture becomes very similar to that of other organizations. Effective power is exercised not by the rank-and-file membership but by executive committees, rival cliques or factions, and —in the larger unions—bureaucrats. Even among the large unions, however, there is a tendency toward overlapping between the top executives and the members of the directorates. And apart from a few exceptions, the unions are usually free from an internal opposition in the form of an effective trade union organization operating among its own employees.

7. "The moment a union or union leaders were to take over the management they would be in management's political shoes and would have to act 'the boss.' They would lose their hold on their members and be confronted speedily by a union movement opposing them" (Drucker, 1950, p. 111-112). Where workers' representatives have been given formal representation in management (as in Yugoslavia, Poland, Germany, and France), they have tended to become divorced from the unions (Sturmthal, p. 170, 190).

B. *The Myths of Ultimate Authority*

THE GROWTH of strong organizations has been paralleled in most countries
by the development of procedures and ideologies which place "ultimate
authority" in the hands of voters, stockholders, association members and
representative assemblies. The traditional conception of the democratic
state tells us that ultimate authority is in the hands of the voters. Modern
corporate law tells us that the ultimate control of a corporation is exercised
by a corporation's owners, namely, its stockholders. The modern idea of
democratic associations tells us that in trade unions, trade associations
and other associations authority is in the hands of the rank-and-file
membership. The modern theory of representative democracy explains
that whereas the actual power of voters, stockholders and association
members may be in fact limited, the authority to rule may be exercised
on their behalf by their elected representatives in legislative bodies,
general councils and boards of directors.

To some extent these ideologies and procedures may have the effect
of slowing down or counter-balancing the growing power of the administrators. To some extent they serve as myths which disguise or legitimize
the growing exercise of power by administrators. In any case they should
not be allowed to conceal the growing separation between "ultimate
authority" and actual power. The authority to do things "ultimately" is
by no means as important as the ability to do things in the first instance.
The actual power of these so-called sovereigns is infrequently used and
indirectly applied. They may influence decisions but they do not make
them; they may reign but they do not rule.

1. THE VOTERS IN ELECTIONS

In a dictatorship people go to the polls to vote for a single candidate
or a single list of candidates. Voting for other candidates is usually
outlawed.

But even in a modern democracy the voter has no wide freedom of
choice. The decision for whom to vote is limited, in effect, to the
candidates who are placed on the ballot by organized political parties;
"write-in" candidates are usually of no significance in political campaigns. The choice of party candidates, in turn, is usually determined
not by the members of a party as a whole but by a small group in some
"smoke-filled room." Where party primaries are conducted for the
purpose of using electoral methods to nominate a party's candidate, the

choice is usually between a number of candidates, each one of whom has been named by small groups of competing party factions who make their choice in other "smoke-filled rooms." The formulation of party platforms and the conduct of party campaigns, moreover, are highly organized operations far beyond the control of rank-and-file party members and individual voters.

In a major sense, however, the voters do decide something. On the assumption that the votes are properly counted, they decide who occupies elective office (although in some highly disciplined political parties the higher party council can force an elected member of the legislature to resign and then replace him by someone of their own choice.) But this does not mean that the voters necessarily know for what they are really voting. One cannot blithely assume that many voters are capable of gleaning insight into real issues from the exaggerated claims, counter-claims, charges and countercharges of the typical election contest. One cannot assume that many are really interested in doing so. Apart from widespread apathy, many voters make their decisions on the basis of blind allegiance to tradition, habit, and group affiliation or emotional response to symbols and images waved in front of their eyes by experts in human manipulation.

Furthermore, it is beyond the province of voters to determine in any detailed manner just what their elected representatives will do after they enter office. Election promises and the provisions of campaign platforms are notoriously vague. Even should they happen to be specific, changing conditions and changing problems (apart from a change of heart) provide ample basis for an elected representative or official to behave in a manner unforshadowed by the "voters' mandate." Attempts to make the electoral process serve as a more meaningful guide to government policy have led to the occasional use of such instruments as the "recall" and the "referendum." Yet as a practical matter, these devices can be used only at rare intervals. When used, the recall turns out to be merely a negative device for removing someone from power, incapable of providing positive guidance. The referendum is a more positive instrument, but as such it is used by the actual wielders of power not by the voters.[8]

2. THE OWNERS OF CORPORATIONS

Traditionally, the owner of a machine is someone who has the legal authority to use it in any way he desires. With the coming of the ad-

8. An interesting review of the difficulties in interpreting referenda and plebiscites is found in Friedrich, 1941, p. 536-563.

ministrative revolution, a growing proportion of machinery and other
assets is owned by corporations. The corporations, in turn, are owned
by stockholders. Only in the rarest of instances will all the stock be
owned by members of a family or some other small group. In the larger
corporations, the ownership of stock is spread rather widely, since the
dispersion of stockholding has proved to be a useful way of raising capital
and developing public support. In turn, the dispersion of stockholding
has led to a divorce between ownership and control, between the legal
authority to control property and the actual power to make such control
effective.

As far back as 1918 this revolutionary change in the nature of private
property was pointed out by Walter Rathenau: "The claims of ownership are subdivided in such a fashion and are so mobile that the enterprise
assumes an independent life as if it belonged to no one . . . the depersonalization of ownership, the objectification of enterprise, the detachment of
property from the possessor lead to a point where the enterprise becomes
transformed into an institution which resembles the state in character"
(1921, p. 120-121). A decade and a half later, Rathenau's observations on
German corporations were verified by Adolph Berle and Gardner Means
in their classic study of American corporate enterprise. The two authors
made a careful analysis of the 200 largest American nonbanking corporations at the beginning of 1930. They found that five major types of control could be distinguished and classified the 200 companies as follows:

Type of Control	*Per Cent of Total Wealth*
Almost complete ownership	4
Ownership of a majority of stock	2
Use of proxies	14
Use of such legal devices as pyramiding, non-voting stock, and voting trusts	22
Self-perpetuating officials	58
Total	100%

The authors concluded that "the concentration of economic power
separate from ownership had, in fact, created economic empires and had
delivered those empires into the hands of a new absolutism, relegating
owners to the position of those who supply the means whereby the new
princes may exercise their power (Berle and Means, 1932, p. 69-118).
Although this flamboyant language does not really identify the "new
princes," there are few today who would contest their well-founded conclusion that little economic power over private corporations is wielded
by stockholders as a whole.

Legally, of course, the stockholders of a corporation have as much power as the voters in a democratic state. They can oust the "self-perpetuating officials" and elect new representatives. Thus, the threat of their doing this may influence the actions of the officials.

In actual fact, the stockholders of corporations are usually even further removed from power than the voters in a democratic state. Many stockholders register their stocks in the names of their brokers. A growing proportion of stockholders own stock through the instrumentality of fiduciary institutions—insurance companies, pensions, trusts and investment trusts (Harbrecht).[9] In any case, the stockholders' legal representatives are elected or reelected. In most cases, such elections are modelled after the practice of the dictatorial state—routine ratification of a single list of candidates. The difference is the large number of stockholders who do not take the trouble to vote and are not compelled to do so by the corporate managers. "The widely publicized proxy fights and battles for control of management which enliven the financial pages are actually the rarest exception in corporate life. Even those, as a rule, commonly concern the small corporations. Not once in a decade is the control of a minor giant thus threatened. Managements of the major giants are, for practical purposes, impregnable" (Berle, 1959, p. 63).[10] But when a proxy contest does take place, it is usually when a stockholder "has accumulated large holdings of voting stock though less than a majority but does not have that relationship with management which enables him through them to secure the votes of the small stockholders who habitually and blindly follow management lead" (Aranow and Einhorn; Karr). The contest itself turns out to be an expensive conflict between competing groups of minority interests.

3. THE MEMBERS OF ASSOCIATIONS

In trade unions, cooperatives, fraternal organizations and trade associations, the ultimate authority usually lies in the hands of the members. Yet meetings of the entire membership usually occur but infrequently. In the interim, power is exercised by a small number of administrators and other activists.

When the general membership is polled on specific issues, a significant

9. Harbrecht estimates that in 1957 institutions, not individuals, owned at least 27 per cent of all corporate securities in the United States. The percentage seems to be rapidly increasing.

10. A more detailed study of American stockholders shows that out of 3,000 companies with stock registered on American exchanges, the number of proxy contests per year amounts to less than one per cent—24 in 1956 and 12 in 1957 (Livingston).

proportion of members usually never takes the trouble to answer. When general meetings are called, a large proportion of the members usually stays away.[11] Among those who do attend, one or two minority groups usually monopolize the time and work out the decisions among themselves. Apathy also extends to the payment of dues. A study of a large British trade union, for example, reveals that during the period from 1935 to 1947 about 80 per cent of the national membership were in arrears on dues payments. The entire 80 per cent were therefore, in accordance with union rules, declared "ineligible for official position in the union" (*Joseph Goldstein*, p. 81-89). Moreover, in some organizations the administrative group dictates who is entitled to come to general meetings and who is entitled to vote. By such devices they can perpetuate themselves in power and make a joke of the ultimate authority of rank-and-file members.

This is not to say that no significance can be found in the "democratic mold" in which many of these associations are cast. As Hazard has pointed out in his study of the Soviet political apparatus, there is even significance in the "democratic forms" developed by Stalin to please the masses and expand Soviet influence among foreign leftist groups. Yet in the Russian political system the outward democratic forms are "counterweighted by totalitarian controls" (1957, p. 9). The democratic forms represent the rules of the game, devised in accordance with the cultural expectations and propagandistic needs, whereby minority elements run the show.

Realistic studies of the operations of associations invariably reveal such pictures as the following:

With respect to trade associations:
The effective as well as much of the legal power in the organization rests with the officers, boards of directors and paid staff (Pearce, p. 33-35; 384).

With respect to a national business organization:
The Chamber of Commerce thus illustrates sharply the symptoms of "centralized control" characteristic of modern large-scale business organizations, though many features of its formal organization show the impress of the democratic mold (Truman, p. 136).

With respect to trade union leaders:
Such officials and their immediate associates, through their greater familiarity with the organization's affairs, through their power to name the membership of key committees, and through other advantages derived from their position, play a disproportionately large role in determining policy (Taft, p. 364).

11. It has been estimated that attendance by a quarter of the members at local union meetings is considered good (Millis and Montgomery, p. 246-247).

Thus, while details may vary considerably, the general pattern is very similar: the same separation between ultimate authority and effective power that we find in the case of voters and stockholders.

In one of the most stimulating analyses of the various reasons for this separation, David Truman lists eight factors. The first is organization itself. "Organization . . . implies varying degrees of participation by the membership in the process of decision making. . . . [It] creates or recognizes various roles in a group, some of which involve more intimate and direct participation in the solution of the group's problems than do others." The other factors are the development of managerial skills on the part of active minorities, the influence of strong minority financial interests, the fact that leadership is a time-consuming activity which can be ill afforded by most members, the unequal distribution of innate leadership talents, custom, conflict situations favoring quick or secret action by minorities, and widespread demands for minority leadership (Truman, p. 139-155).

4. THE REPRESENTATIVE ASSEMBLIES

In view of the obvious difficulties faced by the holders of ultimate authority whenever some of them may try to exercise their authority, it is generally held that actual power in any democratic organization should be exercised by their representatives. Thus the idea of "pure democracy" yields to that of "representative" democracy. The key institution in representative democracy is the elected assembly: the legislative branch of a government, the board of directors of a corporation or the national council or representative convention of a trade association, trade union, political party or church.

At the time when representative assemblies were much younger, a favorite subject for political debate was the extent to which an elected representative should be limited to advocating the views of constituents. Some held that the elected representative must be an instructed agent bound by an imperative "mandate." Others maintained, in the words of Edmund Burke, that a representative should sacrifice his "unbiased opinion, his mature judgment, his enlightened conscience" to no set of men living. Today, however, we hear the former point of view only in the heat of battle when specific pressure groups are trying to determine a legislator's vote on a specific issue. The idea that a representative should be limited to "representing" the view of constituents (views which will often be conflicting and, on many important subjects, nonexisting) is no longer seriously advanced.

Yet if representatives are detached from the people they are presumed to represent, they may also be detached from the basic decisions governing the organizations they are presumed to direct. When we look at the representative assembly of any large organization, we shall always find widespread lamentation that "we can't keep up with things" and that "power has been usurped" by the fulltime managers and employees. This is particularly evident in legislative bodies. The great bulk of government decisions, including many of the most important ones, are invariably made not in the legislature but in the executive departments, cabinets and the presidential offices. The role of the legislature has more and more become one of formal ratification—with but minor changes—of legislative proposals that have been drafted elsewhere or of executive action that is taking place or may even have taken place already. The function of public criticism and the airing of complaints may still remain. But even this function has been taken over to a considerable degree by the operation of special auditing agencies (maybe nominally responsible to the legislature) and special investigating committees or commissions.

When legislatures do play a major role in determining the course of government activity, this is usually because they serve as an instrument through which is channeled the power exercised by others. When this power is exercised by conflicting interest groups, it may lead to "stalemate" in government policy—as often happens in the Federal Government of the United States. Where this power is exercised by many squabbling political parties who are unable to reach agreement, it may result in the breakdown of national government and a constitutional crisis. When legislative leaders themselves become key factors in government decisions, this is usually the result of further organization within the legislative assembly, organization which concentrates power in the hands of a minority of committee chairmen, a small steering committee or a cabinet.

In any large association or corporation a similar situation is usually found. The general board of directors is usually far too large a body to operate effectively. Top-level control usually passes to a small executive committee or another form of organized directorate.

In constitutional government, we are told, certain fundamental authority (sometimes referred to as "powers") is reserved to legislatures alone and cannot be exercised by other agencies of government. Yet in the Federal Government of the United States of America, constitutional restrictions have not prevented the growth of a "broad area of overlapping" between legislative and executive activities. Within this area executive officials can choose between seeking legislative sanction or acting on their own. When they decide upon the former, it is usually because they see the legislative process not as a source of superior power but as an instrument which they can manipulate to build public support and influence public opinion. Within this area of choice many decisions which are often regarded as "exclusively legislative"—such as appropriating funds, making treaties, declaring war and repealing undesirable provisions of law—are made by executive officials in the pursuance of their established duties.[12]

c. *The Myths of Central Omnipotence*

FOR THOSE who may be disillusioned by the evident weakness of voters, owners, association members and representative bodies, it is very easy indeed to jump to the other extreme and conclude that larger organizations are always dominated by some single small group or individual. The idea of central omnipotence attests to deeply rooted sentiments that somewhere there must be always an all-powerful, albeit invisible, Guiding Hand. As Victor Thompson has suggested, the "primitive monistic ideal" may help adults in organizations duplicate childhood experiences of subordination to, and dependence on, an all-powerful parent (p. 20, 95). There is less insecurity in facing a world ruled by a cruel or even erring parent or god than in facing the harsher prospect of no central control at all. Many people prefer "to suffer with interpretations that give their world meaning than to relax in the cave without an Ariadne's thread" (Riesman, p. 255). Even for one who may not need such consolations, the idea that everything is run from a single spot behind the scenes "gives one standing as an inside dopester. For individuals with a strong strain of frustrated idealism, it has the right touch of hard-boiled cynicism" (Dahl, 1958, p. 463).

It is not easy to detect the dispersion of power within organizations. The outward trappings of power are worn, and flaunted, by presidents, directors and governing councils. The operations of the other power wielders are less visible to the outsider. One of the reasons, apart from the baffling intricacies of organizational operations, is that bureaucrats often try to disguise their power by assuming the stance of "your humble and obedient servant," a posture well designed to protect them from the dangers of high visibility and leave them more free to handle things behind the scenes. The same outward impression is promoted by top executives who find that it is easier to augment their own power by

12. Various details on the broadening "area of overlapping" and the dwindling area of the "exclusively legislative" are provided in *Gross*, 1953, Chapt. 9, "To Have or Not to Have a Bill."

helping focus public attention, glory and possible censure on members of directorates.

Moreover, a familiar stratagem in any campaign to weaken those who hold positions of power is to accuse them of being much more powerful than they are, thus arousing the resentment of opponents and rivals. This approach is reinforced by power holders, usually members of directorates, who find that one way of trying to accumulate more power is to exaggerate the amount they already have. We thus find widespread propagation of carefully developed myths of the central omnipotence of some single oligarchy or person.

1. THE "IRON LAW" OF OLIGARCHY

During the early years of the twentieth century, the Italian-Swiss sociologist Michels studied the operations of the Socialist parties and the labor unions in Europe. Michels came to the conclusion that, despite their avowed allegiance to democratic principles, the real power in these organizations was always concentrated in the hands of a small minority. In organizations not committed to democratic principles, he reasoned, minority control must be even more evident. He buttressed his findings with liberal support from Mosca, the Italian political scientist who maintained that "in all human societies which have arrived at a certain stage of development and civilization, political control . . . is exercised always by a special class or by an organized minority . . . which monopolizes power and enjoys the advantages that power brings" (1939, p. 50, 325). He drew inspiration from the work of the Italian economist and sociologist Pareto and his theory that "every people is governed by an elite, a chosen element in the population" (1935, para. 246).

Thus encouraged, Michels formulated his famous "iron law of oligarchy." In its purest form this "law" relates only to individual organizations:

> Organization implies a tendency to oligarchy. In every organization, whether it be a political party, a professional union or any other association of the kind the aristocratic tendency manifests itself very clearly. The mechanism of the organization, while conferring a solidity of structure, induces serious changes in the organized mass, completely subverting the respective positions of the leaders and the led. As a result of organization, every party or professional union becomes divided into a minority of directors and a majority of directed (Michels, 1949, p. 32).

Yet Michels also broadened the "law" to cover society as a whole:

> . . . the majority of human beings, in a condition of eternal tutelage, are predestined by tragic necessity, to submit to the dominion of a small

minority, and must be content to constitute the pedestal of an oligarchy
. . . (p. 390).

When democracies have attained a certain stage of development, they undergo a gradual transformation, adopting the aristocratic spirit, and in many cases also the aristocratic forms, against which at the outset they struggled so fiercely. Now new accusers arrive to denounce them as traitors; after an era of glorious combat and of inglorious power, they end by fusing with the old dominant class; whereupon once more they are in their turn attacked by fresh opponents who appeal to the name of democracy. It is probable that this cruel game will continue without end (p. 408).

The Achilles' heel of Michels' formulation lies in his failure to penetrate sufficiently into the internal operations of organizations. In part, this is due to his neglect of government agencies and business corporations. If he had extended his studies to cover the latter groups, he surely would have been more aware of the significance of top executives, bureaucrats and trade union leaders. In many political parties and trade unions, these three centers of power emerge, if at all, only in a blurred and incomplete fashion. The only one of them to be identified by Michels is the bureaucrats, at which point he transfers his attention momentarily to the state. But without examining the operations of any state bureaucracy, he naively and lightly assumed that the bureaucrats are "an army of slaves" who willingly and completely serve the interests of their masters (p. 186).[13]

The intellectual relation between Michels and the Marxists is clear. Marxism also sees history as a continuing conflict between ruling classes and other classes competing for central power. Before Michels, however, the Marxists usually maintained that the victory of the proletariat, the largest of all classes, would mean democratic rule. Michels claimed to complete and reinforce the materialistic conception of history by pointing out that such a victory would merely mean the substitution of a new oligarchy in place of an old one. This refinement was given life some years later by the Lenin-Stalin conception of the Communist Party as the "vanguard" of the working class. Confronted with the exigencies of political rule, however, the Russian Marxists introduced many refinements in the "iron law." Instead of assuming a single minority which could rule by itself, they recognized the necessity of alliances with other groups: as in Russia with peasants and merchant leaders during the days of the New Economic Policy, in colonial countries with representatives of the rising bourgeoisie, and in European capitalist countries, after

13. The fact that bureaucracy is touched upon only lightly by Michels (and indeed is but a peripheral element in his book) did not prevent the American publishers from writing a jacket blurb calling it a "classic study of bureaucracy."

Hitler's ascent to power in Germany, with any capitalist groups willing to enter an anti-Fascist Popular Front.

Yet insofar as its approach to individual organizations is concerned (and this is the heart of the "iron law"), the traditional Marxian concept is as limited as that of Michels. Top executives are not recognized. Bureaucrats are regarded as mere instruments in the hands of the capitalists. Trade unions are regarded as important during the period of capitalist rule and as serving no function other than to prepare the way for the overthrow of capitalism.

In the field of corporate organization, Berle and Means performed a function similar to that of Michels. Just as Michels exposed the fallacy that political parties or trade unions are run by the rank-and-file, Berle and Means exposed the fallacy that corporations are controlled by all their stockholders. Yet while centering attention upon a "controlling minority," they did not analyze its composition. They made no effort to differentiate between boards of directors, executive committees of boards of directors, and top salaried officials. They did not recognize the existence of bureaucrats and trade union leaders within the corporations. Thus they found it possible to talk about "economic empires," "a new absolutism," and "new princes" without noting the dispersion of actual power within these economic empires.

This same bland abstention from attention to the internal operations of organizations is found in the vigorously argued thesis of C. Wright Mills, that the United States of America is dominated by "the leading men in each of the three domains of power—the warlords, the corporation chieftains, the political directorate . . ." (1956, p. 8-9).

At times Mills notes the existence of other centers of actual or potential power. But in order to substantiate his central theme, he exaggerates their dependence upon the ruling oligarchy within the organization. He finds that the top executives are enslaved by the open expectation of rising from their Number Two position to the charmed circle of the directorates although he himself demonstrates that entry into the directorate level is possible only for a small minority. He denies that "a genuine" bureaucracy exists and maintains that bureaucrats are pawns in the hands of the "power elite." He charges that trade union leaders are usually spineless nonentities who can be found "walking backwards into the future envisioned by the sophisticated conservatives" (1948, p. 233).

With Mills, as with the Marxists, the charge of central omnipotence is a clear call to action by those who, as Mills sees it, have not properly used the potential power which lies at their fingertips. He wants more power in the hands of trade union leaders and bureaucrats and, to a lesser extent, top executives. For him, the present dispersion of organizational power is small (in his more flamboyant moods he would even say nonexistent) because the dispersion which he regards as necessary and desirable is so much larger.

The only modern thinker to locate central omnipotence at a level below that of the members of directorates is Burnham, who descends to the top executives in order to find the ruling oligarchy of his "managerial society." According to Burnham, the genuine managers are "the operating executives, superintendents, administrative engineers and supervisory technicians who are in charge of the actual technical process of producing (in the case of government agencies, the administrators, commissioners, and bureau heads)." Burnham purports to find in these people a strong "drive for social dominance, for power and privilege, for the position of ruling class." He finds that this particular group of managers "will exercise their control over the instruments of production and gain preference in the distribution of products, not directly, but through their control of the state which in turn will own and control the instruments of production. The state—that is, the institutions which comprise the state—will, if we wish to put it that way, be the single 'property' of the managers. And that will be quite enough to place them in the position of ruling class" (1941, p. 71-72; 77-95).

There is no need at this point to review all the many criticisms that have been made of the "elite" theories. As Dahl has pointed out, many of these theorists confuse a potential for control with actual control based upon unified action. A similar confusion flows from the assumption that control on some issues implies control on all issues (1958, p. 363-365). Yet the basic criticism, in our judgment, is that these theorists have not identified enough "elites." They have not entered sufficiently into the operations of organizations to note the development of many oligarchic groups. They have failed to note the fact—spelled out in section A of this chapter—that large-scale organization itself inevitably results in the dispersion of interorganizational authority and power among many different centers, rather than in their concentration at any one point. Thus, if we want to talk about an iron law of organization, we must talk about "organized polyarchy." If we want to use language closer to that of Michels, we must change his formulation to "the iron law of multiple oligarchy."

2. THE PROPAGANDA OF ONE-MAN RULE

The idea of one-man rule has had much less theoretical backing than that of the single oligarchy. Thus Mosca finds that although one person may stand "at the helm of the states" he would certainly not be able to govern "without support of a numerous class to enforce respect for his orders and to have them carried out . . . he certainly cannot be at odds with the class as a whole or do away with it." On this, none of the other theorists of single oligarchy would disagree with Mosca. For a full justification of one-man absolutism, one would have to go back to the absolute sovereign of Hobbes or perhaps the tyrant of Aristotle.

Its lack of popularity among modern theorists has not prevented the myth of one-man rule from achieving considerable prominence in the practical politics of Fascist and Communist movements. Mussolini called the state "a violin in the hands of a maestro." He and his supporters lost no opportunity to identify the maestro as Il Duce himself, the infallible leader who would revive the ancient glory of the Romans. In Germany, thousands of Nazis declared with Goering that Adolph Hitler was "simply infallible" and "must possess any quality attributed to him in its highest perfection" (*Germany Reborn*, p. 79). During the Stalin period in Russia, Stalin was transformed into a veritable god-king by statues, portraits and ceaseless eulogy of his wisdom and infallibility. In all these three cases, the myth of personal omnipotence was used as a device for strengthening the power of specific constellations of minority groups in the party, in the army, the secret police and government and industrial enterprises.

Yet few sober students are misled by these myths. The political scientist and the historian usually realize that the so-called absolute dictator generally provides a classic example of the man riding on a tiger. If the dictator departs from established channels of action and the established expectations of those groups upon whose support he relies, he is apt to move quickly from the top of the tiger to its insides. The very violence and bloodshed which the dictator uses in dealing with competitors are evidence not of his absolutism but of the existence of competition.

Hence, as the historian penetrates into the actual operations of the so-called one-man absolutism, he finds major differences between the reality and the myth. In the case of Russia, for example, there is little support for the contention that the shift from the Stalin to the Khrushchev period was simply from one-man control to collective control. Stalin himself was the "organization man" par excellence. Stalin "developed a system of competing and overlapping bureaucratic hierarchies . . . the Party, the secret police, the armed forces, state administration, and industrial administration." While these were subject to Stalin's direction, "they also operated as centers of influence in their own right. . . . Behind the monolithic façade of Stalinist totalitarianism, the plural pressures of professional bureaucratic interests found expression" (Fainsod, p. 578-

579). They represented forces which found still more expression under Stalin's successors.

In the case of fascist Germany, Trevor-Roper claims that Germany might have won World War II if its degree of central control had been as great as that which one might assume from Nazi propaganda on the power of Hitler. The real picture, he maintains, was one of confusion:

> Only policy, not administration, was effectively controlled at the center. . . . In Nazi Germany, neither war production nor manpower nor administration nor intelligence was rationally centralized. . . . The structure of German politics and administration instead of being as the Nazis claimed, "pyramidal" and "monolithic," was, in fact, a confusion of private empires, private armies and private intelligence services. In truth, irresponsible absolutism is incompatible with totalitarian administration" (1956, p. 2).

But what about the masterful business entrepreneur who carries all before him by the sheer force of his personality? What about the "massive brain in the swivel chair" who snaps out one decision after another as trembling subordinates file in and out?

As many observers have pointed out, this stereotype of the successful businessman has changed radically since its prevalence in the nineteenth century and the early decades of the twentieth. Yet it is doubtful if it was ever fully based on reality. In fact, we can apply to the "business despot" the same criticism which Bentley made in 1908 with reference to one-man "despotism" in government. "Can we then say that the despot has 'absolute' power? Surely not, without giving a technical and closely-limited meaning to 'absolute.' He must get his information from other people . . . he must leave an immense mass of detailed work to his lieutenants to perform, which means at least the rudiments of a division of power. . . . There will be established lines on which these functions will be conducted. There will be limits to the activities of bureaucrats and despots alike, which cannot be exceeded without penalties" (Bentley, p. 314-315).

As an organization gets bigger, each individual in it becomes—in a certain sense—smaller. The Big Boss of early industrial capitalism was no exception to this rule. The pressure of outside forces has forced upon him a civilized veneer and, at times, the trappings of an industrial statesman. The pressure of executives and bureaucrats within the organization has knocked out of him the "I am God," "I am the Law," "I know it all" approach. With the growth of expertise and power throughout the organization, it has become clear that he does not know so very much. A god who is less than all-knowing must move down from the Heavens and become more of a mere mortal.

For genuine one-man rule we can go to only two places. The first is the authoritarian manager of a single unit within a larger organization. Here, by refusing to delegate authority to others, by keeping his hands on every petty detail, a bureaucrat can indeed at times succeed in setting up an absolute monarchy. This is indeed one of the factors contributing to the dispersion of intra-organizational power.

The second place is a small organization in its entirety. Here an authoritarian manager can sometimes succeed in concentrating all significant power in his own hands. The smaller the organization, the more this is possible. Yet if the organization grows larger, the continuation of one-man rule heralds the downfall of the "boss," the organization or both. Or else the boss's total control exists mainly in his own mind. As more and more important things are decided by others, he satiates his will to power by exercising greater and greater control over details of lesser and lesser importance.

Chapter 4

THREATS TO MANKIND

ALTHOUGH the administrative revolution has made possible many achievements that people scarcely dared to dream of in past epochs, it has also created—or been associated with—major threats to man as an individual and to society as a whole.

These threats are usually discussed in a spirit of bland abstraction from the facts concerning organizations and their administration. They are a favorite subject for the swapping of proverbs and purely speculative philosophizing.

On the other hand, both administrators and serious students of administration often shut their eyes to these problems. The practice and study of administration can become an ivory tower in which people can hide themselves from the implications of the administrative revolution.

For my part, I am convinced that administration cannot be fully understood without viewing it in the broader perspective of society and culture as a whole. The task of this chapter, therefore, is to consider the threats of the administrative revolution to the individual, to society and to the very continuation of human life on this planet—particularly as revealed in the burgeoning literature of antiorganizational revolt.

Answers to these problems, however, cannot be rationally discussed without a serious effort to understand the behavior and internal life of organizations and their administrators. Hence all direct discussion of "what might be done" is reserved for one of the last chapters in the book, "The Challenge of the Administered Society" (Chapt. 30).

A. *The Dehumanization of Man*

IN THE EARLY DAYS of the Industrial Revolution there arose a vigorous literature of protest against the degradation of labor in filthy factories and sweatshops and of life in teeming urban slums. In the more advanced societies of the world these horrors have considerably diminished. There is reason to expect they may be eliminated. The leaders of developing nations often believe they can partially skip this stage, or at least ameliorate conditions through welfare services.

But the literature of revolt was never limited to physical conditions. It also accused large-scale organizations of committing the following "crimes" against the individual:

- treating him like a cog in a machine
- subordinating him to the organization
- alienating him from truly human relations with others, and
- promoting mental breakdown

While the other charges have become weaker, these have become stronger. They are heard both in developed and developing economies. They have swelled into a formidable literature of revolt against organizations, bureaucrats and administrators.

Little research has yet been undertaken to provide the evidence backing up these charges, let alone help formulate them more precisely. Thus most of the literature in which they are contained is really "literature." It is penned mainly by reformers, satirists, commentators and artists, although some of them may don the robes of sociologist, psychiatrist, or economist.

Much of this indictment is excellent literature. It seems to ring true. It depicts an important aspect of life in the modern world, even though the colors may sometimes seem unduly somber. It reflects widespread fears and anxieties, themselves a part of life in the administered society. It raises questions that demand attention.

1. THE "FRACTIONATION" OF WORK

As far back as in the days of Adam Smith, economists noted that with the growing division of labor the worker's "dexterity at his own particular trade seems in this manner to be acquired at the expense of his intellectual, social and marital virtues" (Smith, p. 735). Karl Marx observed that the system of concentrating individual work upon minute parts of a total production process "converts the laborer into a crippled monstrosity, by forcing his detailed dexterity at the expense of a world of productive capabilities and instincts; just as in the States of La Plata they butcher a whole beast for the sake of his hide or tallow. Not only is the detail work distributed to different individuals, but the individual himself is made the automatic motor of a fractional operation . . ." (Marx, *Capital*, p. 396).

The monotony of fractionated work has also tended to remove the worker from creative participation in the work process. But as Drucker has pointed out the problem of monotony is minor; in many circumstances, in fact, monotony has its virtues. The more serious problem is that "the worker has not enough relation to his work to find satisfaction in it. He does not produce a product. Often he has no idea what he is doing or why. There is no meaning in his work, only a pay check" (1946, p. 158).

Merton has carried this thought further in his observation that "the splintering of work tasks involves *loss of public identity of the job.*" Can one's wife, children or friends find any social meaning, any claim to respect or deference in one's work in turning three screws, watching four gauges or aligning five parts of a part of a part? This absence of social meaning goes further toward alienating the worker from his job and in making his wage his chief symbol of social status (1957, p. 319).

With only minor adaptations this analysis applies as much to the white collar worker, technician and manager himself as to the manual worker. The clerk may have even less contact than the worker with the goods or services which are produced; he deals with paper-work and routines. The technician immerses himself in the labyrinth of technique; he too often tends to become an example of what Veblen called "trained incapacity." The manager occupies himself more and more with the production of power, prestige, profits and relations with people; he has less and less to do with the goods or services which his organization produces.

The effect on personality is particularly striking in the professional world. Here the division of intellectual labor has led to an unbelievable degree of specialization and subspecialization. The deeper the professional man burrows into his specialty, the greater the social distance which is created between himself and his fellows, including other professionals. On the credit side, this may serve as a tight little island of emotional security, protected against all intruders by a Maginot line of impenetrable jargon. On the debit side, this often also insulates him from creative contact with the real problems of real life, which usually defy neat classification in terms of disciplines and subdisciplines.

2. SUBORDINATION TO THE ORGANIZATION

As an abstract proposition, one might assume that a person working in a narrowly specialized area could both apply his creative spirit within this area and function as an independent individual outside it. However, a growing body of social criticism suggests that with many or even most people exactly the opposite may be the case. Albert Schweitzer is only one of many who have claimed that "over-organized societies" have "shattered" the human spirit (Gollancz, p. 216). David Riesman and his associates (1951) maintain that the typical "character type" in the modern world has become the "other-directed person." This type has a "built-in radar set" which gives him continuous messages on what is expected of him. Although he enjoys a higher standard of living than his predecessors, he pays for this improvement by having to live in "a centralized and bureaucratized society and a world shrunken and agitated by the contact —accelerated by industrialization—of races, nations and cultures." His main concern is not with action but with relations with other people. He manipulates them or is manipulated by them. He becomes the victim of "false personalization" or "enforced privatization." The messages from his radar set tend to dominate his life.[1]

The same basic idea has been further developed by those who have written about the "mass man" and the "organization man." According to Lewis Mumford, the human being produced by modern civilization tends to become

> . . . a mass man: incapable of choice, incapable of spontaneous, self-directed activities: at best, patient, docile, disciplined to monotonous work to an almost pathetic degree, but increasingly irresponsible as his choices become fewer and fewer: finally, a creature governed by his conditioned reflexes—the ideal type desired, if never quite achieved, by the advertising agency and the sales organizations of modern business or by the propaganda office and the planning bureaus of totalitarian and quasi-totalitarian governments (1951, p. 14).

In 1959 a general of the U.S. Strategic Air Command issued "a directive dividing each squadron into groups of three to five men and assigning a non-commissioned officer to find out just what 'the airman does with his off-duty time, whom he associates with and to consel him

---

1. The "other-directed" person is contrasted with "the tradition-directed personality," who is to a large extent influenced by the culture of his society as transmitted to him by the small number of individuals with whom he comes into contact, and the "inner-directed personality," who has inside of him a "psychological gyroscope" of his own.

in the areas where he shows a weakness.' Everything from the airman's automobile to the cut of his hair was to be looked into." When the directive was publicly criticized, the Air Force quickly withdrew it. The general who had issued it ruefully described the system as "only what any father would be doing for his son." In commenting upon the rescinded order, an editorial in *The New York Times* (December 17, 1959) hinted that the new order may have done little more than describe more vividly a policy that had been in force for some time. But neither the general nor the editorial writer pointed out that the "big brother" or "big father" approach was not the invention of the Air Force. The generals merely borrowed it from large corporations which have long followed the practice of keeping close track of the private lives of administrative personnel. In these organizations personal advancement—once one gets past the barrier of initial appointment—is often made conditional upon the type of person one marries, his use of leisure time, the kind of friends he associates with, and a host of other personal characteristics having no direct relationship with the job he is supposed to perform.

The tyranny of the organization has also served as a theme used by modern artists in surrealist painting, in music, in poetry and in the dance. Its most vivid development, however, is found in the novel. In the early 1930's Aldous Huxley wrote his well-known *Brave New World*, a projection into a future six or seven hundred years away. This was a world in which individualism was destroyed by the "nightmare of total organization." A little less than twenty years later, after the world had a chance to view the works of both Nazism and Stalinism, George Orwell published his *1984*. The difference between the two worlds is that for Huxley individualism was eradicated by a scientific caste system and the abolition of free-will through methodical conditioning and the use of drugs and various hypnotic techniques. Orwell's dictators achieve the same objectives through terror and espionage. Looking back upon his prophecies from the vantage point of 1958, Huxley concludes in *Brave New World Revisited* that they "are coming true much sooner than I thought they would" and that both democratic and communist regimes are moving toward a society organized along Huxley or Orwell principles.

A picture of modern society which is in many ways even more terrifying is presented in the strange and nightmarish novels of the Czechoslovakian writer, Franz Kafka. In *The Castle* K. wanders aimlessly in the lower levels of a labyrinthine bureaucracy peopled by strange faceless creatures whose private lives are dominated by their own conceptions of the anonymous occupants of the unseen, unvisited Castle. *The Trial* recounts the experiences of another K. who is arrested on charges that are never specified. Even on the last pages, when a knife is finally plunged into K.'s aching heart, the reader still does not know the identity or the motives of those who have dominated, and finally ended, K.'s life.

A softer, but still rather devastating, picture is painted by William H. Whyte in his analysis of the person who not only *works* for The Organization but who *belongs* to it as well. This is "The Organization Man." While he may give occasional lip-service to the Protestant Ethic of individualism and risk-taking, his life is conducted for him by the new Social Ethic which glorifies the virtues of belongingness, togetherness, conformity and adjustment to the group. "The Corporation Man is the most conspicuous example. But he is only one, for the collectivization so visible in the corporation, has affected almost every field or work." The seminary student, the doctor, the physics Ph.D., the research intellectual, the young engineer and the young lawyer—they are all being molded into organization men who find a refuge from the harsh uncertainties of freedom within the bosom of the organization and who soon become past masters at the great art of "playing it safe." If an organization man should try to resist, if he should reassert some measure of his own individuality, he faces a dilemma. "It is not a case of whether he should fight against black tyranny or blaze new trails against patent stupidity. That would be easy—intellectually, at least! The real issue is far more subtle. For it is not the evils of organization life that puzzle him, but *its very beneficence.* He is imprisoned in brotherhood" (1956, p. 12). It might be added that there are still stronger bonds than beneficence and brotherhood. Many individuals throw themselves completely into their organizational work. For the organization, which serves for them as a symbol and substitute for mother, wife and self, they are willing to sacrifice family relations, friendships, leisure, personal development and individuality itself. It is no exaggeration to say that they "love that organization." In place of the light ardors of adolescence and early marriage they are consumed by passionate dedication to an organization which swallows them up in its all-enveloping embrace.

3. SOCIAL- AND SELF-ALIENATION

With the growth of closer relations between the individual and the group, one might think that the result would be closer relationships between people. Critics of the administrative society grant the new closeness but strongly maintain that these relationships are becoming increasingly nonhuman.

"Due to the bigness of the apparatus to be administered, and the resulting abstractification," observes Fromm, "the bureaucrats consider neither with love nor with hate, but completely impersonally; the manager-bureaucrat must not feel, as far as his professional activity is concerned; he just manipulates people as though they were figures or things. . . . Everybody is to everybody else a commodity, always to be treated with a certain friendliness, because even if he is not of use now, he may be later . . ." (1955, p. 136, 139). Fromm calls this alienation.

Still more serious is the tendency toward man's alienation from himself. "The alienated person is out of touch with himself as he is out of touch with any other person. . . . His sense of self does not stem from his activity as a loving and thinking individual but from his socioeconomic role. . . . He experiences himself, not as a man, with love, fear convictions, doubts, but as an abstraction, alienated from his real nature, which fulfills a certain function in the social system."[2] Or else as a thin substitute for a deeper sense of self, he plays a series of roles in relation to others, roles which have the function of winning friends and gaining approval (*Ibid.*, p. 120-122; 142-143).

A parallel tendency is found in the trend toward the dehumanization of cultural values. Entertainment becomes a highly organized mass activity which emphasizes escapism. Education becomes preoccupied with techniques and utilities. The humanities decline as a field for study and development. Intellectualism becomes suspect. The materialistic values of wealth, efficiency and status become dominant. The academic pedant who teaches Shakespearean drama within the confines of textual exegesis, and thus misses contact with one of the great adventures of the human spirit, also contributes to the dehumanizing process. The fact that he may be a stalwart defender of the humanities against the natural sciences, the professions and such new intruders as business and public administration is merely a pathetic example of the ease with which, in a materialistic society, the forms of humanism may be honored by those who destroy its substance.

4. FRUSTRATION AND NEUROSIS

Anyone with a modicum of organizational experience knows how easily organizational life can lead to frustration and how numerous are the opportunities it provides for the venting of aggression upon others. Argyris (1957) has summarized a vast amount of research which gives depth and meaning to this common-sense observation. In fact, he has

2. In this sense the meaning of "alienation" is close to that assigned it in the nineteenth century when it was regarded as a form of self-estrangement just a little less serious than insanity. This meaning is still preserved in the use of "alienist" to refer to a doctor who deals with the insane.

formulated the thesis that formal organization itself requires "behavior that tends to frustrate, place in conflict, and create failure for psychologically healthy individuals." In part, the result may be a variety of defense reactions (such as daydreaming, aggression, ambivalence, regression, projection), apathy and disinterest toward the organization, and the creation of informal groups to sanction the defense reactions, apathy and disinterest. Another result may be a further stimulus to climb the organizational ladder and reach heights where individual goals are presumably less in conflict with those of the organization. Unfortunately, most of the research work which Argyris draws upon to substantiate his hypothesis deals with people at the lower levels of the bureaucratic hierarchy. Insufficient attention is thus given to the innumerable factors making for frustration and "management ulcers" at the higher levels of the bureaucracy and among the top executives and members of the directorates.

Organizational life at all levels provides abundant opportunity for people to solve their internal conflicts through such neurotic solutions as hostility and aggression, fixation and compulsiveness, compliance and helplessness, withdrawal and isolation, sublimation and displacement. In turn, neurotic behavior in organizations unquestionably gives rise to more frustration, more failure, more internal conflicts—thus promoting additional neurotic behavior. Nor should this be regarded as something which necessarily interferes with organizational performance. Neurotic drives are often the basis of organizational success. In fact, the large-scale organization often provides the ideal framework within which the neurotic personality—and on rare occasions even the psychotic personality—can attain positions of leadership.

If a serious conflict may exist between the needs of individuals and the demands of organizations, perhaps this conflict extends to the administered society as a whole? Thus Sigmund Freud has suggested that in the modern world culture and civilization may themselves come into conflict with human needs. He thus arrives at the concepts of "social neurosis" and the "pathology of civilized communities" (1953, p. 141-142).

This theme has been developed further by Fromm, both a follower and a critic of Freud. Fromm (1955) suggests that in the modern world normalcy itself may be pathological. He holds that the widespread failure to obtain freedom, spontaneity and a genuine expression of self is a "socially patterned defect." He enthusiastically quotes Spinoza's observation that greediness and ambition are forms of departure from sanity. His conclusion is that our over-organized society has become an insane society.

B. *The Sickness of Society*

THE ADMINISTRATIVE REVOLUTION has had a shattering effect upon society by removing the props from beneath many established and long-cherished ideas concerning the nature of society.

The new constellations of organizational power have reduced to a state of insolvency the conventional models of capitalist and socialist economics. In neither case have new conceptions been fashioned to take their place.

They have often been associated with the rise of dictatorships and the decline of democracies. They have rendered the traditional models of political democracy increasingly irrelevant.

The ideological vacuums thus created would not be so serious if they were merely aesthetic defects in the architecture of modern thought. Yet the breakdown of established ideas has occurred at a time when administered society itself shows signs of breakdown and indeed appears to be drifting—sometimes hurtling—toward utter self-destruction. Under these circumstances the collapse of principles is tragic and the need for new guidelines on the future of the administered society is imperative.

1. THE INSOLVENCY OF "CAPITALIST" AND "SOCIALIST" PRINCIPLES

When one appraises the traditional principles of capitalist and socialist economics, one finds valuable assets in both.

The classical and neoclassical capitalist economists have developed impressive techniques of analyzing the price system as a means of resource allocation. They have formulated many useful conceptions and precisely-stated generalizations concerning economic behavior under specified conditions. Their work helped rationalize the development of large-scale industrial organization. It has subsequently served as an effective "counterbalance to radical or bureaucratic illusions concerning what can be accomplished through centralized planning and as a valuable rationalization for conservative political movements." The Keynesian dissenters have helped to preserve classical and capitalistic principles by explaining how free market forces could somehow or other result in depression. They have helped rationalize and design public measures to combat depression through fiscal and monetary policies, thus promoting the further development of large-scale government organization.

They have crystallized the basic concepts of national economic accounting and promoted pioneering activities in economic statistics (Gross,
1957, p. 80-81).

Yet despite these unquestioned assets, capitalist economics cannot
meet its current liabilities. Although it has held forth the promise of
explaining economic behavior, it is not able to explain the operations
of an economy dominated by large corporations, trade unions and government regulatory agencies. It has few trustworthy instruments for
dealing with economic life which does not conform to its narrowly
circumscribed competitive conditions. It has few instruments capable of
dealing with monopolies, cartels and trade agreements. It has barely begun
to approach the problem of analyzing economic development in underdeveloped countries. It usually closes its eyes to the large-scale private
and public organizations whose very existence demonstrates the remoteness between the classical and neoclassic economic model and the
economic reality. The major needs it can satisfy are the appetite for
statistics, the eternal demand for rationalizations to legitimize the predetermined decisions of private or public organizations, and the desire
of economists themselves to perfect this or that technical speciality.
It has also proved a useful device for rationalizing opposition to major
industrial investment in underdeveloped countries, where the marginal
revenues of an individual project will often be less than the marginal costs.
In helping prevent broad programs of economic change, marginal analysis
thus helps keep underdeveloped countries on a marginal basis. For those
who participate heavily in these and similar benefits, capitalist economics
is a going concern, and no amount of evidence will change their minds.
For those who seek guidance in the real world of administered economies,
it cannot meet its debts as they come due. In this sense, capitalist economics
is insolvent.

In making this appraisal, I am using insolvency in the sense given
to it by equity courts: namely, inability to meet debts as they mature.[3]
This is quite different from the bankruptcy conception of insolvency:
assets worth less than liabilities. A corporation which is insolvent in the
equity sense may be very far from bankruptcy. In the same way a system
of thought which is currently insolvent may include very considerable
assets which can be made more productive through reorganization and
incorporation within a broader framework.

The assets of traditional socialist economics are also significant. So-

3. For the concept of insolvency as applied to systems of thought, I am indebted to Peter Drucker's discussion of the insolvency of personnel management
(1954, p. 287-288).

cialist thought maintains that private activities should be subordinated to the general interests of society through nationalization (or other forms of public control). It suggests that central planning or central decision can make up for the irrationalities of unplanned behavior. It holds forth the hope of rationality and cooperation as a form of social action. It stresses the inescapable connection between economics and the rest of society. It recognizes the importance of group interaction and group conflicts. It has directed attention to the distribution of economic power and the condition of the underprivileged. It has provided a highly emotional rationale for the international socialist movement (now declining), for the international communist movement (which seems to be spreading), and for ambitious new elites in underdeveloped countries.

Yet socialist principles are even further than capitalist principles from keeping their promises. If a government nationalizes a company or an industry and then turns to socialist theory for a guide as to what to do next, it can get no help. The founders of socialism were so preoccupied with the problems of obtaining power that they completely neglected the very practical question of what to do with power after it has been obtained. It is not very relevant to criticize the Russians for abandoning Marx in the administration of their national economy. Neither Marx nor the multitudinous Marxians who came after him had much to say about how a socialist economy should be administered. Socialist economics is also insolvent.

If one listens carefully to some of the debates between American and Russian statesmen, one might come to the conclusion that the world stands at the crossroads. Their speeches are filled with references to grand choices between competing systems. One would think that on the basis of performance of these different economic systems, the countries of the world have to choose between some form of modern enlightened capitalism and some form of socialism, either the more democratic or the more dictatorial variety.

Yet this choice itself is as empty as the great principles of capitalist and socialist economics. The two systems are not so far apart. If one wants to continue to use the words "capitalistic" and "socialistic," one must realize that both systems represent a certain combination of the two elements. These old-fashioned terms themselves hardly provide a significant basis for the classification, description and analysis of the differences between the huge administered economies of the modern world. The "great choice" itself has vanished.[4] This formulation of "the"

4. "A faith in grand alternatives is, in one sense, obsolete. Socialism and capitalism, planning and non-planning, welfare state and laissez-faire—these are not the alternatives open to Western societies" (Dahl and Lindblom, p. 517).

problem can only be a liability to those interested in decisions that must be made in shaping the structure of any modern economy. This approach is not merely insolvent, it is bankrupt.

2. THE RISE OF TOTALITARIANISM

One of the great paradoxes of the administrative revolution is that it has intensified ancient conflicts between democratic and authoritarian ways of life.

On the one hand, it has brought unprecedentedly large numbers of people to higher levels of education, self-awareness and freedom from grinding poverty. It has created a continuous revolution of rising expectations of material comfort, self-development and political liberty.

On the other hand, in large-scale bureaucratic organization, coupled with scientific methods of communication, persuasion and terror, it has created unprecedented instruments of power over people. Social conflicts and personal frustration have repeatedly created situations in which relatively small minorities have been motivated to use these instruments in destroying political liberties.

This latter trend has been accelerated in the half century following the end of World War I. During this period millions of people were killed in the gas chambers, torture chambers and concentration camps of the German Nazis and the Italian and Japanese fascists. Other millions died in the carnage of World War II, which spelled the doom of these regimes. But the decline of fascist totalitarianism saw the rise of communist totalitarianism. Between the two wars the only successful communist regime was in the Soviet Union, but after World War II communist totalitarianism was established in China and in Poland, Hungary, Czechoslovakia, Yugoslavia, Bulgaria, Rumania, Albania, and Cuba. These regimes now seem rather firmly established in a vast area embracing more than half of the world's population.

It is a serious error to assume that all communist regimes are alike in all respects—perhaps even more serious than the simplistic equation of communism with fascism. It is also nonsense to assume that in any communist regime there can be a total concentration of power in the hands of any one man or small group. This point was discussed in the preceding chapter. It will be developed at greater length in "The General Environment" (Chapt. 18).

But in their two-pronged approach to democratic ideology all communist totalitarian regimes are surprisingly alike.

On the one hand, they both make a sharp attack on the "false democracy" of the so-called "bourgeois" or "capitalist" governments.

They charge that it is merely a façade behind which a capitalist dictatorship enslaves the great majority of workers, peasants and intellectuals. They charge that such a system is incapable of providing appropriate employment opportunities and living standards for the great masses of the people. This can be done properly only by a dictatorship of the proletariat or a united front of "people's parties," either of which is to be led by the communist party.

At the same time, they both claim that they themselves are the true democracies, the "people's democracies." In the short run, whatever constraints they may place upon political liberty, are placed there in the interests of the people. In the long run, when there is no longer any threat of capitalist dictatorship from within or without, there will no longer be any need for dictatorial countermeasures by the people's representatives. Whether or not the state will go so far as to wither away (as stated in the Marxist ideology of an earlier era), they claim that the people's democracies will in time become still more democratic.

3. THE BREAKDOWN OF THE DEMOCRATIC MODEL

There is no great difficulty in finding the weaknesses in the democratic pretensions of the "people's democracies." It is very easy for people in Western Europe and North America to point out condescendingly that the existence of mass elections and an elected legislature is not enough to provide true democracy. The true democratic model calls for a choice between opposing candidates. This model is perverted when voters are presented with a single list of communist party candidates. The democratic model requires freedom not only to speak against the policies of the dominant party but also to organize an opposition. This model is subverted by the suppression of open opposition parties and by the totalitarian policy of preventing the operation of any organizations that may become centers of opposition power.

But it is much harder—if not impossible—to counter totalitarian pretensions with the traditional model of political democracy.

The traditional model assumes certain conditions which cannot be found—and which few people would really want to establish—in the Western democracies. It assumes that elections really direct the affairs of a nation. One would indeed have to close his eyes to the realities of political life in order to convince himself that this is what happens in the administered societies of the United States of America, England, France, Italy, Western Germany and other "democratic" nations. As already pointed out in our discussion of the weakness of "ultimate authority," the electoral process comes to grips with major issues only in the most general way and on selected occasions. Legislative assemblies dwell on the periphery of genuine decision-making, rarely coming close to or staying long at the vital center.

As a limiting influence on some abuses of administrative power, as an opportunity for the expression of dissident views, democratic forms and procedures are of tremendous value. But these forms and procedures have only an occasional and remote relation to the world of cabinets, kitchen cabinets, chief executives, presidents and vice-presidents, bureau and division chiefs, experts, technicians, and bureaucrats of all sorts. The bargaining activities of big groups and big lobbies which make national policy through agreements and conspiracies of their own, which can operate through government agencies or outside of government channels—this world is not recognized in the democratic model. As an explanation of what happens in the democratic nations the traditional model of popular control through electoral systems, legislatures and competing parties, is insufficient. As a guide to the adaptation and improvement of the basic institutions of governmental action in developed countries, it cannot help very much. It can help even less when applied to a wide variety of developing countries, particularly those with little national tradition and extremely low levels of education. In short, the traditional democratic model has broken down as a viable and complete alternative to totalitarianism.

c. *The Possibility of Self-Destruction*

THERE WAS A TIME when the dinosaurs were the largest and most powerful of all the beasts of the world. Yet as conditions changed, the dinosaurs failed to change; they perished. All that is left behind are some old fossils which serve as reminders of their ancient grandeur.

The fate of the dinosaur may well serve as a precedent for that of many of our large modern organizations. As organizations become very large, they tend to lose their dynamism. Their leaders fail to adapt to new conditions; their members resist change. Many of their subunits continue to go through the motions of established activity even after the purpose of such activities has vanished.

Kenneth Boulding explains this tendency in terms of what he calls "the principle of increasingly unfavorable internal structure." As an organization increases in size beyond a certain point, "it becomes more and more difficult to maintain an adequate system of communication between those people who are directly in contact with the environment of the organization (foremen, salesmen, parish priests, deacons, privates, instructors, local organizers) and those who are in major executive positions . . . if the information system is inadequate, however, information which is essential for the survival of the organization does not get transmitted to those who are mainly responsible for its policies" (1953, p. 23-25).

From this point of view, the tendency to organizational growth leads inevitably in the direction of collapse. On the other hand, the organization which does not grow perhaps comes even closer to a stage of breakdown. While growth itself is an essential part of any form of life, either physiological or organizational, the cessation of growth is itself a form of decay. Thus both the expanding organization and the static organization seem to be confronted by destruction. While this might seem paradoxical at first glance, it is merely a reformulation in terms applicable to social organizations of the second law of thermodynamics. This law asserts that there is a tendency for entropy—that is, the unavailability of energy for specific purposes—to expand within every system.

As we look back again at the dinosaur, it seems unlikely that he really died of old age. The probability is that he was killed.

From this point of view Boulding's parallel becomes even more uncomfortable. Organizations, closely associated with their economic suppliers, are amassing weapons of destruction capable of eradicating animal and plant life on this planet. Preparation for a new war has become the largest single long-range planning activity in the world. The assumed inevitability, probability or possibility of a third world war has become a guiding principle for the operations of a very considerable number of members of directorates, top managers, bureaucrats and trade union leaders. This possibility is so much taken for granted that people who talk about the necessity for peace or disarmament are looked upon with a suspicion which may, in fact, be sometimes justifiable. Disarmament proposals and "peace offensives" have often been seen as devices to lull the enemy into dropping his defenses and prepare the ground for victorious military action.

Nor need war come merely because some administrators duly launch an offensive. If an American or Russian radar man should mistake a dead satellite, a stray meteor or a ghost electronic echo on a radar screen for an incoming ballistic missile, he might easily provoke the launching of a barrage of countermissiles. In the space of but a few hours the whole world could be a blast-shaken shambles of fire and radioactivity.

But this possibility of unwanted self-destruction is not limited to accidents. As Herman Kahn has pointed out, it can also be brought about by "unauthorized behavior of either man or equipment . . . psychopathic or irrational individuals, mechanical or human failure, sabotage, irresponsible behavior, and so on" (1960, p. 154). These possibilities will multiply as membership in the "nuclear club" is enlarged and many countries will be capable of starting the "doomsday machine"[5] in motion. From the point of view of the physical power it has been able to amass, the administrative revolution reached a new and historic peak when a few countries became capable of destroying the world. A still higher peak, by this same standard, will be reached when this capacity is shared by many others.

Whether this power of destruction will in fact be used, or when it may be used or the possible extent of the devastation—these are subjects on which many people differ sharply. Yet there is no dispute anywhere in the world on the possibility that this power *may* be used and that it *may* destroy all human life on this planet. On this, both the optimist and the pessimist, the idealist and the cynic will agree. The possibility of total self-destruction is the final threat spawned by the administered society.

5. The term "doomsday machine" is here used for the process of attack and retaliation not, as in Kahn, to the extreme case of one explosion that could destroy the world.

Part II

THE DEVELOPMENT OF ADMINISTRATIVE THOUGHT

Chapter 5

THE ANCESTORS

ONLY IN THE TWENTIETH CENTURY has administrative thought emerged as a differentiated field of sustained writing, conscious observation, abstract theory, and specialized terminology. This has been both a product of the administrative revolution and a factor that has helped spin still faster the wheel of administrative innovation and historical change.

Yet for tens of centuries considerable thought has been given to organizations and their governance. Only by thoughtful and deliberate effort was it possible to build and operate the world's earliest armies, churches, governments, empires and other complex enterprises. The nature of this achievement may be inferred from the remaining records concerning these organizations. But this belongs to the history of administration, not of administrative thought.

When we look for recorded administrative thought in the more general sense, we find that in most cases it is part of the rich tapestry of philosophic (or even religious) commentary on man and his relations to fellowmen, state, and society. At times we find flashes of intellectual lightning that directly illuminate major aspects of administration. At other times (as with the great political philosophers) we find writings that, while relating to organizations and their administration, are presented in a broader context and with a different vocabulary than is usually used today. In fact, so many aspects of political philosophy and political economy are relevant to our field that we must satisfy ourselves with but a few typical illustrations.

It is interesting to note that many of the ancestors served as advisers to government rulers. Some gained significant experience in administrative posts, sometimes rather high ones. Most of them learned in practice how great the demand had always been for thinkers who provide "the ruler with a rational explanation of what he, the ruler, had already done" or of what he would like to do (Parkinson, 1958, p. 9). While we need not go so far as does Parkinson in contending that "the book comes afterwards to defend the deed," we must not automatically presume that the thinkers discussed below shaped administrative affairs in the societies in which they lived. Many of them, in fact, suffered the traditional anguish of the adviser, seeing their most cherished ideas ignored, misunderstood, or perverted. It would not be possible, without historical analysis of the society in which each lived, to make a judgment concerning the balance between "shaping" and "being shaped."

A. *Advice to Rulers*

ONE OF THE GREAT TRADITIONS in ancient literature has been advising rulers on the conduct of affairs. Much of this advice is embedded in great religious texts such as the *Mahabhrata* and the Old Testament, where it often appears in the form of parables or maxims. Some is found in the more worldly writings of such philosophers and commentators as Confucius, Liu Shao, Plato and Aristotle. Some is presented in a long series of "what to do and how" treatises. Many of these—such as Kautilya's *Arthasastra*,[1] Nizam Al-Mulk's *The Book of Government*,[2] Machiavelli's

---

1. Kautilya was a minister and King-maker who helped overthrow the Nanda dynasty in India and place Chandragupta Maurya on the throne. His *Arthasastra* (available in translation by Shamasastry, Mysòre: Mysore Printing and Publishing House, 6th edition, 1960) is a comprehensive treatise that attempts to set forth general principles and detailed rules for the management of a despotic state's internal affairs and foreign relations. It is claimed to have been written by Kautilya in the period 321-296 B.C., but may in fact have been written by others in later years.

2. Nizam Al-Mulk served as vizier in the late eleventh century A.D. to the sultans of the Saljuq dynasty in Persia. At least part of *The Book of Government* seems to have been written in an effort to restore himself to royal favor. Shortly after the book's completion around A.D. 1690, he was slain by one of the assassins whom he had denounced in the book.

The Prince,[3] and Taylor's *The Statesman*,[4]—are extremely realistic. While some of this realism is applied to detailed techniques in such areas as warfare, espionage, palace guards, prostitutes, taxes, and letter-writing, much of it is of more general and perennial applicability.

1. BE WISE

Solomon was not the only wise man to hold that "wisdom is more precious than rubies" and that by wisdom "princes rule and nobles, even all the judges of the earth" (*Proverbs*, 3:15, 8:16).

Perhaps the fullest conception of this view is found in the philosopher-king conception of Plato (428-348 B.C.): "Until philosophers are kings, or the kings and princes of this world have the spirit and power of philosophy, and political greatness and wisdom meet in one, and those commoner natures who pursue either to the exclusion of the other are compelled to stand aside, cities will never have rest from their evils—no, nor the human race, as I believe . . ." (*Republic*, Book V).

In his later years, after bitter experience as an adviser to Dionysius, the tyrant of Syracuse,[5] Plato is less perfectionist. In his last work, *The Laws*, written in the serene disillusionment of old age, Plato describes the "second best community." Here he assumes that the rulers will be something less than philosophers and that they will be dragged downward by the "sinews" or "cords" of their baser instincts. As a counteracting force to bring them back to the paths of wisdom, Plato turns to the "leading string, golden and holy, of 'calculation' entitled the public law of the State." The other cords are hard and inflexible. But the "golden cord," flexible and gentle, with the help of those who are ready to subordinate themselves to the common good, will lead people toward a society based on temperance, moderation and harmony.

3. Machiavelli served for fourteen years as a middle-level bureaucrat in republican Florence. When the Medici came to power in 1512 and ousted the republican officials, Machiavelli retired to a farm and wrote *The Prince*. He hoped that the book, dedicated to Lorenzo de Medici, would pave the way to a new appointment. The effort failed; the book won him more enemies than friends. But together with *The Discourses*, it won him a firm place in the history of political science.

4. Henry Taylor was Permanent Under Secretary in the British Colonial Office. He wrote *The Statesman* in 1836 to "divert the attention of thoughtful men from forms of government to the business of government."

5. Dionysius invited Plato to Syracuse to advise on establishing a model government along the highest philosophic lines. When the two disagreed, Plato was offered for sale in the slave market. Bought by a friend who set him free, he returned to Athens with less illusions than when he had left for Syracuse.

The Confucians also stress the importance of administration by men of wisdom. Confucius (551-479 B.C.) himself tended to see wisdom as flowing from literary scholarship. A practical-minded disciple like Mocius (c. 470-390 B.C.) finds that wisdom comes from using procedures and systems developed by specialists.

> Whoever pursues a business in this world must have a system. A business which has attained success without a system does not exist. From ministers and generals down to the hundreds of craftsmen, every one of them has a system. The craftsmen employ the ruler to make a square and the compass to make a circle. All of them, both skilled and unskilled, use this system. The skilled may at times accomplish a circle and a square by their own dexterity. But with a system even the unskilled may achieve the same result, though dexterity they have none. Hence every craftsman possesses a system as a model. Now, if we govern the empire, or a large state, without a system as a model, are we not even less intelligent than a common craftsman? (1928, p. 226).

Occasional attention is given to the possiblity of expertise in general administration itself. Thus in one of the Socratic dialogues "recorded" by Xenophon, a battle-scarred soldier protests to Socrates (c. 470-300 B.C.) that despite his military experience he has not been chosen as a general. Instead, he complains, the people have chosen "Antisthenes, who has never served in a marching regiment, nor distinguished himself in the cavalry and understands nothing but money-making."

Socrates points out that Antisthenes, in addition to knowing how to raise money and being eager for victory, has been very successful in organizing a chorus. The soldier is outraged. He insists that "there is no analogy between the handling of a choir and of an army."

In reply, Socrates observes that although Antisthenes "knows nothing about music or choir training, he showed himself capable of finding the best experts in these. . . . Whatever a man controls, if he knows what he wants and can get it, he will be a good controller, whether he control a chorus, an estate, a city or an army."

"Really, Socrates," cries the soldier, "I should never have thought to hear you say that a good businessman would make a good general."

Socrates counters by listing the common functions of both a businessman and a general. "The management of private concerns," he summarizes "differs only in point of number from that of public affairs. . . . Neither can be carried on without men, and the men who are employed in private and public transactions are the same. . . . Those who understand how to employ them are successful directors of public and private concerns, and those who do not, fail in both" (Xenophon, III, p. 183-189).

Like Socrates (as reported by Xenophon), Plato also saw management, or rule, as an element common to different types of organizations.

King, statesman, master, householder—all are concerned with the management of people. This art deals not with the management of people as mere individuals, but rather with people organized into groups. It is the art of "man-herding," of collective management. Its two main divisions are compulsory management and voluntary management. The tyrant knows only the former. The true statesman practices the art of "voluntary management of herds of voluntary bipeds." The most important thing about this art is based upon scientific knowledge. Since only a few people can ever obtain this knowledge, true government will always be in the hands of a small body or an individual. The masters of this "royal science"—which might be called politics, economics or management—weave together into one royal web the other arts and sciences. They also weave together the different types of peoples, both the brave and the temperate, who comprise the human herd (*Statesman*).

The first serious effort to distinguish among various types of people was made between A.D. 240 and 250 by Liu Shao, a retired Chinese official in *The Study of Human Abilities*. "Of all wisdom," writes Liu Shao, "there is nothing more valuable than to know men." Everyone thinks he can understand men. "But when we see men examining other men, we may conclude that knowledge is not obtained." The reason is that people of ability recognize qualities they share but have difficulty in appreciating other qualities. Liu Shao's observations on this point have been summarized as follows by his American translator (1937, p. 77):

The Ability	*What It Recognizes*	*What It Does Not Recognize*
The man of sublime behavior	The constants of human nature	Strategy
The legalist	Uprightness	The adaptability of strategy
The strategist	Strategy	Obeying the law
The man of instrumental ability	The working of a plan	The origins of institutions
The astute man	Strategy	The constancy of doctrines
The practical man	Progress	The transforming power of virtue
The critic	Reprimanding	The variations of masterfulness
The man of words	Retort	Rhetoric and style

Moreover, the standards men use in judging others are rambling and confusing. "Therefore, the chance that good abilities and those who can recognize them should meet is hardly one in ten thousand. The chance that one is able to recognize good abilities and also be in high position so as to be able to employ them is hardly one in a hundred. The chance that one should be in high position, and have the facilities for recommending such men is hardly one in ten" (*Ibid.*, p. 151).

A still more humble conception concerning human wisdom—one that is echoed in many ancient works—is contained in the words of a high Persian official in a famous book written to prepare his son for possible kingship: "Do not be puffed up with your own learning and virtue, nor think that you already know everything. Account yourself as being of the company of the foolish, for you only become wise when you realize your own unwisdom . . ." (Kai Kaus, 1951, p. 32).

Many centuries later Henry Taylor, the Victorian official who never went to a university, ridiculed the idea that an academic or literary background prepares men for high public office. He argued that the wisdom of independent thought is unfavorable to statesmanship. "The business of a statesman is less with truth at large than with truths commonly received. . . . His presumptions should be in favor of such opinions as are likely to be shared by others. . . . His object should be, first, to go with the world as far as it will carry him; and from that point taking his start to go farther if he can . . . (*The Statesman*, p. 44). Above all, the essence of administrative wisdom lies in understanding the importance of acting through others. "The importance of his operations vicariously effected ought . . . to predominate greatly over the importance which can attach to any man's direct and individual activity. . . . But it is a snare into which active statesmen are apt to fall, to lose, in the importance which they attach to the immediate and direct effects of their own activity, the sense of that much greater importance which they might impart to it if they applied themselves to make their powers operate through the most effective and widest instrumentality. The vanity of a statesman is more flattered in the contemplation of what he does than of what he causes to be done . . ." (*Ibid.*, p. 33).

2. BE GOOD

"Be good" is also one of the most time-honored aphorisms on the management of men. At times, it is seen as the companion of "Be wise." At other times, it is seen as the ultimate value. Still greater differences, naturally, are found in the specification as to just what is "good."

The approach to administration developed by Confucius and his followers is based upon a fusion of politics with ethics. This provides a delightful blend of lofty moral principle and homespun practicality. One of Confucius' disciples, Tsekung, once asked Confucius what are the prerequisites for successful government. "People must have sufficient to eat," Confucius replied. "There must be a sufficient army; and there must be confidence of the people in the ruler."

"If you are forced to give up one of these three objectives," asked Tsekung, "what would you go without first?"

"I would go without the army first," Confucius replied.

"And if you were forced to go without one of the two remaining factors, what would you rather go without?" asked Tsekung again.

"I would rather go without sufficient food for the people. There have always been deaths in every generation since man lived, but a nation cannot exist without confidence in its ruler" (Lin Yutang, 1943, p. 11-24).

Confidence can exist only when good men conduct the affairs of government. "When the ruler himself does what is right, he will have influence over people giving commands, and when the ruler himself does not do what is right, all his commands will be of no avail."

The ruler or the administrator must be a "good person" in all his relationships. Above all, he must be true to himself. "There is only one way to gain confidence in one's authority: if a man is not trusted by his friends, he will not have confidence in those above him. There is only one way to be trusted by one's friends; if a man is not affectionate toward his parents, he will not be trusted by his friends. There is only one way to be affectionate toward one's parents: if a man, looking into his own heart, is not true to himself, he will not be affectionate toward his parents. There is only one way for a man to be true to himself. If he does not know what is good, a man cannot be true to himself" (*op. cit.*, p. 121, 199).

For the Taoists and the Buddhists, however, the Confucian conception of "good" is too worldly. As believers in nonworldliness, passivity and mysticism, they take direct issue with the rationalism and practicality of the Confucians. While Confucius called for wise men in government, Lao Tse said "Banish wisdom, discard knowledge and the people shall profit a hundredfold. . . . Exalt not the wise, so that people shall not scheme and contend." While Confucians called for diligence and energy, Lao Tse wrote "In managing human affairs, there is no better rule than to be sparing—that is, never do too much" (Lin Yutang, 1948, p. 56-271).

Yet below the surface of this philosophy "do little or nothing," one can often find a deep current of practical wisdom on how to do things effectively. Lao Tse's verse on rulers supplies us with a gem-like picture of a certain type of extremely effective management:

> Of the best rulers
>   The people (only) know that they exist;
> The next best they love and praise;
>   The next they fear;

And the next they revile.
When they do not command the people's faith,
Some will lose faith in them,
And then they resort to oaths!
But (of the best) when their task is accomplished, their work done,
The people all remark, "We have done it ourselves."
(*op. cit.*, p. 114.)

Indian philosophy provides a strange blend between otherworldliness more otherworldly than Taoism and practicality more practical than Confucianism. The ultimate aim of human life is *moksha,* which can be translated as release from the bondage of human existence. But three wordly objectives are also recognized: *dharma,* religious and moral duty; *arthra,* material possessions, and *kama,* pleasure and love. While ancient Indian literature includes many treatises on each of these four aims, those dealing with *dharma* relate most directly to the role of the "good" in worldly life. In *The Code of Manu* (probably written sometime between the sixth and second centuries B.C.), Manu says, "I will declare the duties of Kings and show how a king should conduct himself. . . ." The king's first duty is to preserve *dharma* by the merciless, although just, use of punishment:

> Punishment alone governs all created beings, punishment alone protects them, punishment watches over them while they sleep: the wise declare punishment to be identical with the law . . .
> If the king did not, without tiring, inflict punishment on those deserving to be punished, the stronger would roast the weaker, like fish on a spit.
> The whole world is kept in order by punishment . . . (Brown, 1958, p. 26-39).

In the great epic poem, the *Mahabhrata,* probably recorded in its present form during the third and fourth centuries A.D., *dharma* during normal times is seen mainly as the duty to be righteous. "One becomes a king for acting in the interests of righteousness and not for conducting himself capriciously. . . . If the king acts righteously, he attains to the position of a god. On the other hand, if he acts unrighteously, he sinks into hell . . ." (*op. cit.*, p. 35-48).

3. BE BOLD

At times, the very boldness of the leader or ruler is elevated to the level of a major principle. In the *Mahabhrata* this principle, like many others, is often illustrated by animal fables. For example, a mouse lived in the jungle in the same tree with a wildcat who was always trying to catch him. One day the wildcat himself was caught in the meshes of a net placed by a trapper. The mouse rejoiced and paraded around boldly in front of his trapped enemy. Suddenly the mouse was threatened by an owl in a branch above and by a mongoose on the ground. He promptly asked to be sheltered in the bosom of the cat, and in return, promised to gnaw through the meshes of the net in order to save the cat from the trapper. The cat agreed. The mouse jumped to safety between his paws. But instead of carrying out his promise at once or even after the owl and the mongoose had disappeared, he postponed action as long as possible, using the claws of his enemy as a protection against the dangers of the jungle. Only when the trapper was seen approaching did he gnaw through the mashes and release the cat. The obvious moral of the tale is the importance not only of temporary expedients but also of bold and shrewdly-timed alliances (Zimmer, 1956, p. 87-89).

The case for boldness is also stated more abstractly in the *Mahabhrata:*

> No man can reap good without incurring danger. If, again, he succeeds in preserving his life amid danger, he is sure to earn great benefits. A king should ascertain all future danger; when they are present, he should conquer them; and lest they grow again, he should even after conquering them, think them to be unconquered (Brown, p. 45).

Executive boldness is also a main theme with Machiavelli (1469-1527). In reviewing the rise of such leaders as Moses, Cyrus, Romulus and Theseus, he observes that "they owed nothing to fortune but the opportunity which gave them matter to be shaped into what form they thought fit; and without that opportunity, their powers would have been wasted, and without their powers, the opportunity would have come in vain" (*The Prince*, Chapt. VI).

Machiavelli clearly prefers boldness to the cautiousness and timidity of the moderates. To drive his point home, he compares the handling of public affairs with the "management" of women:

> . . . Fortune is a woman, and it is necessary, if you wish to master her, to conquer by force; and it can be seen that she lets herself be overcome by the bold rather than by those who proceed coldly. And, therefore, like a woman, she is always a friend to the young, because they are less cautious, fiercer, and master her with greater audacity (*Ibid.*, Chapt. XXV).

A somewhat different model of executive energy is presented by the Victorian, Henry Taylor, who urges that bold action be subjected to the control of outward order, calmness and gentlemanly equanimity. Yet a "man of business" should resist the temptation to deal with the easiest matters first. Rather, he should "deal first with the question of greatest difficulty, being that which most requires to be encountered in the bloom of novelty, with the unblunted edge of conscious energy"

(*The Statesman*, p. 64-67). Moreover, a comfortable marriage (and one that brings wealth, if he be not wealthy by inheritance) will help him concentrate his energies upon public affairs. "A statesman's almost incessant engagements hardly admit, unless upon the call of passion, any other occupants of his affections than such as, being inmates of his house, fall, as it were, into the chinks of his time" (*Ibid.*, p. 60).

4. BE WILLING TO COMPROMISE

All rulers, the ancients realized, are buffeted by opposing pressures and opposing principles. If they hew too strongly to principles of virtue, they may fail in their efforts. "Be not righteous overmuch; neither make thyself over wise," warns Solomon." Why shouldest thou destroy thyself?" (Ecclesiastes, 7:6). The Confucians, however, translated the necessity of compromise into a principle of virtue itself. For them, the Golden Mean between extreme forms of action becomes the essence of goodnss.

The same idea is found in most Greek philosophy. Abstract virtue must be tempered by practical wisdom. Goodness flows from harmonious action. With Aristotle, the "golden mean" is the kingpin in both his ethical and his political system. The basic policy for rulers is moderation, "nothing in excess." He then translates this general principle into specific advice to the rulers of different types of government. Democracies, which usually attack the privileges of the rich, should spare the rich. Aristocracies, similarly, should prevent the circle of privileged aristocrats from becoming too small. Oligarchies should encourage and help the poor. They should also compensate for their narrow basis of public support (in contrast with democracies) by the quality of their organization. Tyrannies have a basic choice. They can behave in the traditional fashion —that is, break the spirit of their subject, breed mutual distrust, and render their subjects incapable of action by impoverishing them or keeping them constantly occupied with public works or with wars. Or else the tyrant can preserve himself by turning his tyranny, at least in part, into kingship. He can do this by behaving with personal dignity and moderation, showing himself as the steward of public revenues and courting the favour of the masses as well as the notables (*Politics*, Book V).

The spirit of compromise is also found in the advice of Nizam Al-Mulk:

> The king should so wage war against his enemies that there remains room for peace; he should so contract friendships that they can be broken, and so break them that they can be mended. He should not drink wine for the sake of intoxication. Let him not be constantly jocular, not altogether austere . . . Then we will possess both worlds. In all things

he should take the middle course, for the Prophet (upon him be peace) said, "the best of things is the middle of them" (*The Book of Government*, p. 251).

A different aspect of the problem is revealed in Henry Taylor's discussion of the enforcement of standing rules and regulations. He points out that some officials "are accustomed, with too much regard to their own convenience and too little to the specialties of cases, to insist upon adherence to system or precedent." Unless we would spoil the meat to save the salt, officials should realize that "personal individualities may, from time to time, be of such moment as to make it well worthwhile to set aside the general rule on account of them" (*The Statesman*, p. 68-69).

5. BE UNSCRUPULOUS

As we move further along the road of "realistic" advice, we find a current of thought which suggests that true wisdom may be found not only in being bold but also in departing from commonly accepted notions of goodness and moderation. Thus the more "practical" ancients advise using any means that may be justified by the ends that are sought.

Han Fei Tsu justifies such an approach on the ground that the ruled themselves may behave badly:

> In ruling the state, the sage does not count on people doing him good, but utilizes their inability to do him wrong. If he counts on people's doing him good, within the boundary there, will never be enough such persons to count by tens . . . (Lin Mousheng, p. 110).

In his commentaries upon the way different kinds of governments should be run, Aristotle includes advice to tyrants on how to maintain their rule. The tyrant "sows distrust among his subjects, he takes away their power, he humbles them." He may also behave more like a monarch. He should "adorn and improve his city, as though he were not a tyrant but a guardian of the state." But like all monarchs he should not allow any one person to become too great. "If one is promoted, then two or three should be also, so that they may look sharply after one another. If, after all, someone has to be made great, he should not be a man of bold spirits; for such dispositions are ever most inclined to strike. And if anyone is to be deprived of power, let it be diminished gradually, not taken from him all at once" (*Politics*, Book V).

While the Indian concept of dharma emphasizes righteousness and moral behavior in normal times, classic works of Indian philosophy prescribe entirely different behavior for periods of disaster and emergency. For such periods they propound the law of the jungle. This is done with vivid bluntness in such general maxims as these from Book XII of the *Mahabhrata:*

> Both kinds of wisdom, straight and crooked, should be within call of the king.
> Might is above right; right proceeds from might; right has its support in might as living beings in the soil. As smoke the wind, so right must follow might. Right in itself is devoid of command; it leans on might as the creeper on the tree.
> If thou art not prepared to be cruel and to kill men as the fisher kills the fish, abandon every hope of great success.

In keeping with this general approach, the strategems of deception and treachery are raised to the level of principle. One of the basic rules of conducting both foreign and domestic affairs is that of *maya,* the creation of an illusion. In the Vedic myths the gods themselves use *maya* when they assume the form of animals or ordinary men. For those who cannot rely on such magic feats, Book XII of the *Mahabhrata* provides detailed maxims:

> Carry your enemy on your shoulder until you have got from him what you want. Then throw him off and shatter him, like an earthen jar against a rock.
> When he lifts his hand, ready to strike his enemy, he should accost him in a friendly way. He should address him even more gently while delivering the deadly blow. And when he has cut off his enemy's head, he should pity and bewail him.

In his *Arthasastra,* Kautilya applies these principles to specific problems of government. In the field of foreign affairs he sets forth an international political geometry in his science of the *mandala,* the circle of states. This science is based on a model of concentric circles. Each king must regard his own country as standing in the center. Surrounding him is a circle of enemies, his immediate neighbors. Around the enemies he must build a circle of friends, who will threaten his enemies. But around them will be a ring of remoter danger comprising those states which may supply reinforcements to his enemies. Foreign policy consists of adjustments in the various concentric rings. These adjustments are made on the basis of power: "for it is power that brings about peace between any two kings; no piece of iron that is not made red-hot will combine with another piece of iron."

In the management of domestic affairs Kautilya emphasizes the difficulty of finding men of high character to serve as ministers and other officials. Men "are naturally fickle-minded, and like horses at work, exhibit constant change in their temper." They are apt to be unfaithful and to plot rebellion. Above all, they are given to stealing:

> Just as it is impossible not to taste the honey or the poison that finds itself at the tip of the tongue, so it is impossible for a government servant not to eat up, at least, a bit of the king's revenue.

He also recognizes the difficulty of finding out what actually happens:

> Just as the fish moving under water cannot possibly be found out either as drinking water, so government servants employed in the government work cannot be found out while taking money for themselves.

Kautilya's solution for these problems consists, in part, of detailed administrative control. This involves precise predetermination of the form, place, time, and costs of all work and daily examination of results. Severe fines and punishments must be meted out for errors and carelessness. In larger part, however, he outlines an elaborate system of spying and allurements. The king should create a network of spies to check on the activities of both ministers and officials. These spies must not only provide the king with information. They should also test ministers and officials by subjecting them to various temptations. With considerable relish, Kautilya defines five forms of administrative espionage and four types of allurements.[6]

In the Western World Machiavelli's stress on "the ends justify the means" has been one so widely known that "Machiavellian" has entered some Western languages as a synonym for "unscrupulous." And truly there is something which will always shock many people in Machiavelli's basic advice to rulers:

> How we live is so far removed from how we ought to live that he who abandons what is done for what ought to be done will rather learn to bring about his own ruin than his own preservation. . . . Therefore it is necessary for a prince, who wishes to maintain himself, to learn how not to be good, and to use this knowledge or not use it, according to the necessity of the case . . . (*The Prince*, Chapt. XV).

Yet the only difference between Machiavelli and his Indian predecessors, apart from the former's use of illustrative material from European history, is Machiavelli's fervent patriotism. His elucidation of "the law of the jungle" adds little to that set forth in the *Mahabhrata* and the *Arthasastra*.

6. For further commentary on Kautilya, see D. Brown, *White Umbrella*; "The Art of Politics: Kautilya," p. 49-63: and Zimmer, *Philosophies of India*, Chapter I of Part II, "The Philosophy of Success," p. 87-139.

Centuries later the Victorian gentleman, Henry Taylor, tried to reconcile the necessity of "official lies" with the code of truth-telling. Admitting that members of a government must publicly support measures with which they disagree, he suggests that "no government has ever been formed, any one member of which has been other than a liar." He justifies such lies on the ground that there is a difference between private and public morality. "Falsehood ceases to be falsehood when it is understood on all hands that the truth is not expected to be spoken." Above all, the primary test of right and wrong is "the balance of all the consequences, near and distant, obvious and involved." Statesmen, therefore, must be expected to weigh all these consequences. Having spoken so bluntly, Taylor then confesses that he has "written this chapter with a trembling hand" (*The Statesman*, p. 80-85).

6. BE WELL-ADVISED

Whether they seek to be wise, good, bold, moderate or unscrupulous, rulers must seek the help of advisers. "Where no counsel is, the people fall; but in the multitude of counsellors there is safety" (Proverbs, 13:1, 14). The king must lay his problems before the elders. "Let him daily worship aged Brahmans, who know the Vedas and are pure; for he who always reveres aged men, is honored even by the evil spirits" (Brown, p. 30). Nizam Al-Mulk quotes from the Koran to show that even Mohammed, the Prophet, was instructed by God to advise with others. "Since God commanded him to seek advice and even he needed counsel, it is obvious that nobody can need it less than he" (*The Book of Government*, p. 95). Al-Mulk goes on to warn against allowing "people of the veil to have any say except in matters concerning their own underlings and servants. He quotes the Prophet's command: "Consult women, but whatever they say, do the opposite, and that will be right" (*Ibid.*, p. 188-191).

It is important to pick advisers carefully. Thus, for one Indian thinker, one may consult with military men on *how* to conduct war but not on *whether* to declare war:

> Military officers are not to be consulted in the determination of policy. They are only too ready to clutch at war. Strife is the law of their being. They are not to have a hand in the formation of policy lest they involve the state in needless wars. Besides, if they are placed in control of civil policy, they may grow dangerously proud and powerful (Prasad, p. 235-236).

Machiavelli emphasizes the role of the ruler in the use of advisers. In addition to choosing the best possible advisers, the ruler must ask the right questions of his advisers and encourage them to speak freely. "He ought to be a great asker and a patient hearer. . . . Wise counsels, from whoever they come, must necessarily be due to the prudence of the prince, and not the prudence of the prince to the good counsels received" (*The Prince*, Chapt. XXIII).

Machiavelli also advises on how to advise. He cautions "not to undertake to advocate any enterprise with too much zeal." An adviser runs serious risks if he appears to be the sole source of a course of action which ends unsuccessfully. Better to gain the "great credit which you will have if, after having modestly advised a certain course, your counsel is rejected, and the adoption of a different course results unfortunately." He also touches the ever-ticklish problem of how to propose drastic changes in the status quo. His solution is simple: "retain the semblance of the old forms." Most men are more interested in appearances than in realities and are more influenced by the things that seem than by those that are. Thus, in all innovations it is useful to retain as much as possible of the previously existing forms (*Discourses*, Chapts. XXXV, XXV).

A more idealistic statement on the proffering of advice to rulers is made by Castiglione in his famous attempt to set forth the ideal personality of the Renaissance gentleman, or courtier. Courtiership, with all that it involved in command of the arts, is not an end in itself. Rather, the end of courtiership is to go so far in winning the good will of the prince that "the Courtier, without fear or danger of displeasing the Prince, can tell him and always does tell him the truth concerning everything proper for him to know" (*The Book of the Courtier*, p. 50).

A classic statement of the practical administrator's objection to unsolicited advice from "ignorant" observers is recorded under the name of Lucius Paulus, a Roman General (229?-160 B.C.). After observing that commanders should be counseled chiefly by people present at the scene of action, Paulus continues as follows:

> If, therefore, anyone thinks himself qualified to give advice respecting the war which I am to conduct—let him not refuse assistance to the State, but let him come with me to Macedonia.
> He shall be furnished with a ship, a tent, even his traveling charges will be defrayed, but if he thinks this is too much trouble, and prefers the repose of a city life to the toils of war, let him not on land assume the office of a pilot. The city itself furnishes abundance of topics for conversation. Let it confine its passion for talking to its own precincts and rest assured that we shall pay no attention to any councils but such as shall be framed within our camp.[7]

7. Quoted on frontispiece by Leonard Drohan in *Come With Me To Macedonia*, New York: Knopf, 1957.

In an age when criticism was still less to be avoided, Henry Taylor suggested a more positive way of dealing with unrequested advice from people in positions of formal authority:

> He who objects to what is proposed or written in the transaction of business should consider himself under an obligation to propose and execute something to be substituted; for every political measure is in the nature of an alternative, and is not to be pronounced good or bad except as it is better or worse than some other equally definite course of proceeding which might be adopted instead of it (*The Statesman*, p. 70).

On the other hand, Taylor found much greater value in suggestive criticisms from people who lack formal authority and are close to events. "Official criticism is chiefly valuable when exercised by the inferior functionary upon the work of the superior, who will be enabled to weigh the comment undisturbed by deference for the authority of the commentator" (*Ibid.*, p. 71). Whether or not the inferior functionary will be disturbed by the authority of his superior is a point Taylor does not mention.

B. *Administrative Education*

THE APHORISM that managers and leaders are born, not made, has probably been most widespread precisely in those societies where birth does not bestow the mantle of authority. In monarchies, where the legitimate king of the future *is* born (and even where there may be confidence in his inherited abilities), it has generally been recognized that he must be *made* also. Even in the earliest monarchies this led to considerable speculation on the kind of education most befitting a future king.

But kings, no matter how well trained, also need help—particularly when trying to maintain or expand their power in the face of an ambitious or even rebellious aristocracy. This, in turn, led in the past to the proffering of advice on the training of skilled servants, civil and otherwise.

1. RULERS

Much of ancient Indian political thought, which invariably takes monarchy for granted, centers around the question of how to educate young princes. Thus, in the Code of Manu we find this curriculum:

> From those versed in the three Vedas let him learn the threefold sacred science: the primeval science of gorvernment, the science of dialectics,

and the knowledge of the Supreme Soul: from the people the theory of the various trades and professions (Brown, p. 30).

One Indian author lays down a somewhat fuller curriculum distinguished not only by gentlemanly breadth but also by attention to laughter, strategy and the art of love:

> The Veda, archery, medicine, sacrifices, astronomy, grammar, the origin of writing, the performance of sacrifices, eloquence, rhetoric, the art of love, interest, purity of families, the ten names, computations, chess, dice, the study of origins, music and song, the art of playing on the conch, dancing and laughter, the art of prestidigitation, education, the making of garlands of flowers, massage, the science of precious stones and valuable materials for clothing, silk, sealing, weaving, wax work, strategy, sewing, sculpture, painting, arrangement of garlands, interpretation of dreams, interpretation of the flight of birds, horoscopes of boys and girls, the training of elephants, the art of playing on the tambourine, the rules of battle array, the domesticating of horses, the carrying of the lance, jumping, running and fording a river (Prasad, p. 218).

As one might expect, Kautilya's approach is more practical. One of his first principles in the training of crown princes is the selection of proper teachers. The first part of the day shall always be devoted to learning the military science. The second part can then be divided between the "sacred canon," philosophy, economics and politics. The teachers of economics shall be "the heads of the administrative departments." The teachers of politics shall be "those versed in its theory and practice." The prince shall also learn self-discipline and self-control "at first from the teachers: afterwards he shall constantly associate with those of mature learning, for discipline depends upon such associations" (Ghoshal, p. 121).

Plato presented a much more elaborate program for the training of his philosopher-kings. He prescribes a series of four "barrier examinations" at the ages of twenty, thirty, thirty-five, and fifty. Until the age of twenty there shall be universal compulsory education beginning at an early age, with emphasis upon gymnastics, music and individual sciences. Those who excel will enter a ten-year program in which they will learn the relations between the various sciences and develop their powers of dialectical reasoning. At the age of thirty those who have distinguished themselves will study philosophy for another five years. Those who survive this test will then be sent into the world and "compelled to hold any military or other office which young men are qualified to hold; in this way they will get their experience of life, and there will be an opportunity of trying whether, when they are drawn all manner of ways by temptation, they will stand firm or flinch." This phase will last fifteen years. Then at the age of fifty "those who still survive and have distinguished themselves in every action of their lives and in every branch of knowledge come at last to their consummation." These will be the rulers. They will also have the task of bringing up in each generation others like themselves to take their places (*Republic*, Books V, VII).

2. OFFICIALS

While the Confucians directed their advice to rulers, their educational activities produced "the scholars, officials and statesmen who carried on the functions of the government and the state. . . . While in medieval Europe the scholar had no way of advancement except through the Church, the Chinese system of civil service examinations enabled the Confucianist scholars themselves to control the channels of civil and social advancement" (*Encyclopaedia of the Social Sciences*, Vol, IV, p. 199).

The Confucian approach to education, therefore, was directed toward preparing students to pass the examinations. For the Confucian literati the purpose of such examinations was not to test any special skills. It was rather to test "whether or not the candidate's mind was thoroughly steeped in literature and whether or not he possessed the *way of thought* suitable to a cultured man and resulting from cultivation in literature. . . . All the grades were intended as tests in penmanship, style, mastery of classic writings and finally . . . in conformity with the prescribed mental outlook" (Weber, *Religion of China*, p. 121).

For centuries monarchs sought help from scholars who were able to train officials who could serve well as the "king's men" and counterbalance the power of the feudal nobility. The German Cameralists[8] were perhaps the only scholars who equalled the Confucians not only in supplying such help but also in developing a formal literature. The Cameralists flourished from the middle of the sixteenth century to the end of the eighteenth. Like the British mercantilists, they believed in far-reaching governmental control of the economy. Unlike their English brethren, however, they involved themselves directly in the education of officials to carry out mercantilist policies.

The Cameralists recognized the similarity between public and other forms of administration. "The great management of the state," observed Johann von Justi, "rests virtually upon the same rules which other management must observe. In both establishments the ultimate purposes are

8. The word "kamera," which is the root of the German *kameralwissanschaft* refers to the room, or chamber, in which a government official works.

to acquire 'means,' to assure what has been acquired, and to use reasonably the goods possessed. The housekeeping of the state is merely of incomparably greater extent than that of a private person" (Small, 1909, p. 303). They therefore concerned themselves almost exclusively with state agencies and procedures needed for collecting revenues, promoting industry, dispensing charity, protecting the public health, building public works, controlling colonies and administering justice.

Above all, the Cameralists concentrated on the development of trained public officials. A ruler, according to Georg Zincke, a foremost Cameralist, "must have the knowledge necessary to insure good management. . . . It follows that a prince needs genuine and skillful cameralists. . . ." The universities themselves became the training grounds. Cameralism itself was installed as a major field of study. Instruction was based on Von Justi's principle that "some will want to make a career in the manufacturing system, some in the bureau of taxation and revenue, some in forestry or the forestry bureau, and all must have opportunity to get detailed instruction in the selected specialty" (*op. cit.*, p. 253, 307). Zincke, von Justi and other Cameralists served as public officials and professors at the same time. From these beginnings grew the tightly-organized, carefully-selected Prussian civil service.

The British Civil Service was developed by practical-minded men who took little time out for general observations. Besides, it was based upon the principle that the best way to learn about government was to work in government. This philosophy was given general expression in Henry Taylor's statement that "when the student shall have attained to four and twenty years of age, more or less, the sooner he is in office the better; for it is only there that some essential processes of his education can be set on foot, and it is in youth only that they can be favorably effected. An early exercise of authority is, in the case of most men, necessary to give a capacity for taking decisions" (*The Statesman*, p. 31). However, Taylor had serious doubts about the British practice of relying upon general education programs at the universities. He quoted with approval Francis Bacon's early complaint that there is "no education collegiate" designed to the end of preparing students for entry into government. He argued for a curriculum which would give special attention to historical case materials, law and political economy. He went still further by proposing that the student be asked to deal with questions of executive agency action which have been discussed in Parliament. On the basis of the public documents and other available information, the student should be asked to present:

1. The material facts of the case as drawn from the evidence,

2. The various views and opinions which have been or might be adopted upon the matter,
3. The conclusions of his own judgment, with his reasons,
4. If he concludes for legislation, a draft of the law by which he would exercise his purposes, and
5. A draft of the speech with which he would introduce his proposed law to the notice of the legislature (*The Statesman*, p. 29).

c. *Formal Organization*

IN ADDITION to their advisory and educational activities, the ancestors of administrative thought often discussed various aspects of formal organization. At a higher level of abstraction they dealt with the legitimation of formal authority by rulers of the state, and at a somewhat lower level with the number of rulers and patterns of hierarchy and specialization. In one way or another—but increasingly with the coming of the administrative revolution—they focused attention on the concept of organization.

1. LEGITIMATION OF AUTHORITY

How to get the authority of the rulers accepted by the ruled?

This is an age-old problem of rulers, leaders and administrators in all cultures. Apart from the use of force, ritual, and charismatic appeal, rulers have usually found it necessary to convince people that their authority is "legitimate" and should be accepted. The need to do this has been particularly acute whenever their authority has not been fully established or has been threatened by internal or external opponents. In either case, they have invariably made use of arguments and ideologies developed or dressed up for them by political philosophers.

At the risk of perpetrating minor violence upon a body of thought embroidered with delicate distinctions (and particularly upon theories of sovereignty), I find that all the arguments used to legitimize authority are based upon one or more of five simple themes. These may be summarized briefly.

First of all, authority has been justified on the ground that *power* itself is its own justification. In declaring that "might makes right," Callicles (in the *Gorgias*) and Thrasymachus (in the *Republic*) are much more than straw men for Plato to attack. Through them Plato recorded a theme that has run consistently throughout the previous and subsequent history of political thought. Sometimes it has been stated openly and brutally, as in the *Mahabhrata* and *Arthasastra*. More often it has been embellished with nationalistic glorification. It has been supported by euphemistic observations that freedom consists of submission to the powerful or that those whose power enables them to survive in the struggle for existence are unquestionably the fittest to rule.

The second is *wisdom*. At the very least the rulers know more than their inferiors. Their knowledge is based on superior ability, on truths handed down from previous generations, or on the help of wise men, magicians or scientists. Ultimately, the ruler may be considered omniscient or infallible.

The third is *goodness*. In a negative sense the authority of the rulers is the only protection against the evils of disorder or anarchy. More positively, the authority stems from their deep concern with the true interests of the people. They may even be the great defender of the common good or the "good old" ways of life. Custom itself is sometimes regarded as the proof of goodness. Thus hereditary privilege is good because it is part of the established order.

The fourth theme is *divinity*. In its earliest and purest form the rulers themselves are gods—either by their very nature or by apotheosis. In baser form the rulers are the vicars or representatives of one or more gods on earth. Ruling by divine right and divine grace, they have a godly share of power, wisdom and goodness.

The fifth theme is *consent*. Authority is most acceptable when the ruled themselves (or at least some part of them) sanction it by some formal act of acceptance. This act may be incorporated in some ancient covenant or contract, or it may be periodically repeated through various devices of selection and election.

It should be noted that there has never been any necessary connection between the themes used to justify highest authority and the particular form or rule which is being justified. The Divine Right of Kings has been used against rule by priests. Wisdom has been used to justify both the "separation of powers" and their centralization. Popular consent and service to the general will have been used to support monarchy and dictatorship. *Vox dei* and *vox populi* have been used, both separately and in conjunction, to legitimatize almost every form of rule. The only serious hesitation that may be observed is with the open use of the divinity theme to obtain the support of disbelievers or the open proclamation of "might makes right" by those who themselves believe in nothing else.

The fluidity with which these different themes have been combined, recombined, and applied to ever changing situations is often a result of intellectual audacity in the construction of myths. One of the most famous of all such myths is the "needful falsehood" proposed by Plato to obtain acceptance of his Philosopher-kings by the masses:

"Citizens," we shall say to them in our tale, "you are brothers, yet God has framed you differently. Some of you have the power of command, and in the composition of these he has mingled gold, whereof also they have the greatest honor. Others he has made of silver, to be auxiliaries. Others again who are to be husbandmen and craftsmen he has composed of brass and iron. . . . When a man of brass or iron guards the State, the State will be destroyed . . ." (*Republic*, Book III).

2. THE NUMBER OF RULERS

It was a widespread custom among ancient Greek philosophers to classify governments in accordance with the number of rulers: one, few, or many. Plato and Aristotle developed this idea further by distinguishing between pure and corrupt forms of each. In its simplest form Aristotle's basic classification, not much different from Plato's, is as follows:

NUMBER OF RULERS	FORM	
	Pure	*Corrupt*
One	Monarchy	Tyranny
Few	Aristocracy	Oligarchy
Many	Constitutional government (or polity)	Democracy

Moreover, both Plato and Aristotle noted the tendency for one organizational form to transform into another. Monarchy or aristocracy tend to turn into oligarchy. In turn, oligarchy tends to be transformed into democracy and democracy into tyranny. The wheel turns a full circle only when tyranny is stabilized through the establishment of a monarchy, which then broadens into an aristocracy. Both of them tend to favor an enlightened aristocracy.

Neither Plato nor Aristotle, however, gave much attention to the structure of rule in organizations other than governments. Plato is willing to subordinate family ties (and eliminate them completely in the case of the guardians) in order to achieve the higher rationality of the all-encompassing government structure. Aristotle makes a sharp distinction between political rule, on the one hand, and the rule of a household—over wife, children and slaves—on the other hand. In fact, he chides Plato scornfully for presuming that the management of a government, household and slaves is all the same. Yet Aristotle does not find economic activity worthy of serious attention and confines himself almost entirely to government. His passing comments on the handling of slaves, women, and children, however, indicate that he takes one-man rule for granted in both household and economic operations.

Machiavelli deals with the number of top administrators in a somewhat broader context. Thus, in addition to discussing the top organs of government, he discusses "the uselessness of several commanders in one army, or in a city that is besieged." He quotes approvingly a Roman general who objected to being appointed commander of a military expedition: "In important affairs it is necessary for success that the principal authority should reside in one man only." He adds his own sardonic comment on the practice of the day: "This is just the contrary of what is done by our princes and republics of the present day; who confide to several commissaries and chiefs the administration of places subject to them, which creates an inconceivable confusion. . . . It is better to confide any expedition to a single man of ordinary ability, rather than to two, even though they are men of the highest merit, and both having equal ability" (*Discourses*, Book 3, Chapt. XV).

3. HIERARCHY AND SPECIALIZATION

The first recorded advice on the division of authority within organizations is found in the Old Testament story of Jethro, a father-in-law of Moses. Visiting his son-in-law in the desert, Jethro noted that large numbers of people stood around all day waiting to bring their personal grievances before Moses. "The thing that thou doest," he protested, "is not good. Thou wilt surely wear away both thou and this people that is with thee; for this thing is too heavy for thee; thou are not able to perform it thyself alone." He then followed up his criticism with two specific proposals. The first dealt with Moses' own functions:

> Hearken now unto my voice, I will give thee counsel, and God shall be with thee. Be thou for the people to God-ward, that thou mayest bring the causes unto God: And thou shalt teach them ordinance and laws, and shalt show them the way wherein they must walk, and work they must do.

The second proposal was more specific:

> Moreover, thou shalt provide out of all the people able men, such as fear God, men of truth, hating covetousness; and place such over them, to be rulers of thousands, and rulers of hundreds, rulers of fifties, and rulers of tens: If thou shalt do this thing, and God command thee so, then thou shalt be able to endure . . . (Exodus, XVIII).

According to Exodus, Moses took immediate action. "And Moses chose able men out of all Israel and made them heads over the people rulers of thousands, rulers of hundreds, rulers of fifties and rulers of tens. And they judged the people at all seasons: the hard causes they brought unto Moses, but every small matter they judged themselves" (*Ibid.*).

Jethro's second proposal has echoed repeatedly in the ears of administrative thinkers. In classically simple form it contains the idea of the division of labor and the delegation of authority along hierarchic lines. One modern writer has even gone so far as to proclaim that the motto "Bring the hard causes to Moses, but judge the small matters yourself" expresses "in a form that no human thought can improve . . . the law, written or unwritten, which governs those who exercise delegated authority . . ." (Mooney, p. 21).

On deeper examination, however, Jethro's detailed advice seems to suffer from the typical defect in the work of outside experts: the failure to adapt proposals to the special characteristics of the organization advised. He seems to have ignored the possibility of recognizing natural tribal leaders in the appointment of Moses' chief officers. Thus, Buber charges that Jethro tried to graft onto "the resistant cellular structure of the community . . . [an] amorphous system of division by decades [which] will never agree with the genuine forms of life of a people settled on the soil" (Buber, p. 1, 99-100).[9] It was perhaps in realization of this weakness that the scholars who retold the same story without Jethro in the Book of Deuteronomy (probably some hundreds of years after the Book of Exodus was written) have Moses choose not merely able men but "the chiefs of your tribes, wise men and known . . ." (*Deuteronomy*, I:15).

In Plato's *Republic,* the entire state is organized into an elaborate three-level hierarchy. At the top are the philosopher-kings or guardians, who represent an aristocracy of intelligence and knowledge. At the second level, we find the warriors and auxiliaries who are motivated by spirit and courage. At the bottom are the artisans, who are motivated by appetite and desire and who specialize in material pursuits. These three levels parallel the "three souls" within every individual: the rational, the spirited and the appetitive, similar in many ways to the Freudian superego, ego, and id.

Aristotle, in contrast, emphasizes division of function rather than hierarchical levels. He is among the first to distinguish clearly between the deliberative element in the state (the legislative), the magistracies (the executive) and the judicial functions. He identifies such major executive functions of government as defense, finance, religion, justice and public works. He maintains that the specific division of executive functions and the powers of executive officers cannot be fixed in general terms but must

9. Although Buber's comment is well taken, the Israelites—far from being "settled on the soil" in the period under discussion—were still wandering in the desert.

be suited to the specific constitutional structure of a given state. He points out the effect of size on the degree of specialization that can be afforded. He identifies the problem of whether such a function as the maintenance of order should be centralized or decentralized (*Politics*, Book VI).

4. THE ORGANIZATIONAL CONCEPT

In a penetrating analysis of European and American political thought, Sheldon Wolin has stressed the long tradition of emphasis on "matters that concern the community as a whole" and "the welfare of the whole society." In contrast, he finds that since the French Revolution there has been a tendency for social scientists to withdraw attention from the polity or society as a whole and focus rather upon corporations, trade unions, associations and other organizations (1960, p. 429-434). Attention is thus called to the slow emergence of the concept of an organization as a form of human behavior.

Although the early political philosophers often discussed aspects of formal organizational structure, their recorded thought reveals no clearly-articulated concept of an organization. They tended to identify the affairs of state and the structure of government with the community or polity as a whole. Although distinctions were occasionally made between the management of household slaves, and kingdoms, although the existence of non-State associations or "political factions" were sometimes recognized, these other groups received no serious attention. The agencies of government were seen more as part of the polity than as separable and differentiated structures.

The first major theoretical departure from this point of view is found in the concept of the corporation.

Under late Roman law a corporation was an association possessing a legal personality separate and distinct from its members. Not only could it exercise legal rights but it could attain immortality by continuing to own property even after all of its founders had died and been replaced. Yet it was both a single "body" (or corpus) and a group, thus providing a fusion between the idea of one and the many. In medieval Europe the use of the corporate form spread to include not only universities, cities, and communes, but also segments of the Catholic Church. Often, the term "corporation" merely provided a handy way of referring to a single organization.

The idea of the corporation developed in two directions. On the one hand, it was used by pluralists who favored the growth of many types of independent or quasi-independent associations.

"Political theorists who desired to attack the concentration of authority in the hands of a single individual in church or state were attracted by the idea of a body corporate, recognized as a person in a legal sense. This idea served for a time as an intermediate state between the single individual and the whole body of individuals" (Gettell, p. 141).

On the other hand, the corporate idea was often defined in such a way as to subordinate individual corporations to the higher authority of Church or State. Innocent IV (who became Pope in A.D. 1243) was the first to maintain that the personality of a corporation is merely a "legal fiction." He proclaimed that this fiction can be brought into being only by fiat of higher authority—that is, by the Pope. This "fiat doctrine" was eagerly taken up by secular rulers, and it became an accepted principle that no corporation would be created except by charter from the sovereign" (Levy, p. 3-13). The subordination of separate corporations became still more important for those who regarded all of mankind as one huge corporate entity, one great body politic. The theorists of Catholic Church supremacy held that "mankind constituted a Mystical Body, whereof the Head was Christ" and from this "deduced the proposition that upon earth the Vicar of Christ represents the one and only Head of this Mystical Body . . ." (Gierke, 1958, p. 22).

With the coming of the Renaissance, the Enlightenment and the industrial and administrative revolutions, the concepts of an organization as something distinct from the community or polity as a whole became somewhat more articulate. The theological debates surrounding the Reformation centered to a considerable extent around the desirability of different and competing forms of church organization. Legal theorists devoted considerable thought to the development of many forms of limited liability business corporations. The concept of the "separation of powers" became a way of differentiating among different groupings of government organizations. Pluralists and syndicalists began to differentiate sharply between various groupings of organizations, propose various roles for specific associations and offer utopias in the form of small organized communities. Saint-Simon (1760-1825), who might be called the first non-Catholic organization theorist,[10] found in the emerging patterns of capitalist industry a hope for stability and progress in the aftermath of the French Revolution. This hope was embodied in the consciously and rationally developed organization. By and through organizations, "Man shall henceforth do consciously, and with better directed and useful effort, what they have hitherto done unconsciously, slowly, indecisively and too ineffectively" (*Selected Writings*, p. 70). The success of organ-

10. Although born a Catholic, Saint-Simon tried to found a new religion dedicated to the cause of improving the lot of the poor.

izations would depend largely upon the skills of scientists, artists and industrial administrators.[11]

At the same time, the bipolarity inherent in the medieval concept of
the corporation was continued. The organization came to be looked upon
not only as "an intermediate state between the individual and the whole
body of individuals," but also as an instrument for the more systematic
control of the entire community. Saint-Simon envisioned not only a
multitude of organizations, but also the incorporation of such organizations into organized and planned society. The "positivism" of Saint-
Simon's follower, Comte (1798-1857), the father of modern sociology,
inspired many of the subsequent efforts at the scientific study of organizations. During the same period the admiration of Marx and other socialists
for the productive powers of the capitalist corporation led them to the
idea of a society which would be organized and administered like one big
corporation. Although this idea was not based upon any direct examination of how capitalist organizations actually operated, it became a fundamental concept underlying many varieties of nineteenth- and twentieth-
century socialism.

d. *The Enlightenment*

ALL THE ANCESTORS of administrative thought operated on the explicit
premise that by the exercise of reason men could devise feasible and consistent means for attaining desirable ends. It was on this basis that they
offered advice to rulers, concerned themselves with administrative education and studied formal organization.

During the great intellectual upsurge of the Enlightenment this premise became an explicit and articulate principle that energized the philosophy, politics, science and art of Western Europe and North America.
Copernicus, Galileo, Bruno and Kepler destroyed the old image of man
and his planet as the center of the universe. While this was a shattering
blow to many illusions, it opened up new vistas of observation and discovery. By the time of Descartes, Spinoza, Newton, and Locke, rationality became a widespread article of faith. Both man and his universe were
seen as behaving in accordance with natural laws; there was nothing accidental or arbitrary in nature. By discovering these laws and acting in
accordance with them, man could control his irrational impulses and win

11. The relation of Saint-Simon to more recent organization theory is dealt
with not only by Wolin (1960, p. 376-382) but also by Alvin Gouldner (1959).

true freedom. Somewhat later, the prophets of the Enlightenment placed less emphasis on the authority of natural law and showed more confidence in the rational endowments of every individual, which were to be developed by education and freedom from oppressive controls. "*Sapere aude!* Dare to use your own understanding! is thus the motto of the Enlightenment," declared Immanuel Kant. "Nature has placed no bounds on the perfecting of the human faculties," wrote Condorcet, "and the progress of this perfectability is limited only by the duration of the globe on which nature has placed us." In the nineteenth century the program of enlightenment itself led to less faith in man's innate rationality and goodness, more recognition of divisive interests and more attention to the promotion of material benefits by the deliberate control of human behavior. Throughout this entire development superstition, supernaturalism and the dead hand of tradition were persistently countered by sober, skeptical and scientific calculation.

The Enlightenment provided the broad set of cultural values within which the industrial and administrative revolutions emerged and grew. In its many and changing forms it supplied the justification and inspiration for modern science and technology. It provided the rationale for people to attempt larger tasks by working together in organizations and seeking the enhancement of organizational power. Finally, if we look closely enough, we can find in the Enlightenment the seed germs of scientific management, human relations, managerial decision-making and other concepts of modern administration. Without exception the pioneers of administrative thought addressed themselves to the extension—each in his own way—of the rule of reason.

Chapter 6

THE PIONEERS:
THE GOSPEL OF EFFICIENCY

*B*Y THE TWENTIETH CENTURY, with the administrative revolution having already made over the face of society in the highly industrialized fourth of the globe, the pressure of new and more complex administrative problems presented a formidable intellectual challenge.

On a day-to-day basis this challenge was met—as similar challenges had been met in previous centuries—by the intuitive wisdom of practical administrators interested in building more powerful, more enduring, more efficient, and more effective organizations.

But this time, in contrast to previous centuries, a growing number of people started to apply to administration the methods of scientific observation which had already yielded dramatic and highly applauded results in the physical sciences. They tried to collate the growing mass of intuitive ground rules into clearly enunciated principles. The first of these pioneers were solitary voices in the wilderness. But they slowly won a growing host of enthusiastic converts among both practical men and abstract thinkers. What began as a small trickle became a broad stream of writing, research, discussion, and instruction.

The idea of efficiency provided a unifying theme in the work of the earlier pioneers. Frederick Taylor rallied support to the study of improved administrative methods by deploring the "great loss which the

whole country suffered through inefficiency in almost all our daily acts."
Max Weber hailed "monocratic bureaucracy" as "capable of attaining
the highest degree of efficiency" and thus "formally the most rational
means of carrying out imperative control over human beings." Attention
to efficiency was usually associated with a search for a value-free approach
to administration. Weber urged social scientists in general to aim at "ethical neutrality." Luther Gulick proclaimed that "in the science of administration, whether public or private, the basic 'good' is efficiency."
Lyndall Urwick sought neutral principles which "can be studied as a
technical question, irrespective of the purpose of the enterprise, the personnel composing it, or any constitutional, political or social theory underlying its creation." This emphasis on neutrality made it possible for
people with many different viewpoints or interests—reformers and re-
actionaries, the proponents and opponents of expanded government functions—to find a common meeting ground in the study of administration.

While a complete list of the founders and propounders of the gospel
of administrative efficiency would include many others, five men deserve
special attention: Frederick Taylor, Henri Fayol, Max Weber, Luther
Gulick, and Lyndall Urwick. Each of them made substantial contributions
to the development of administrative thought. Each exerted widespread
influence. The writings of each, although in many ways "out of date,"
are still worthy of sustained attention and deep respect.

Before reviewing the work of these four men, it is interesting to note
their backgrounds:

Taylor (United States of America)	Engineering Private business, middle management
Fayol (France)	Engineering Private business, top management
Weber (Germany)	Law, economics, sociology Consultant to government University professor
Gulick (United States of America)	Political science Public service, mainly research and advice
Urwick (England)	History (at Oxford) Military service Private business, middle management Public service, mainly research and advice

It is also interesting to note that each of them was personally and deeply involved in various aspects of administration. Fayol was the only one who personally shouldered top-level administrative responsibility for a sustained period of time. Yet as advisers and researchers, Taylor, Weber, Gulick and Urwick were able to obtain a "ringside" view of administrative activity in a large variety of undertakings.

A. *Taylor: More from Workers*

How TO GET more work out of workers, who are naturally lazy and engage in systematic soldiering?

This was the question that Frederick Taylor (1856-1915) asked himself in the early 1880's when he rose to foreman in the machine shop of the Midvale Steel Works in Philadelphia. At first, he tried to answer this question by applying the familiar techniques of engineering to one of its traditional subjects: the improvement of machinery. After a long series of experiments, he developed high-speed cutting steel, improved the design of machine tools, and set forth specific methods for the most efficient use of the improved tools. This inquiry itself brought him into a somewhat newer field, the use of tools by workers. From here, only one more jump was needed for Taylor to plunge directly into the analysis of work methods, a field which previous engineers had rarely entered.[1]

The written record of Taylor's achievements in this field is found in three basic documents: "Shop Management," a paper presented to the American Society of Mechanical Engineers in 1903; "The Principles of Scientific Management," which Taylor wrote in 1909 when his work was becoming an object of public attention, but which was not published until

---

1. Even the first pioneer had his predecessors. The most significant of Taylor's predecessors was not an engineer but rather the English mathematician, Charles Babbage (1792-1871). In trying to build one of the world's first calculating machines, Babbage spent many years visiting workshops and factories both in England and on the Continent. This led to the writing of his *On the Economy of Machinery and Manufactures,* first published in London in 1832. Here he tried to apply to industry "those principles of generalization to which my other pursuits had naturally given rise." This led him not only into economics but also into a pinpoint analysis of the amounts of labor needed for separate parts of a production process. Another predecessor—one who gave Taylor direct personal encouragement—was Henry R. Towne, an American industrialist and engineer. Towne was one of the first to promulgate the idea among engineers that "the matter of shop management is of equal importance with that of engineering" (*Transactions of the American Society of Mechanical Engineers,* Vol VII, 1886). He was also an originator of one of the piecework plans which Taylor criticized.

1911; and his 1912 "Testimony before the Special House Committee," which consisted largely of a justification of his views in the light of public attack. These three documents have been published in one volume, *Scientific Management*, with a foreword by Harlow S. Person.

1. THE ANALYSIS AND PLANNING OF WORK PROCESSES

Before Taylor, many manufacturers had used "piecework" systems under which workers received higher wages for producing more output. Taylor heaped scorn on such systems, charging that the employers had no way of knowing how much work could really be accomplished in a given period of time. The incentive effect of higher wages was vitiated by being dependent on the initiative of the workers themselves. Management by "initiative and incentive," although the best type of management in ordinary use, could only "drift" toward the goal of improved efficiency.

Taylor proposed that managers use scientific research methods to discover the best way of performing every piece of work. This would enable management itself to determine how much work should really be accomplished in a given period of time. It would also involve far-reaching changes in the specifications for tools and materials, the selection and training of workmen and the supervision of work. When this foundation has been laid, and only then, would it be possible to make proper use of bonuses and premiums for higher individual output. He maintained—and demonstrated—that through this combination of methods it would be possible to obtain dramatic increases in efficiency.

Management, and management alone, can be responsible for carrying these methods into effect. Although it is important to obtain the cooperation of the workers, it must be "enforced cooperation." Taylor drives home this point as follows:

> It is only through *enforced* standardization of methods, *enforced* adaptation of the best implements and working conditions and *enforced* cooperation that this faster work can be assured. And the duty of enforcing the adaptation of standards and of enforcing this cooperation rests with the *management* alone (*Scientific Management* "Principles of Scientific Management," p. 53, Taylor's italics).

A. *Work study*. Before Taylor, detailed knowledge concerning methods of work was the province of the workmen themselves, particularly the master craftsmen. As Taylor himself pointed out, "the knowledge which every journeyman has of his trade is his most valuable possession. It is his great life's capital. . . ." Taylor's first innovation was to gather in this great mass of traditional knowledge, record, tabulate it, improve upon it through analysis and experimentation, and then finally reduce it to "laws, rules and even mathematical formulae."

Taylor did this by applying to the movements of workers' bodies the same methods of careful observation which he had used in studying metal-cutting machines. In one of his first experiments he gave a young man a stop watch and a carefully prepared set of forms. This man spent two and a half years analyzing the motions of individual workmen. Every operation was broken down into its smallest components and carefully timed. It was found that even among the best workmen some used more economical motions than others. Thus it was possible to build up an ideal method based upon the best elements of various workers. Beyond that, it was also possible to "eliminate all false movements, slow movements and useless movements" and to develop methods that none of the workers had ever thought of before. Minimum allowances of time for fatigue and unavoidable delays could also be stated mathematically. In this way Taylor felt that one could scientifically discover "the one best method" for accomplishing work in the shortest possible time. He was tremendously encouraged by the fact that after three years average output per man in the machine shop had doubled.

B. *Standardization of tools.* Such increases are usually possible, Taylor maintained, only if, in addition to determining the best methods, management also standardized tools in the light of the needs of specific jobs. In an historic experiment at the Bethlehem Steel Works on the shovelling of coal, Taylor found that the average shovel load varied from about 16 to 38 pounds. Further experiments showed that good workers were able to shovel more tons per day if they used a shovel carrying a load of from 21 to 22 pounds. Subsequently, Taylor found that with different types of material to be shovelled, about fifteen different types of shovels were needed. From then on, when workers arrived in the morning, they received written instructions on what to shovel and what shovels to use. After three and a half years, 140 men were doing the work formerly handled by 400 to 600 men.

C. *Selection and training of workers.* Taylor insisted that each worker should be given the job for which he was best suited. "Now one of the very first requirements for a man who is fit to handle pig iron as a regular occupation," observed Taylor, "is that he shall be so stupid and so phlegmatic that he more nearly resembles in his mental make-up the ox than any other type. . . . There is work for each type of man, just as, for instance, there is work for the dray horse and work for the trotting horse. . . . [T]here is no type of work, however, that suits all types of man" (*Ibid.*, p. 59, 175).

It is therefore essential to find realistic ways of judging the capacities of different workers—to sort out the oxen, dray horses and trotting horses. But even the suitable man cannot be left to himself in the job for which he is most suitable. Management must give him formal training and specific instructions on precisely how to perform the prescribed motions with the standardized tools and materials.

D. *Supervision and planning.* Taylor found considerable opposition to his methods on the part of foremen and gang bosses, who had risen to their present position under different conditions and resented his methods. He soon came to the conclusion that his system imposed too large a burden upon the traditional foreman and that the "military type of organization"[2] under which every worker was responsible to only one superior should be abandoned.

As an alternative, he followed his usual system of dividing work into its component parts, and divided the task of foremanship into eight separate functions. He proposed that each worker receive his daily orders and help directly from eight different bosses, each of whom would limit himself to his own particular function.

Of his eight "functional foremen," only four were to serve on the shop floor: inspector, repair foreman, speed boss, and gang boss. The other four would sit in a specially established "planning room" and deal, respectively, with routing, the preparation of instruction cards, time and cost records, and discipline.

This division fitted into Taylor's feeling that planning functions must be given special status in the organization. At one point Taylor even recommends that "the shop, and indeed the whole works, should be managed not by the manager, superintendent or foreman, but by the should be carried on by the various functional elements of this depart- should be carried o by the various functional elements of this department, so that, in theory at least, the works could run smoothly even if the manager, superintendent and their assistants outside the planning room were all to be away for a month at a time" (*Ibid.*, "Shop Management," p. 110).

E. *Payment in accordance with output.* Having indicated how the methods—and thus the rate—of production can be planned in advance, Taylor and his associates went on to develop ever-new systems of paying workers in accordance with their output instead of the mere number of hours worked. The essence of all these various plans was the payment of extra sums or "bonuses" to workers who meet or exceed the defined

2. Taylor's conception of military organization was not entirely up-to-date. During the very period that Taylor wrote about military command, steps were being taken to introduce the general staff concept in the American army.

"task," otherwise referred to as "standard time," "norm," or "bogy."[3] The "task" was usually based on the amount of time taken by an able and well-trained worker. To this basic time was added an allowance for unavoidable delays and for rest periods.

Above all, each worker should be paid in accordance with his individual output rather than the output of the group to which he belongs. "When workmen are herded together in gangs," writes Taylor, "each man in the gang becomes far less efficient than when his personal ambition is stimulated. . . . Individual efficiency falls almost invariably down to or below the level of the worst man in the gang . . ." (*Ibid.*, "Principles of Scientific Management" p. 72-73).

2. THE OPPOSITION TO TAYLORISM

Taylor repeatedly pointed out that the execution of his ideas required a revolutionary change in the thinking of managers and workers. The difficult and painful nature of this change, however, was not something which he had predicted on the basis of abstract analysis. From the very beginning it was brought home to him by the continual obstacles placed in his path by both managers and workers.

A. *The resentment of managers.* As already pointed out, Taylor's methods were often resented by foremen and gang bosses. But this resentment was not limited to the lower levels of management. The higher ranks also took umbrage. They did not appreciate his scornful comments on "rule of thumb" method. Those who had fought their way to high managerial positions without the benefit of higher education were sensitive to Taylor's stand that, unless assisted by highly trained experts, they were unqualified to manage.

It is interesting to note that Taylor had to leave his first position at the Midvale Steel Works, where he had performed his first pioneering experiments in the machine shop, because of friction with the company's managers. At Bethlehem Steel, where he performed still more important experiments, the anti-Taylor sentiment among operating chiefs was so strong that he was able to keep his job only because he received personal protection from a member of the Board of Directors (Copley, 1923, Vol. 2, p. 22). But after three years he received a letter from the company President; the letter read, *in toto,* "I beg to advise you that your

---

3. Although the etymology of the term "bogy" is not entirely clear, it is probably connected with the word "bogyman," a devil or phantom. If the bogyman is the most frightening part of nursery tales, the bogy in incentive wage plans has often turned out to be one of the most frightening parts of life in a factory.

services will not be required by this company after May 1st, 1901" (Nadworny, 1955, p. 11).

B. *The trade union attack.* The resentment of workers was even deeper than that of the old-fashioned managers. They resented being studied by men with a stop watch in their hands. They resisted being asked to behave like machines and move mechanically in accordance with preordained patterns. They disliked having comradely work relationships broken up by wage systems that put every worker on his own and fomented individual rivalry. They reacted against Taylor's effort to transfer to management the craftsman's knowledge of his trade.

The leaders of the crafts unions saw Taylorism as leading to a breakdown of craft skills and thus of craft unionism itself. They saw it as strengthening employers at the very time when employers in the United States were conducting a bitter "open shop" campaign against trade unions.

In 1912 the unions struck back at Taylor by obtaining an investigation of his methods by a special committee of the House of Representatives. In 1915 they succeeded in having added to an Army Appropriations Act an amendment forbidding the use of stop watches or the payment of premiums or bonuses in Army arsenals. This law stayed on the statute books until World War II.

A still stronger blow was struck by the investigation conducted for the United States Commission on Industrial Relations by Professor Robert Hoxie. The Hoxie report concluded that the approach of Taylor and his associates dealt only with the mechanical and not with the human aspects of production. It also charged that time study and task-setting were "the special sport of individual judgment and opinion, subject to all the possibilities of diversity, inaccuracy and injustice that arise from human prejudice." The selection of workers to be timed, the determination of "normal times" and the fixing of allowances to be added for delays —all these were largely arbitrary, rather than scientific decisions (Hoxie, 1915, p. 40, 56).

3. THE "SCIENTIFIC MANAGEMENT" MOVEMENT

In his earlier days Taylor usually referred to his bundle of administrative techniques as "the task system" or "task management." In 1910, however, a new and more popular label was provided by Louis Brandeis (later Supreme Court Justice), who represented Eastern shipping concerns in a struggle against a projected increase in railroad rates. The railroads had applied to the Interstate Commerce Commission for a rate increase, basing their plea on a recent increase in wages. Brandeis appeared before the Commission and contended that without any increase in rates the railroads could maintain their profits by introducing more efficient methods of operation. He supported the position by using Taylor's ideas. But Brandeis felt that he needed a term which would be more popular than the severe-sounding "task system." He chose "scientific management" (a term previously used only occasionally by Taylor) as *the* label (Nadworny, p. 35).

Taylor welcomed the broader and more appealing nomenclature. Soon after, he declared that "management is a true science, resting upon clearly defined laws, rules and principles." Nor was he concerned about the breadth of the phrase. He felt that his own work covered the entire sphere of industrial management. He was convinced "that the same principles can be applied with equal force to all social activities: to the management of our homes; the management of our farms; the management of the business of our tradesmen, large and small; of our churches, our philanthropic institutions, our universities, and our government departments" (*Scientific Management,* "Principles of Scientific Management," p. 8).

The railroad rate case gave Taylor's ideas not only a popular label but also a tremendous amount of public attention. He himself became more active than ever before, not only as an adviser but also propagandist. His closest associates—Henry Gantt, Frank B. Gilbreth and Lillian Gilbreth, Horace Hathaway, Sanford Thompson, and Harrington Emerson—published countless articles and many books. They and innumerable followers served as advisers to hundreds of companies, thus developing the profession of "efficiency expert" or "management consultant." Engineering schools began to give courses on "shop management" and "industrial management." Schools of business administration followed suit. Many special disciplines, each partly rooted in "scientific management," emerged from the welter: production engineering (or production management), cost accounting, personnel management and industrial psychology.

In brief, scientific management became something of a "movement." In an age of growing achievement in the physical sciences, it offered the hope of resolving industrial problems also through the use of objective principles. For young and imaginative engineers it provided an *ethos* and a mission in life. The movement soon became replete with popularizers, traditionalists and dissidents. After the initial period of resistance it conquered the citadels of old-fashioned industrial management in the United States, and had a tremendous effect on industrial practice. It had a major influence on the growing reform and economy movements in public administration. It even began to win support among some trade union leaders, albeit conditioned upon trade union participation in the setting of norms.

The movement also became international. It soon spread to Germany, England, France, Sweden and other European countries—where once again it faced the initial opposition of trade unions. Its greatest success, however, was in Russia. Immediately after the Bolshevik revolution of 1917, Lenin referred to "the Taylor system" as "a combination of subtle brutality of bourgeois exploitation and a number of its greatest scientific achievements. . . ." Yet the new regime "must at all costs adopt all that is valuable in the achievements of science and technology in this field" (1946, Vol. III, p. 332-333). He and Trotsky sponsored a state-led "scientific management" movement aimed at promoting labor discipline and higher productivity. The movement seems to have been supported by all the contending factions at the higher levels of the Russian Communist Party. Taylor's basic ideas were then built into the curriculum for the education and training of the engineers who subsequently tended to monopolize managerial posts in Soviet industry.

B. *Fayol: More from Managers*

LIKE TAYLOR, Henri Fayol (1841-1925) was an engineer whose technical achievements were impressive. In his earlier days he performed outstanding work in overcoming the fire hazards in coal mining and in analyzing the geological formation of French coal deposits. Again like Taylor, he concentrated on industrial administration, but maintained that the basic principles of administration were applicable to all forms of organizations.

But here the similarities end and the differences between the two men (who might be called the founders of modern administrative thought) begin. When Fayol rose from a technical post to become general manager of his company in 1888, the problem he faced was how to save a mining company which was on the verge of bankruptcy. To deal with it, he could not limit himself to work methods and work planning. He focused his mind more and more on what is to be expected from managers. He based his conclusions not on "scientific" observations but on personal experience during many years of high administrative responsibility.

In 1900 and again in 1908 Fayol set forth his first views on administration in papers presented before engineering and mining conferences.

His major work, *General and Industrial Management*,[4] appeared in 1916. Two years later, at the age of seventy-seven, he retired from his company. He devoted the seven remaining years of his life to founding a center of administrative studies and trying to apply some of his ideas to public administration in France.

1. A GENERAL APPROACH TO ADMINISTRATION

Fayol was the first writer to develop what might be called a "general approach" to administration. As a top executive himself, he looked at administration from the top down. This gave him a much broader perspective than Taylor, who was first and foremost a technician. This wider perspective is found in his views on the essence of administration and on the need for administrative training and theory.

A. *The elements of administration.* Fayol defines administration in terms of five elements. "To administer," he writes, "is to forecast and plan, to organize, to command, to coordinate and to control. . . ."

But administration is "neither an exclusive privilege nor a particular responsibility of the head or senior members. . . ." It is spread throughout an organization. Even workers may participate to some degree in administrative activities. As one goes up the "scalar chain" of an organization's hierarchy, the relative importance of administrative responsibility and administrative ability increases.

Administration, however, is only part of "government." To govern is to conduct the undertaking toward its objective by seeking to derive optimum advantage from all available resources. This calls for the smooth working of six essential functions, of which administration is only one:

4. This work first appeared as "Administration Industrielle et Generale" in the *Bulletin of the Societe de l'Industrie Minerale*, 1916, third issue. It was subsequently republished in France in 1925 and translated into English in 1929 and 1949. The latter, the most widely used English edition, is *General and Industrial Management*, translated by Constance Storrs, with an introduction by L. Urwick. It should be noted that this brief book was planned as the first part of a larger work which was to summarize Fayol's personal observations and experience and deal with the administrative "lessons" of World War I. The latter half was never completed. Fayol's other major publication is "The Administrative Theory of the State," an address presented to the Second International Conference of Administrative Science at Brussels in 1923. This was translated by Sarah Greer and appeared in the collection, *Papers on the Science of Administration*, edited by L. Gulick and L. Urwick. Since Fayol always used the French word "administration," it is unfortunate that some of the translators have translated this as "management." The subsequent quotations from Fayol will all use "administration" instead of "management."

(1) technical (or technological) activities; (2) commercial activities (buying, selling and exchange); (3) financial activities (search for and optimum use of capital); (4) security activities (protection of property and persons); (5) accounting activities (stocktaking, balance sheet, costs, statistics) and (6) administration (which operates only on personnel and not directly on either materials or machinery). At times, however, Fayol seems to depart from this initial categorization and to write about administration as something which itself deals with the integration of the first five activities (*General and Industrial Management*, p. 3-13).

B. *The need for administrative training.* Fayol criticizes civil engineering colleges in France for not including administration in their syllabi. Administrative ability cannot be developed through technical training alone.

But administrative training should not be limited to engineers. "Everyone needs some concepts of administration; in the home, in affairs of State, the need for administrative ability is in proportion to the importance of the undertaking, and for individual people the need is everywhere greater in accordance with the position occupied. Hence there should be some generalized teaching of administration: elementary in the primary schools, somewhat wider in the post primary schools, and quite advanced in higher educational establishments."

Where the school ends, the company or the government agency should take over. "A sign of good administration is the steady, methodical training of all employees required and at all levels. . . . If the manager preaches by example in introducing his subordinates as much as possible to the general problem of administration, if he prevails upon the engineer to instil a little science into the foreman in exchange for experience, and gets the foreman to try and teach workers, there is every chance that the concern will soon rejoice in a fine personnel."

Fayol's plea for administrative training at all levels, starting as low as elementary school, covers everything except the highest levels. The top executives and board members are seen as teachers, not students. In this, he follows in the footsteps of the ancient philosophers who devised plans for the training of officials and crown princes but stopped short before ever hinting that reigning kings themselves might benefit from additional education (*op. cit.*, p. 14-16, 80-96).

C. *The need for administrative theory.* "But why," asks Fayol, "is there not enough teaching of administration?"

"The real reason," he replies, "is the absence of theory; without theory no teaching is possible."

There is no shortage of personal theorizing, Fayol points out. But this leads to "the most contradictory practices under the aegis of the same principles." It is no substitute for "a collection of principles, rules, methods, procedures, tried and checked by general experience." Without such a collection "the most undesirable practices may be indulged in with impunity." Unfortunately, most higher managers with vast experience have "neither time nor inclination for writing and most often depart without leaving either doctrine or disciples" (*op. cit.*, p. 14-16).

Fayol's purpose, therefore, in writing *General and Industrial Management* is to start the process of theory formulation. "I hope," he adds modestly, "that a theory will emanate from it."[5] This done, the foundation will be provided for the teaching of administration in both school and work place. In fact, such a theory would put an end to the "general groping prevalent in the isolation of our households" and allow the home to "play the part which befits it in the administrative training of youth" (*op. cit.*, p. 96).

2. FLEXIBLE PRINCIPLES

Fayol was resolved that, unlike other top managers of his acquaintance, he would not depart without leaving a body of doctrine behind him. Accordingly, he set out to propound a considerable number of general principles. Using them as the framework for one of his chapters, he listed fourteen principles specifically: division of work, authority, discipline, unity of command, unity of direction, subordination of individual interests to the general interest, remuneration, centralization, scalar chain (line of authority), order, equity, stability of tenure of personnel, initiative, and *esprit de corps*. He also formulated quite a number of principles in the course of analyzing the five elements of administration: planning, organizing, command, coordination, and control.

In discussing principles, Fayol takes pains to dissociate them "from any suggestion of rigidity." He maintains that "there is nothing rigid or absolute in administrative affairs; it is all a question of proportion." All principles of administration are flexible. Their proper adaptation to specific circumstances "is a difficult art requiring intelligence, experience, decision and proportion."

Moreover, there is no limit to the number of administrative principles. There is a place for any new principle whose worthiness is confirmed by experience. All old ones can be changed in the light of experience.

A. *The body corporate.* The major task of organization, according

5. In 1923, seven years later, when he wrote "The Administrative Theory of the State," Fayol felt more confident and referred to his ideas as "*The* administrative theory."

to Fayol, is to develop the personnel capable of carrying out the six essential functions of an enterprise. In dealing with this task he warns against comparing the personnel of an organization to an "administrative machine." This might suggest that "like the mechanical gearing, the administrative one is incapable of transmitting movement without losing power." This is false, because every intermediate executive "must be a generator of power and ideas."

Fayol prefers to regard the administrative structure as a "body corporate" and compares the managerial function with the nervous system of an animal. The growth of a corporate body is limited by both the strength of this managerial function at its center and the activities of other organizations. Corporate bodies of similar size resemble each other in general hierarchical structure.

Every organization, no matter what its size, should provide an appointed place for every employee and see that every employee is in his appointed place. For this purpose the organization chart is "a precious managerial instrument." It enables managers to grasp the organic whole at a glance, better than could be done by lengthy description. It facilitates finding weak points and noting how a change at one point may have repercussions elsewhere (*op. cit.*, p. 54-60, 77-78).

B. *One head per body*. Fayol's most vigorously stated principles are the "unity of command" and the "unity of direction." He maintains that "an employee should receive orders from one superior only." He insists that there should be "one head and one plan for a group of activities having the same objective. . . . A body with two heads is in the social as in the animal sphere a monster and has difficulty in surviving."

Fayol points out with grave concern the tendency for "dual command" to "worm its way into the social organism on the most plausible pretexts." Among the more understandable reasons are the imperfect demarcation of departments and the natural intermeshing of functions. But "in no case is there adaptation of the social organism to dual command. Either dual command is itself eliminated or the organism withers away."

This point of view leads to a direct criticism of Taylor's ideas of having workers receive instructions from a large number of "functional foremen." Fayol grants the need for more specialists in the planning and direction of work but insists that their use be reconciled with the unity of command. The reconciliation can be effected by regarding these specialists not as additional foremen but as "the staff" of the foremen.

In criticizing Taylor on this point, Fayol stresses his admiration for Taylor's work on high-speed steel and "minute and precise methods in conditions of work" (*op. cit.*, p. 24-26, 66-70). One cannot help but speculate how the two men might have struck it off together had Taylor worked in a plant managed by Fayol.

c. *Many brains to help*. Although a single head is needed at the top, Fayol maintains that apart from some small organizations no top manager can either know enough or have enough energy to handle all the administrative burdens thrust upon him. "Hence the need to fall back on the staff, wherein lies a reserve of physical and mental strength, competence, and time, on which the manager may draw at will." Staff members may thus be expected to serve as "an adjunct, reinforcement and sort of extension of the manager's personality."

Staff work involves assistance to managers in four types of activities: correspondence, interviews and other current matters; liaison and control; preparing plans and developing improvements in every sphere of activity. The first two of these activities are more widely recognized. The latter two are "often deplorably neglected." It has not yet become established custom "to regard the staff as an organ of thinking, studying and observation, whose chief function consists, under administrative impetus, in preparing for the future and seeking out all possible improvements. In order to carry out this role, staff members should be free of all responsibility for running the business" (*op. cit.*, p. 63-64, 68-70).

d. *Matching authority with responsibility*. Fayol defines authority as "the right to give orders and the power to exact obedience." He also distinguishes between the "official" authority which derives from the office a person holds and its necessary complement, the "personal" authority based on his intelligence, experience, moral worth and other personal abilities.

It is a natural tendency for people in an organization to seek more authority and to fear responsibility. This fear of responsibility paralyzes initiative. Accordingly, special steps must be taken to induce people to accept responsibility. In any case, it is essential to pin down the degree of responsibility of all people who wield authority.

Yet the linking of authority and responsibility is far from simple. "It is increasingly difficult to isolate the share of the initial act of authority in the ultimate result and to establish the degree of responsibility of the manager. The measurement of this responsibility and its equivalent in material terms elude all calculation" (*op. cit.*, p. 21-22).

e. *The "gangplank."* Although Fayol places great emphasis on formal organization, he is quick to point out the dangers of excessive formalism. "It is an error to depart needlessly from the line of authority, but it is an even greater one to keep it when detriment to the business ensues."

Thus, communication between two subordinates in different departments may be disastrously lengthy. One can reach the other only by sending a message up a long ladder of command and waiting until it then descends to its destination. He illustrates this problem with the accompanying figure:

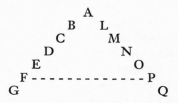

It is much better for F and P to make use of a "gangplank" between them than to use A and all the other intervening layers as intermediaries. This can be done without violating the line of authority *if* the immediate superiors, namely E and O, authorize such a relationship and are kept informed of what may be agreed upon. If a disagreement develops between F and P, they must then turn the matter over to their superiors.

Fayol hazards the conjecture that there is less use of the "gangplank" in government agencies than in private business. One reason is that the aim of the organization is often more vague in a government agency. Hence "each section tends to regard itself as its own end, neglects its relationship with other sections, and becomes isolated, cloistered, aware only of the line of authority." Another reason is that the supreme authority himself, the A at the top of the pyramid, fails to encourage his own direct subordinates to use the "gangplank" themselves (*op. cit.*, p. 34-36).

F. *Planning in business and government.* Fayol was probably the first writer to present a broad conception of organizational planning. He maintains that detailed planning is necessary at all times in order to avoid "hesitation, false steps, untimely changes of direction." It is above all necessary "in difficult moments." "The best of plans cannot anticipate all unexpected occurrences that may arise, but it does include a place for these events and prepares the weapons which may be needed at the moment of being surprised."

Fayol's discussion of planning includes copious reference to the practices of his own company. Here the plan, in keeping with his conception of "government," was extremely broad, covering the technical, commercial, financial, accounting, security and managerial activities. It was based on a survey of the past history and the present situation of the entire business. It consisted of "a series of separate plans, called forecasts, monthly, weekly, daily forecasts, long-term forecasts; and there are yearly forecasts, ten yearly forecasts, special forecasts, and all merge into a single programme which operates as a guide for the whole concern."

At times, Fayol uses the word "plan" and "forecast" interchangeably. Yet an important difference between the two is indicated when he declares that although an organization's plan must be continuously adjusted, "it is the law to which one bows" (*op. cit.*, p. 43-49).

Fayol was also one of the first to call for planning on a national scale. If foresight is needed in business, it is even more needed in government. In developing this point, however, it is clear that Fayol advocates the orderly handling of existing government functions rather than an extension of government functions.

From this vantage point Fayol deplores the lack of foresight in the French State. "The annual forecasts (budget) are rarely completed early enough to be of use and long-term forecasts are rare, and in this immense undertaking demanding great foresight life is somewhat from hand to mouth. . . ." The basic reason for this sad situation is the "lack of stability of ministerial tenure" (*op. cit.*, p. 52-53).

G. *Human relations.* Since the term "human relations" did not come into use until much later, one might get the impression that the "classical" writers on administration did not deal with the subject. This was not the case. Taylor, in fact, clearly recognized that administration dealt with people. He also had a clear conception concerning workers. He saw them as people who (a) are naturally lazy, (b) resist work more effectively when operating in groups, (c) must be subjected to sharp discipline, (d) can best be motivated by the incentive of higher wages, (e) can do much better when properly instructed and (f) differ markedly among each other in native ability and capacity. Many of these conceptions, particularly the latter ones, have entered into subsequent theories and techniques of human relations.

Fayol's ideas concerning human relations were, as one might suspect, much broader than those of Taylor. As already pointed out, personnel is for Fayol the essence of organization. The confusions that develop under dual command and the difficulty of a top manager's handling all his burdens without assistance are seen, at least in part, as psychological problems.

More specifically, in the last five of Fayol's specifically listed principles, he deals with quite a number of human problems in administration. In discussing the principle of "order," he holds that organizational order demands "precise knowledge of the human requirements and resources of the concern and a constant balance between these requirements and resources." Under the principle of "equity" he notes that workers aspire to "equity and equality of treatment." Equity, he holds, results from "the combination of kindliness and justice." In discussing "stability of tenure of personnel" he holds that "instability of tenure is at one and the same time cause and effect of bad running." Yet the discussion deals more with tenure as a technical prerequisite for learning a job than as an answer to inner emotional needs. Under "initiative" he identifies "thinking out a plan and ensuring its success" as one of the "keenest satisfactions" that an intelligent man can experience and one of "the most powerful stimulants of human endeavor." To encourage initiative, superior officers must show much tact, some integrity and the ability to sacrifice personal vanity.

Under "*esprit de corps*" Fayol emphasizes the need to build a sense of harmony among the personnel of a concern. To do this, a manager must set a good example and must himself show high personal integrity and moral character. Nor should he follow the motto of "divide and rule." "Dividing enemy forces to weaken them is clever, but dividing one's own team is a grave sin against the business." In this connection he looks back to an earlier decade, 1860, when unorganized industrial workers were "without cohesion, without common bond, a veritable cloud of individual dust particles." Since then "the union has produced collective associations, meeting employers on equal terms." Similarly, he welcomes the trend for competing firms to develop friendly relations and settle common interests by joint agreement (*op. cit.*, p. 36-42).

c. *Weber: Rationality from Bureaucrats*

WHEN WE MOVE on from Fayol to Weber, we turn to one who looked not only at the administration of single organizations but also at the structure of society as a whole. A founder of modern sociology and the greatest scholar among the pioneers of administrative thought, Max Weber (1864-1920) was one of the towering thinkers of the early twentieth century. "In the present era of scientific specialization, he appears already like a man of the Renaissance, who took all humanity for his province. . . . He studied law and economics; he became a specialist in the interpretation of religious doctrines and he was a notable biblical scholar; he had a thoroughly technical grasp of ancient Roman land-surveying methods, medieval trading companies, and the modern stock exchange; he became a specialist in the comparative history of urban institutions; he examined in detail the farm-labor problems of East German agriculture; he developed a systematic framework for an interpretation of ancient Mediterranean civilization and of the political development of Western Europe; he made a special study of the medieval origins of Western music; and he analyzed in detail the social and

psychological conditions of productivity in a West German textile mill.
. . . And throughout his career he was as much immersed in the methodological controversies of the social sciences as in the political controversies
of his time and country" (Bendix, *Max Weber, An Intellectual Portrait*,
p. 469).

A major theme underlying most of Weber's work was the evolution
of various civilizations in terms of the balance between rationality and
magic. This led him to study different kinds of organizations—economic
enterprises, governments, religious orders, associations, and parties—in
terms of their reciprocal relations with society as a whole. In the later
years of his life he tried to consolidate his many historical studies in a
grand opus, *Wirschaft und Gesellschaft (Economics and Society)*. Unfinished at his death, this work depicts the development of Western
rationality through the instrumentalities of capitalism, science and bureauc
racy.[6] Its first part has been translated by Henderson and Parsons under
the title *The Theory of Economic and Social Organization*. Different
sections from the same work, along with representative selections from
other works, have been made available in the Gerth and Mills translations
under the title of *From Max Weber: Essays in Sociology*.

1. TRADITIONAL, CHARISMATIC, AND LEGAL AUTHORITY

One of Weber's most widely acknowledged contributions to social
science has been the formulation of three "pure" or "ideal" types of
legitimate authority: traditional, charismatic, and legal (or rational)
authority. For Weber, the ideal type concerns the *is* rather than the
should be. Yet "it is not a description of reality, but it aims to give
unambiguous means of expression to such a description. . . . It offers
guidance to the construction of hypotheses" (*Methodology of the Social
Sciences*, p. 90). As a logically controlled and unambiguous conception,
an ideal type is more removed from historical reality than less precise
concepts. The task of the researcher is to analyze the distance between
them and reality and the extent to which they are found in various
combinations.

Traditional authority rests on "an established belief in the sanctity
of immemorial traditions and the legitimacy of the status of those exercising authority under them." Those who exercise authority do so under

6. Also unfinished at the time of his death were the lectures published in English under the title of *General Economic History* and a series of volumes (of
which the 1904 *Protestant Ethic and the Spirit of Capitalism* was the first) on the
sociology of religion.

rules that "have always existed," but may also exercise personal preroga-tive. Obedience is given not to the rules but to the rulers, not to superiors but to chiefs. New rules are not enacted, they are "found." The only documents in the administration of law are the "documents of tradition: namely, precedents." Resistance, when it occurs, is directed against "the person of the chief or a member of his staff. The accusation is that he has failed to observe the traditional limits of his authority" (*The Theory of Economic and Social Organization,* p. 341-342).

The most primitive types of traditional authority are "gerontocracy," and "patriarchalism." In the former control is exercised by a council of elders; in the latter, by an individual. With the development of an administrative staff, traditional authority turns into "patrimonialism," under which "members" are now treated as "subjects." The monarch has full personal control over the resources used by the royal household. He delegates this control to others through "benefices," i.e., rights to use his lands or to collect taxes, fees, usufruct and/or rentals due to the chief. In "decentralized patrimonialism," or feudalism, the power of the chief is limited by the rights of nobles. The latter are tied to the chief by not only "benefices" but by "fiefs," i.e., contracts to provide personal loyalty and military services in return for lands, territory, offices and/or a set of governing rights.

Charismatic authority rests on "devotion to the specific and excep-tional sanctity, heroism or exemplary character of an individual person, and of the normative patterns or order revealed or ordained by him." The term "charisma" (gift of grace) is taken from the vocabulary of early Christianity. Here it is applied to supernatural, superhuman, or extraordinary qualities of a leader. Among the holders of charisma are the sorcerer, the prophet, the leader of hunting and booty expeditions, the warrior chieftain, the so-called "Caesarist" ruler, the personal head of a party and the demagogue. Those subject to this authority are "followers," not "subjects." "Charismatic authority repudiates the past, and is in this sense a revolutionary force. It recognizes no appropriation of positions of power by virtue of the possession of property, either on the part of a chief or of socially privileged groups. The only basis of legitimacy is personal charisma, so long as it is proved; that is, so long as it receives recognition and is able to satisfy the followers of disciples" (*op. cit.,* p. 262).

Although pure charismatic authority is foreign to everyday routine, it can escape being a transitory phenomenon only by being routinized. The first task of routinization is to provide for succession by (a) finding a new charismatic leader with specific characteristics, (b) oracles or by drawing lots, (c) designation of successor by original charismatic leaders or a charismatically qualified staff, (d) heredity, (e) personal transmission through such ritual acts as anointing, consecration, "laying on of hands" or coronation, and (f) plebiscites. Routinization also involves the growth of administrative staff and some form of fiscal organization.

Legal authority rests on "a belief in the legality of patterns of normative rules and the right of those elevated to authority under such rules to issue commands. . . . Obedience is owed to the legally established impersonal order. It extends to the persons exercising the authority of office only by virtue of the formal legality of their commands, and only within the scope of the authority of the office" (*op. cit.*, p. 328). Legal norms may be established on a variety of bases, by agreement or imposition, on grounds of expediency or rational values. These norms are abstract rules intentionally established, and then applied to particular cases, with formally provided opportunities for appeal. Written documents are the heart of the process; all final decisions are supposed to be recorded in writing. Although the supreme head of a system of legal authority may enjoy authority on traditional or charismatic grounds, the administrative staff is much larger and better trained than under traditional or charismatic systems. In contrast with legal authority, the other two systems place major obstacles in the way of rational, stable and calculable action. Thus Weber often refers to legal authority as rational or legal-rational authority.

2. THE BUREAUCRATIC ADMINISTRATIVE STAFF

"For all types of authority," wrote Weber, "the fact of the existence and continuing functioning of an administrative staff is vital. . . . It is, indeed, the existence of such activity which is usually meant by the term 'organization' " (*op. cit.*, p. 383). The nature of this activity and of the staffs themselves varies with the type of legitimate authority.

The most rational form of administrative staff, according to Weber, is the pure or "monocratic" bureaucracy.

> It is superior to any other form in precision, in stability, in the stringency of its discipline, and in its reliability. It thus makes possible a particularly high degree of calculability of results for the heads of organizations and for those acting in relation to it. It is finally superior both in intensive efficiency and in the scope of its operations, and is formally capable of applications to all kinds of administrative tasks.
>
> The development of the modern form of organization of corporate groups in all fields is nothing less than identical with the development and continual spread of bureaucratic administration. This is true of church and state, of armies, political parties, economic enterprises, organizations to promote all kinds of causes, private associations, clubs, and many

others. Its development is, to take the most striking case, the most crucial phenomenon of the modern Western state. However many forms there may be which do not appear to fit this pattern, such as collegial representative bodies, parliamentary committees, soviets, honorary officers, lay judges and what not, and however much people may complain about the "evils of bureaucracy," it would be sheer illusion to think for a moment that continuous administrative work can be carried out in any field except by means of officials working in offices. For bureaucratic administration is, other things being equal, always, from a formal technical point of view, the most rational type. For the needs of mass administration today, it is completely indispensable. The choice is only that between bureaucracy and dilettantism in the field of administration (*op. cit.,* p. 337).

Although Weber made various lists of the characteristics of pure bureaucracy, these may best be dealt with in relation to the subdivision of labor, hierarchy, and rules.[7] Thus, first of all, labor is divided into offices, or spheres of competence and responsibility defined by law and administrative regulations. Each office is supposed to be the sole or primary occupation of the incumbent. Although the incumbent will usually enjoy tenure, he cannot personally own the office or the means of production and administration. His appointment and job placement are based upon his technical qualifications and, presumably, special training. His acceptance of an appointment is based on a free contractual relationship.

Second, a pure bureaucracy provides for a hierarchic separation between super- and subordinate offices. The hierarchic structure provides for (a) the supervision of lower offices by higher ones, (b) a stable and carefully delimited distribution of authority, (c) varying degrees of social esteem, (d) fixed salaries paid in money and graded in accordance with responsibility as well as social status, (e) promotions and career advancement on the basis of both seniority and achievement, and (f) appeal and grievance machinery.

Third, a pure bureaucracy operates in accordance with general rules. Although office holders may be free from such rules in their personal affairs there is systematic control over their official actions. The dominant norms are concepts of straightforward duty without regard to personal considerations. Personal favors, arbitrariness, grace and gratitude cannot be openly avowed. Every act of personal discretion—even those which are aimed at preserving or enhancing the officials' power—must be justified by impersonal ends.

Many of the ancient bureaucracies developed under the patrimonial forms of traditional authority. "Bureaucracy has first developed in patri-

7. In accordance with the discussion in "More Bureaucracy" in Chapt. 2.

monial states with a body of officials recruited from extra-patrimonial sources. . . . Those with permanent functions are household officials of the chief." But under the pure type of traditional authority, a bureaucracy lacks such essential features as a clearly defined sphere of competence, a rational ordering of superior-subordinate relations, appointment and promotion on the basis of free contract, technical training as a regular requirement and fixed salaries paid in money. Under pure charismatic authority the work of administrative staff is performed by disciples and followers. As charisma becomes routinized, a tendency toward bureaucratization may be discerned. But staff members will often be elected instead of appointed or appointed on the basis of personal loyalty rather than competence. Even under legal authority, the pure type of monocratic bureaucracy may not be immediately reached. The collegiate principle, indeed, may play an important role in establishing rational specialization of functions and enduring structures independent of the person. Later, "collegiate administration disappears as soon as progress in the means of communication and the increasing technical demands of administration necessitate quick and unambiguous decisions, and as soon as the dominant motives for full bureaucratization and monocracy . . . push to the fore." Collegiate bodies below the level of ultimate authority may then survive only in the form of advisory committees that serve to "put the concrete experience of interested groups into the service of a rational administration of expertly trained officials" (Gerth and Mills, p. 236-239). By this stage pure monocratic bureaucracy may be reached.

Weber also tried to identify the various factors and conditions that have contributed to the growth of modern bureaucracy. The proper soil for bureaucratization has always been the quantitative and qualitative development of administrative tasks (already discussed in Chapt. 2). In warfare the task of winning victory or avoiding defeat brought into being military bureaucracies and concepts of discipline that have had profound effects upon nonmilitary organizations. A money economy, although not indispensable for bureaucracy, makes it possible to pay fixed salaries and draw a sharp distinction between the property of the organization and the official. It also offers a better basis for the income of the organization. "Today it is primarily the capitalist market economy which demands that the official business of administration be discharged precisely, unambiguously, continuously, and with as much speed as possible. Normally the very large, modern capitalist enterprises are themselves unequalled models of strict bureaucratic organization. Business management throughout rests on increasing precision, steadiness, and, above all, the speed of operations. . . . The extraordinary increase in the speed by which public announcements, as well as economic and political facts are transmitted exercises a steady and sharp pressure in the direction of speeding up the tempo of administrative reaction toward various situations. The optimum of such reaction time is normally attained only by a strictly bureaucratic organization" (*op. cit.*, p. 215).[8] Finally, he dealt at great length with the influence of religion, values and "ideal interests." He pointed out the "paradox of unintended consequences" in the effects of Confucianism and Puritanism. The former exalted the goal of material welfare, while the latter rejected it. Yet the Chinese failed to achieve their goal, and the Puritan mentality contributed to material well-being through the growth of capitalism, legal authority and bureaucracy (*The Religion of China*, p. 226-249).

In appraising the consequences of modern bureaucracy, Weber identified the democratic and levelling effect of impersonal appointments, various effects upon university education, the difficulty of the highest officials in controlling a bureaucracy, and the many points of tensions between bureaucracies and democratic ideals. He also makes a major qualification concerning the rationality of the super-rational bureaucracy. Its rationality is merely formal rationality, which deals with the adaptation of means to the given and clearly established ends of an organization. "Substantive rationality," on the other hand, deals with meeting the basic needs of people in a nation. In both economic activity and law there is a continuous tension between formal and substantive rationality. The consideration of substantive rationality brings us to a level beyond the precise and rational calculation of bureaucrats. At this level Weber himself contributed occasionally to the literature of antiorganization revolt. He pointed out that "material goods have gained an increasing and finally an inexorable power over the lives of men" and referred to modern men as "specialists without spirit, sensualists without heart" (*The Protestant Ethic and the Spirit of Capitalism*, p. 181-182). During a debate in 1909, he voiced his misgivings about the inexorable trend of bureaucratic administration:

> It is horrible to think that the world could one day be filled with nothing but those little cogs, little men clinging to little jobs and striving towards bigger ones—a state of affairs which is to be seen once more, as in the Egyptian records, playing an ever-increasing part in the spirit of our present administrative system, and especially of its offspring, the

8. Weber paid repeated homage to the "Taylor system" and the "American system of scientific management" as pioneer efforts in "the rational conditioning of work performance" (Gerth and Mills, p. 261). He also largely adopted Taylor's approach to workers' aptitudes, skills and incentives for work (*The Theory of Social and Economic Organization*, p. 261-262).

students. This passion for bureaucracy . . . is enough to drive one to despair. . . .[9]

D. *Gulick-Urwick: Architecture*

WORLD WAR I gave a tremendous impetus to the legal-rational gospel of efficiency. At a technical level the followers of Taylor developed more mature techniques of work study and production management, testing and selection of workers, and cost accounting. At a more general level the principles of Fayol were developed into sweeping principles concerning the architecture of "monocratic" bureaucracy.

As examples of the principles of formal organization, one can hardly do better than to turn to the work of Luther Gulick and Lyndall Urwick. Both of them authored significant formulations of organizational principles, formulations far superior to those of a host of lesser imitators. Although they concentrated on certain formal aspects of administration, they were both aware of broader approaches to the subject and even encouraged the presentation of other viewpoints. Both served on public bodies charged with producing state papers on important aspects of administration. Both were indefatigable publicists, propagandists and promoters of the gospel of neutral principles directed at raising the level of organizational efficiency.

In 1937 Gulick and Urwick cooperated in editing *Papers on the Science of Administration*.[10] Of the eleven papers in this collection, two—"Note on the Theory of Organization" and "Science, Values and Public Administration"—were authored by Gulick. Another two—"Organization as a Technical Problem" and "The Function of Administration, with special reference to the work of Henri Fayol"—were written by Urwick. From among the long list of their other publications, special reference might also be made to Gulick's *Administrative Reflections on World War II*, and Urwick's *The Elements of Administration*.

9. Quoted in Bendix, *Max Weber, An Intellectual Portrait*, p. 464.
10. This publication was initiated by Gulick as part of his service on the Committee on Administrative Management, set up by President Franklin D. Roosevelt during the late 1930's. Gulick felt that a collection of basic essays on administration was needed to facilitate the work of the committee's staff. The other two members of the President's Committee were Louis Brownlow, Chairman, also a pioneer in public administration, particularly at the municipal level, and Charles Merriam, an outstanding political scientist, and one of the first to recognize the significance of Taylor's ideas for government operations.

1. FROM FAYOL'S ELEMENTS TO POSDCORB

As a framework for his neutral principles, Gulick uses Fayol's five elements of administration: planning, organization, command, coordination and control. In so doing, however, he separates forecasting from planning in order to give it special emphasis.

Gulick goes much further in expanding Fayol's categories. "What is the work of the chief executive?" he asks.

His answer is POSDCORB, a verbal artifact made up of the initial letters of seven types of administrative activities:

Planning, that is working out in broad outline the things that need to be done and the methods for doing them to accomplish the purpose set for the enterprise;

Organizing, that is the establishment of the formal structure of authority through which work subdivisions are arranged, defined and co-ordinated for the defined objective;

Staffing, that is the whole personnel function of bringing in and training the staff and maintaining favorable conditions of work;

Directing, that is the continuous task of making decisions and embodying them in specific and general orders and instructions and serving as the leader of the enterprise;

Co-ordinating, that is the all important duty of interrelating the various parts of the work;

Reporting, that is keeping those to whom the executive is responsible informed as to what is going on, which thus includes keeping himself and his subordinates informed through records, research and inspection.

Budgeting, with all that goes with budgeting in the form of fiscal planning, accounting and control" (*Papers*, "Note on the Theory of Organization," p. 13).

In this list of seven activities, three—planning, organizing, and co-ordinating—are taken over bodily from Fayol. Fayol's command appears under the heading of direction. His control is covered in part by budgeting and reporting, which serve as instruments of both planning and control. In staffing, Gulick separates out for special mention an activity which Fayol largely included as part of organization.

Whatever its merits or demerits, POSDCORB served as a convenient starting point for innumerable writers interested in dealing with different aspects of administration or, to use a term which soon came into wide use, with different administrative processes. Many writers on public or business administration took this list and—through additions, subtractions and amendments—adapted it to meet their tastes and needs.

2. ORGANIZATIONAL PRINCIPLES

Despite their interest in dealing with administration as a whole, most of the Gulick-Urwick principles deal with the architectonics of formal organization. Eight of the most widely popularized principles deserve attention at this point.

A. *Fitting people to structure.* Urwick defines organization as "determining what activities are necessary to any purpose (or 'plan') and arranging them in groups which may be assigned to individuals." It should be undertaken "in a cold-blooded, detached spirit," like the preparation of an engineering design, without reference to any individuals who may now be in the organization. Every effort must then be made to find or fit people to the structure (*Elements of Administration,* p. 34-39).

B. *One top executive.* Urwick warns against the use of committees for purposes of administration. He quotes approvingly from the *Report of the U.S. President's Committee on Administrative Management:*

> For purposes of management, boards and commissions have turned out to be failures. Their mechanism is inevitably slow, cumbersome, wasteful and ineffective and does not lend itself readily to cooperation with other agencies. . . . The conspicuously well-managed administrative units in the Government are almost without exception headed by single administrators (p. 32).

In line with this point of view, Gulick—who, as a member of the President's Committee, probably wrote the above passage—played an active role in trying to work the principle of one-man administrative responsibility into the structure of the many boards and commissions in the U.S. Federal Government.

C. *Unity of command.* Gulick reiterates Fayol's maxim that "A man cannot serve two masters." Although rigid adherence to this principle may have its absurdities, these are "unimportant in comparison with the certainty of confusion, inefficiency and irresponsibility which arise from the violation of this principle" (*Papers,* "Note on the Theory of Organization," p. 9).

He himself, however, provided an exception to this principle in the case of field office specialists. According to the principle of "integrated dual supervision," for example, an engineer in a field office can be subject to the "administrative supervision" of the field office manager and to the "technical supervision" of the chief engineer in the central office[11] (*Administrative Reflections on World War II,* p. 91-96).

---

11. In this connection Gulick reviews the widely dispersed activities of war-

D. *Staff: special and general.* The Gulick-Urwick principles of staff assistance to executives deserve special attention. They were formulated during a period when it became increasingly clear that higher executives needed the help of larger and larger numbers of experts and specialists. This immediately raised the question of the relation between these specialists and the regular "line officials." Moreover, the multiplication of staff experts confronted higher executives with difficult problems of coordination. Drawing not only upon Fayol but also upon military experience with staff-line arrangements, Gulick dealt with each of these problems.

The first problem is that of special staff. Here, Gulick insists, the task of staff experts is to "devote their time exclusively to the knowing, thinking and planning functions." They must get results only by persuasion, by the "authority of ideas." They must not be given administrative authority or responsibility. (*Papers*, "Note on the Theory of Organization," p. 30-31).

The second problem is the executive's difficulty in supervising a large number of subordinates, including special staff experts. Most public officials and business, Urwick maintained, are overwhelmed with everyday work. They have no time to read, think, meet their subordinates and develop the "personal touch" essential for leadership. Surveying the vast duties heaped on the shoulders of the President, the President's Committee on Administrative Management came to a similar conclusion. "The President," they reported bluntly, "needs help."

The Gulick-Urwick answer to this problem is to provide help through "general staff" as distinguished from "special staff" assistance. As in military organizations, general staff officials may assist their superiors in their central tasks of command, control and coordination. As distinguished from special staff officials, they are not limited to the proffering of advice. They may draw up and transmit orders, follow up on operations and iron out difficulties. They should help coordinate the work of staff specialists without themselves taking on any specialized functions.

In so doing, they act not on their own but as direct agents or representatives of their superior and within the confines of decisions made by him. They thus relieve the top executive from the burdensome detail of administration. They allow him to exercise a larger span of control. They free him to concentrate upon the most important matters.

---

time agencies. He concludes that in order to avoid "multiple and nonintegrated supervision," dual supervision must rest on a clear distinction between "(a) the teamwork functions of action which must be supervised and directed locally, and (b) the methodology of technical operations which may be held to standards and supervised by central technical services and staff agencies."

Urwick recognizes that in civilian life a secretary or assistant who acts on behalf of a top executive will often be regarded as "encroaching" upon the authority of officials senior to himself. In military organizations, however, where staff officers are "almost invariably junior in rank to their commander's principal subordinates. . . . it is clear that their actions are in virtue of their appointment, their functions, and involve no assertion of unjustified authority" (*Ibid.*, "Organization as a Technical Problem," p. 64). Urwick does not indicate how this difficulty can be met in civilian organizations, where status is usually determined by jobs rather than by personal rank. Gulick and his colleagues on the President's Committee for Administrative Management provided a partial answer. They proposed that general assistants to the President be men with a "passion for anonymity."

E. *The basis of subdivision.* In assigning functions to groups of people, the first principle is homogeneity. In the simplest of all cases this homogeneity may be based on the identity or similarity of four factors: the purposes they serve, the processes they use, the persons or things they deal with, or the place where they work. In most cases, however, a choice must be made as to which of these principles—purpose, process, persons or things served, or place—should be given precedence. Units established on various principles are woven together to form the "tangled fabric" of larger organizations (*Ibid.*, "Note on the Theory of Organization," p. 15-30).

F. *Delegation.* Urwick maintains that "lack of the courage to delegate properly and of knowledge how to do it is one of the most general causes of failure in organization." Jethro's advice to Moses should be heeded by modern administrators. In larger organizations, they must even delegate the right to delegate. In checking on operations they should operate on Taylor's "exception principle"—that is, should concern themselves only with significant exceptions to the standards that have been set[12] (*Elements of Administration*, p. 51-52, 110, 125).

G. *Matching responsibility with authority.* While Fayol emphasized the need to promote a sense of responsibility Urwick deals with both sides of the authority-responsibility relationship. It is not enough to hold people accountable for certain activities. It is also essential to delegate to them "the necessary authority to discharge that responsibility." On the other side, "the responsibilities of all persons exercising authority should be absolute within the defined terms of that authority. They

12. On this subject, as on many others, Urwick leans heavily on James Mooney and A. C. Reilly, *Onward Industry*, 1931, later revised and published as James Mooney, *Principles of Organization*.

should be personally accountable for all actions taken by subordinates." In contrast to Fayol's observation that the measurement of responsibility "eludes all calculation," he sets forth the widely quoted principle that "at all levels authority and responsibility should be coterminous and coequal" (*Elements of Administration*, p. 45-46, 125).

H. *Span of control*. According to Urwick, "No supervisor can supervise directly the work of more than five, or at the most, six subordinates whose work interlocks." This is the administrative counterpart of the psychological conception of the "span of attention." When the number of subordinates increases arithmetically, there is a geometrical increase in all the possible combinations of relationships which may demand the attention of the supervisor[13] (*Elements of Administration*, p. 52-53).

Gulick identifies various factors that may influence the optimum span, particularly the capacity of an individual executive, the nature of the work performed, the stability of an organization and geographical proximity to those who are supervised. He is less categorical about the maximum number of subordinates, but no less confident concerning the general validity of the principle (*Papers*, "Note on the Theory of Organization," p. 7-9).

13. To support this formulation Urwick relies heavily on a mathematical analysis of minimum and maximum relationships between a supervisor and varying numbers of subordinates as presented by V. A. Graicunas in "Relationship in Organization," which is included in *Papers on the Science of Administration*.

Chapter 7

THE PIONEERS:
NEW BEGINNINGS

*A*LTHOUGH THE GOSPEL of administrative efficiency obtained a wide following, from the very beginning it provoked intellectual competition, if not opposition. The trade-union attack on Taylorism was followed by an increasing awareness of the limitations of "scientific management." Both teachers and practitioners grew restless with the narrowness of the principles presented so confidently by Fayol, Gulick and Urwick. At first, it was charged that their principles, although theoretically sound, simply did not work out in practice. And it was not long before their theoretical validity itself was challenged. Still more significant than this challenge, many new lines of thought—entirely outside the framework of the efficiency gospel—were initiated.

These new beginnings are much harder to categorize than the gospel of efficiency. The new pioneers did not dispute the importance of efficiency as a goal, but they held that other goals must also be considered. They did not challenge the ultimate desirability of laws and principles, but they suggested the previously promulgated laws and principles were false or oversimplifying and that they should be at least revised, if not rejected *in toto*.

In part, it might be said that the second group of pioneers demanded a new approach to "human relations." It might in addition be said that they went further in developing the "process approach" to administration, with attention to such fundamental processes as communication and decision-making. Yet each of these characterizations would be incomplete. No label more specific than "new beginnings" could be broad enough to encompass the multihued content of this second stream of administrative thought.

The best way to illustrate the richness of these new beginnings is to summarize the work of five people: Mary Follett, Elton Mayo, Fritz Roethlisberger, Chester Barnard and Herbert Simon. Each of these made seminal contributions to the growth of a new discipline. Each must be included among the "great names" of administrative thought.

Before reviewing the work of each, it is interesting to note their personal backgrounds.

Mary Follett U.S.A.	Political science and economics Community work and public service Occasional lecturer on business administration.
Elton Mayo Australia and U.S.A.	Psychology and philosophy Industrial research University professor
Fritz Roethlisberger U.S.A.	Chemical engineering and philosophy Industrial research University professor
Chester Barnard U.S.A.	Top executive in private business and philanthropic foundation Occasional public service Occasional lecturer
Herbert Simon U.S.A.	Political science Business administration and psychology Occasional government service University professor

As with Taylor, Fayol and Urwick, each of these five enjoyed close contact with administrative life—although Barnard, like Fayol, was the only one who had sustained personal experience with top-level administative responsibility. All five, moreover, including the three full-time university professors, were "field jumpers."

A. *Follett: Dynamic Integration*

ADMINISTRATION is one of the very few fields of human thought in which a woman has been an outstanding pioneer. Mary Follett (1868-1933) deserves to be ranked alongside such a trail-blazer as Florence Nightingale.

Although less known to the public at large (and even, apparently, little known to some writers and teachers on administration), her achievements are no less significant than Nightingale's. Mary Follett may not have been as experienced an administrator and behind-the-scenes operator as Florence Nightingale, whose major triumphs included the revitalization of hospital administration as well as the founding of modern nursing.[1] But she was no less an innovator, and her intellectual horizons were much broader.

Mary Follett was among the first to recognize the psychological aspects of administration and to deal with them on the basis of modern psychological thought rather than with glib references to the mysteries of human nature. She was the first to perform the unladylike task of inserting the nasty word "power" into the vocabulary of administration. She breathed a sense of dynamism and creative democratic spirit into the more static concepts of "scientific management" and organizational principles. She was probably one of the first to indicate how business management might develop into a genuine profession.

Like many others, Follett came to administration in a roundabout way. After studying economics, she entered political science by preparing an intensive historical survey of the post of the Speaker of the U.S. House of Representatives and the growing political power associated with it. (*The Speaker of the House of Representatives*, 1896). She then became active in many forms of community work, particularly adult education and vocational guidance. Her interest in social problems led to a book on democratic government and community activity (*The New State*, 1920). The community work brought her into public service as a member of the Massachusetts Minimum Wage Board. Here she met many business men and labor leaders and became familiar with management-labor disputes. These experiences led to a book on the psychological processes by which the views and interests of conflicting groups may be integrated (*Creative Experience*, 1924).

By this time her attention was drawn more and more to business administration. She made contact with many thoughtful businessmen in both the United States and England, men who were seeking an ideology more satisfying than mere money-grubbing and broader than Taylor's "scientific management." She found men who joined her in seeing business as "pioneer work in the organized relations of human beings" and who "were willing to try new ways the next morning. . . ."

In trying to develop and support some of these new ways, she pro-

1. Florence Nightingale's battles for administrative reform are vividly portrayed by Cecil Woodham-Smith in her classic biography, *Florence Nightingale*.

duced a series of lectures and articles replete with practical wisdom, deep flashes of intuition, undepartmentalized thinking, and an all-pervading spirit of democratic dynamism. One of these lectures was included by Gulick and Urwick in *Papers on the Science of Administration*. Others were published in various collections edited by Henry Metcalf of the Bureau of Personnel Administration. The most complete and representative set of her papers was edited by Metcalf and Urwick and published as *Dynamic Administration, the Collected Papers of Mary Parker Follett*.[2]

To present a summary of Follett's thinking on administration is a difficult task. She herself never attempted a systematic formulation. Her thinking was very much akin to her conception of the process of social action—a continuous emerging and becoming. Nevertheless, it is possible to single out certain concepts from her writings that have been particularly influential.

1. CONFLICT AND INTEGRATION

In *Creative Experience* Follett wrote that it is possible "to conceive conflict as not necessarily a wasteful outbreak of incompatibilities, but a normal process by which socially valuable differences register themselves for the enrichment of all concerned" (p. 300). In one of her first essays on business administration, "Constructive Conflict," she carries the same theme still further by considering how "we can set conflict to work and make it do something for us." She posits three ways of dealing with conflict. One is domination, which means a victory for one side or the other. The second is compromise, which means that each side gives up something in order to have peace. The third—and most constructive—is integration. In a true integration of conflicting views, a place is found for each desire and neither side sacrifices anything. In fact, both sides gain.

The first steps toward integration are to bring a conflict into the open and discover its most significant aspects, rather than merely the most dramatic ones. This requires a judicious examination of the symbols that are used and the realities to which they actually refer. It involves both breaking the demands and interests of both sides into their constituent parts and finding "the whole demand, the real demand, which is being obscured by miscellaneous minor claims or by ineffective presentation." It involves dropping general or theoretical dispute and centering upon

2. In their joint introduction, Metcalf and Urwick acclaim Follett as a "political and business philosopher of the first rank." It is testimony to the intellectual breadth of Urwick and Gulick that they both promoted the writings of someone whose basic approach was so different from their own.

proposed activities. These steps can lead to a "revaluation of interests" and a "revaluation of desire." We should "never allow ourselves to be bullied by an 'either-or.' There is often the possibility of something better than either of two given alternatives."

Above all, integration requires awareness that human behavior is not linear but circular. B does not merely react to what A does. He also reacts to his own anticipation of what A may do on his own and of how A may react to something B does. Yet the actual response is still more circular. "I can never fight you. I am always fighting you plus me. . . . Employees do not respond only to their employers, but to the relation between themselves and their employer. . . . Circular behavior on the basis of integration gives us the key to constructive conflict."

One of the many obstacles to integration is that "most of us are trying to get power over." This form of power is evidenced in the use of persuasion as well as of compulsion. While we can never get rid of "power over," we should "develop the conception of power with, a jointly-developed power, a coactive, not a coercive power." A business should be "so organized that a workman has an opportunity of influencing you as you have an opportunity of influencing him." If the possibility for reciprocal interaction exists, power-with may be built up and integration achieved ("Constructive Conflict" and "Power," *Dynamic Administration*).

2. THE LAW OF THE SITUATION

For Taylor, Fayol, Gulick and Urwick, the major way of getting people to do things is command or direction—the giving of orders. Such basic concepts as the unity of command, the span of control and authority are all formulated with reference to linear relationships in which A tells B what to do.

Follett does not deny the necessity of order-giving. In fact, she even deals with *how* orders should be given. Habit patterns and mental attitudes must be built up by training. The time, place, and circumstances are also important. Nor is the long-distance order very effective. "One might say that the strength of favorable response to an order is in inverse ratio to the distance the order travels."

Yet people resent being bossed: "Psychology, as well as our own observation, shows us not only that you cannot get people to do things most satisfactorily by ordering them. . . . The more you are 'bossed' the more your activity of thought will take place within the bossing pattern and your part in that pattern seems usually to be opposition to the bossing."

This difficulty cannot be solved merely by the arts of persuasion. To reason with subordinates, even to convince them—this too may be regarded as an act of domination and may become part of the "bossing pattern."

How can we avoid the two great extremes, she asks, of too great "bossism" in giving orders and practically no orders given? "My solution," she replies, "is to depersonalize the giving of orders, to unite all concerned in a study of the situation, to discover the law of the situation, and obey that." By this approach A does not give orders to B. Both do whatever the situation requires. The orders "should be the composite decision of those who give and those who receive them." A may exercise initiative in identifying the problem and in analyzing the situation. But the possibility of destructive friction between A and B is reduced. B's energies are canalized into helping make the decision and carry it out, rather than being drained away in open or suppressed resentment.

This is the path of fact control, not personal control. The objective analysis of alternative paths of action determines what shall be done. "Orders come from action, not action from orders." In operating positions the most effective method will be standardized until a better method is found. "Men follow standard practice rather than obey arbitrary commands."

At first thought, Follett's "depersonalization of orders" seems somewhat reminiscent of Taylor's mechanical approach to work and workers. It seems hard to reconcile this with her emphasis on the human and personal aspect of administration. Follett herself recognizes the paradox and tries to solve it. By studying the entire situation and trying to determine what action it requires, we are, in fact, "repersonalizing." Human relations take place in and through a whole situation. "We cannot have any sound relations with each other as long as we take them out of that setting which gives them their meaning and value" (*op cit.*, "The Giving of Orders" and "Leadership Theory and Practice").

3. THE CONFUSION BETWEEN POWER AND AUTHORITY

Gently but firmly, Follett chides management writers and political scientists who talk about "the delegation of power" or the separation, transfer, or conferring of power. They are guilty, she maintains, of confusing power and authority.

Power is defined by Follett as "simply the ability to make things happen, to be a causal agent, to initiate change." Its sources and uses should be carefully studied. In any case, whether it is good or bad probably depends on the purposes for which it is used.

Nor can power be either delegated or conferred. It is not "a pre-existing thing which can be handed out to someone, or wrenched from someone. . . ." It is rather "self-developing capacity." The manager cannot share power with his division heads. But "he can give them opportunities for developing *their* power." He can encourage them to integrate their activities in order to achieve "jointly developing power. More power, not division of power, should always be our aim; more power for the best possible furtherance of that activity, whatever it may be, to which we are giving our life." The great advantage of "power with" is that it leads to more power than "power over."

Authority, on the other hand, is vested power, the right to develop and exercise power. It *can* be conferred. But to confer authority is not to delegate it. Authority should not be seen as something that flows downward, like water from a tank on the roof of a building. A person's authority flows from the function, from the job to be performed, and from the changing situations in which he finds himself. No president or general manager should have "any more authority than goes with his function. Therefore I do not see how you can delegate authority except when you are ill or take a vacation. And then you have not exactly delegated authority. Someone is doing your work and he had the authority which goes with that particular piece of work. Authority belongs to the job and stays with the job." But since the operation of any organization calls for the interweaving of many different functions, authority is not a static thing like a pile of bricks. In the ideal organization it "is always fresh, always being distilled anew."

Because of the necessity for expertise, authority is widely dispersed within the larger, more modern organizations. The idea of "functional authority" or "pluralistic authority" is thus more important than the older notion of "ultimate" or "central" authority. Moreover, a change is taking place in the conception of the expert's role. We used to think that a staff expert merely gives advice. "But a new relation has entered in of recent years; there is something emerging which is neither orders nor advice." The opinions of staff "advisers" are being given "much more weight than mere advice in the ordinary acceptance of that word."

A certain form of central authority, Follett readily admits, is necessary. But this should not be overemphasized. And it should be seen not as the chief executive but as "a technical expression of scientific management indicating the point where knowledge and experience on the method in question are brought to a focus." This question brings her back to the old question of sovereignty, which she struggled with in her writings on political science. She now concludes that "the only legitimate boss, sovereignty, is, I believe, the interweaving experience of all those who are performing some functional part of the activity under consideration." This is much more than transferring the seat of sovereignty from the ruler to the people. She is not satisfied with mere consent on the part of the governed. In fact, she points out that what we often see in business today is "the consent of the governors," whereby higher executives spend most of their time consenting to plans submitted by their subordinates. Neither form of consent is enough. What is really important is participation at all levels, interweaving and integration.

Thus Follett inveighs against thinking of organization in terms of "over" and "under." She enthusiastically quotes certain telephone company officials who saw themselves in terms of their specific jobs rather than their hierarchical location. The ideal attitude is that people work "with" others, not under or over them (*op. cit.,* "Power," "Responsibility in Business Management," "Leader and Expert," and "Psychology of Consent and Participation").

4. CUMULATIVE RESPONSIBILITY

Follett's concept of authority necessarily implies a revision of the more traditional concept of responsibility. Responsibility, like authority, stems from function and situation. One should not ask *"To whom* is he responsible?" but rather "For *what* is he responsible?"

As the result of the diffusion of function, final or ultimate responsibility, like final authority, is "partly an illusion. You will not find the pot of gold at the foot of that rainbow." How then can the work of different people and units in an organization be unified? The answer is found in the ideas of cross-functioning, group responsibility and cumulative responsibility. Each individual function should not be seen in isolation. It must be seen in terms of its interdependence with, and contribution to, other functions. Each subexecutive, because of his function, has the responsibility to integrate his work with other subexecutives rather than merely pass on the task of coordination to hierarchical superiors. This requires organizational arrangements for intimate cross-relations, rather than too much reliance on "always running up and down a ladder of authority." This interweaving of responsibility should start at the earliest stages and at the lowest levels. "You cannot always bring together the results of departmental activities and expect to coordinate them. . . . Strand should weave with strand, and then we shall not have the clumsy task of trying to patch together finished webs."

Follett draws two significant conclusions from this analysis of responsibility. The first is that lower level executives should be regarded as responsible for helping to formulate general policy. She takes issue with those who maintain that the production manager should subordinate departmental policy to general policy. In fact, she doubts whether there really is such a thing as a departmental problem, one that can be considered purely one of production or distribution. Each small part has a potential contribution to make to the whole, "not to a stationary whole, but to a whole a-making."

The second conclusion is that workers also have a role in management. Just as there is no sharp line between planning and executing, "the distinction between those who manage and those who are managed is somewhat fading." In one sense, workers inevitably take part in management whenever they use their own judgment in deciding how to carry out orders. In another sense, progressive management tries to develop on the part of workers not only a sense of individual responsibility but a sense of joint responsibility. Employees and their elected union representatives have a major contribution to make to the management of a company. This contribution should be solicited and given not on the basis of the Golden Rule, but on the higher principle of genuine community of interest. Hence "employee representation should be considered as an aspect of organization engineering. . . . It should be an integral part of a certain plan of organization. . . ."

But this pluralistic conception of responsibility should not lead to haziness. "To be honest and clearcut in delimiting function is, I believe, essential to the success of the redistribution of function." For example, a Works Council may be regarded as an advisory, a judicial, or even a legislative body—but never an executive body. In dealing with executive functions, it may be harder to "fix" responsibility. Yet the effort must be made. When things go wrong, "we have to discover how far each one concerned has contributed to the failure or partial failure. . . ." The purpose of allocating responsibility for a failure, however, is not to distribute reprimands. It is rather to discover ways of doing better in the future, to give education instead of blame (*op. cit.*, "Responsibility in Business Management," "Business as an Integrative Unity," and "Influence of Employee Representation").

5. PLANNING AS COORDINATION

Although favoring "collective planning on a national or even international scale," Follett feels that central government planning imposed from the top down is doomed to failure. "The opposite of laissez-faire is not coercion but coordination" and "coordination is by its very nature a process of auto-governed activity . . . the reciprocal relating of all the factors in a situation." Thus a National Planning Board "ought not to arrogate to itself the task of coordinating." Its task, rather, should be to facilitate the coordination process.

In addition to reciprocal relating, she offers three additional principles for national or international planning. The first is direct contact between the responsible people concerned, particularly between the responsible heads of industry. This may often mean "cross relations between heads of departments instead of up and down the line through the chief executive." The second is coordination in the early stages before policies have been formed. "The process of the interpenetration of policies must begin before they are completed, while they are still in the formative stage." Third, coordination must be viewed as a continuing process. Only through continuous machinery can it be clear that problems are faced rather than solved. Finally, all these principles must be underpinned by information based on continuous research. "The information of itself would be a form of control, for there would be a tendency to act in accordance with information given if it were accepted as accurate."

According to Follett, national planning need not be in opposition to individualism. If national planning is based on the principle of "the interpenetration of authority instead of a super-authority," it could "give scope to individual initiative . . . by showing it the way to combine effectively with other individual initiatives . . . by a process not of compromise but of integration" (*op. cit.*, "Individualism in a Planned Society").

6. A PROFESSION IN THE MAKING

Follett sees certain tendencies in the direction of the professionalization of business management. Among these are the developments of "scientific management," the growth of specialization, the decline of arbitrary authority, the trend toward conscious control of business cycles, and the recognition that management is a more fundamental element in industry than either stockholders or bankers. But a true profession is based on the motive of service and a foundation of science. Here much more should be done.

A. *The ideals of service.* With respect to service, Follett attacks the old idea that a businessman makes money for himself in the daytime (or in his younger years) and then renders service to the community by sitting on a civic committee at night (or after amassing enough money to afford being unselfish). "Our work itself," she maintains, "is to be our greatest service to the community." The services of businessmen are as essential as those of doctor, lawyers, teachers, and engineers.

They are also every bit as high and noble. The real service of businessmen is not merely the production and distribution of manufactured articles. It is "to give an opportunity for individual development through the better organization of human relationships. . . . The *process* of production is as important for the welfare of society as the product of production."

The service implies high standards of accomplishment. Personal standards are important—particularly when they express a sense of style, "the love of work, the craftsman's and artist's joy in work well done." But they are not enough. They must be broadened into group standards. These standards must be developed, enriched and maintained. Businessmen should educate the public to appreciate these standards. When there is a clash between company and professional standards, an integration should be made. "It is unfair," she maintains, "to think that all businessmen have only as high a code as is compatible with keeping profits at a certain level. I have known businessmen who were willing to make sacrifices to maintain certain standards." Follett does not find any basic inconsistency between the service motive and the profit motive. Motivation is a complex and multiple process. None of the professions have given up the money motive. The more motives the merrier.

B. *The scientific foundation.* With respect to science, two major steps are needed. First of all, "the scientific standard must be applied to the whole of business management." It must include not only operations, but also management itself. It must deal not only with the technical side, but also with the personnel and human relations side. In fact, the technical side itself cannot be properly understood if divorced from the human side.

The second step is to develop an organized body of knowledge. This involves intensive and continued research and the "organization of the knowledge obtained by research." We should analyze managers' jobs and managerial waste "somewhat corresponding to the analysis of workers' jobs in the Taylor system." This can lead to standardized—but progressively evolving—managerial methods and techniques. Above all, there should be systematic recording of executive experience in individual plants. Just as an efficient company makes a systematic follow-up of new production processes, it should make a "systematic follow-up of decisions, of new methods, of experiments on managing." To profit from such experience each company should have a management research analyst, "an official, one of whose duties should be to classify and interpret managerial experience with the aid of the carefully kept records which should be required of every executive." It is also essential to compare the experience and experiments of different companies and different countries. Conferences, journals and "sifted bibliographies" can be extremely helpful. It would also be useful to classify and cross-index the business policy case studies collected by the Harvard Business School.

In the difficult pioneer work of developing standards of service and building a body of organized knowledge, managers themselves must play the major role. "All professions have been developed by the work of their own members." The manager must contribute to the development of his profession not merely by activity in a management association. "The way in which you give every order, the way in which you make every decision, the way in which you meet every committee, in almost every act you perform during the day, you may be contributing to the science of management" (*op. cit.*, "How Must Business Management Develop in Order to Possess the Essentials of a Profession," and "How Must Business Management Develop in Order to Become a Profession").

B. *Mayo-Roethlisberger: Human Relations*

IN 1925, when Follett issued her call for intensive research within organizations, an ambitious research project was already under way at the Western Electric Company's Hawthorne plant near Chicago. Its purpose was to measure the effect of improved lighting on workers' output. Although the investigators conducted their study with the thoroughness of Taylor himself, after two and a half years they found no direct statistical relation between the two. Still eager to pin down such a relation, they turned for help to Elton Mayo and Fritz Roethlisberger of the Harvard Graduate School of Business Administration. A former medical student who had deserted medicine for psychology and philosophy, Mayo (1880-1949) was then engaged, along with Harvard biochemists, in studying fatigue in industry.[3] Roethlisberger (1898-   ) was his research assistant. With their encouragement, and with the participation of many others from Harvard and Western Electric, a new study was started in 1927. This led to a series of studies that *in toto* lasted more than five years. The resulting "Hawthorne studies" were soon to become an historic landmark in administrative thought. Having a much wider impact than Follett's writings, they helped bring into being the so-called "human relations" school. They served as inspiration for scores of empirical studies of human behavior in organizations and for new approaches to administrative education. They achieved the distinction of being dis-

3. Many details of Mayo's unusual career have been summarized by Urwick (1960).

torted by followers who sought devices for the manipulation of workers and by critics who ignored their historic contribution and concentrated upon their weak points alone.

Not a researcher himself, Mayo's major role in the Hawthorne studies was to emphasize the desirability of studying workers' behavior in all its complexity. Physiological, physical, economic, and psychological factors—all were to be included. All conclusions were to be skeptically tested against concrete experience. This he called the "clinical approach." He also brought to the studies an interest in obsessive and neurotic behavior derived from his familiarity with the writings of Pierre Janet and Sigmund Freud. As they became available, Mayo used the results of the Hawthorne studies as a springboard for speculation about administration and also about the broader problems of social organization. His growing interest in the larger problems of society is indicated by the "trend line" suggested by the titles of his major works: *The Human Problems of an Industrial Civilization* (1933), *The Social Problems of an Industrial Civilization* (1945), and (still incomplete at the time of his retirement) *The Political Problems of Industrial Civilization* (1947). In a sense, Mayo was a social reformer with a vision of a better society that could be attained not through any specific panaceas but through the leadership of forward-looking administrators, particularly businessmen. Roethlisberger, in turn, concentrated more upon the empirical studies and their interpretation within the focus of single organizations. He is best known for the classic *Management and the Worker* (1939),[4] written in collaboration with William J. Dickson of Western Electric, *Management and Morale* (1941), and *Training for Human Relations* (1954). Roethlisberger has guided many empirical studies by students and associates and has been active in developing methods for training students and administrators in social skills.

1. THE "GREAT ILLUMINATION"

The new studies at the Hawthorne plant first attempted to measure how new output was affected by certain changes in physical working conditions: rest pauses of different lengths and frequencies, with and without lunches, and different lengths of both work day and work week. The researchers placed five girls in a separate Relay Assembly Test Room

---

4. This is the definitive presentation of the Hawthorne studies. A more detailed analysis of one of the studies (the Relay Assembly Test Room) is provided by another Harvard researcher, T. North Whitehead in *The Industrial Worker* (1938). An interpretive study is provided by the same author in *Leadership in a Free Society* (1936).

and placed an observer in the room to keep accurate records and maintain a friendly atmosphere. During the first few months physical conditions were maintained without change in order to get the girls accustomed to the test room. In this period hourly output rose. Then conditions were gradually improved: hours were decreased below the original 48-hour week; rest periods of different lengths and frequencies were introduced. Hourly output rose steadily—usually more than enough to counterbalance the decline in hours per week. Weekly output declined only when hours per week fell to less than 42.

After a year and a half of charting these changes, it was decided to withdraw all the improvements and return to the original conditions at the beginning of the experiment. This was done in the famous "Period XII." As a result, hourly output fell somewhat. But it nevertheless remained far higher than a year and a half earlier at the start of the experiment. Moreover the return to a 48-hour week—which represented more than a 14 per cent increase in working hours—brought weekly output to new heights. In the next period, hours were reduced and rest periods brought back. Hourly output then rose very sharply, so much so that despite the decline in hours it brought weekly output to its peak.

By this time, according to Roethlisberger and Dickson, the investigators were puzzled. "The general upward trend in output independent of any particular change in rest pauses or shorter working hours was astonishing. The improvement in mental attitude throughout the first two years of the experiment was also perplexing. Neither one of these developments could be related to the kind of working day in any simple one-one correlation. . . . To what could this improved output, on the one hand, and improved mental attitude or morale, on the other, be related?" (*Roethlisberger and Dickson*, 1939, p. 86-87).

Perhaps the reason could be found in the changed operation of Hawthorne's incentive wage plan. When the girls had worked in the regular relay assembly department, they had received bonuses in accordance with the output of a group of approximately one hundred employees. In the Relay Assembly Test Room, although the bonus system was technically the same, it was based on the work of only five employees. Thus the relationship between group output and individual pay was closer than before.

In order to isolate the influence of wage incentives, two supplementary experiments were conducted. First, five other girls were organized into a Second Relay Assembly Test Room identical in every way to the first except for the change in wage incentive. The women in this room were operators who had always been paid on an individual piece-work basis. This system was continued. These supplementary experiments convinced the investigators that neither wage incentives alone, nor all the changes in physical conditions taken together, could explain the increases in output in the first two years of the Relay Assembly Test Room. More important, they concluded that they had been mistaken in their first effort to "maintain a controlled experiment in which they could test for the effect of a single variable while holding other factors constant. . . ." The effort to keep all other factors constant "in itself introduced the biggest change of all." This was the change in human attitudes and sentiments.

One source of this change was a radical change in the nature of supervision. Previously, they had been under strict supervision. But in the test room, where the official observer and other experimenters took over most supervisory functions, the atmosphere became more relaxed. The girls were allowed to talk freely. Changes in conditions were discussed with the girls in advance, instead of being arbitrarily announced by superior authority. "In the endeavor to keep the major variables in the situation constant and the girls' attitude cooperative, the investigators inadvertently altered the social situation of the group. Thus, as a consequence of setting up an experiment to study the factors determining the efficiency of the worker, they abrogated most of the rules intended to promote and maintain efficiency" (*op. cit.*, p. 182-183).

Second, the girls received more attention. The fact that they were studied became a source of pride. Important visitors streamed through the test room. They even "became the focus of considerable attention from top management" (*op. cit.*, p. 180-181).

Third, the girls had grown into a close-knit group. They cooperated not only with the experimenters but with each other. They grew more and more to enjoy their interpersonal relationships at work. Out of this grew "new group loyalties and solidarities" (*op. cit.*, p. 58-59).

In short, the human relations between workers and their supervisors and among the workers are important influences on workers' behavior, at least as important as physical working conditions and monetary incentives. It is this idea that many commentators have hailed as the "great illumination." In part, its greatness stems from the blindness of the industrial psychologists and engineers who had been preaching the gospel of efficiency in accordance with Frederick Taylor's conceptions of human motivation. Many years later Roethlisberger himself suggested that the Hawthorne studies simply represented "the systematic exploitation of the simple and the obvious" (1941, p. 7). Yet with due allowance for Roethlisberger's modesty, the essence of outstanding research and theory in administration is the explicit formulation of relationships that are, from the point of view of an administrator's intuitive wisdom, simple and obvious.

2. SENTIMENTS AND THE "INNER REFERENCE"

In 1928 the investigators started a special study of human attitudes and sentiments in the plant. For this purpose interviewers asked employees "to express frankly their likes and dislikes about their working environment." By the time this project was ended in 1930 over 21,000 interviews had been recorded and analyzed.

At the beginning the interviewers tried to limit the content of the interviews. But sometimes, "regardless of what the interviewer said, the employee's thoughts tended to gravitate toward one idea." At other times "a particularly reticent person became remarkably communicative if just the right topic could be touched upon in conversation." Accordingly, a new interviewing technique was adopted: the indirect approach. With this technique, the employee followed his own lead. The job of the interviewer, after a brief initial explanation of the program, was mainly to listen attentively and display a real interest in everything the employee said. He was never to suggest answers. Under this system the length of the average interview grew from half an hour to an hour and a half.

As the interviewing program continued, it was found that "frequently there was no simple and direct relation between the complaint and the object toward which the complaint was directed. . . . Certain grievances, although directed toward some object or person, were not due to some deficiency in the object criticized but rather were expressions of concealed, perhaps unconscious, disturbances in the employee's situations. Such complaints had an inner as well as an outer reference, and the inner reference could be reached only by a further study of the person who made the complaint. To put it in other words, the latent content of a statement, that is, the attitude of the complainant, was in many instances, just as important to understand as its manifest content" (*Roethlisberger and Dickson*, 1939, p. 266). This was illustrated on a number of occasions when the conditions objected to were changed but the complaint continued anyway.

But here again, as with the Relay Assembly Test Room, certain unforeseen results led them to acclaim the project a success. First of all, the interviews seemed to have a marked effect in reducing tensions and raising morale. The employees "appreciated being recognized as individuals who had valuable comments to make." They obtained a real "lift" from expressing themselves freely and at length. Seriously-felt grievances became more bearable or even disappeared. At times, even when no corrective action whatsoever was taken, employees were convinced that conditions they had complained about—such as "poor food" in the company restaurants—had actually been improved.

Second, the interviewing program "created a change in supervision over and above that which came from the participation of supervisors in conferences." The reason given is that for the first time the supervisors knew that "his methods were being made the subject of research and that his subordinates were being invited to express their opinions about him."

Third, the interviewers felt that "they had acquired a new and improved way of understanding and dealing with their fellow-men." They learned that the behavior of workers cannot be understood apart from their feelings and sentiments. They concluded that these feelings and sentiments derive from both an employee's personal history and his social situation at work (*op. cit.*, p. 226-229). They found that social structure was "an intricate web of human relations bound together by a system of sentiments" (Roethlisberger, 1941, p. 44).

3. SOCIAL ORGANIZATION vs. THE "RABBLE HYPOTHESIS"

As a result of their interviewing experiences, some of the interviewers started to analyze the social situation in various departments. But it was soon decided that any careful analysis of the social relations between workers called for a concentrated study of a single group.

In November 1931, therefore, the project leaders established the Bank Wiring Observation Room. Here fourteen men—nine wiremen, three solderers and two inspectors—worked together for seven months under careful observation. This time, however, instead of taking over supervisory functions themselves, the investigators included as objects of the study the behavior of four supervisory officials who came into contact with the workers: group leader, section chief, assistant foreman, and foreman.

The findings on output might seem, at first blush, to substantiate Taylor's charge that workers engage in "systematic soldiering." The wiremen and solderers were guided by their own standard of a "day's work," a standard considerably below the management's "bogey." The workers themselves were capable of producing far more. Yet anyone who exceeded the informal group standard was subjected to strong social pressure. As a result, some of the ablest workers were among the lower producers. The highest producer was one of the least capable.

Yet the wages of the workers in the observation room were carefully related to individual output. If they had produced more, they would have made more money. By restricting output, they deliberately held down their own wages. This was at odds with Taylor's conception of workers' behavior.

Moreover, the workers habitually frustrated the system of production records that had been carefully established in accordance with the principles of "scientific management." But their purpose was not to obtain more money. Rather, they wanted to give the impression of a fairly uniform rate of output. One way of doing this was by "saving up connections" when their output was high and reporting them on days when their output was low. Another way was to manipulate the reported figures on net working time. This was done by exaggerating the amount of time lost by supply shortages, defective materials and other factors presumably beyond the employees' control.

Finally, the lower ranks of supervisory personnel—the group chief and section chief—tolerated both output restriction and records falsification. They also winked at other infractions of company policy and rules. As a result, the channel of upward communication to the foreman was broken down. "The group chief and section chief . . . did not dare to give the foreman an objective account of the facts. It was even doubtful if they could have done so; their own hopes and fears were too much involved. The outcome was that departmental records became distorted." But the foreman could not find out the facts for himself. "When he entered the room, the behavior of the men underwent a sudden change; they acted as they were supposed to while he was present" (*op. cit.*, 1939, p. 458).

In interpreting output restriction, Roethlisberger and Dickson refuse to accept Taylor's explanations that workers are simply lazy or uncooperative. They reject the idea that the workers were expressing hostility against the company, which is said to have had "a long record of fair dealing with its employees." Nor could the restriction have been controlled by the immediate supervisors. The roots were much deeper.

Roethlisberger and Dickson find that output restriction, although inconsistent with the "logic of efficiency," is rooted in the "logic of sentiments." They define the logic of sentiments as "that system of ideas and beliefs which expresses the values residing in the interhuman relations of the different groups within the plant." These ideas and beliefs stem not only from the formal organization but also from the many informal groups that inevitably develop side-by-side with the formal organization. It is in these informal groups, which may work with or against the formal organization, that workers obtain a significant degree of position and status.

This analysis is bolstered by a detailed study of the informal organization within the Bank Wiring Observation Room. First of all, the group as a whole held the following ideas concerning individual behavior:

1. You should not turn out too much work. If you do, you are a "rate buster."
2. You should not turn out too little work. If you do, you are a "chiseler."
3. You should not tell a supervisor anything that will react to the detriment of an associate. If you do, you are a "squealer."
4. You should not attempt to maintain social distance or act officious. If you are an inspector, for example, you should not act like one.

An individual's status in the group was determined largely by his conformity to these sentiments (*op. cit.*, p. 522).

Moreover, the group as a whole was divided into two cliques. The clique which conformed more closely to the group's norms regarded itself as superior to the other. The output differences between individuals seemed to be determined by the exigencies of inteclique friction, in which many other factors also appeared. For the "deviants," those not fully accepted in either clique, output tended to be one of the ways of expressing resentment or resistance against their ostracism.

The sentiments of the informal organization are also related, according to Roethlisberger, to the larger social situation. The plant technologists propose technical innovations which often impair the workers' status, social codes, interpersonal relations and traditions of craftsmanship. The supervisors try to induce the workers to conform to the rules of the technical organization. Both technologists and supervisors are seen as a source of interference and constraint. "Resistance to such interference was the chief external function of the bank wiremen's informal organization" (*op. cit.*, p. 547).

If there is more social organization in the factory than meets the eye, Mayo contended, the same is true for society as a whole. Society also is a vast and complex network of organized groups. Our understanding of society, however, has been impeded by the "rabble hypothesis," the assumption of the classical economists that "mankind is a horde of unorganized individuals actuated by self-interest. . . . For many centuries the rabble hypothesis, in one form or another, has bedeviled all our thinking on matters involving law, government or economics. From this theory has evolved the conviction of a need for a Leviathan, a powerful state, which by the exercise of a unique authority shall impose order on the rabble." This theory is valid, and the so-called laws of economic self-interest apply, only in a period of social breakdown when social organization has failed (Mayo, 1945, p. 41-44).

4. THE SOCIAL EQUILIBRIUM

Both Mayo and Roethlisberger used the concept of social equilibrium as "a way of thinking which, if followed, prevents us from making a simple cause-and-effect analysis of phenomena in which a relation of interdependence obtains" (Roethlisberger, 1941, p. 184-185). They used L. J. Henderson's definition of equilibrium as "a state such that if a small (not too great) modification different from that which would otherwise occur is impressed upon a system, a reaction will at once appear tending toward the conditions that would have existed if the modification had not been impressed."[5] Instead of regarding social equilibrium as based upon the interrelation of a small number of factors, they followed Henderson also in "mutual dependence analysis," the simultaneous measurement of many specific variables, "as few as we may, as many as we want."

By this approach a "steady state" is one in which a cooperative system can continue to operate indefinitely, even in the face of external adversity, just as long as internal equilibrium is maintained. Thus Mayo explains the continuously high performance of the girls in the Relay Assembly Test Room not on the basis of any one factor, either economic or social. His explanation is rather that "by strengthening the 'temperamental' internal equilibrium of the workers, the company enabled them to achieve a mental 'steady state' which offered a high resistance to a variety of external conditions" (Mayo, 1933, p. 72).

This approach enables Roethlisberger to pin down the concept of "morale." Instead of being a quality attaching to an individual or a group, morale is "a dynamic relation of equilibrium between individuals and the organization they serve." Just as health can be understood only by thinking about the physical organism as a physio-chemical system, so morale can be understood only by thinking about people in their relations with another as part of a social system (Roethlisberger, 1941, p. 192-193).

Mayo applies the equilibrium concept to external conditions as well. In society as well as in smaller groups, human collaboration "has always depended for its perpetuation upon the evolution of a nonlogical social code which regulates the relations between persons and their attitudes to one another." Modern industry has violated such social codes by

5. *Three Lectures on Concrete Sociology*, p. 21. Henderson's definition is a restatement of Pareto's concept of social equilibrium. The debt to Pareto is established more fully in Henderson's *Pareto's General Sociology*.

insisting upon "a merely economic logic of production." In the factory this leads to the restriction of production. In the larger community it leads to social disintegration and disorganization. The most blatant forms of such disorganization are delinquency, suicide, neurosis and obsessions. Deeper, although less obvious, are "anomie" (Durkheim's term for the sense of emptiness, futility and planlessness), and acquisitiveness. Mayo refers sympathetically to R. H. Tawney's attack on modern society for viewing the acquisition of wealth as its highest aim (*The Acquisitive Society*), but he suggests that acquisitiveness is merely a symptom of disequilibrium. The problem of industrial civilization "is not that of the sickness of an acquisitive society; it is that of the acquisitiveness of a sick society" (Mayo, 1933, p. 138-147).

5. SKILL AS A "WAY OF LEARNING"

According to Mayo, science originated in the observations of people who were practicing various skills. Thus medical knowledge first developed as an outgrowth of the clinical work of practicing physicians. Knowing in the sense of *connaitre*, "to know from experience," preceded knowing in the sense of *savoir*, "to know as the product of abstract thought" (Mayo, 1945, p. 15-22). At a later date the relation between skill and knowledge becomes a two-way affair. In the behavioral sciences, which are still immature, "skill and knowledge, instead of helping each other out, seem to have difficulty in getting together. Each cultivates its own garden . . ." (Roethlisberger, 1954, p. 9). Since administrative theorists tend to overemphasize the latter, it is necessary to pay more attention to skills and their development. Any skill, particularly administrative skill, is "manifested at a particular point as a complex capacity acquired by experience in responding appropriately to particular, concrete and whole situations." Rather than being a static set of techniques, it is "the way an ordinary mortal goes about improving his response to an external object and situation . . . an internal way of learning rather than an external technique to be learned." The key characteristics of skillful behavior are balanced growth through time and a conscious awareness that makes it possible to discriminate between objects and situations (*op. cit.*, p. 15-20).

Both Mayo and Roethlisberger insist that social skills have lagged behind technical skills. The social skills are those through which the administrator becomes "the guardian or preserver of morale through the function of maintaining a condition of equilibrium which will preserve the social values existing in the cooperative system." In a negative sense, such skills are quite different from the specialist skills which do not involve cooperative phenomena, the skills of engineers, chemists and physicists. They are also different from the specialist skills of accountants, economists, personnel men, production control men and others who come much closer to cooperative phenomena. In more positive terms these are the skills of the successful practical administrators. Unfortunately, since these people usually operate on the basis of intuition instead of theory, they find it difficult to communicate their skills to others. Through adequate research into administrative experience, these skills can be formulated, communicated, practiced and applied. In this process, theory is essential; for "although theory without practice is idle speculation, practice without theory is incommunicable."

Roethlisberger places great emphasis on skill in diagnosis. "Cost control, quality control, production control, measuring the performance of workers, salesmen, foremen—all these are diagnostic aids to the administrator." But the techniques of diagnosing human situations are less well developed. Here people tend to use saws instead of hammers, to analyze human problems with nonhuman tools. Managers must learn how to think of cooperative phenomena in terms of social conditioning, informal patterns of behavior, sentiments and beliefs and equilibrium analysis. Above all, they must learn the skills of patient listening (Roethlisberger, 1941, p. 137-159, 175-194).

Mayo sees the lag in social skills as a threatening factor in social disequilibrium. In an age of rapid development of the physical sciences and economics, "our administrative elite has become the addict of a few specialist studies." Their technical competence is accompanied by "utter social incompetence." Too many operate on the "unthinking assumption" that every participant in an organization "will be a devotee of systematic economics and a rigid logic." They fail to understand that the industrial workers want "first a method of living in social relationship with other people and, second, as part of this an economic function for and value to the group" (Mayo, 1933, p. 173-175).

Mayo feels that the resulting disequilibrium is inevitable if the social composition of administrative leaders inside and outside of government remains stable. The vigor needed to maintain or restore social equilibrium is possible only (in Pareto's terms) if there is a "circulation of the elite," that is, a continuous upward flow of new arrivals from lower social and hierarchical strata. The development of such a constantly reinvigorated elite is the basic social problem in both Russia and the United States of America. In Europe the difficulty is simply lack of circulation due to ancient barriers against an upward flow. In the United

States of America, although the upward flow takes place, people arrive at positions of high authority in total ignorance of the problems of maintaining social equilibrium. To overcome this ignorance and develop the required social skills, a new approach to administrative education is needed. The universities of the world "have not yet begun to think about the discovery and training of the new administrator." They must recognize that careful training is a prerequisite for developing an administrative elite capable of dealing with the human problems of sustained cooperation (*op. cit.*, p. 161-180).

c. *Barnard: Executive Responsibility*

ONE IS ALWAYS SURPRISED when a highly successful man of affairs plays the role of a theoretician, and even more so if he succeeds. This happened with Henri Fayol, the first general theorist in modern administrative thought. It happened again with Chester Barnard (1887-1961), the outstanding theorist in the field.

Barnard came to administrative theory after many years of experience as president of a large public utility, the New Jersey Bell Telephone Company. He had also been active in many government, civic, and philanthropic organizations. In 1937 he was invited to give a series of lectures on administration at the Lowell Institute in Boston. These were subsequently published in *The Functions of the Executive* (1938), which still stands as an outstanding classic in administrative literature. Ten years later Barnard published *Organization and Management* (1948), a more loosely organized collection of papers and lectures. His last published writing is "Elementary Conditions of Business Morals," based on a lecture given in 1958.

In these two books Barnard tries to build a rounded theoretical system. While he does not achieve the simplicity and clarity of Fayol's uncompleted work, he goes far deeper than anything ever hinted at in Fayol. He also brings to bear upon administrative theory powers of intellectual analysis invigorated by contact with philosophy, political science, economics, sociology, psychology and the physical sciences.

In making the case for theory in this field Barnard observes that on practical matters experienced executives from different fields have so much in common that they "are able to understand each other with very few words." But as soon as the discussion becomes somewhat more abstract "the common understanding seems invariably to disappear." The reason is that executives suffer from "the lack of an accepted conceptual scheme with which to exchange their thought."

1. CONSCIOUSLY COORDINATED COOPERATIVE SYSTEMS

The usual concept of an organization, Barnard points out, is that of "a group of persons, some or all of whose activities are coordinated." This, he feels, is an unworkable concept, since it implies "membership." Every person is a member of various groups. Moreover, some of the most important participants in certain organizational activities—such as stockholders, creditors, customers, suppliers and subcontractors—can hardly be called members. If the group concept means anything at all, the hard core of meaning is the "system of interactions." To obtain a workable concept, therefore, it is better to focus directly on the interactions and regard an organization as "a system of consciously coordinated personal activities of two or more persons."

In this sense, an organization is not a material object. It can be only indirectly symbolized by reference to the equipment or even the people that may be involved. It is a system composed of the activities of human beings, a system in which the whole is always greater than the sum of its parts and "each part is related to every other part in some significant way." As a system, it is held together by some common purpose, by the willingness of certain people to contribute to the operation of the organization, and by the ability of such people to communicate with each other.

With the exception of the state and the church, all organizations are partial systems. They are dependent upon larger and more comprehensive systems. The most comprehensive formal organizations are included in "an informal, indefinite, nebulous, and undirected system usually named a 'society'" (Barnard, 1938, p. 65-123).

The best-known type of formal organization is "scalar" or hierarchical. Coordination is achieved through the subordination of its parts to central authority. "Freedom is lessened in order that friction, strike and disruption may be reduced, security and power thereby being attained and conserved." A "lateral" organization, in contrast, achieves coordination by agreement. Its members bargain and compete with each other. Lateral organizations may be formed by agreement among scalar organizations—as with international federations. "Inherently such a system lacks its own formal means of preventing friction, strife and disruptive action" (Barnard, 1948, p. 149-160).

2. THE CONTRIBUTION-SATISFACTION EQUILIBRIUM

By why, asks Barnard, should an individual want to contribute his activities to the operations of any particular organization? Although the individual has but a limited freedom of choice, he stands outside all organizations and parcels out his contributions among those which give him the greatest return in the form of personal satisfactions. "If each man gets back only what he puts in, there is no incentive, that is, no net satisfaction for him in cooperation. What he gets back must give him advantage in terms of satisfaction; which almost always means return in a different form from what he contributes" (*op. cit.*, p. 58).

Thus the existence of organization depends upon the maintenance of an equilibrium between contributions and satisfactions. This equilibrium conception is developed with greater sophistication and detail than in the writings of Mayo and Roethlisberger, who in fact relied upon Barnard as well as upon Pareto. Contributions, Barnard points out, are always activities—such as, the work of employees and managers. The contributions of customers, investors and suppliers should not be seen in terms of money, capital or supplies but rather in terms of the *transfer* of money, capital or supplies.

The satisfactions which an individual receives in exchange for his contributions may be regarded—from the viewpoint of the organization—as inducements or incentives. A primary function of executives is to handle the "economy of incentives" within an organization. Yet Barnard firmly disassociates himself from viewing contributors to organizations as "economic men." He did not begin to understand human behavior in organizations, he reports, until he had relegated "economic theory and economic interests to a secondary—though indispensable—place." Even in well-managed business concerns "business decisions" are constantly being made that are not based upon economic motives . . . there is not enough vitality in dollars to keep business running on any such scale as we experience it, nor are the things which can be directly purchased with money an adequate incentive" (*op. cit.*, p. 14, 15).

In analyzing the multiplicity of satisfactions, Barnard identifies four "specific inducements:" (1) material inducements, such as money, things or physical conditions; (2) personal nonmaterial opportunities for distinction, prestige and personal power; (3) desirable physical conditions of work; (4) ideal benefactions, such as the pride of workmanship, sense of adequacy, altruistic service for family or others, loyalty to organization and patriotism, and aesthetic or religious feelings and the satisfaction of the motives of faith or revenge.

In discussing the relationship among these specific inducements, Barnard maintains that "material rewards are ineffective beyond the subsistence level except to a very limited proportion of men; that most men neither work harder for more material things nor can be induced thereby to devote more than a fraction of their possible contribution to organized efforts." He observes that "insufficiency with respect to the nonmaterial inducements leads to the attempt to substitute material inducements for nonmaterial." Such a substitution can be effective only to a limited degree and for a limited period of time.

Barnard also spells out four types of "general incentives": (1) Associated attractiveness based upon compatibility with associates; (2) The adaptation of working conditions to habitual methods and attitudes; (3) The opportunity for the feeling of enlarged participation in the course of events; (4) The condition of communing with others, a condition based upon personal comfort in social relations and the opportunity for comradeship and for mutual support in personal attitudes (1938, p. 142-149).

Barnard uses "efficiency" in the specialized sense of an organization's "capacity to offer effective inducements in sufficient quantities to maintain the equilibrium of the system" (*op. cit.*, p. 93). One of the best tests of efficiency is survival. The survival of any organization depends both upon its internal equilibrium and upon "an equilibrium between the system and the total situation external to it." In this connection, Barnard wryly observes that "successful cooperation in or by formal organization is the abnormal, not the normal, position. What are observed from day to day are the successful survivors among innumerable failures. . . . In our Western civilization, only one formal organization, the Roman Catholic Church, claims a substantial age. . . . Failure to cooperate, failure of cooperation, failure of organization, disorganization, disintegration, destruction of organization—and reorganization—are characteristic facts of human history" (*op cit.*, p. 5).

3. INFORMAL AND FORMAL ORGANIZATION

Barnard maintains that there are "informal organizations related to formal organizations everywhere." This includes the organization of executives as well as of workers.

The difference between formal and informal organizations is that while the former is a system of consciously coordinated activities, the latter is unconscious. It is also indefinite and rather structureless.

The relationship between the two forms of organization are very intimate. On the one hand, it is informal organization which gives rise to formal organizations. On the other hand, once formal organizations are established, they inevitably create and require informal organizations, which not only condition them but vitalize them. Thus, the one can scarcely exist without the other.

At times, informal organization may operate against either the purposes or the methods of the formal organization with which they are associated. Yet there are three positive functions that informal organization alone can perform for formal organizations. One is to perform "the communication of intangible facts, opinions, suggestions, decisions that cannot pass through formal channels without raising issues calling for decisions, without dissipating dignity and objective authority, and without overloading executive positions" (*op. cit.*, p. 225). The second is to maintain cohesiveness in formal organization through regulating the willingness to serve and the stability of objective authority. The third is to help maintain the feeling of personal integrity, of self-respect, of independent choice. This feeling is derived from the fact that "the interactions of informal organizations are not consciously dominated by a given impersonal objective or by authority as the organization expression. . . ." It may be regarded as "a means of maintaining the personality of the individual against certain effects of formal organization which tend to disintegrate the personality" (*op. cit.*, p. 122). Barnard also points out that individuals who cannot maintain a sense of self and a sense of ability to make choices of their own are incapable of functioning effectively in a cooperative system.

4. THE ACCEPTANCE CONCEPT OF AUTHORITY

For Barnard authority is "the character of an order in a formal organization by virtue of which it is accepted." Hence the decision as to whether an order has authority or not does not reside in those "persons of authority who issue orders." The decision lies instead with the persons to whom it is addressed. Even in the extreme case of armies or dictatorial regimes, the final test of authority is the acceptance or consent by individuals.

Communications will be accepted as authoritative only if they live up to four standards: (a) intelligibility; (b) consistency with the purpose of the organization; (c) compatibility with the personal interests as a whole of those to whom the order is addressed; and (d) feasibility.

The acceptance of authority within organizations is facilitated by the "zone of indifference" of individual contributors to the organization. That is, for each individual there is a certain area, either wide or narrow, within which he will accept orders willingly. This zone is recognized by experienced executives, who will in most cases give only those orders which will be obeyed. To do otherwise would be to open themselves to the charge that they do not know how to use authority or are abusing it. Conformance to all orders within the zone of indifference is also supported by "organization opinion" and "group attitudes." The strength of these attitudes derives from the fact that "denying the authority of an organization communication is a threat to the interests of all individuals who derive a net advantage from their connection with the organization."

The communal support for authority is facilitated by "the fiction of superior authority." This fiction enables individuals to place the responsibility for decisions upon others; it also underscores the fact that arbitrary or merely temperamental flouting of objective authority harms the organization as a whole. Yet this fiction of superior authority does not eliminate the underlying veto which lies in the hands of those who receive orders. This veto will always be exercised if those in positions of authority show ineptness, ignorance of conditions or failure to communicate what ought to be said. On the other hand, people will generally grant much greater authority, far outside the usual zone of indifference, to those superiors who unite the formal authority of position with the superior ability, knowledge and understanding which gives them also the authority of leadership. Above all, "objective authority cannot be imputed to persons in organization positions unless subjectively they are dominated by the organization as respects their decisions." In other words, the authority of organizational superiors is validated by their subordinates only if it is clear that these superiors are themselves responsible to the organization.

5. THE MORALITY CONCEPT OF RESPONSIBILITY

Barnard defines responsibility as "the power of a particular private code of morals to control the conduct of the individual in the presence of strong contrary desires or impulses." Responsibility is determined not by any single code, but by a complex set of moral, legal, technical, professional, and organizational codes.

These codes are effective less because of external sanctions than because of a person's feeling of obligation and the painful sense of internal guilt which arises when an obligation is abrogated.

Some of the most difficult administrative problems arise whenever there are conflicts between codes which have substantially equal validity or power. These conflicts stem from the complexity of internal organizational codes and from an individual's participation in different organizations with conflicting codes. Code conflicts become much more serious at the higher ranks of executive responsibility, which are differentiated from the lower ranks mainly by conditions of greater moral complexity.

One response to conflicting codes is "paralysis of action, accompanied by emotional tension and ending in a sense of frustration, blockade, uncertainty or a loss of decisiveness and lack of confidence." Failure of many executives often derives not from their technical incapacities but from this paralysis of action.

Another reaction is to conform to one code and violate another, which may have the effect of destroying the second code. This can be harmful for the organization unless an acceptable justification or substitute is provided.

A third solution is "moral creativity," finding substitute action which satisfies immediate needs, and yet conforms to all code requirements. The distinguishing mark of the "executive responsibility," Barnard says, "is that it requires not merely conformance to a complex code of morals but also the creation of moral codes for others."

Barnard concludes his analysis of executive responsibility with this poetic description of the role of morality in organizations:

> For the morality that underlies enduring cooperation is multidimensional. It comes from and may expand to all the world, it is rooted deeply in the past, it faces toward the endless future. As it expands it must become more complex, its conflicts must become more numerous and deeper, its call for abilities must be higher, its failures of ideal attainment must be, perhaps, more tragic; but the quality of leadership, the persistence of its influence, the durability of its related organization, the power of the coordination it incites, all express the height of moral aspiration, the breadth of moral foundations.
>
> So among those who cooperate, the things that are seen are moved by the things unseen. Out of the void comes the spirit that shapes the ends of men (*op. cit.*, p. 258-284).

In his last published writing Barnard returns to this theme. "Management decisions," he maintains, "are concerned with moral issues." Yet the best known moral principles—Judaeo-Christian ethics, the Ten Commandments, the Sermon on the Mount, the Golden Rule—seem to have "little application or relevance to the moral problems of the world of affairs." Management morality relates not only to strictly personal questions, but also to the "good of the organization," "interests of society" and prescriptions of public law. "There are circumstances where it would be immoral from the standpoint of responsible representative behavior, not to do things immoral and even illegal from a personal point of view." Yet theologians, religious leaders and philosophers have not concerned themselves with the moral problems of representative and executive behavior. "It is simply not known to any wide degree what are the number and the character of the moral problems that are faced by those who do the world's work . . ." ("Elementary Conditions of Business Morals").

6. THE COMMUNICATIONS NETWORK

A cooperative system is held together, according to Barnard, by the ability of contributors to communicate with each other. Hence a primary function of executives is to establish a communications system. From this point of view, the formal organizational structure is to be regarded as a communication network. The "lines of authority" are fundamentally the channels of formal communication. Every executive is, in fact, a "communication center." A major problem involved in large-scale organization is the problem of the growing complexity and difficulty of communication.

It is interesting to note that Barnard's pioneering presentation of communication as an essential part of administration comes from one who served as president of a large organization engaged in supplying communications services. However, Barnard does not venture into the theories of communication and information transmission which were themselves developed under the auspices of telephone agencies. In fact, he confines himself to such formal principles as these:

1. Channels of communication should be definitely known. This is done by fixing and publicizing the authority of both position and person.

2. Objective authority requires a definite, formal channel of communication to every member of an organization. In other words, everyone in an organization must have a definite, formal relationship of subordination or superordination to someone else in the organization.

3. The line of communication should be as direct or short as possible. The shorter the line, the greater the speed and the less the error.

4. The complete line of communication should usually be used. The bypassing of intermediate points leads to conflicting communications, misinterpretations and the undermining of responsibility.

5. The competence of the persons serving as communication centers, that is, officers, supervisory heads, must be adequate. At the major centers of communication the competence to handle complex communications cannot be expected from one person only. Hence the necessity for assistants, deputies and staff experts. In most important organizations, the highest executive authority is itself an organized group rather than an individual.

6. The line of communication should not be interrupted during the

time when the organization is to function. This requires elaborate pro-visions for "the temporary filling of offices automatically during incapac-ity or absence of incumbents."

7. Every communication should be authenticated. This means that the person communicating must be known actually to occupy the position of authority concerned, that the communication is actually an authorized communication from this person and that he is within his authority.

In a large organization, the application of these principles is a complex task. In small suborganizations, most of them operate automatically. The only exception is the fifth principle concerning the competence of the leader, something that is "never to be taken for granted even in simple organizations" (1938, p. 82-95, 161-184).

7. STRATEGIC FACTORS IN DECISION-MAKING

Barnard looks at organizations as systems of decision-making as well as of communication. Organizational decision-making is far more rational than individual decision-making. Organizational action is based more upon deliberation and calculation rather than unconscious and auto-matic response. Even automatic responses in organizations may be the result of carefully analyzed prior decisions on procedures and methods.

The difficulty in studying organizational decision-making is that "there is little direct opportunity to observe the essential operations of decisions." Many people participate in any one decision, a single decision is usually merely a small point in a long sequence of decisions. Only a small part of decisions may be identified as a result of formally given orders. Most of them "produce no direct evidence of themselves and . . . knowledge of them can only be derived from accumulation of indirect evidence."

The decision-maker, according to Barnard, must distinguish between those facts which may affect the accomplishment of an organization's purpose and those which are more or less irrelevant. This can be done only through a search for "strategic factors." The strategic factor is "the one whose control, in the right form, at the right place and time, will establish a new system or set of conditions which meets the purpose . . . the determination of the strategic factor is itself the decision which at once reduces purpose to a new level, compelling search for a new strategic factor and a new situation." Barnard indicates his indebtedness for the concept of the strategic factors to John R. Commons' analysis of the "limiting factor" in economic activity. He also quotes with approval Commons' observation that while the volitional control of strategic factors may be regarded as the "cause" of certain actions, the "effects" are derived from the complementary factors also (Commons, 1934, p. 627-633).

The aim of technique, according to Barnard, is to assist in the accurate discrimination of strategic facts. Unfortunately, there has been uneven development of these techniques. The technical methods of discrimination among physical parts of the environment are far more developed than those relating to economic factors. "A similar disparity exists between the economic and the other social factors of the environment. There exists in the social field no such powerful magnifier as the balance sheet which rivets the attention on the significance between income and outgo, nor any invention of general applicability that approximates in precision money of account that lies back of the balance sheet." This "unbalance in the discrimination of the facts of the environment" has serious consequences. Since we have fewer methods of analyzing the present, we often turn to the past instead. Instead of asking what something is *now* worth, we ask what did it cost. Instead of looking at the past and the future as simply a means of trying to understand the present, we often confuse what has been with what is (1938, p. 185-199, 206-211).

Yet the solution of this difficulty cannot be found merely through logical techniques. It is also essential to develop nonlogical mental processes. These are the processes of mind which are "not capable of being expressed in words or as reasoning. . . . This may be because the processes are unconscious or because they are so complex and so rapid, often approaching the instantaneous, that they could not be analyzed by the person within whose brain they take place." The rigorous, logical work of the exact scientist, the mathematician, the lawyer, and the accountant, is relevant only to materials that consist of precise information. For materials of a speculative type or of a hybrid character, it is to a large degree irrelevant to apply the logical reasoning processes. Such material "cannot bear the weight of ponderous logic." Moreover, in organizational situations the mere logical formulation of a problem or statement of a hypothesis may itself have a major effect in changing the situation that is being analyzed and rendering the formulation or the hypothesis inaccurate" (*op. cit.*, p. 301-322).

8. NATIONAL AND WORLD PLANNING

Debates concerning national economic planning and planning for world government, according to Barnard, have usually ignored the realities of behavior in complex organizations. Most plans are based upon great uncertainties with respect not only to the future but also the past and the present. Detailed blueprints are illusory—except with respect to certain aspects of plans for physical structures. The planners inevitably make many mistakes. They "will necessarily operate unconsciously as the agents of a 'spontaneous automatism'—intellectual, emotional, and political—that is more subtle and even more hidden than the 'unseen hand' of unplanned economic systems." The planners try to escape their own freedom of choice by seeking "constantly to devise rules, norms, formulas and organization by which decisions are made for them." They must necessarily limit the freedom of others. Although "we cannot have freedom without order," we "cannot have order and all our freedoms too." (1948, p. 176-193).

Genuine planning is "a process of developing and applying knowledge and intelligence to our affairs." The most feasible type of planning is strategic planning, which involves instrumental action and cause-and-effect reasoning, functional planning, which relates to the creation or maintenance of systems, and evolutionary planning, which involves attainment of a future system through a series of intermediate systems. Any plan is much more than what may be expressed in formal documents. It is "not a plan until it is accepted as a basis of action." Every plan includes such elements as (1) ends to be attained, (2) feasibility, (3) the "givens" of the situation, (4) commitments, (5) positive provision for uncertainties and (6) responsibility for action. Any plan for internal organization should recognize "the informal organization of the world as the indispensable base for any stable organization" (*op. cit.*, p. 134-175).

D. *Simon: "Satisficing" Man*

THE OVERRIDING GOAL of Herbert Simon (1916-   ) has been to develop a value-free science of human behavior. In this respect, he is close to Taylor, Gulick, and Urwick. Yet in his earliest work he refused to accept the dicta of these earlier pioneers. His first work on administration, completed when he was a young political scientist, was the booklet he wrote with Clarence Ridley, *Measuring Municipal Activities* (1938), still a minor classic in municipal administration. At the University of California's Institute of Public Administration he then went on to publish various studies on the ideal caseload for social workers, the measurement of fire insurance risks, and metropolitan consolidation.

As his work progressed, he became more and more disenchanted with the "proverbs" of the earlier pioneers. He worked his way toward the belief that a science of man "must accommodate his dual nature as a social and a rational animal." He suggested "two principal mechanisms—the mechanism of influence and the mechanism of choice." The writings of Barnard—and Barnard personally—encouraged him in this approach. Many of Barnard's ideas are echoed and expanded in Simon's two major books on administration, *Administrative Behavior* (1947) and *Public Administration* (1950), written with Donald Smithburg and Victor Thompson. In recent years Simon has given less attention to influence and more to decision-making. This shift is evidenced in *Centralization vs. Decentralization in Organizing the Controller's Department* (1945) with Harold Guetzkow, George Kozmetsky, and George Tyndall; *Models of Man* (1957), a collection of sixteen mathematical journal articles, together with a series of unifying comments; *Organizations* (1958) with James March, which summarizes major approaches to organization theory; and *The New Science of Management Decision* (1960). In concentrating upon decision-making, Simon has deliberately turned away from other vital aspects of administrative and organizational behavior and from the broader problems of the relation between organizations and their environments. Specializing in the computer simulation of individual decision-making, he has become one of the world's outstanding pioneers in psychological research and theory on the cognitive aspects of thought processes and in the development of "thinking machines."

1. THE ATTACK ON "PROVERBS"

Simon will long be reread with pleasure for his free-swinging attacks on the Gulick-Urwick principles as homely proverbs, myths, slogans, pompous inanities, and "terms not unlike those used by a Ubangi medicine man to discuss disease." In this attack Simon gave expression to the widespread disenchantment of many people, both academicians and practitioners, who were disturbed by the yawning gulf they often saw between the prescribed principles and effective practice.

The unity of command. Unity of command, according to Simon, is an illusion. Subordinates accept orders not only from their formal superiors but also from all sorts of specialists. Any effort to have the views of specialists follow the formal lines of hierarchic authority would be so time-consuming as to break down the channels of communication. Actual authority is "zoned" in accordance with special fields, much along the lines of Taylor's "functional foremanship." The principle of unity of command is made more defensible, however, by whittling it down to the following: "In case two authoritative commands conflict, there should be a single determinate person whom the subordinate is expected to obey." Yet in this form the principle solves fewer problems (1947, p. 22-26).

Staff, auxiliary and line units. Simon, Smithburg, and Thompson attack four widely-accepted ideas concerning staff, auxiliary and line units.

First, they brush aside the distinction between auxiliary units, which are supposed to serve line units by supplying men, money, equipment and supplies, and staff units, which are supposed to assist the chief executive. These are both "overhead units." The only real distinction between them is in the nature of the activities. Second, they scoff at the idea that the activities of line units are more important than those of overhead units. This false issue is like the question of whether heart or lungs are the more important part of the body. Third, they make a frontal attack on the idea that overhead units do not exercise authority over line units, that auxiliary units merely serve and staff units merely advise. "Overhead units do exercise authority; they do control and command." Finally, they pinprick the idea that staff units are more closely identified with the executive than line units. The closest confidants of the executive will usually be "an informal group which may well include, or perhaps be limited to, line personnel."

Some of these myths, however, "help to bridge a gap between the way people feel they should be treated in organizations and the way they are actually treated." The myth that staff units merely advise makes it easier for them to give orders to people who believe in the unity of command, who want to accept authority from only one source. The myth that staff units are a part of the executive is particularly important whenever a staff specialist holds a lower rank (or is younger) than the person who is supposed to accept his authority (*Public Administration*, 1950, p. 280-291).

Authority and responsibility. Simon and his colleagues also take issue with the thesis that "authority be commensurate with responsibility," or at least with its popular interpretation. If this principle means that a unit head must have authority to direct his subordinates without any interference from others, it is merely another way of proclaiming the doctrine of unity of command. If it means that he must be given all the money and other resources that are needed, it ignores the inevitable interdependence of activities and the necessity of mobilizing limited resources by winning the cooperation of other units (*op. cit.*, p. 281-287).

The span of control. Simon attacks the principle of the span of control on the ground that one can also state a contradictory proverb which is equally plausible: "Administrative efficiency is enhanced by keeping at a minimum the number of organizational levels through which a matter must pass before it is acted upon." He demonstrates that a narrowing of the span of control, desirable from one point of view, usually has the undesirable effect of hampering communication by increasing the number of organizational levels. Neither proverb, he laments, casts light on how to reconcile these conflicting considerations (1947, p. 26-28).

The bases of organizational grouping. Simon attacks Gulick's analysis of the grouping of activities on the basis of purpose, process, clientele, or place. There are serious ambiguities, he points out, in these terms. There is "no essential difference between a 'purpose' and a 'process,' but only a distinction of degree. A 'process' is an activity whose immediate purpose is at a low level in the hierarchy of means and ends, while a 'purpose' is a collection of activities whose orienting value or aim is at a high level in the means-end hierarchy." "Clientele" and "place" are "really not separate from purpose, but a part of it" (*op. cit.*, p. 28-35).

People as "special purpose mechanisms." In *Organizations* Simon joins with March in criticizing Taylor's "scientific management" as a whole. They refer to this body of thought as limited to such physiological variables as physical capacity, motion, speed and fatigue. For March and Simon, this body of thought "would transform a general-purpose mechanism, such as a person, into a more efficient special-purpose mechanism." In so doing, it concentrates on repetitive tasks involving a minimum of problem solving and presupposes exclusively monetary motivation. Even within these limitations, it suffers from serious defects. Only in a minority of cases have production engineers succeeded in synthesizing time standards from standard data on component units. Nor have they established clear specifications for data analysis. The human organism, even when regarded as merely a neurophysiological machine, has proved too complex for even the best of Taylor's followers. The ideas of scientific management are probably better adapted to genuine, rather than human, machines. As such, indeed, they have contributed significantly to the development of modern machine building and automation (*Organizations*, p. 12-22).

2. EFFICIENCY: "FUNDAMENTAL" TO "LOW LEVEL"

In *Administrative Behavior* Simon maintains that "the fundamental criterion of administrative decisions must be a criterion of efficiency rather than a criterion of adequacy." This criterion "dictates that choice of alternatives which produces the largest results for the given application of the resources." Adequacy, in contrast, is the absolute measure of accomplishment. Simon defends the efficiency criterion against those who complain against "mechanical" and "ruthless" efficiency or charge that efficiency "directs all attention to the means and neglects the ends." His answer is simply this: that the truly efficient administrator gives proper weight to all of the ends and values that are relevant to his activity. Only by keeping his eye on all of these values can he properly address himself to application of the efficiency criterion.

In *Public Administration* Simon and his colleagues start the process of limiting the use of the efficiency criterion. The first condition of its use is that the human and material resources that he proposes to employ must be "scarce." This scarcity expresses itself in the value of foregone alternatives—that is, in "opportunity costs." But where there are ample resources, no opportunities are lost through their use and there is no reason to stress efficiency. The second condition is that the administrator himself be *neutral* as to how resources are used, just so long as they will achieve the greatest possible results. Any bias toward certain ways of doing things, as contrasted with others, will interfere with the application of the efficiency criteria. Simon and his coauthors also recognize other important criteria that commonly compete with efficiency. Rationality, which is defined as the adaptation of means to ends, may be oriented toward the achievement of adequacy or effectiveness instead of efficiency[6] in the use of resources. Another criterion is responsibility, or responsiveness of the organization to people or values. Discussions of administration are often rendered incomprehensible by the use of the term "efficiency" to refer to all of these ideas or merely as an all-embracing term of approval.

Subsequently, Simon downgrades efficiency as an operational criterion for decision-making. In his introduction to the second edition of *Administrative Behavior* he finds the efficiency criterion applicable "largely to rather low-level decisions," since higher level "outputs" and "results" do not lend themselves to measurement and comparability. In his work on rational choice, as set forth in *Models of Man*, he finds himself dealing more and more with the compromises that people make between multiple goals or values. This analysis brings him to a breaking point with the supremacy of the efficiency criterion.

3. THE MECHANISM OF INFLUENCE

For Simon, the people in organizations are decision-making mechanisms. Administrators exercise "influence" (or "power") over subordinates by helping to determine the factual premises or the value premises on which decisions are based.

The first decision which an organizational participant (whether employee, consumer or stockholder) makes is whether or not to partici-

6. "Adequacy" or "effectiveness" is used to refer to the quality or quantity of output, "efficiency" to an input-output relation.

pate, that is, to contribute his work or money. Here Simon takes Barnard's idea of equilibrium and restates it as follows: "Each participant will remain in the organization if the satisfaction (or utility) he derives from the net balance of inducements over contributions (measured in terms of their utility to *him*) is greater than the satisfaction he could obtain if he withdrew. The 'zero point' in such a 'satisfaction function' is defined, therefore, in terms of the opportunity cost of participation." By thus emphasizing foregone alternatives, Simon brings Barnard's equilibrium much closer to the equilibrium of the economists.

While refining Barnard's conception of equilibrium, Simon also distinguishes between the decision to participate and the decision to produce. In deciding to participate or not, one is guided by personal considerations. Once this decision is made, personal goals are to some degree subordinated to the goals of the organization. High morale develops whenever the mechanism of influence creates the kind of inducement-contribution equilibrium in which employees are willing "to participate in a truly active way and to devote their full energies to the organization's task. . . ."

"Internal influence" operates through the process of an individual's identification with the organization. While such identification is always limited by an individual's background and outside influences, it is accelerated by the encouragement of loyalty to one or another part of the organization, if not to the organization as a whole. Informal influences are also important.

One of the most important "external influences" is authority, which he defines as "the power to make decisions which guide the actions of another." Authority cannot be fully understood as a legal phenomenon or as based on formal sanctions alone. A person will accept orders not merely because of the fear of punishment but also because of willingness to achieve the organization's purpose, a disinclination to accept responsibility, a psychological willingness or desire to follow a leader or the social sanctions imposed by the group to which he belongs. Many subordinates will often ask themselves "How would my superior wish me to behave under these circumstances?" He thus anticipates the exercise of authority, a phenomenon referred to as the "rule of anticipated reactions."[7] Under such circumstances explicit authority may need to be exercised only to reverse an incorrect decision where reactions are improperly anticipated. Where no corrections are made, the evidences of authority in terms of sanctions will be very slight. Moreover, authority

7. For this idea Simon expresses his indebtedness to Carl J. Friedrich's *Constitutional Government and Democracy*, p. 589.

is by no means limited to the relationship created when a hierarchical superior asks his subordinate to do something or when the subordinate anticipates what his boss wants him to do. Modern society gives more and more authority to functional status and less and less to hierarchy. Members of organizations "are becoming more and more accustomed to accepting the proposals of functional specialists—and to feeling that they ought to accept these proposals." This acceptance flows from confidence in the competence and good faith of the authority wielders.

Other external influences are training, advice, and communications that direct attention. Training may take place both at the level of indoctrination, which is training in values, and at the level of knowledge and skills, which are more related to factual premises. In either case it "changes the person in such a way that he will act as desired by his own motivation rather than by the stimulus of moment-by-moment instructions." Advice and information are continually flowing in all directions in organizations. They provide people with indispensable facts, estimates, and judgments. The selection of people who can most readily identify with the organization, who are already trained and who are most susceptible to authority, advice, and information make the task of influence all the easier.

In *Public Administration* Simon and his colleagues give so much attention to conflicting influences that at one point they warn against giving the impression that "administration is nothing more than a continuous battle among contending groups." They show how conflicts develop as a result of empire building, differences in background, differing group identifications within the larger organizations. They recognize the importance of outside pressures; they point out that leadership and coordination involve a large amount of conflict reconciliation. They also warn the reader not to regard conflict as necessarily or inherently bad (with apparently no awareness of Follett's thoughts on the subject). Conflict may serve to bring a wide range of specialized competence to bear on individual decisions. It may be the means for bringing into the view of high level administrators issues that otherwise would escape attention, thus preventing them from "being decided anonymously at obscure levels of the bureaucracy."

In *Organizations*, March and Simon summarize recent thinking on individual or group conflict within organizations, with some attention to conflict within individuals and between organizations. They maintain that an organization reacts to conflict by four major processes: problem-solving, persuasion, bargaining, and "politics." They defer problem-solving to their consideration of rational choice and more or less ignore both persuasion and "politics." They survey efforts to develop criteria for bargaining through the theory of games. They come to the pessimistic conclusion that "with rare exceptions" bargaining theory has operated in an empirical vacuum. They maintain that no general theory of bargaining can be developed unless serious empirical research is developed to "match, in terms of energy and competence, the mathematical efforts of the past ten years."

4. COMMUNICATION: BARRIERS AND AIDS

Simon defines communication as "any process whereby decisional premises are transmitted from one member of an organization to another." This is a two-way process, including both the transmittal *to* a decisional center and the transmittal of the decisions reached *from* the center to other parts of the organization. This process moves "upward, downward; and laterally throughout the organization." Placing much less emphasis than Barnard upon the formal network of authority, Simon finds that informal channels are much more important in the transmission of information.

Simon also goes much further than Barnard in dealing with the difficulties in the communication process. Serious blockages may occur in any one of the three steps in the communications process: initiation, transmission or reception. Much of language—particularly academic or organizational jargon—is simply not commonly understandable. A person's perception of a message depends upon his own preconceptions and frames of reference. Status differences exert a considerable filtering and distorting influence. Geographical distance makes direct contact difficult. Many communications are slanted by the senders or censored, if not completely pigeonholed, by others. The pressures of work make it impossible to give adequate attention to all communications.

Because of the difficulties of intraorganizational communication, most organizations need certain specialized communications activities. Information is gathered through special intelligence units; these may deal with the collection of information from the outside environment as well as the transfer of internally produced information. The most distinctive bureaucratic activity is the storage of information in some form or organization "memory" such as files, libraries, and computing machines. Finally, information is distributed through general circulars, hierarchical channels, screening devices, and elaborate procedures for review and clearance. One of the reasons for the proliferation of committees and conferences is their utility in the spreading of information. One of the great values of training—through the conference method or through formal instruction—is that it can deal directly with some of the basic barriers to effective communication by promoting a common organizational language and shared frames of reference. An excellent analysis of the services provided by accountants, in terms of the information needed at different points in the organization, is provided in *Centralization vs. Decentralization in Organizing the Controller's Department.*

5. "SATISFICING" vs. MAXIMIZING AND OPTIMIZING

In dealing with his greatest love, the decision-making process, Simon attacks the assumptions of total rationality underlying the theories of choice in economics, game theory and statistical decision-making. These theories, he charges, are founded on at least three unrealistic assumptions: (1) the decision-makers omniscience concerning the existence of all possible alternatives and the future consequences of all possible alternatives, or at least the probability distribution of consequences; (2) his unlimited computational ability; and (3) his carrying in his head of a "complete and consistent preference ordering" of all possible consequences.

Simon asserts that any theory based on such assumptions is "fundamentally wrong" as either a descriptive or a normative model. He maintains that actual human rationality is neither perfectly rational nor irrational. Rather, it involves "bounded rationality." Of all possible alternatives people perceive only a few. Of all possible consequences they predict only a few and may be wrong at that. Nor is the aspiration level inflexible. "As the individual in his exploration of alternatives finds it *easy* to discover satisfactory alternatives his aspiration level rises; as he finds it *difficult* to discover satisfactory alternatives his aspiration level falls." Thus he need not compare marginal increments in order to make decisions. Instead of insisting upon "optimal" solutions, he is satisfied with "good enough" or "somehow muddling through." Since he has not the wit to "maximize," he is obliged to "satisfice." A major function of organizations is to compensate for the limited rationality of individuals. The purpose of administrative theory is to fill a gap in the rationality of organizations.

If these limitations are accepted, Simon thinks then that it is possible to build a mathematical model of rational choice. The model is similar to a linear programing model, but with primary concern for determining program feasibility rather than discovering the optimal program. Many of the ideas in servomechanism theory can also be used. In developing these ideas, he assumes (a) that the organism can plan only relatively short behavior sequences, (b) that its needs are not insatiable, and (c) that since it possesses storage capacity, the exact amount of satisfaction of any particular need is not critical at any particular time. This leads him to the conclusion that "blocks of the organism's time can be allocated to activities related to individual needs (separate means-ends chains) without creating any problem of over-all allocation or coordination or the need for any general 'utility function.' The only scarce resource in the situation is time, and its scarcity measured by the proportion of the total time that the organism will need to be engaged in *some* activity, can be reduced by the provision of generous storage capacity."

Simon makes a major distinction between programed and unprogramed decisions. The former are those that are more repetitive and routine. In organizations these may be increasingly handled by the mathematical techniques of operations research. With the help of the electronic computer these decisions may often be automated. The result will be a decline in the ranks of middle management and an increased tendency toward centralization of decision-making.

Even with nonprogramed, or novel and unstructured decision-making, according to Simon, there is a great role for the electronic computer, partly in automating such decisions; even more, in understanding how human beings make them. The best way to study thought processes is to simulate them with a computer program:

> A human being can think, learn and create because the program its biological endowment gives him, together with the changes in that program produced by interaction with his environment after birth, enables him to think, learn and create. If a computer thinks, learns and creates, it will be by virtue of a program that endows it with these capacities . . . that analyzes, by some means, its own performance, diagnoses its failures, and makes changes that enhance its future effectiveness.

In addition to reviewing the burgeoning work in this field, Simon has been personally active in developing computer programs for heuristic problem solving. He has concentrated upon the computer simulation of problem-solving processes, maintaining that such processes are composed of simple symbol-manipulating operations. He relates this work to organization theory by postulating that the same processes can be used to account for administrative decision-making. By illuminating the nature of thought processes, it may "provide us with the means for improving substantially the effectiveness of humans in performing such tasks" (*The New Science of Management Decision, passim*).

Chapter 8

CONTRIBUTORS FROM OTHER FIELDS

*T*HE WORK OF THE PIONEERS in administrative thought was paralleled and followed by an unprecedented increase in almost all fields of intellectual activity.

In turn, this has meant the development of a vast amount of concepts, generalizations, methods, and knowledge with great implications—either direct or indirect—for the understanding of administration.

In all of these fields these implications have at times been ignored. In some, they have been recognized only by an occasional few. In still others, they have been exaggerated by those who regard their own specialty as the "mother hen" of all administrative thought or find all of "management science" in a single approach. In any case, the progress made throughout these many fields has been so great that those who concentrate upon any aspect of administrative thought have rarely been able to exploit the riches available to them. The very abundance of intellectual activity in the mid-twentieth century has produced a built-in —and probably inevitable—cultural lag.

Administrative thought has at times been called "applied social science." As an antidote against administrative formalism, this is a useful label. But it would be extremely misleading if regarded as conferring monopolistic rights upon the social sciences. Many significant contributions to administrative thought have been made from established fields entirely outside of the social sciences and from newly established fields that cannot be appropriately regarded as a part of the social sciences alone.

In this chapter I shall suggest the nature of these contributions. In so doing, however, I shall not attempt a comprehensive review of any area. I shall confine myself to a presentation only of those aspects of these areas which seem most significant for administration. Only thus is it possible to give some idea of the vast network of ideas from which our efforts to understand administration must obtain sustenance.

A. *The Social Sciences*

IN EACH of the social sciences there are those who have directly entered the study of administration and established significant strongholds on some part of its vast area. The more obvious entrants may be schematically illustrated as follows:

Political scientists	⟶ Public administration
Economists	⟶ Managerial economics
Psychologists	⟶ Industrial psychology
Sociologists	⟶ Industrial sociology
Anthropologists	⟶ Applied anthropology

The magnitude of these ventures is attested to by the various associations and journals established by those in the right-hand column.

Yet it would be a serious error to think that the major contributions of social scientists to administrative thought are limited to these direct entries. Those whose work is only indirectly relevant to administration are often precisely those whose work is most significant for the understanding of administration. This may be called the "phenomenon of indirect relevance." This phenomenon is illustrated by all the social scientists quoted in Chapters 2, 3, and 4: Bentley, Michels, and Mosca (political science); Marx, Berle, Means, and Gordon (economics); Freud and Fromm (psychology); Weber (sociology); and Fortes and Evans-Pritchard (anthropology).

Even within the special fields listed in the right-hand column the more creative work has tended to fan out in many directions and achieve more general relevance. This tendency has been accentuated by three major trends in modern social science: (a) the direct observation of human behavior; (b) the development of systematic theory, often referred to as "model building"; and (c) an overlapping of interests and inquiries that render the traditional division of "fields" (or any one-way classification) increasingly unsatisfactory for purposes other than the allocation of budgets and professorships.

1. POLITICAL SCIENTISTS

The literature of public administration, largely "applied political science," deals so directly with our central subject that it can hardly be classed a "contributor from another field." It is therefore discussed in the next chapter. Here we will concentrate on political science in the broader sense.

It would be helpful if this review could be initiated by pointing to a modern tradition of political philosophy dealing impressively with the "political order" and the aims that should guide the operations of governments. This cannot be done. As Wolin (1960) has pointed out, political philosophy has declined. Political scientists have done little either to revitalize the sagging ideals of political democracy or to help develop the practical politics of achieving a peaceful world order. The few remaining exponents of political philosophy spend their time juggling the remnants of frayed and decayed ideologies.

The other side of the coin is the shining example of modern political science at its best: the increasingly realistic dissection of political action. Instead of dealing abstractly with "the State," modern political scientists have become increasingly pluralistic. In the spirit of Bentley's *The Process of Government* (1908), but with much more conceptual flexibility, they have identified the various groups and institutions that participate in the process of government. A wealth of penetrating studies have been made on the interactions of private groups with public agencies. Many of these have been invigorated by the influence of Lasswell (1936, 1950) and Merriam (1950) in stressing the importance of power, symbols and myths. Brilliant studies have been made on the operations of legislative bodies, political parties and courts. Important experiments have been made in applying marginal utility analysis and game theory to national and international politics.

Nor have political scientists confined themselves entirely to "public government." In the light of Merriam's comparison between "private" and "public governments" (1944), they have made at least suggestive entries into the government of the large private corporation (Latham, 1960). They have started to indicate the elements held in common by political and economic processes (Dahl and Lindblom, 1953). They have studied the operations and influence of mass communications industries. They have ranged freely over all the social sciences in an effort to develop interdisciplinary approaches to the formation of public policy. They have analyzed international power politics without hiding the brutality and cynicism involved. They have studied the slow processes through which the United Nations and other international organizations have been built. They have made realistic analyses of governmental processes in other countries, an area previously monopolized by a sterile legalism. These include an important series of studies on modern dictatorships. Many exhibit an increasing use of sociological perspectives, particularly with respect to industrially underdeveloped countries (Almond and Coleman, 1960). These represent vigorous efforts to break away from nationalistic and culture-bound conceptions and to understand the growth of government agencies in societies at all levels of economic and political development. However, the outstanding book on government's role in economic development, *Economic Planning in Underdeveloped Areas*, has been written by an economist (Mason, 1958).

These developments have been paralleled by a growth of interest in a more systematic approach to political theory. Easton has stimulated much greater attention to the need for integrating research with theory. In so doing he has stressed the inadequacy of the equilibrium concepts that underlie much of existing theory (1953, 1956). He also urges that political theory be linked with clearly stated moral values. Similarly, Wolin asks political scientists to rise above fragmented study and focus on the polity and community as a whole. Finding that there is as yet "no public-interest theory worth the name," Schubert calls for a vigorous orientation in this direction (1960). The fact that none of these men has yet tried to carry out his own prescription does not detract from their value in pointing the way. Their prescriptions probably express the inclinations of many political scientists, and the results may well be seen in another decade.

None of the people mentioned above has been a specialist in public administration. Nor does much of their work go very far into the internal structure and administrative processes of government agencies. Yet almost all of their work has tremendous significance for public administration, probably more so than some of the public administration literature as such. In fact, since these general studies deal with the political environment in which *all* organizations operate, they are of great significance to the study of *all* forms of administration.

2. ECONOMISTS

Under the self-imposed taboos of classical and neo-classical economics, the role of a business manager in a competitive economy is merely one of passive adaptation to market stimuli. In Veblen's vivid words:

The hedonistic conception of man is that of a lightning calculator of pleasures and pains, who oscillates like a homogeneous globule of desire of happiness under the impulse of stimuli that shift him about the area, but leave him intact. He has neither antecedent nor consequent. He is an isolated definitive human datum, in stable equilibrium except for the buffets of the impinging forces that displace him in one direction or another. Self-imposed in elemental space, he spins symmetrically about his own spiritual axis until the parallelogram of forces bears down upon him, whereat he follows the line of the resultant. When the force of the impact is spent, he comes to rest, a self-contained globule of desire as before (1919, p. 73-74).

Similarly, orthodox Marxism rules administrative discretion out of existence. Under capitalism, entrepreneurs are driven by inexorable historical forces and the managers who work for them are merely pawns and mouthpieces. The administration of government itself, as seen by Lenin in his most historic official document, *State and Revolution,* (1917) is mainly a matter of accounting and control. And "the accounting and control necessary for this have been simplified by capitalism to an extreme and reduced to the extraordinary simple operations—which any literate person can perform—of checking and recording, knowledge of the four rules of arithmetic, and issuing receipts."

In the U.S.A. many of the first educational programs in business administration grew in departments of economics. Thus instruction in business administration was often dominated, at least in its early days, by those intellectually committed to the proposition that such a subject did not exist, or by those who feared that if it came into being, it would impair traditional concepts of economics. Yet as these programs matured, and as economists came more and more to grips with the realities of the world, these men began to make many substantial contributions to administrative thought.

The most direct contribution is in the small but growing field of managerial economics. Here the best example can be found in the work of Joel Dean. In *Managerial Economics* (1951) Dean analyzes certain typical economic problems that confront the administrators of large industrial corporations. Special emphasis is placed upon alternative approaches to profits, costs, and pricing policy. Many of Dean's concepts are applicable to other types of organizations, but he makes no effort to apply them more broadly. Nor are there many who have done significant work in the wake of Dean's pioneering study.

If we look for more economics that is directly relevant to administration, we are led naturally to the "theory of the firm." But if we expect very much here, we are apt to be disappointed. For the most part we find here elegant elaborations of *a priori* propositions first stated by Cournot in 1838 and not backed up by any significant amount of empirical observation. In the 1930's and subsequently, the discoverers of imperfect competition made a few minor concessions to observed facts but, in the main, continued the tradition of writing about "should be" in the mood of "is." More recently, there have been a few attempts to initiate an empirical approach to the price and output policies of firms. Among these one of the most significant older works is J. M. Clark's *The Economics of Overhead Cost* (1923). In the same tradition Wiles has analyzed the totally different price policies of different kinds of producers (1961) and the allocation models followed by different Communist countries (1962). Cyert and March have done pioneer work in moving toward a theory of the firm based on empirical studies of actual decision-making in firms (1963). Harbison and Myers have pioneered in a comparative study on management and economic development in a variety of countries and cultures. Yet the bulk of the new work in this field is doggedly prescriptive. This does not necessarily destroy its interest for administrative thought. It merely moves it into the more general realm of the normative approach to decision-making and preferential behavior, a field which will be discussed subsequently in its own right.

When we move from direct to indirect relevance to administration, we find more significant contributions in institutional economics and statistical studies of economic developments. The works of Veblen (1899), Tawney (1927), Karl Polanyi (1957), and Mason (1958) have given us indispensable historical background on the growth of the modern industrial system. Commons (1934, 1951) carried this approach further by analyzing the legal and social foundations of business enterprises. A broad approach to the structure of industry was developed in considerable detail by the various reports of the Temporary National Economic Committee (a joint committee of the U.S. Congress). Berle and Means (1932) demonstrated the separation of ownership from management, a line of analysis that has been extended by Gordon (1945), Berle (1954, 1959), Harbrecht (1959), and Mason (1960). Boulding provides an "outside" analysis of some of the problems of large-scale organization (1953) and calls for major extensions in traditional theories of the firm (1960).

A number of across-the-board studies of Russian management have been made by Bienstock, Schwarz and Yogow (1944), Berliner (1957), and Granick (1954, 1960). The later Granick study has the merit of comparing Russian with American industrial managers. Yet work of this type has not yet reached the point where direct empirical studies have been made of actual decision-making on a broad scale within a single company or sector. Nor have investigators yet attempted serious studies of the administration of a cartel, a holding company, or a trade association.

Despite the attention given this subject at the "should be" level, we have had no serious studies of how specific managers have faced their recurring every-day problems of competition and cooperation.

Of potentially great significance to administrative theory is the new area of economic growth and development. Here economists have directed themselves to the problem of analyzing those factors which determine rapid economic change. Their work has been seriously vitiated, however, by a simplistic assumption that the volume of capital available for investment is the decisive factor in economic growth. The importance of entrepreneurship may be recognized without making any attempt to deal with what it is that entrepreneurs really do. Thus Hagen tackles entrepreneurship from the important (albeit also limited) viewpoint of personality development (1962). Hirschman points out that "development depends not so much on finding optimal combinations for given resources and factors of production as on calling forth and enlisting for development purposes resources and abilities that are hidden, scattered or badly utilized" (1958). But he cannot bring himself to recognize administration or institution-building as dynamic factors that have been missing from previous oversimplifications. Similarly, the economists who document the need for government planning usually fail to come to grips with the managerial context of planning.

Finally, we cannot ignore the tremendous progress made during recent decades in the compilation of national economic data. National economic accounting has provided sophisticated tools for policy-making both by large organizations and by government agencies. Many of these accounting concepts in these areas, as will be demonstrated later in Part Five, "The Purposes," can be extremely useful in analyzing organizational activity and judging organizational performance. Moreover, as with the studies of political behavior, the ever-growing flood of reports on economic behavior provides invaluable background on economic development.

3. PSYCHOLOGISTS

Unlike managerial economics (which has belied its broad name by limiting itself to the economics of business organizations), industrial psychology has belied its narrow name by dealing with psychological aspects of nonindustrial organizations as well.

Industrial psychology is "a field of specialization concerned with methods of selecting, training, counseling, and supervising personnel in business and industry" (Morgan, 1956, p. 633). This field of specialization grew up with the encouragement of the followers both of Taylor, who wanted to design machines and people to fit together, and of Mayo and Roethlisberger, who felt that psychology was a key to understanding the operations of industrial enterprises. Rather well supported by large organizations, it has yielded a huge amount of publicly available research. These range from studies of morale and attitude studies to elaborate analyses of fatigue, turnover, lighting, machine design, and personnel applications to a growing assortment of tests and training techniques (Blum, 1952; Viteles, 1953; Likert, 1962).

Nevertheless, we may here again see the phenomenon of indirect relevance. The broader fields of social and individual psychology have much greater significance for the understanding of administration. Moreover, industrial psychology has matured beyond the level of mere gadgetry only when thoroughly infused with the deeper concepts of social and individual psychology.

One of the keystones of social psychology is found in Floyd Allport's deflation of institutional fictions and analyses of organizations in terms of individuals' interactions (1924, 1962). Other crucial elements, no less basic to any understanding of administration, are found in the concepts of social norms, social status, social role, and the social aspects of perception and communication. Kurt Lewin's pioneering analyses of small group behavior in terms of personal energies in the "psychic field" (1948) has led to the subdiscipline of group dynamics. Much of the work in this field (see Cartwright and Zander, eds., 1953), and particularly the more recent work on social power (Cartwright, ed., 1959), has relevance for larger organizations also. Special mention might be made of the work on communication networks (Bavelas, 1950) and the introduction of "planned change" (Lippitt et al., 1958). Sociometry has provided increasingly valuable tools for identifying the matrices of personal interrelations within organizations (Bales, 1950, and Weiss and Jacobson, 1955). Any good text on social psychology (such as Krech and Crutchfield, 1948, or Hartley and Hartley, 1952) provides splendid background for the analysis of administration.

Individual psychology has been no less productive. With their explorations of the unconscious aspects of human behavior, Freud and the neo-Freudians have opened new vistas for the understanding of human behavior in organizations. Psychiatrists and psychoanalysts have often been brought into the realm of large-scale organization by being asked to deal with acute problems of personal strain and tension—particularly during and after World War II. Some of them responded to this challenge by addressing themselves directly to central questions of organizational and administrative behavior, as in the case of the work done under the auspices of the Tavistock Institute of Human Relations in England and the Mental Health Institute of the University of Michigan. From Tavistock have come outstanding observational studies on the Glacier Plant in England (*Jaques*, 1951), the Ahmedabad plant in India (*Rice*, 1958, 1963) and work groups in British coal mines (*Trist et al.*, 1963).

Probably even more relevant to the behavior of human beings in organizations are the theories of motivation and personality. Horney (1950), Fromm (1955), Rogers (1951), Maslow (1954) and Murphy (1958) have placed major emphasis upon the variety of human needs and interests and upon human potentialities for self-development in associations with others. They have thus gone a long way toward revealing the limitations in simplistic assumptions concerning "economic man" or "rational man." Erikson (1956) has explored the individual's search for identity. Many psychologists (Adorno *et al.*, 1950) have joined in the effort to understand the roots of authoritarianism. Rokeach (1960, 1961) has identified the basic differences between authority and authoritarianism. All of this work represents a growing tendency among psychologists to look at "ordinary" people instead of concentrating upon the psychopathic fringes.

In experimental psychology there is a similar tendency to get away from an overconcentration upon rats and from oversimplifying experiments with individuals. With considerable personal impetus from Simon, increasing attention is being given to experiments relating to thought processes and decision-making. While this has diverted attention from the closely connected subject of feelings and emotions, it has led to impressive beginnings in the laboratory study of bargaining and group decision-making. New developments in learning theory (Mowrer, 1958, and Bruner *et al.*, 1956) have implications for learning processes in organizational situations and the adaptation of administrators to rapidly changing conditions. Tolman (1951) has made classic studies of purposeful behavior. In *Plans and the Structure of Behavior* (Miller, Galenter, and Pribram, 1959), a group of experimental psychologists have developed a "subjective behaviorism" replete with implications for the planned behavior of organizations.

4. SOCIOLOGISTS

The term "industrial sociology" has no referents as clearly pinned down as "managerial economics" or "industrial psychology." One of the reasons (apart from the fact that industrialists have probably bought fewer services from sociologists than from economists and psychologists) may be that almost all of sociology has considerable significance for the administration of all organizations.

There is still considerable significance in the writings of the older sociological "giants" on the division of labor (Durkheim), conflict and power (Simmel), socialization (Cooley), and social equilibrium and the circulation of the elites (Pareto). Of even greater significance today are the general sociological studies of modern industrial society. Merton's analysis of latent and manifest functions (1957) has promoted widespread attention to bureaucracy. In *American Society* (1960) Williams has prepared one of the few across-the-board studies of an entire society, a venture not yet undertaken on the same scale in any other country. A more literary approach, replete with stimulating imagery, on the impact of large-scale organization on society is provided by Riesman and his associates (1951). Bendix (1956) and others have analyzed stratification and authority in society as a whole and in industry in particular. Hartmann (1959) has provided a valuable analysis of authority in German industry. Innumerable studies have been made of leadership in all sorts of groups and organizations.

Another outstanding aspect of modern sociology has been the emphasis upon intensive empirical investigation. In *The American Soldier* (*Stouffer et al.*, 1949) American sociologists conducted a monumental survey of soldiers' attitudes, opinions and beliefs. Many impressive studies have been made of community structures and of human interaction in small groups.

Still more significant to those interested in administration has been the rich series of empirical studies of single organizations. Although none of these has as yet been conducted on the grand scale of the Hawthorne and Glacier studies or *The American Soldier* they have yielded a rapidly accumulating body of observational data. Many of these studies are subsequently referred to in this book (and almost all of them appear in the annotated bibliography of empirical studies). Among the more important are those by *Argyris* (1953), *Bakke* (1950), *Blau* (1955), *Dalton* (1959), *Gouldner* (1954), *Janowitz* (1960), *Lipset* (1956), *Selznick* (1949), *Stanton* and *Schwartz* (1954), *Walker* and *Guest* (1952), and *Whyte* (1947).

These books comprise a "must" reading list for those interested in empirical reports on administrative styles, leadership, conflict, power and social structure in organizations. They also serve as a demonstration to people in other disciplines of what can be accomplished by a theory-oriented approach to case studies. Although most of the authors used their individual studies as springboards for imaginative generalizations (sometimes overly-oriented toward proving or disproving something written by Weber many decades earlier), the data as a whole still await further general analysis. Homans (1950) has used a number of such studies in formulating a theoretical analysis concerning the relations between activity, interaction, norms and sentiments. Dubin (1958, 1961) has used these studies to develop still more general ideas concerning the organization and direction of work.

Modern sociology is also distinguished by the impressive efforts made by some of its leaders to establish general conceptions that can help unify all of the social sciences. The most significant efforts in this direction have been undertaken by Talcott Parsons. In *The Social System* (1951) Parsons provides a morphological analysis of the structure of systems as a "second-best" alternative to dealing with dynamic processes. In *The General Theory of Action* (1954), along with Shils and a group of collaborators from psychology and anthropology, he aims at "the establishment of a general theory in the social sciences." Here the point of reference is more dynamic: the action of an individual actor or a collectivity of actors. Although the Parsonian terminology often becomes a rather confusing morass and the Parsonian concepts often lose contact with the empirical data they are supposed to illuminate,[1] this work has had a deep influence on research and theory. This influence has extended far beyond the realm of sociology.

5. ANTHROPOLOGISTS

During the last days of Western colonialism, which may be roughly dated as the period between World Wars I and II, "applied anthropology" rose rapidly. European colonial administrators became increasingly convinced that systematic knowledge concerning African and Asiatic societies might help them avoid serious difficulties. Anticolonial independence movements unquestionably contributed to this conviction—just as unionization in the U.S.A. during the same period stimulated the systematic study of human relations. Anthropologists were also employed to assist in the administration of government programs dealing with minorities (such as the American Indians). During World War II they served in a similar capacity with respect to "enemy aliens," the cultural aspects of psychological warfare, and the administration of occupied territories. Within a decade or so after World War II, as the colonies achieved independence, applied anthropologists shifted their attention to the adjustment of the same areas to rapid technological and organizational development. At the same time, many began to find a new area of focus in the study of organizations in industrial societies.

The older form of applied anthropology has yielded one of the classic empirical studies of organizational behavior. Leighton's *The Governing of Men* (1945) not only analyzes an organization under stress but also indicates the importance of deeply-held belief systems. In another volume

1. For a delightful attack on Parsonian remoteness and obscurity (which can be appreciated even by Parsonians), see "Grand Theory" in Mills, 1959.

(1949) Leighton reports on the frustrations of social scientists working for government on the appraisal of enemy morale. In *Anthropology and Administration* (1956) Barnett summarizes a number of years' experience in trying to build anthropological advice into the structure of the government agency responsible for certain Micronesian islands in the Pacific.

An increasing number of empirical studies are being yielded by the anthropologists' new interest in organizations. Among the more significant is Caudill's case study of a small mental hospital (1958). In shifting their attention from primitive to modern societies, however, the anthropologists tend to adopt the concepts and techniques of sociology and psychology. Unfortunately, this has usually been a process of replacement rather than addition, with the traditional anthropological concepts being discarded. Thus the anthropologists have so far told us very little about values and belief systems in large-scale organizations and have completely neglected the role of ritual, ceremony, and "modern magic" in complex bureaucracies. The same comment can be made about the larger area of "nonapplied" anthropology. A preoccupation with primitive societies, out-of-the-way communities, and minority groups has produced a blind spot: contemporary culture in its broader aspects.

Nonetheless, anthropology's greatest contribution to administration has been its illumination of the similarities and differences of the various cultural environments in which organizations operate. The social anthropologists,—from Radcliffe-Brown and Malinowski to Kroeber, Redfield, and Linton—have enlarged Western man's perspective of the world. They have provided many enlightening studies of primitive political institutions. Malinowski was one of the first to develop the modern concept of an institution (1945), Radcliffe-Brown one of the first to develop the "structural-functional" method of analysis (1952). In a manner particularly relevant to the study of administration, Chapple and Coon present a broad framework for analyzing the growth of economic, political and religious organizations and "tangential associations" (1947). Sapir (1949) and Whorf (1956) have analyzed the way in which language in various cultures structures and affects both perception and thought. Hall (1961) has related the cultural aspects of communication more directly to the problems of organizations operating across cultural boundaries. On the basis of Harvard University's cross-cultural study of human values, Kluckhohn has attempted to get beyond cultural relativism and identify the elements that enter into the value systems of all cultures (1956).

6. HISTORIANS

Although the term "applied history" may not have ever been used before, the phenomenon itself is ancient. The physical monuments that the leaders of powerful organizations may leave behind in the form of pyramids and skyscrapers are not always as satisfying as the anticipated respect of generations to come. Hence they are often interested not only in making history but in having it written the way they would like others to read it.

And so we have "official" and "semiofficial" histories. Most of them are histories of states and political leaders. A growing number are written about corporations, universities, and other organizations. Some are as replete with approved adulation as court biographies or as carefully censored as the "doublethink" histories in George Orwell's *1984*. Some are documented presentations which through their apparent candor and strenuous objectivity will, like Caesar's *Gallic Wars*, provide a "subtle apology and attempted vindication" (Hoselitz, 1959, p. 32).

During World War II many agencies of the U.S. Government undertook histories of individual agencies. One of the most valuable (*Cline*, 1951) reviews the transformation of the War Department's prewar War Plans Division into the Operations Division, a much more effective planning staff and "command post." The U.S. Bureau of the Budget (1946) has provided a somewhat more cursory but less heavily-censored review of the civilian agencies involved in wartime economic mobilization.

Not all histories of organizations are official. Some are written by former members who have freed themselves from restrictions on what can be said, as with Nourse's report (1953) on the U.S. Council of Economic Advisers. Such freedom does not necessarily bring with it lack of personal justification; documents of this type must be regarded as raw data to be carefully evaluated by others. Some organizational histories are painfully reconstructed decades or centuries later from fragmentary data. Others are written currently on the basis of whatever information outsiders can obtain, with the occasional help of participant-observers. This brings us, of course, to the entire set of empirical studies of organizations, every one of which can be regarded not merely as a case study but as a case *history*. Seeing these studies as histories reminds us that history is written by all social scientists, not only by historians. More important, it helps us see these studies in the double perspective of the time they are written and the period under study.

The greatest wealth of historical material on administration is largely written without particular emphasis on organizational frameworks. Since political events have thus far attracted the bulk of historians' attention, it is only natural that they have written copiously about the activities of government. Thus there is a tremendous amount of historical material available on the rise and fall of Chinese and Indian dynasties, the Roman and Byzantine Empires, and the growth of European States. Those historical works purporting to concentrate on administration—such as Tout's

Chapters in the Administrative History of Medieval England (1920)—
usually deal with restricted aspects of formal structures and procedures.
The great interpretive histories—such as Weber's *General Economic
History* (1927) or *Religion of China* (1951) or Wittfogel's *Oriental
Despotism* (1957)—are much less restricted. Histories of broader scope
often provide more information about organization than do the formal
histories of bureaucracy. Thus Albert B. White's *Self-Government at the
King's Command* (1933) relates the little-known story of how the early
British Kings found a supplement to a salaried bureaucracy in local services forced and cajoled out of the citizenry against their will. The biographies of government leaders provide still more personal and more
dynamic material, but usually disassociated from any systematic framework of analysis. The administrative history of governments will probably have to be rewritten in terms of new concepts that enable a deeeper
probing into organizational behavior and governance. Leonard White
came close to this in many parts of his impressive trilogy *The Federalists*
(1948), *The Jeffersonians* (1951), and *The Jacksonians* (1954). Schlesinger came still closer in *The Coming of the New Deal* (1958, p. 538-
539). His analysis of President Franklin D. Roosevelt's leadership style
helped to overturn the idea (emanating from critiques by formalistic
public administrators) that Roosevelt was a "good politician but a
wretched administrator."

Outside of government one of the richest fields of historical research
has been in the study of the development of the business corporation.
Here we have the benefit of at least three classic legal surveys: Gierke's
monumental study of the German corporation (Maitland, tr., 1958);
Davis's *Corporations* (1961), and Levy's *Private Corporations and Their
Control* (1957). In addition, there is a rich and growing body of historical studies on entrepreneurial history. An outstanding illustration of
how such studies can be used as the basis for looking at the management
of organizations is provided by Dale's studies of the DuPont, General
Motors, National Steel, and Westinghouse Electric corporations (1960).

B. *Other Established Fields*

THERE ARE MANY connecting links between administration and the well-
established fields of philosophy, mathematics, the natural sciences, the
professions, and literature.

On the nature of these links, we find extreme viewpoints. Those who see administration as a "trade school" subject do not recognize any links. Those who prefer to "stick to their last" view such links skeptically.

On the other hand, those who appreciate the concept of administration as the guidance of organizations often see important connections with their own "last." They may develop ideas of considerable significance for administration or, on occasion, desert their own field to become experts on administration. Finally, there are those who deal with certain aspects of administration, or ideas important to administration, without ever being aware of the connection.

1. PHILOSOPHERS AND MATHEMATICIANS

Although many of the ancestors of contemporary thought were philosophers, the progressive differentiation of new disciplines has meant an increasing remoteness from the central core of philosophic inquiry. This remoteness is nowhere more clear—or more poignant—than in ethics, the very stronghold of ancient philosophy. The philosophers seem to have been thrown off their balance by cultural relativism, the Freudian id, the Einsteinian universe, the clash between competing ideologies, and the widespread disillusionment with the older ideologies of the good life. No modern philosophers worthy of attention have risen to the challenge so sharply presented by Barnard in his call for a non-individualistic ethics that relates directly to the era of the organization man and the administrative revolution.

This does not mean that small beginnings cannot be discerned. The general theory of value developed by Perry (1926) and carried forward by Pepper (1958)—with its emphasis on human interests—has implications of considerable significance. "Axiologists" have called for a scientific approach to human values and preferential behavior (Morris, 1959). Edel (1955) has developed the idea of a valuational base which represents a fusion of local elements and those universal needs that can be empirically revealed in biological and psychological terms. But these are largely methodological, or quasisubstantive formulations.

In an age of science and technology it is only natural that philosophers should move from the Good to the True. Modern philosophy has given considerable attention to the nature of propositions that may be asserted concerning the world. It has thus given significant impetus to the study of semantics and linguistics, although many philosophers themselves seem to spend much of their time in semantic entanglements. Nagel has analyzed scientific method in all modern sciences (1961) and has dealt directly with many of the problems faced by the analysts of organizations and their administration. Mead (1934) has developed some of the basic concepts in social psychology. Dewey and Bentley (1949) have developed the transactional approach to scientific inquiry, emphasizing the interpenetration of organism with environment instead of causal interaction between independent entities. The philosophers, however, have not yet caught up with the philosophic implications of general systems theory and cybernetics.

Contemporary forms of logic and mathematics have already played a major role in information theory, cybernetics, and decision theory. Operations research, in fact, has become a major field of applied mathematics. These developments have, in turn, stimulated logicians, mathematicians, and statisticians into fashioning new and more refined concepts and techniques. For the most part, however, the new mathematical techniques are little more than applications of those that have been laboriously and imaginatively designed to meet the needs of physics and engineering. Very few mathematicians have yet gone very far in studying social science and few social scientists have become expert mathematicians. Perhaps it remains for a philosopher of science to formulate the various kinds of mathematics needed for the more rigorous study of complex social systems with large numbers of variables that cannot be "frozen." In the meantime small beginnings are being made in computer programing theory and Simon's "combinatorial analysis."

2. NATURAL SCIENTISTS

Operations research has provided a field of service which has already attracted many physicists and chemists into the analysis of organizational problems. General systems theory has provided a formal way for natural scientists in any fields to relate their ideas to the concept of human and social organization.

Apart from these recent developments, however, natural scientists have persistently developed ideas which have had profound effects on the study of organizations and their administration. The mechanistic ideas of classical physics probably provided the foundation for the mechanistic ideas of the earlier administrative theorists. The field theory of gravitational force directly inspired the field theory of Lewin as applied to small groups. Cannon's study of homeostasis in the blood-stream (1939) had a direct effect upon those making the earlier studies of social equilibrium in the factory. Thompson's *On Growth and Form* (1961), one of the great classics of biology, has recently served as an inspiration for the study of the growth of corporations (*Haire*, 1959). Williams' studies of *Biochemical Individuality* (1956) may yet give great impetus to methods of coping with organizational individuality. Selye's *The Stress of Life* (1956) is replete with implications for organizational growth, stress and adaptation. In fact, many new developments in physics, chemistry and biology may suddenly and unpredictably suggest new approaches in the social sciences as a whole—and through them to administration in particular.

It is entirely possible, however, that many of the connections will ultimately be still more direct. The physiological investigations of factory fatigue, for example, led directly to questions of motivation, organization, and administrative policy. New studies of fatigue and neurophysical energy might lead to findings of direct value in understanding energy disbursements of individual members of organizations and the development of social power.

3. PROFESSIONALS

The great established professions of law, engineering, and medicine have had particularly close relations with administration. These relations have centered around the professional services rendered by lawyers, engineers, and doctors, their entry into posts of administrative responsibility, and their direct involvement in administrative thought and education.

From the earliest days of the administrative revolution lawyers were needed to advise on the legal aspects of organization-building. Engineers were needed to provide technological guidance. Somewhat more belatedly, as administrators became concerned with industrial accidents, disease and absenteeism, "industrial medicine" came into being and doctors entered large-scale organizations in a service capacity.

In both law and engineering, however, the role of adviser and therapist was too limited for the more able and ambitious practitioners. In increasing numbers, lawyers and engineers began to man top executive posts in public and private organizations. In law this tendency was strengthened in many countries by the close relation between law and political science, with public administration being regarded as an offshoot of jurisprudence. Judicial administration, however, has never been more than a minor point of focus. Like the lawyers, engineers have been mainly concerned with the administration of organizations that need, rather than supply, their professional services. This tendency has been reinforced by the growing demand for technology-oriented administrators at both the middle and top executive level. In the wake of Taylor's "scientific management" it was reinforced still further by programs of instruction and research in industrial engineering, industrial management, production management, systems engineering, or systems management. In the earlier days most of these programs were narrowly technological. More recently, they have tended to include "human engineering" and "man-machine systems" within their scope.

Physicians, on the other hand, have been increasingly placed into administrative positions in organizations producing medical services. This has led to considerable initiative on the part of the medical profession in exploring the problems of hospital administration. Their work in this connection has been enriched by the psychiatrists and psychoanalysts who have at times tried to use their clinical and therapeutic skills in diagnosing organizational ailments and administrative problems.

Similar tendencies may be seen on the part of the less developed professions. Those professions whose services are largely supplied through organizations give increasing attention to the administration of such organizations. Hence the expansion of teaching and research in educational administration, nursing administration, social work administration, library administration, and similar fields. Those professions that supply services needed for the internal operations of organizations tend to look more and more toward the broader problems of their clients. Hence the interest of accountants in developing managerial accounting or in supplying consultant services dealing with management in general. In fact, the intensity of its approach to the study of administration can be regarded as one of the indicators of the seriousness of an occupational group's efforts to obtain fuller recognition or strengthen the foundation of its professional status.

The above comment, obviously, is particularly relevant to so-called professional managers or management consultants. Earning salaries or fees through administrative activities makes someone a "professional" only in the sense that an athlete who loses his amateur status is regarded as a "pro." It does not qualify one as a "professional" in the sense that lawyers, engineers, or physicians are professionals. In this sense of the term, money-making by itself may merely establish one as a quack. Genuine professional status is based, rather, upon an organized body of knowledge, a code of ethics governing services to clients, and a systematic approach to training and acceptance into the profession. By these standards there is not as yet—for either active practitioners or for consultants— any established profession of administration or management. It is only the increasing intensity with which the many associations of administrators have approached the study of administration that makes it possible to glimpse the future possibility of the slow growth of genuine professionalism in this field.

4. BELLE-LETTRISTS

It would be a mistake to think that all references to literature have been postponed until the end of this chapter. Many of the writings referred to under other rubrics are highly literary in nature. I am not referring to documents in which fancy words are used to cover up lack of content. I am thinking, rather, of those social science documents—unhappily too few—in which high literary style is used in the presentation of observed fact, the creation of "atmosphere," the expression of insight and the stimulus of the reader's imagination. I am also referring to the large and growing "literature of antiorganizational revolt," already discussed in Chapter 4.

Moreover, special contribution to the understanding of organizations and their administration can be obtained from novels, plays, and other forms of *belles-lettres*. As representations of human behavior "in the round," the novel and the drama may be much more "true" than the pallid cross-sectional representations obtained through scientific analysis. The difference between art and science is merely that they use different kinds of fictions in dealing with reality. Waldo suggests that literature can transmit emotional comprehension of administration, as distinguished from intellectual perception. It may also, he points out, help people extend their perspectives, see administrators as others view them, provide emotional release from administrative tensions, indicate the limits of rational analysis and focus on the psychological and moral aspects of decision-making (*Perspectives on Administration*, p. 77-106). In an enthusiastic review of John Hersey's *A Bell for Adano*, Rowland Egger finds that the novelist "has said more that is valid for all sincere and humble men everywhere who are honestly trying to discharge their administrative mandates than is contained in all the pompous tomes which have so far appeared on the subject of public administration (Egger, "A Fable for Wise Men"). In another book review, Stephen Bailey goes still further: "Most cartoonists, many novelists, poets and playwrights, some painters and musicians, and even a few literary critics have a far deeper insight into political man, or more accurately, into man in a political or administrative context, than all but a thimbleful of political scientists and public administration experts" (Bailey, "A Frank Statement of Affairs").

To find such insight we need not limit ourselves to the literature that satirizes bureaucracy or presents realistic portrayals of the struggle for power in governments, corporations, and universities. These are merely the more obvious examples that illustrate the principle of indirect relevance. The literature of greatest significance for the understanding of administration is not necessarily the "applied" or obvious variety. It is found mainly in the work of the greatest dramatists and novelists, such as Shakespeare, Tolstoy, Dostoevsky, and Mann, who have always been far ahead of scientists in revealing the nature of man and his behavior.

c. *The Newer Fields*

ONE OF THE EXCITING THINGS about intellectual life in the mid-twentieth century is the frequent development of new subjects or disciplines. People from different academic or professional fields pool their thoughts on a common problem, develop new concepts or apply old ones in a new way, form an association, publish a journal—and a new field is born.

Many of these new fields are initiated in a burst of grandiose claims of "breakthroughs" and exaggerated applications to irrelevant situations. This seems particularly true of those—like information theory, cybernetics, operations research, general systems theory, and information retrieval—which are somehow or other related to administration. Some operations researchers, for example, have seen all of "management science" in the use of their restricted techniques. Apart from the exaggerations which can normally be expected to accompany creative work, many of these claims have the appearance of high pressure sales talks designed to obtain funds from gullible administrators. Yet initial puncturing of inflated claims should not lead to premature disenchantment. Each of these fields is in a very early stage of growth. As they mature, many of them may in time become increasingly meaningful for administration. The serendipity pattern[2] may well apply; any one of them may unexpectedly give rise to new discoveries, even new fields, that we cannot now anticipate. At the very least they create an intellectual disequilibrium that helps prevent either academics or administrators from relapsing into the deadening calm of intellectual self-satisfaction.

1. INFORMATION THEORISTS

With the attention given to the important role of communication in administration by Barnard, Simon, and others, many separate aspects of communication have been developed within various disciplines. As already pointed out, political scientists have analyzed mass communication in political systems. Sociologists have traced the flow of communica-

2. An interesting explanation of the "serendipity pattern" of obtaining valid, but unsought, results is provided by Merton (1957, p. 103-108).

tion in communities and nations. Psychologists have studied communication patterns in small groups.

Far more attention, however, has been obtained by the work of communication engineers in establishing "information theory," which might be regarded as a highly specialized part of electrical engineering. Starting with the pioneer work of Shannon and Weaver for the Bell Telephone Company (1948), electrical engineers have analyzed the process of transmitting signals over telephone, telegraph and radio systems. They have broken the communication process into five parts: (a) the source of the message, (b) the transmitter, which operates on the message in some way to produce a signal suitable for transmission over the channel, (c) the channel, or medium used to transmit the signal to the receiver, (d) the receiver, which decodes the original message from the signal transmitted over the channel and (e) the destination to which the message was sent. They have devised exact methods of quantifying signal sequences and the capacity of channels to handle them. This helps in the solution of many complex problems with respect to the optimum use of channel capacity, methods of coding and decoding and the speed, accuracy and cost of transmission. The term "binary digit" (referred to as *bit* or *binit*) is used as a measure of the relative frequency of a certain sequence among all signal sequences of the same length. This form of measurement is useful *only* by ignoring whatever may be expressed by the signal sequences. It does not deal with meanings, with semantics (the relation between symbols and referents) or with the response of recipients to the messages received. In other words, the "information" theory of the engineers does not deal with the human aspects of information.

The information engineers, however, have at times spread misinformation about their own work. Their skill in the precise language of mathematics has not been matched by an ability to cope with the greater ambiguities of the word-language in which mathematics is embedded. "We see over and over again that, in spite of the official disavowal of the interpretation of 'information' as 'what is conveyed by a signal sequence,' 'amount of information,' officially meant to be a measure of the rarity of kinds of transmissions of signal sequences, acquires also, and sometimes predominantly, the connotation of a measure . . . of the kinds of facts . . . designated by these signal sequences" (Bar Hillel, 1955, p. 94). Shannon and Weaver themselves (1949, p. 95) contribute to this ambiguity by stating that their use of the word "communication" involves "not only written and oral speech, but also music, the pictorial arts, the theatre, the ballet, and in fact all human behavior." Norbert Wiener (1950, p. 7-8) has done his share by equating the engineer's kind of "information" with meaning.

Although engineering information theory cannot be directly applied to the broad problem of communication within and among organizations, it has had an important impact upon computer technology. It has suggested analogies of considerable use to geneticists and neurologists. It has provided new technical concepts—such as channel capacity, overload, noise, and redundancy—which can be adapted for use in analyzing individual mental processes and interpersonal communication. The maturation of general administrative theory—by providing a stronger basis for the necessary adaptations—can facilitate an even fuller exploitation with respect to organizations and their administration.

Like engineering information theory, information retrieval has also originated in response to the needs of certain large-scale organizations. In this case, the problem lay not on the transmission but on the reception side: how to cope with the information crisis created by "the over-production of information relative to the capacity for its storage, analysis, and distribution to the point of need" (Gross, 1962). Technical and research executives in the chemical and metallurgical industries particularly found that they could no longer rely on old-fashioned filing and library methods to keep them posted. Forward-looking librarians (Shera, 1957) became convinced that the traditional forms of library documentation had to be supplemented by newer methods. A growing number of scientists and technologists took time out from their own frantic efforts to keep up with the flood of information to help design general methods of providing information services to both users and producers of scientific information (Kent, 1962).

In a narrow sense, information retrieval deals with methods of using computer technology in expanding the capacity of organizations, associations or nations to store, analyze, and distribute scientific information. It includes the storage of coded information on data processing machines searching for and finding whatever information a potential user may need, and using translating machines to help reduce language barriers. It also includes the transmission of the required information by photostats, radio facsimile, closed-circuit television, and other modern methods of rapid, long-distance communication. In a broader sense this new field also includes the more traditional techniques and skills of documentation experts (particularly systems of classifying, annotating and abstracting), without which the computer technology can never be properly exploited.

Despite many overenthusiastic claims for what can be accomplished by mechanized retrieval methods, the connection between administration and information retrieval in the broader sense has thus far been largely ignored. It has been touched upon only insofar as it may promise (with good reason) to revolutionize filing systems. But the more important aspects of informational retrieval in organizations is centered around the administrator's dual problem of (a) handling information that is not, cannot, or should not be recorded in documents, and (b) determining what kind of information, documentary or not, should be stored or retrieved. When those involved in administrative thought and information retrieval make more progress in working on this common problem, it will probably be easier to develop and administer the extremely complex information retrieval systems needed to meet the needs of industries, researchers or nations as a whole.

2. CYBERNETICISTS

Cybernetics, according to one of its founders (Wiener, 1948, p. 19), is concerned with "the entire field of control and communication theory, whether in the machine or in the animal." More specifically, this field originated in the effort to develop automatic control systems for the regulation of industrial machinery using vast quantities of power. This was done by vastly extending the servo-mechanism control devices previously used in devices such as thermostats. By being hooked up with electronic data processing machines the new control systems are capable of responding quickly and accurately to changes in a large number of variables.

The basis of cybernetics is the concept of a man-made machine system that has a continual input and output and "includes the results of its own action in the new information by which it modifies its subject behavior" (Deutsch, p. 88). This "feedback" provides "orders" that keep the system on its programed course of action. Because of the great complexity of some systems, a component which is not fully understood but must nevertheless be included in the system is referred to as a "black box."

The above concepts have been imaginatively extended both to physical systems in nature and to living systems. They have been enriched by use of the second law of thermodynamics, which holds that there is a tendency for the universe as a whole to run down and approach a state of chaos and sameness governed by the laws of probability rather than by organization. Entropy is the measure of this tendency and negative entropy the measure of the countervailing force of information and organization which appears in certain local enclaves in the universe (Wiener, 1950, p. 12). Both machine and living cybernetic systems may be represented by mathematical models.

The most obvious impact of cybernetics has been in the acceleration of technological change through new machines that can replace routinized mental labor. As with other technological advances, these new "machine brains" change the technological environment of organizations and administrators. The adaptation to these changes over a period of decades will have considerable effects on organizational structure, authority concepts and the dispersion of power within and among organizations. These effects will be still greater if, as Simon predicts (1960, p. 21-24), it will become possible to develop problem-solving machines capable of handling higher level, nonroutine decisions.

A more significant relation between cybernetics and administration is found in the imaginative—albeit potentially misleading—analogies that have been made between self-controlled machine systems and man-directed organizations. In his trail-blazing presentation of cybernetics as a framework for political study, Karl Deutsch reviews the deficiencies of the "classical analogues" of mechanism, organism, and process: "Mechanism and the equilibrium process cannot represent growth and evolution. Organisms are incapable of both accurate analysis and internal arrangement; and models of historical processes lacked inner structure and quantitative predictability. In place of these obsolescent models, we now have an array of self-controlling machines that react to their environment, as well as to the results of their own behavior that store, process, and apply information; and that have, in some cases, a limited capacity to learn. . . . The analogies cybernetics may suggest between communication channels or control processes in machines, nerve systems, and human societies must in turn suggest new observations, experiments or predictions that can be confirmed or refuted by the facts" (1963, p. 79-80). Deutsch then proceeds to indicate how certain engineering concepts from cybernetics can be imaginatively adapted to deal with human systems. This leads to an integrated set of concepts dealing with such challenging subjects as learning, purpose, will, consciousness, autonomy, integrity and meaning. All of these concepts center around the core idea of a self-steering network composed of receptors, effectors and feedback controls (*op cit.*, p. 98-142). The path toward the more fruitful use of such concepts in the understanding of administration will undoubtedly be strewn with simplistic efforts to use cybernetics in developing mechanistic, nonhuman and potentially misleading theories of administration.

3. OPERATIONS RESEARCHERS AND DECISION THEORISTS

"During World War II military management called on scientists in large numbers to assist in solving strategic and tactical problems. . . . Scientists from different disciplines were organized into teams which were addressed initially to optimizing the use of resources. These were the first 'O.R. teams' " (Churchman *et al.*, 1961, p. 6). After the war the use of operations research in military organizations expanded. It also spread rapidly to other fields. Operations research services are provided by most management consulting firms and by a growing number of special units in large organizations. Operations researchers often call themselves "management scientists," the latest variation on Taylor's "scientific management."

The central aim of operations research is to provide decision-makers with a quantitative basis for choosing among possible alternative courses of action. While they like to use the fullest possible help from computers, their emphasis is upon rational calculation by men who have mastered all mathematical techniques that may be relevant to any given problem. After formulating a problem, their basic approach is to construct a mathematical model (usually based on calculus, linear algebra, or probability theory) to represent the system under study. They then derive a solution from the model and try to test both the model and the solution. They are then in a position to indicate to decision-makers the boundaries within which discretion may be rationally exercised.

The methods of operations research have been extremely helpful in dealing with such problems as determining inventory levels, allocating limited resources to different activities, and dealing with waiting-time and replacement processes. The indispensable prerequisites seem to be large-scale operations and a large amount of available data. Under these conditions the operations researchers have proved able to develop many valuable solutions—even in the face of risk and uncertainty.

If decision-making is regarded as the essence of administration and operations research the scientific approach to decision-making, it is easy for operations researchers to regard themselves as dealing with the basic problems in the guidance of organizations. One of them, in a presidential address before an operations research society, went so far as to suggest that operations researchers be used as a general guide to national economic planning in underdeveloped countries (Ackoff, 1957). This grandiloquent presentation (which was in truth a more sober statement than many made by operations researchers in discussing their contribution to the management of business enterprises) was fortunately countered by an experienced operations researcher with a better sense of perspective. The counter-blast pointed out that "operations research is the art of sub-optimizing, i.e., of solving some lower-level problems, and that difficulties arise and our special competence decreases by an order of magnitude with every level of decision we attempt to ascend. The sort of explicit simple model which operations researchers are so proficient in using can certainly reflect most of the significant factors influencing traffic control on the George Washington Bridge, but the proportion of the relevant reality which we can represent by any such model or models in studying, say, a major foreign-policy decision, appears to be almost trivial. . . . Overselling has become the besetting vice and danger of our discipline. Nothing is as likely to bring operations research into disrepute as exaggerated hopes and claims . . ." (Hitch, 1957).

The popularity of operations research has unquestionably contributed to the expansion of decision-making theory in general. Initially, operations researchers used such available techniques as linear programing, probability theory and game theory—with liberal borrowing from information theory and cybernetics. Many economists have moved into the picture and sought to relate economic theory to "managerial analysis" (Baumol, 1961) and to revitalize old-fashioned econometrics by moving from the use of calculus to the use of the mathematical theory of linear spaces. If this has taken economists still further away from the empirical study of firms and economics, it has at least given them a franker orientation toward dealing with prescriptive rationality in any situation whatsoever. Many mathematicians and statisticians have also paid more attention to the theoretical developments related to decision-making under conditions of risk, uncertainty, limited information, and competition. One of the most dramatic developments has been in game theory, which at the beginning was mainly limited to zero-sum games (in which each player's loss was the other's gain) between two persons (Von Neumann and Morgenstern, 1953). Many efforts are being made to deal with situations of combined cooperation-and-conflict (Schelling, 1959), many players (Luce and Raiffa, 1961) and group decision-making (Arrow, 1951). As these extensions come closer to the conflict situations faced by administrators, however, their mathematical rigor usually tends to diminish and their formulations tend toward symbolic logic without quantification.

4. GENERAL SYSTEMS THEORISTS

General systems theory deals with any kind of systems—physical, biological, or behavioral. Although using many of the concepts of cybernetics, general systems theorists are primarily concerned with description and analysis rather than control. They seek to discover structural similarities, or isomorphics, that go beyond mere analogies (Bertalanffy, 1955).

Many general systems theorists have busied themselves with such matters as parallels between the process of learning and the process of evolution (Pringle, 1956), mathematical models for the spread of neural impulses, rumors and epidemics, and discontinuity theories in meteorology and psychology (Thompson, 1960). Others have dealt with such methodological questions as the difference between open and closed system (Bertalanffy, 1955), and the use of equilibrium models in the social sciences (Easton, 1956, and Hagen, 1962, Appendix I). Miller (1955) has suggested a number of descriptive propositions concerning energy, information, growth and adaptation in systems ranging from the cell to the organ, individual, group and society.

Above all, the general systems theorists are interested in studying complex systems through some form of synthetic analysis rather than following the traditional scientific method of breaking down complex wholes into simple parts (Ashby, 1958). They seem to feel that the fundamental problem of modern science is the development of a general theory of organization. Toward this end they favor interdisciplinary studies that will help produce "scientific generalists" (Bertalanffy, 1955).

Although very few of the general systems theorists have concerned themselves directly with the administration of human organizations, the applicability of much of their work is clear. Their work abounds with ideas relating to the control, purposes, structure, and operating processes of organizations.

Chapter 9

THE RISING FLOOD

*I*N THE FIRST DECADES of the twentieth century the small trickle of systematic and recorded administrative thought became a broad stream. In the next few decades the stream deepened and widened. By mid-century it became a flood. Fed by contributions from many other fields, the flood is rising rapidly.

This flood is embodied in an almost unbelievable amount of popular, semipopular and abstruse books, articles and reports on administration. It includes the required reading for tens of thousands of students and the "required writing" of hundreds of teachers and researchers. It includes an immeasurable amount of confidential reports written for the edification or justification of administrators.

One of the main streams in this flood has been the development of special techniques of administration—often referred to as "tool" or "bread and butter" subjects. Here, among others, we find the documents prepared by "experts" in producing management, financial management, personnel management, and many other burgeoning specialties.

Another main stream has dealt with the administration of certain types of organizations. Here we find the writings on public administration, business administration, and other important although less conspicuous organizational types.

A third stream is the growing body of thought which takes a much more general approach. Here we find "organization theory" and general theories of administration.

Although the course of this rising flood is still affected by the seminal work of Fayol, Taylor, Weber, Gulick, Urwick, Follett, Mayo, Roethlisberger, Barnard, and Simon, it goes far beyond them. It already includes at least a score of others who, each in his own way, is probably also entitled to designation as "pioneer." It also includes many scores of valiant "hewers of wood and drawers of water."

Because of the broad scope of this chapter an injustice will be done to many who are not mentioned. Nor can I "do justice" to those who are mentioned. But the purpose of this chapter is neither justice nor encyclopedic comprehensiveness. It is merely to indicate the major currents in the rising flood of modern administrative thought.

A. *Special Techniques of Administration*

TECHNOLOGY is often thought of only in terms of such phenomena as the invention of the wheel, the spinning jenny, the steam engine, or —as in more recent times—the revolutionary techniques of metallurgy, chemical synthesis, data processing machinery, nuclear energy, supersonic flight and electronics, and space exploration. These may be called *production technologies.*

There are also new *administrative technologies* which, although less invigorated by scientific research, have already played a major role in the operations of modern organizations. Providing techniques useful in the governance of all organizations, these technologies are applicable, with certain adaptations, to all systems of production.

The initial impetus to the development of administrative technologies came from the "scientific management" movement. Taylor and his associates did not only lay the basis of production management. They also contributed to new approaches in financial management and helped bring personnel management into being. Although initially resisted by old-time administrators, each of these fields won substantial acceptance in almost all types of large-scale organizations. This led to drives for "professional recognition," resulting in the formation of associations, the convening of regular meetings, and the publication of journals. Academic recognition was gradually obtained by the initiation of university courses, programs and—in some cases—even separate faculties or degrees. This led to a great outpouring of textbooks and manuals.

As with all specialists, the practitioners or teachers of these administrative technologies often fall victim to occupational myopia. They have often equated one or more of these tools with administration as a whole. They have usually failed to consider the interrelation of these tools in the governance of an organization.

Also, there is a sharp gap between actual practice and the publicly available literature. Some of the best practitioners do little teaching and less writing. Some of the best writing appears not in textbooks and journals but in the confidential reports of inside experts and outside consultants.

Each of these technologies, however, stands on the verge of a tremendous reinvigoration that will be brought about by new research and theory in administration and all related fields. In some, the process has already begun. Whether this will lead to a spread or contraction of ultra-specialist myopia remains to be seen.

1. PRODUCTION MANAGEMENT

The term "production management," as here used, refers to the administrative technologies that deal with production processes apart from specific production technologies. It includes the work not only of production engineers (or industrial engineers) but also of "Organization and Methods" (O. and M.) specialists in government agencies. These are the people often referred to as "efficiency experts" or "productivity experts."

The hard core of progress in thise area has been the development of the basic techniques of Taylor and his associates: methods analysis, work measurement, and incentive wage plans. This has led to the development of such specific areas as production scheduling, materials handling, quality control, product simplification and standardization, work conditions, worker training, job evaluation, and merit rating. Many of these techniques have been adapted to the more routinized aspects of clerical and white-collar activities with respect to records, payrolls, purchasing, and stock control. A further broadening has led the "efficiency experts" into the areas of plant and office layout, product design, preventive maintenance, safety and suggestion systems (Maynard, 1956; I.L.O., 1959). Changes in any of these areas, it has been shown, may help eliminate the ineffective use of workers' time or deduce the basic content of human labor in any given production process.

During World War II a tremendous boost was given to production management in all its forms by the drive for increased industrial productivity. For war-damaged countries engaged in physical reconstruction and industrially backward nations engaged in the construction of new industries, the engineering aspects of administration seemed of central importance. They also received great attention from national and international agencies engaged in technical assistance programs.

More recently, production management seems to face a paradoxical situation. By helping to reduce human labor to routinized processes, it has contributed to the replacement of human labor by machines that can handle these routines quickly and more cheaply. The role of work study and incentive wage systems thus becomes proportionately smaller. At the same time, the traditional techniques of production engineers and O. and M. specialists are being replaced by those of the operations researchers and the cyberneticist designers of machine and man-machine systems. Thus the very efficiency experts whose activities have struck fear in the hearts of millions of workers are themselves threatened by creeping obsolescence.

The response to this paradox seems double. On the one side, systems analysis and operations research is beginning to enter the curriculum for the training of engineers—although a full fusion with traditional production engineering has not yet occurred. On the other side, the concept of production management tends to broaden to cover administration as a whole. Thus many of the consultant firms in this area call themselves "management consultants." O. and M. offices now often use "M" as a symbol not of "methods" but of "management." How far the reality corresponds with the semantics is a question that can be answered only in specific cases.

2. FINANCIAL MANAGEMENT

The term "financial management" is here used to refer to a wide variety of techniques dealing with the monetary aspects of an organization's activities. It includes those used both by accountants and by experts in budgeting and finance.

Accounting is one of the oldest of all administrative tools. It first developed as a means of simply "keeping the books" on the expenses and revenues of an organization, as well as its property and debts. With the proliferation of corporations and joint stock companies, financial accountants developed their three major instruments: the balance sheet (or position statement), the income statement (or profit and loss statement), and the funds statement. For a long time the basic orientation of accounting was to give "an accounting" to investors and lenders. Similarly, public agencies give a financial accounting to legislatures and associations to their membership. Auditing soon developed as a separate branch of accounting, with both internal and external auditors seeking to prevent or detect fraud and error.

This "stewardship" or "accountability" approach in accounting has always meant a basic emphasis upon the past. Many accountants seem to feel that their major purpose is the careful recording of minute historical details. Indeed, widespread delay in submitting financial reports often suggests an almost-archaeological approach to the remote past.

As against this past-orientation, the newer trends in accounting emphasize the provision of information that will assist in making decisions about the future. Under the stimulous of production engineering, cost accounting grew up as a method of calculating the costs of end and intermediate products (usually referred to as "job order" and "process" cost accounting). These concepts were used in projecting future goals— in the form of standard or budgeted costs—against which performance could be measured. Budget systems were developed to apply them to subdivisions in organizations, various types of activities, and various groups of cost categories. "Flexible budgeting" recognizes cost changes resulting from variations in output volume. These various forms of budgets are increasingly regarded as instruments of internal administration—although in the public sector budgeting is still largely seen as an instrument of external relations. In the private sector this interest in external relations is paralleled by tax accounting, which developed as a means of enabling organizations to handle disputes with government taxing authorities. "Tax avoidance," as distinguished from "tax evasion," has become a recognized legal means of operating an organization in such a way as to incur the lowest possible tax liability.

The literature of accounting is vast and exceedingly complex. It reflects intensive specialization on many aspects of accounting and on the special problems of different sectors of an economy and different forms of organization. Most accounting texts (such as the three volumes of Finney and Miller) have been prepared to train professional accountants, and the specialized language of accounting has created serious obstacles to communication between accountants and the managers of the organizations for which accounts are made. In the business area Bierman (1959) and in the government area Jesse Burkhead (1956, Chapt. 14) have tried to interpret accounting techniques to nonaccountants.

The literature of accounting taken as a whole, however, is but a pale reflection of the skills and methods used by operating accountants. Few authors in the field have dealt frankly with the arbitrary nature of accounting methods and the tremendous room for the exercise of judgment in the classification of transactions. Nor have the writers on budgeting, which is often regarded as extending far beyond accounting, exercised similar frankness. Thus Burkhead's excellent study of government budgeting (1956), while fully recognizing the political environment of the budgeting process, hardly touches upon the strategy and tactics of cost estimating and "budget juggling." In his masterly *Managerial Accounting* (1960) Anthony has gone far in presenting accounting and budgetary problems from the viewpoint of business managers, but has barely hinted at the stratagems actually used in handling these problems.

A little more realistic emphasis is to be found in the literature of corporate finance and controllership. Thus Donaldson's *Corporate Finance* (1957) gives a dynamic picture of many of the choices involved in organizing a corporation, promoting securities, handling working capital problems, determining and distributing income, and moving through the dangerous waters of reorganization, receivership, and dissolution. Many writers on "controllership" (such as Bradshaw and Hull, eds., 1949) have developed a top executive viewpoint on the coordination of the work of accounting, budget, and finance and their integration into the other activities of a business organization. Nevertheless, despite increasing use of the term "managerial accounting," a fully managerial orientation has yet to be developed in the broad literature of financial management.

3. PERSONNEL MANAGEMENT

The term "personnel management" is here used to refer to a large array of techniques designed to assist administrators on some of the human aspects of governing organizations. The field developed under the direct impetus of production engineers in industry and civil service reform movements in government. Although it has not yet achieved the professional status of accounting or production engineering, personnel specialists are important people in most large-scale organizations.

The hard core of the literature in personnel management deals with job analysis, position specification, recruitment, examinations and tests, training, disciplinary action, wage scales, performance rating, and the maintenance of personnel records (Mee, 1951; Jucius, 1955). Most of these subjects are offshoots of production management. Many are closely tied up with the work of industrial psychologists. In government service the earlier tendency has been to use these techniques mainly as a way of reducing external political influence upon the selection, promotion and compensation of personnel. More recently, public personnel specialists have directed themselves more fully to the problems of internal operation (Stahl, 1956; Nigro, 1959).

There have been two major new currents on modern personnel management: human relations and executive development. Since the pioneering work of Mayo and Roethlisberger, the human relations approach has been a major element in most personnel literature. In its minor aspects this has meant considerable attention to improved working conditions, health and welfare benefits, and recreational programs. Its more important aspects have been employee morale, the nature of supervision and leadership, internal communications, and union-management relations. On most of these matters the writers on personnel management in business have taken the lead (Gardner and Moore, 1955; McGregor, 1950; Scott, 1962). This probably stems from the larger amount of research finance by business organizations or schools of business administration.

While the training of employees has always been a part of personnel management, concentrated attention to educational programs for people already holding higher executive positions began only after World War II. Ambitious and increasingly popular training programs were initiated by universities (Andrews, 1959), large corporations (Bridgman, 1959), and such organizations as the Administrative Staff College in England and the management associations in many countries. With the exception of the military, government organizations have usually lagged behind business in this field. Nevertheless, in both the public and private sphere, the literature on executive development has grown steadily. Since it must perforce focus on the broadest problems of administration, it has tended at one and the same time both to widen the perspectives of those dealing with personnel management and to leave the field of personnel management entirely (Mace, 1950; Sofer and Hutton, 1958).

4. OTHER ADMINISTRATIVE TECHNIQUES

In addition to the managerial tools referred to above, there are many others of growing importance.

One set of tools deals with the relationship between the organization and its environment. Here one finds public relations and publicity. These include various techniques of analyzing the opinions and attitudes of various publics, developing favorable relations with various groups, and using the various instruments of personal and mass communication and propaganda (Canfield, 1956; Ferber and Wales, eds., 1958).

A still larger field is that of marketing, which is also oriented toward the mobilization and maintenance of external support. The major marketing techniques are market analysis and research product determination and styling, pricing, advertising, public relations, salesmanship, the development of sales channels, and sales administration (Hansen, 1956; Hepner, 1955).

Another broad area is the provision of certain general services needed by every organization. One significant field is the procurement of materials and equipment and their storage, maintenance, distribution, and replacement (Lewis and England, 1957). Another area is the organization and use of files and archives—sometimes referred to as "records management." Still another is the provision of internal communications through telephone and messenger services and routing systems.

With the passage of time new tools are constantly being developed. This is done through the refinement of specialties within older fields. It is done through the combination of existing techniques. It is also done through the application of other disciplines to management and the sheer invention of new techniques.

B. *Special Types of Organizations*

A SECOND MAJOR CURRENT in modern administrative thought is associated with specialized educational programs designed to prepare people for future work in such broad categories of organizations as government agencies, business enterprises, armies, churches, schools and hospitals.

For a considerable period special programs in public and business administration were opposed by those who saw the best educational preparation for future administrators in a broad general education with emphasis on literature, mathematics and science. They were also opposed by those who favored professional training in one of the established professions. During the period between World Wars I and II, however, special university programs in public and business administration developed rapidly in the United States. After World War II they began to gain a footing in Western Europe—often under the aegis of technical schools or nonuniversity institutions. With the impetus given by technical aid programs for industrially-underdeveloped countries, American and European-style programs in these fields spread rapidly to Asia, the Middle East, Africa, and South America. The new executive development programs also began to spread rapidly.

The only countries in which such programs have not developed are the communist-bloc nations. There orientation toward specific types of organizations is carried to its logical extreme, with special schools usually associated with every sector of an economy. The techniques of production management are the only aspects of administration which are fully recognized as a fit subject for study. Otherwise, the training tends to be technological or political.

The Soviet Union, however, has recently hired Western management consultants to introduce special training programs in industrial management. This may well herald a major new trend among the communist nations.

1. PUBLIC ADMINISTRATION

The major source of the literature on the administration of government has been the political science or government departments of universities. Although many professors of political science have looked down on public administration, there has always been a sprinkling of eminent men like Woodrow Wilson, Charles Beard, and Charles Merriam who gave vigorous encouragement to this "subdomain." From the political science departments, therefore, have come the leading spirits in theory and research and the students who have served as the captive clientele for the documents produced. In the United States some of these departments established special "bureaus" or "institutes" to provide research services for municipal or state government agencies.

A second important source of administrative literature has been the research organizations established outside of the university framework, such as the New York Bureau of Municipal Research (set up in 1906) and the Brookings Institution in Washington, D.C. (set up in 1927). Most of the special research organizations, whether inside or outside the university, have been interested mainly in action-oriented research.

A third source has been government agencies themselves. In England, the United States, and many other countries, there is a long tradition in accordance with which specially appointed boards are asked to prepare proposals on specific problems of government administration. Government agencies have also initiated a large amount of detailed research through full-time research staffs and the hiring of *ad hoc* outside consultants. Some of the documents thus produced, however, are regarded as highly confidential. Most of them are "fugitive documents" in the sense that, although not particularly confidential, they have not been duplicated or, if duplicated, have rarely been tracked down by libraries and recorded in catalogs, bibliographies, or even the review sections of professional journals.

The major orientation in public administration literature has been toward "executive agencies." Judicial and legislative bodies are customarily regarded as being outside the place of public administration and relevant to it only by their interrelations with executive agencies.

The earlier writings in public administration were greatly influenced by "scientific management" and the "gospel of efficiency." They were based upon a rather sharp dichotomy between "policy," which was associated with politics, legislatures, and special interests, and "administration," which was the province of neutral, impartial civil servants. The special administrative techniques were vigorously applied to government organizations. Public personnel management emphasized the development of a nonpolitical civil service system. Public financial management emphasized the significance of detailed budgeting. Public production management dealt with the procedures of public purchasing, licensing, and regulation. On the organization side of O. and M. the Gulick-Urwick principles received major attention and minor variations on POSDCORB were developed. Considerable attention was given to the general division of labor among executive agencies and their relations with each other, with the other branches of the Federal government and with State and local governments. Proposals and principles of formal reorganization were brought forth. Some aimed at strengthening legislative or judicial control over executive agencies. A growing number aimed at strengthening the executive branch as a whole by facilitating Presidential leadership and control. The report of the President's Committee on Administrative Management (1937) clearly belongs in this category. Many of the proposals in the reports of the "Hoover commissions" (1949, 1955) also tended in this direction.

After World War II, as pointed out by Sayre (1951, 1958) many shifts took place. The politics-administration dichotomy was strongly assaulted by Appleby (1949) and others. Principles that had been previously taken for granted were bluntly challenged. The efficacy of formal reorganization as a method of effectuating significant change was itself scrutinized more carefully. Public administration was increasingly brought within the scope of the "newer realism" in political science. Interest groups, informal organization, politics, power, pressure, conflict, strategy, decision-making, and communication—subjects previously rather alien to the literature of public administration—rose to the fore. For some this seemed to equate public administration with the general study of political processes or of the substantive issues involved in the major controversies concerning executive agency policies. This led in part to a "downgrading" of the traditional "tool subjects" and in part to a more flexible and dynamic approach to them.

Throughout this entire period a growing number of empirical studies of specific government agencies were made. The earlier studies tended to emphasize formal organizational structure at the higher levels and external relations. The later ones have tended to reveal more of the internal operations of the agencies and relate them to the dominant pressures in their environment. Among the more significant studies are those by *Fenno* (1959), *Kaufman* (1960), *McMahon et al.* (1939), *Mansfield* (1939), *Neustadt* (1960), *Robson* (1960), and *Somers* (1950). The empirical approach has been strengthened by the preparation of case studies under the Inter-University Case Program (Stein, 1952, 1963; Bock and Campbell, 1962; Bock, 1963).

One of the major concepts now emerging in public administration is that of an organization with a complex internal life of its own. For a long time this was obscured by an external approach which emphasized the executive branch as a whole, the relations among agencies, or merely the top-side and formalistic aspects of an agency's "insides." Now more attention is increasingly being given to problems of internal morale, supervision, cooperation, and conflict. This trend can be illustrated by comparing Kaufman's *The Forest Ranger* (1960) with Mansfield's *The Controller General* (1939), or the more recent textbook of Dimock, Dimock and Koenig (1958) with the first edition of White's *Introduction to the Study of Public Administration* (1926). To a large extent this shift indicates a growing awareness of the relevance of the work done by psychologists, sociologists, and anthropologists.

Another new development is the increasing attention being given to comparative public administration. This is well illustrated by the studies of Riggs (1957, 1961) and Chapman (1959) and the ideas on development administration advanced by Weidner (1961). The challenging work of Riggs unquestionably foreshadows increasing interest in the insights to be gained through the perspectives of sociology and anthropology.

2. BUSINESS ADMINISTRATION

As with public administration, the major source of the available literature on business administration has been the universities. Here, however, the academic sponsorship has been broader based, with writings originating not only in departments and colleges of business administration but also in departments of economics and industrial engineering. Moreover, many of the business administration programs have been closely associated with the work of sociologists and psychologists.

An additional element of breadth has been provided by closer associations with the work of psychologists, sociologists and anthropologists.

Both through greater use of consultants and closer contact with industrial technology, business administration writers have also been closer to the work of operations researchers, decision theorists, and cyberneticists. Moreover, a somewhat larger number of top executives from the business field have ventured into systematic writing on administration. In public administration, while a growing number of writers on the subject have had experience in government service, very few have had personal experience in positions of high authority; Appleby (1945, 1949, 1952), Cleveland (1960) and Dimock (1940, 1945, 1958) are conspicuous exceptions. In the business field, however, there seem to be many more—such as Mooney (1947), Alvin Brown (1947), *Wilfred Brown* (1960), Marrow (1957), Plowman, of Peterson and Plowman (1953) and Randall (1957)—who have carried on the practice-theory tradition of Fayol and Barnard.

The literature of business administration, unlike that of public administration, does not deal very fully with the external relations of business enterprises. Although it pays growing attention to the "public responsibilities" of businessmen (Selekman, 1956; Glover, 1954) it rarely touches upon the activities of business administrators in political campaigns or in the organization of trade associations, holding companies or cartels. It deals only superficially—and more on the prescriptive than the descriptive level—with the strategies of business administrators in their relations with suppliers, banker, clients, and competitors. These important aspects of business administration are rarely recognized outside of their rather limited treatment as part of the techniques of publicity and public relations.

The other side of this coin is that the writers on business administration have gone much further and more intensively into the internal aspects of administration. The subjects of production management, financial management, and personnel management have generally been handled in more specialized writings—usually associated with special courses or departments dealing with these subjects separately. This has left the general writings on business administration much more free of the "tool subjects" than the equivalent writings in public administration. Writers like Newman (1951), Newman and Summer (1961), Petersen and Plowman (1953), Terry (1953), and Koontz and O'Donnell (1955) have taken advantage of this freedom to concentrate on the processes of organization, planning, coordination, direction, and control. Much of the material in these books represents a far more fully developed version of the POSDCORB approach than is to be found in books in the writings of public administration; and much of it has relevance for all types of organizations. Other writers—such as Drucker (1954), Davis (1951), Brech (1953, 1957) and Viller (1960)—deal also with the distinctive profit-making aspects of business organizations.

Reference has already been made to "human relations" and executive development. In business administration, particularly, both of these aspects of administration have moved out of the more narrow framework of personnel management. They have been increasingly viewed as central aspects of administration in the broadest possible sense.

Long-range planning is another field in which business administration writers have gone far beyond those in public administration in theory, research and operating techniques. The philosophy of planning has permeated all of the writings on special administrative techniques. It has become a favorite subject for books—such as those by Goetz (1949), Ewing (1958), and Le Breton and Henning (1961)—and journal articles. More than a dozen documents in the general management series of the American Management Association deal with business plans and planning. Paradoxically, the comparative neglect of government planning in the United States results to a considerable extent from the opposition of business associations that—rightly or wrongly—often equate government planning with a further extension of government into the realms of nongovernment enterprise.

Business administration has also taken the lead in the development of case studies as instruments in administrative education. The various papers in *The Case Methods at the Harvard Business School* (McNair, 1954), as well as the pioneering work of the same school in case study collection, have touched off continual and fruitful debates on the uses and limits of case studies. Some of these papers, such as Gragg's classic essay "Because Wisdom Can't Be Told" (1940), raise much deeper questions concerning the learning process. Thus the debates on the use of case studies have inevitably branched off into significant inquiries into how students and practitioners learn and how teachers can contribute something to their learning processes. This has led .to a growing amount of experimentation and research on role playing, simulation and "management games."

As already indicated, many of the empirical studies by psychologists, sociologists, and anthropologists have been undertaken in business organizations. At the same time, the tradition of the Hawthorne studies has been carried on and extended at the Harvard Business School, often in collaboration with scholars from these social sciences. Some of the fruits of this work are shown in the studies by *Barnes* (1960), *Lawrence* (1958), *Learned* (1951), *Lombard* (1955), *Ronken* and *Lawrence* (1952). *Zaleznik* (1951, 1956) and *Zaleznik et al.* (1958). In the light of the comments at the beginning of this section, it might be noted that all of these studies are "inner-oriented." None deals directly with the external environment of the organization. Much more attention to environmental relations is found in the empirical studies prepared by *Brown* (1960), *Jaques* (1951), *Rice* (1958, 1963) and *Sofer* (1961) as a consequence of the consultative work of the Tavistock Institute of Human Relations.

3. OTHER TYPES OF ORGANIZATIONS

The previous sections have dealt with public and business administration only in the broadest of terms. There is also a growing literature on special types of civilian public agencies—particularly those dealing with public education, public health, public welfare, public works, public lands, police and local government in general. Considerable attention has also been given to various sectors of business enterprise—particularly manufacturing, banking, transportation, distribution and agriculture.

It would be a miracle, indeed, if in an age of mounting specialization the flood of adminstrative thought did not extend also to other types of organizations. Nor has such an extension been merely a matter of going along with the fashions of the day. It has stemmed from the very practical necessities of precareer, midcareer, and top executive educational programs geared to the distinctive administrative problems faced by special types of organizations.

Most of the work done in these specialized fields has originated with people who are primarily specialists in such substantive fields as education, health or social welfare. This has at times meant that when purporting to write about administration they have merely dressed up their regular subject matter in a slightly different form. Or else they have simply borrowed and restated some of the more elementary administrative techniques or the more formal ideas from public or business administration.

More recently, however, there has been a tendency for the writers on the administration of special types of organizations to catch up with the "new beginnings" and the new contributions from the social sciences as a whole and from the new fields of inquiry. This has led to a more balanced and less exaggerated approach concerning the special problems of certain types of organizations and a greater interest in learning more about administration through the full exploitation of theories, research and techniques from any aspect or field of administration. A note of realism, moreover, has been added by the collection of case studies for instructional purposes and the conducting of significant research studies. As already indicated in the previous chapter (and as borne out in the bibliographical report "Research Studies in Organizational Behavior"), a significant proportion of the empirical studies of organizational behavior have been made in military organizations, hospitals, and trade unions.

The number of organizational types and the volume of publication with respect to each are so great that it would be inappropriate at this point to summarize the work in each field. It may be noted, however, that highly specialized forms of administrative thought may have great implications for all types of organizations. This is certainly true of Von Clausewitz's *On War* (1880, republished in English, 1950), which contains many classical and widely applicable passages on strategy, planning, information, and the relation between theory and practice. It is also true of Hart's *Strategy, the Indirect Approach* (1954). Based upon many empirical studies of military operations, this important book presents a non-Clausewitz concept of strategy which, in the author's words "is closely related to all problems of the influence of mind upon mind." Of an entirely different nature, *Explorations in Role Analysis (Neal Gross et al.*, 1958) has not only illuminated important aspects of public school administration; it has also been one of the most significant contributions to the role concept in administration and to the empirical study of role conflict.

c. *General Approaches*

ONE OF THE MOST SIGNIFICANT CURRENTS in the rising flood has been the continuation of the general approaches taken by the pioneers of administrative thought.

As already indicated, the specialists in administrative techniques have usually been interested in applying them across a wide variety of organizations. Similarly, those who have purported to specialize in specific types of organizations have been rather general in their approach. Thus Appleby (1949), in focusing upon public administration, deals with an extraordinarily wide range of different kinds of government agencies. In stressing the distinctive aspects of government organizations, he enters the comparative field by contrasting public with private organizations. Much of what he writes about the relation between policy and administration is relevant to any form of large-scale employment organization. Drucker's "business philosophy" of management by objectives and self-control, together with his pungent critiques of personnel management, "scientific management," and reporting procedures (1954), have even wider implications.

Many other specialists have been much less inhibited in dealing directly with many different kinds of organizations. Thus Mooney in *The Principles of Organization* (1947) has analyzed perpendicular and horizontal coordination, leadership delegation, and authority in business, religious, government and military organizations. Tead, in his *Art of Administration* (1951) has presented a reasoned case for a democratic style of administration. Litchfield (1957) has formulated a number of suggestive propositions for a general theory of administration. James D. Thompson has gone much further in his "Common and Uncommon Elements in Administration" (1962).

Many of the more recent extensions of the general approach fall under the rubric of "organization theory." They are exemplified by the books of Blau and Scott (1962), Etzioni (1962), Haire, ed. (1959), and Victor Thompson (1961). In addition, helpful compilations of writings on organization theory have been made available by James Thompson *et al.* (1959), Dubin (1961, 2nd ed.), Etzioni (1961), Rubinstein and Haberstroh (1960), and Tannenbaum *et al.* (1961).

It would be a mistake to regard recent organization theory as a relatively integrated field of inquiry undertaken by a well-defined community of scholars. It is rather a meetingplace for a large number of theorists and researchers with highly divergent viewpoints and interests. These include a considerable number of sociologists, psychologists, anthropologists, decision theorists, and general systems theorists. Political scientists, economists (except for those who have frankly moved into decision theory) and historians are but sparsely represented.

Nor is modern organization theory, despite a new label, very new. It is rooted in the thought of Barnard, Simon, and the other pioneers. It has been strongly influenced by the work of the great sociologists. As it matures, it will probably sink deeper roots into the heritage of political philosophy and political science.

Nevertheless, there are three new elements whose importance should not be underestimated.

The first is the somewhat sharper formulation of the concept of a human organization. There is both greater agreement and deeper insight with respect to the essentials of organizational structure and action. Although some of the organization theorists are not interested in administration, those who are tend to see administration as "activity related to the creation, maintenance or operation of an organization" (James Thompson *et al.*, p. 7).

The second is a much greater emphasis upon the empirical observation of specific organizations and their administration. Some of the more outstanding empirical studies have already been referred to in this and the preceding two chapters. Hundreds of others have also been made and untold hundreds are now in process or being planned for the near future.

The third is more systematic efforts at theory building. In part, these may consist merely of a formal summarization and classification of past theoretical work, with an effort to map future lines of growth. In part, to use the phrase with which Haire describes the papers in his collection, these are "the ragged leading edge of theoretical development" (Haire, 1959, p. 2). These efforts are extremely varied in scope, point of attack, level of generality, relation to observed data and theoretical rigor. Yet underlying them all is a keen interest, either implied or explicitly stated, in the development of integrating concepts that bear upon both the similarities and differences in organizations and their administration. In fact, the closer one looks the more readily one can see the beginnings of an emerging integration. If this be slow in coming, one of the reasons is that with the upsurge of new research and ideas in this field, there is more to integrate than ever before.

The task of the following chapters is to hasten this process along. In so doing, I shall draw heavily upon the organization theorists whose work has been so summarily referred to in this section.

Part III

THE EMERGING
INTEGRATION

Chapter 10

THE MANAGEMENT OF ORGANIZATIONS

T HE EMERGING CONSENSUS in modern administrative (or managerial)[1] thought seems to include three major elements:

- the identification of administrative (or managerial) activity as having something to do with the guidance or governance of the activities of organizations,
- attention to certain characteristics which all organizations and their administration—when viewed at a high enough level of abstraction— have in common, and
- awareness of the special or unique characteristics which differentiate every single organization—when viewed closely enough—from others.

To set forth this growing consensus involves more than summarization. At many points it requires a synthesis of diverse ideas and their expression in a consistent terminology.

Much of the emerging consensus, however, is concealed by different ways of saying similar things. Accordingly, this chapter is concluded

1. The terms "administration," "administrative" and "administrator" are here used as synonymous with "management," "managerial," and "manager." The reasons for this usage are discussed at the end of this chapter.

with an identification of some key terminological problems and a presentation of one way of meeting them.

A. *The Governance of Organizations*

IN MODERN THOUGHT the term "administration" (or management) usually refers to a great variety of activities engaged in by people who occupy positions of formal responsibility and authority in organizations—that is, by administrators (or managers). Without such words as "public" or "business" in front of it, the term refers to the activity of administrators in all types of organizations, armies, political parties, churches, trade unions and trade associations, as well as government and business organizations. Unless preceded by words like "top" or "lower level," it refers to the administrative activity of supervisors, sergeants, and others at lower hierarchic levels, as well as of presidents, department heads, generals, and boards of directors.

1. ADMINISTRATION AS GOVERNANCE

More specifically, how can we distinguish administrative from other activities?

In colloquial usage there are many ways of answering this question without detailing what administrators do. One of the best answers is that the administrator's activity is "getting things done through (or by) others." Similarly, people will often refer to an administrator as someone who is "in charge of others," has people working "for him," "under him," or "with him," is "responsible for the work of others," or as simply the chief, head, boss or "top dog." This usage has the advantage of clearly excluding various clerical activities and housekeeping services in such fields as supplies, maintenance accounts, files and correspondence.[2] On the other hand, by overemphasizing the administrator's concern with hierarchical subordinates, it diverts attention from his activities relating to the environment of his organization.

If we turn to more formal definitions of administration, we usually

2. The ambiguity created when "administration" is used in one phrase to refer *both* to running an organization and to handling housekeeping services or certain administrative tools is beautifully illustrated in positions with titles such as "Deputy-Administrator for Administration."

find an emphasis upon the two elements of (1) guiding or governing, (2) an organization, a unit of an organization or an aggregation of organizations. These two ideas are expressed in a remarkable variety of terms. Thus by combining any word from the first column with any word or phrase in the second column, we can get a hundred different ways of expressing a similar idea:

Managing	. . . an organization
Administering	. . . the activities of an organization
Governing	. . . organized human behavior
Guiding	. . . an enterprise
Coordinating	. . . an undertaking
Integrating	. . . a group of people
Running	. . . people
Directing	. . . the activities of people
Supervising	. . . subordinates
Controlling	. . . the use of resources

With a little ingenuity the number of combinations may be increased still further. Any combination may then be embroidered, as usually done in formal definitions, by reference to (a) purposes, (b) the physical resources used by people in organizations, (c) some criterion of successful administration, such as effectiveness or efficiency, and (d) processes or activities. Yet a careful examination of formal definitions—even though they may originate in the specialized fields of public or business administration—will usually show an explicit or implicit use of the ideas referred to in the two columns.[3]

3. A sampling of definitions from various sources yields the following:
Public Administration. White, 4th edit. (1955): "The direction, coordination and control of many persons to achieve some purpose or objective." Pfiffner and Presthus (1953): "The organization and direction of human and material resources to achieve desired ends." Millett (1954): "The process of directing and facilitating the work of people organized in formal groups to achieve a desired goal."
Business Administration. Newman (1951): "The guidance, leadership and control of the efforts of a group of individuals towards some common goal." Peterson and Plowman (1953): "A technique by which the purposes and objectives of a particular group of people are determined, clarified and effectuated." Koontz and O'Donnell (1955): "The function of getting things done through others." Terry (1956): "The accomplishment of a predetermined objective through the efforts of other people."
General. Adams (1913): "The capacity of coordinating many, and often conflicting, social energies in a single organism so adroitly that they shall operate as a unity." Tead (1951): "The conscious effort to direct, guide and integrate associated human strivings which are focussed towards some specified end or aims."

They thus provide a basis for distinguishing administrative activities from such nonadministrative activities as (a) spontaneous cooperation among people, (b) influencing others outside of an organizational context, (c) guiding the operations of machines, and (d) providing services which, while they may be used by others in an organization, are not designed to guide or coordinate the activity of others.

There are certain disadvantages to any key term in a shorthand definition. "Governance" may seem to imply that administration is an activity only at the highest levels of organization or that there are no important differences between public and private administration. "Guiding" may imply that the "pilot" is interested only in the external reefs and straits. "Coordinating" and "integrating" may suggest interest only in the internal problems. "Running" and "directing" may overemphasize the power and authority of the administrators. This is why formal definitions must always be handled with care and never taken too seriously. Far more significant is the broad context or network of symbols and meanings.

Although "governance" (or governing) is not commonly used in this context, there are various precedents. Fayol, it will be recalled, refers to "government" as the all-inclusive process of "directing an undertaking." Merriam finds that "obviously there is governance everywhere—government in heaven; government in hell; government and law among the outlaws; government in prison" (1944, p. 1). Ruml maintains that "it is in no sense a figure of speech to refer to a business company as a private government" (1950, p. 220). Eells uses the term in analyzing the "constitutional crisis" within the private corporation (1962).

This usage has many advantages. In the public sphere it helps focus attention on the political aspects of administration, thereby escaping the overconstrict dichotomy between public administration and politics. In the private sphere it facilitates attention to organizations as miniature polities with internal politics of their own. It helps bring out the element common in both political thought concerning sovereignty and administrative thought concerning authority. It suggests that the rule-making, rule-executing and rule-interpreting activities of public agencies may have parallels in private organizations. It suggests going beyond internal *minutiae* and dealing also with the guidance of an organization through the difficulties of its environment.[4]

4. This connotation ties in with the word's origin in the Greek *kubernan*, "to steer or control," which is also the source of the modern "cybernetics." The Sanskrit version is probably *kubhan*, which means "to dance or pirouette." This is not too remote from images of the intricate footwork of administrators in their efforts to maintain a balance among conflicting forces.

2. THE ADMINISTRATORS AND THE ADMINISTERED

Another widely accepted premise of administrative thought is a distinction between those who have and those who do not have administrative responsibility and authority—that is, between the administrators and the administered, the managers and the managed. This distinction is similar to that often made in political science between the rulers and the ruled, the governors and the governed. The governance of an organization cannot be "self-government" in the sense that all members have equal responsibility and authority. A "self-governing" organization, rather, is one whose members may participate to a certain extent in formulating purposes and selecting governing boards and top executives. Although the people so selected may be responsible to all the members (as in many associations and legislative bodies), they nevertheless stand apart from them. In any organization, moreover, there may be significant tension, if not conflict, between the two groups.

Yet this distinction cannot be seen as separating all members of organizations into two classes of people. There are at least four widely accepted limitations that tend to blur the dividing lines between the administrators and the administered.

First of all, most managers are themselves among the managed. All administrators except those at the highest levels of responsibility and authority are subject to the general guidance of other administrators.

Second, most administrators are also involved in a certain amount of nonadministrative activities. At the middle and lower levels of an hierarchy, as Fayol pointed out long ago, the proportion of nonadministrative to administrative activity tends to rise.

Third, formal designations may be rather misleading. On the one hand, people may be given administrative titles merely to justify a salary increase or raise their social status. Some people with titles of "administrative assistant" or "assistant to the administrator" may be engaged in little more than minor clerical work. On the other hand, professionals with administrative responsibilities often prefer to highlight their professional tasks and conceal or even evade their administrative responsibilities.[5]

Finally, administrative activities may be dispersed among various assistants and advisers. There is no clear line of demarcation that can always be drawn among those responsible for guiding an organization or unit and those responsible for helping them do this. As organizations become larger and more complex and as more specialized forms of

5. Note discussion of "The specialist-administrator" in "People-in-Organizations: Formal Aspects" (Chapt. 15).

administrative techniques are used, the circle of those with some form
of administrative responsibility may widen. In highly decentralized and
more democratic organizations it becomes still larger.

3. GENERALISTS vs. SPECIALISTS

There is also a wide consensus on the concept of administrators as
generalists rather than specialists. This concept is particularly applicable
to the higher level administrators, whose responsibilities usually include
the coordination of the work of many specialists or experts. It may also
be applied to other administrators as well—albeit in a more limited sense.
Even though they operate at a lower level of generality, they are usually
involved in the coordination of the work of different people with special
problems and viewpoints. Also, in handling relations with the external
environment of their units, they usually deal with a more varied array
of problems than faced by their subordinates.

At the higher levels of organizations, where both external and internal
relations are highly varied, administrators can never hope to master the
details of all the problems with which they deal. The responsibility of
keeping track of what is going on in many fields makes it impossible for
the administrator to become, or remain, an up-to-date specialist in any
field. In this sense, the top administrator's ignorance of many details is
usually one of his outstanding characteristics. The top administrator who
proudly proclaims that he knows everything that is going on in his
organization (even without reference to its immediate environment) is
invariably deceiving himself. The depth of his belief is probably exceeded
only by the depth of his ignorance concerning those aspects of his organization's activities which he has neglected.

Yet the generalist-specialist distinction is also subject to various widely
accepted limitations.

First of all, identifying someone as a generalist does not tell us what
kind of generalist he is. Certainly, there are many varieties. At one extreme, there is the jack-of-all-trades who knows almost nothing about
anything or flits aimlessly from one problem to another. At the other,
there is the one who is able to fit diverse activities into a general framework.[6]

Second, administrators usually specialize in the problems of the organizations or units they are expected to guide. Administration has no significance unless specifically oriented toward a specific organization. "You

6. Note discussion of different generalist roles in "People-in-Organizations:
Informal Aspects" (Chapt. 16).

can't administer administration."[7] Accordingly, administrators usually try to develop expertise in the specific purposes, problems and procedures of their organizations or units.

Finally, the generalist administrator may be something of a specialist in administration. He may be a specialist in handling one or more of the specialized tools of administration. This is not quite the same, it should be added, as being a professional production engineer, accountant or job analyst; in the former instance the expertise relates rather to the use of experts in these technical fields. The administrator may also be something of a specialist in the more general arts of governance. Expertise of this sort may come from broad experience in a variety of administrative posts, from study and learning and even from research and theory. In this sense, becoming a generalist may itself be a form of intense specialization.

B. *The Common Characteristics*

WHAT DO ADMINISTRATORS do when involved in the governance of organizations?

This question is a tricky one. When we look at administrative activities closely, we may see a variety of activities by the same administrator, a greater variety by different administrators in the same organization and still greater variety in different organizations in different countries and at different periods in history.

Despite this variety, there is growing consensus concerning certain characteristics that are common to all administrative activity. These will now be presented in a series of basic propositions, with a subsequent discussion of some of the more fundamental ideas in these propositions. In the following chapters these fundamental ideas, in turn, will be elaborated upon—but with less effort to remain within the area of the emerging consensus.

1. SOME BASIC PROPOSITIONS

The following propositions do not include all the valid or useful statements that have been or can be usefully made concerning administration. They are mainly of a rather obvious and axiomatic character. Instead of being looked upon as a revelation, they can be taken for granted

7. This is adapted from the title of Wendell Johnson's article "You Can't Write Writing" (1954).

by those who are seriously engaged in the solution of administrative problems, the conduct of administrative research or the improvement of administrative education. They are precisely the kinds of propositions that serve as the articulate or inarticulate major premises of experienced administrators. In one form or another, they are implicitly or explicitly stated in the best of modern administrative research and theory.

1. Administration, or governance, is the complex process through which administrators try to guide the activities of people in an organization toward formulating or achieving some accepted pattern of purposes.
2. The purposes of an organization are multiple, are given different degrees of emphasis by different members of the organization and are constantly changing in response to new situations.
3. The formulation and achievement of such purposes are blocked by conflicts, obstacles or changing circumstances within the organization or in the relations between the organization and its environment.
4. To achieve results, both organizations and their administrators try to cope with this blockage through the development, maintenance and use of power, or influence, with varying degrees of authority and responsibility.
5. In dealing with the members of an organization and with the external environment, administrators engage in or make use of the following:
    —the broad processes of making decisions and communicating information,
    —the fundamental administrative processes of planning, activating and evaluating, and
    —various technical administrative processes relating to production, budgeting and accounting, personnel, distribution of output, general internal services or research.

An aspect of all these propositions is that each can be reduced to the form of "A *is* B." In conformance with customary usage, the "is" may be interpreted as including "has been" and "will be," plus "any place." The word "always" is thus implied. If "always" seems overstrong, let us realize that it means "always to some degree." The propositions themselves are not confined to any particular degree. Nor are they limited to those variables which we are not as yet very adept at measuring, whether by cardinal numbers, scale analysis or other methods.

It will be noted that none of the propositions in the definition appears in the form "A *should be* B." They are not statements of value in the sense that the stater expresses his delight or regret that A is B. Centering on the *is*, they are conceptual and factual statements, not ethical statements.

Nevertheless, these propositions have many "should be" implications. The selection of these propositions from among a host of other possibilities is a way of saying that a serious analysis of administration *should* include these matters as starting points. This act of selection (as well as the selection of administration as a field of analysis) is itself an expression of certain ethical values and goals of the author. If A *is* B, one *should not* operate on the assumption that it is not. If B is composed of varying amounts of X, Y, and Z, one *should* under certain circumstances distinguish between different kinds of B. Moreover, many of these propositions deal even more directly with values. The purposes referred to in the first three propositions provide a basis for describing all organizational goals, "ultimate" as well as "instrumental." Thus they, in essence, assert as a *fact* that people in organizations are deeply concerned with *values*. It implies, as will be made clear later, that administrators are deeply concerned with adjustments among competing values.

These propositions do not constitute a model in the sense of Weber's "ideal type." There is no question of determining how administration at any particular time or place may conform to or depart from the model. There is thus no problem of building a bridge between model and reality to handle the distance that may be observed between the two. If the propositions are valid, *there can be no such distance.*

But are these propositions useful starting points for understanding the practice of administration?

To help answer this question, it is first essential to explain some of the underlying concepts embodied in them.

2. PEOPLE, ORGANIZATIONS, ENVIRONMENTS

Underlying all the propositions is the theme that administration involves people. In administration things are not merely *done*. "Administrators try to guide the activities of people." No matter what specific language be used, this modern approach to administration rips aside the veil of anonymity and abstraction. It breaks away from older ideas of the administrative world as one inhabited solely by structures, diagrams, rules and regulations. It parts company with those who have seen no difference between the management of men and the management of machines and materials. The material resources of an organization are important only because they are used by people (or "human resources"). This approach ties in with the Parsons-Shils view of social action as "the action of an individual actor or of a collectivity of actors" (1951, p. 4). It obliges us to relate the study of administration to the findings, controversies, and problems of all the disciplines and quasi-disciplines which throw any light on the behavior and misbehavior, the greatness and brutishness, the irrationality and irrationality, the predictability and unpredictability of human beings. Nothing human is alien to administration. In this sense "human relations" is not a specialized technique; it is the very kernel of administration!

Moreover, administration involves organizations. The administrators are themselves members of organizations. They try to guide the activities of "people in organizations." They are interested in formulating and achieving the purposes of organizations. It is within organizations and the various formal and informal units or subdivisions of organizations that administrators occupy various "roles" or—what is almost the same—"organizational positions." For purposes of analysis it is often desirable to shift attention from individuals and focus it instead upon these roles or positions.

The administrator himself, it should be added, is often an integral part of a group, not an isolated individual. "The President Roosevelt of history, for example," as Bentley wrote with reference to the first of the American Presidents by that name, "is a very large amount of official activity involving many people" (1949, p. 176).

An organization, in turn, is not a closed system. It exists within a certain environment. According to the basic propositions, the environment may give rise to "conflicts, obstacles or changing circumstances." Administrators try to influence both the organization and its environment. In the form of climate, flora, fauna, and all sorts of physical resources, nature is a part of every organization's environment. Man is usually a more active part. The human environment is as broad as the community, state, society, and culture in which an organization operates. More narrowly, an organization's environment also takes the form of the "superior" organs of any larger organization to which it belongs. It consists of "outside" individuals, groups and organizations acting to influence it in one way or another. These outsiders—which may include controllers and opponents as well as clients, suppliers, and advisers—enter into direct relationships with the organization. Often, their interaction goes so far as to be called "intervention." Hence we cannot reserve exclusively to the members of an organization the privilege of participation in its activities. Outsiders, as well as administrators and other members, may also be involved in shaping the pattern or an organization's purposes and the choice of measures designed to achieve them.

These three interrelated concepts of *people* in *organizations* in *environments* are an integral part of the emerging consensus in modern administrative thought. We have probably passed the stage when a serious thinker in this field could ignore the human basis of administration, the organizational framework, or the ecology of organizations.

Nevertheless, much still remains to be done in analyzing these three basic elements. In the five chapters of Part IV, "The People," I shall go somewhat beyond the present consensus and develop these concepts on the basis of the progress already made in various fields of intellectual effort.

3. PURPOSES

The importance of purposefulness in the administration of organizations is universally recognized. In administrative life it is reflected in repeated exhortations to "clarify our objectives," "figure out just where we're going," or "get those fellows down there (or up there) to understand what our purposes really are." It is indicated by the large number of terms that are used to convey more or less similar ideas concerning purpose: objective, goal, target, norm, aim, end, intention, and function. One or another of these terms is used in most formal definitions or administration. The theme of purposes runs throughout the basic propositions.

The first proposition, it should be noted, refers to "formulating or achieving . . . purposes." This recognizes that higher level administrators may be more involved in broader or longer range purpose formulation, with lower level administrators often paying major attention to intermediate purposes or means. The proposition expresses the modern rejection of the idea that administration must necessarily be limited to narrowly conceived means of attaining fixed and predetermined purposes. It expresses the widespread acceptance of the inevitable interrelating of means and ends. It recognizes that administrators are often concerned with both and that the process of achieving purposes may itself lead to some kind of reformulation.

Throughout the propositions runs a strong emphasis upon the multiplicity of organizational purposes. This multiplicity reflects the diversity of interests by both members and outsiders and the many links in any purpose chain designed to satisfy any given interest. Any one purpose, moreover, may be "given different degrees of emphasis by different members of the organization." Purposes are "constantly changing in response to new situations."

Although the individual members of an organization usually have many differing individual purposes, these different purposes are brought together into an "accepted pattern of purposes." At one extreme, this pattern may consist of widespread dedication to common goals. At the other extreme, it may reflect *quid pro quo* bargains which give different returns to different members as rewards for their cooperation. Similarly, some purposes may be accepted with enthusiasm, some only through pressure. Some may be but grudgingly acceptable.

One of the great forward strides in modern administrative thought has been the increasing attention to the various categories of organizational purpose. Even those who see efficiency or profitability as the major purpose base their claim on the thesis that it serves to unify other purposes. Many kinds of purposes are thereby recognized. More explicit recognition has been provided by various classifications of objectives (Mooney and Reiley, 1931, p. 3-4; Davis, 1951, p. 90-126). There is now widespread acceptance of the idea of "a hierarchy of purposes" or "pyramid of values," as first presented by Waldo (1948, p. 204-205).

The kinds of performance purposes most frequently referred to may be listed as follows.

1. The satisfaction of various interests
2. Output of services or goods
3. Efficiency or profitability
4. Investment in organizational viability
5. Mobilization of resources
6. Observance of codes
7. Technical or administrative rationality

In Part V, "The Purposes," this set of purpose categories is presented as the "global matrix" of organizational purposes. Each of the seven elements is broken down into many component elements, together with a presentation of the many different terms used to express the same ideas. The fourth element—investment in the organization itself—provides a direct link with desired changes in the organization and its relation to the environment. Accordingly, the desired performance pattern of any organization may be expressed in some combination of these elements and sub-elements. Similarly, it is shown, the same concepts are used in formulating criteria for evaluating the performance of organizations and administrators. This effort at synthesis is feasible only because of the groundwork already laid by many writers in various disciplines.

4. PROCESSES

The "process approach" to administration is one of the great unifying trends in modern administrative thought, if not in all scientific inquiry. Yet to understand what is meant by this term, and by the reference to "complex process" in the first proposition, we must distinguish among three complementary concepts of process.

A. *Change and becoming.* The first concept is that of the administrative process as a continuing, ever changing activity. By this approach the realm of administration is one of flux and becoming, like the universe as Heraclitus saw it many centuries ago: "Into this same river you could not step twice, for other waters are flowing." It consists not of separate actions as disparate entities, but of interlocking activities. One activity blends into another. It is hard to find the beginning and still harder to find the end. Every achievement creates certain difficulties. Every solution creates new problems. Neither people nor purposes ever remain immobile. Organizations are born and they die. Their members enter and leave; of those who remain, some grow wiser and all get older. If the process of change is not evident from outside or is not formally legitimized, it takes place beneath the surface. This does not imply losing sight of the more static aspects of administration. They must be included as an essential part of the picture—just as the shifting sandbars and leafy banks are part of a rushing river. As Commons wrote about economics, "The organization of activity is merely the more stabilized aspect of activity. The form is part of the process" (1951, p. 21). Or, as put more positively by L. L. Whyte, "there is no sharp division between structure and process, because structure is a limiting case of process" (1950, p. 19-20).

To analyze and describe a process is far from easy. It is like trying to capture the flow of action on a football field with a still camera. We can make meaningful efforts to record what is going on only if we have instruments comparable to a battery of movie cameras equipped with color film and telescopic and panoramic lenses. But even thus the dynamics of motion, causation, and uncertainty are apt to elude us as spectators. The players and the captains "feel" what is happening. But even they probably never learn what is happening all over the field or why certain things have happened.

B. *The processes of various disciplines.* In his puny efforts to understand the ongoing flow of events, man tries to slice up his universe into various specific processes: physical, chemical, physiological, psychological, sociological, political, economic, administrative, and many others. Each of these represents a different aspect of, or a different way of thinking about, the same ongoing stream of action and becoming. Hence a strong emphasis upon the boundaries of academic disciplines—while helpful in the proper division of labor, funds and prestige within institutions of higher learning—can easily lead to aridity, sterility, and a breakdown of intellectual vigor within any discipline. This is particularly true in the field of administration. If one feels constrained from bringing to the study of administration concepts that have been developed by economists, political scientists, sociologists, psychologists, anthropologists and even biologists, mathematicians, and logicians, one cannot undertake a creative and meaningful study of administration.

This interweaving of "disciplinary processes" may be illustrated by a few comments concerning the interrelationship between administration and economic and political processes. The economic process is generally regarded as relating to the production, exchange, utilization, or accumulation of wealth or of goods and services. Yet the overwhelming bulk of goods and services are produced by organizations. These organizations could not operate unless they were administered. Thus, administration is an inevitable part of the economic process. From a broader point of view, the economic process can be seen as one of decision-making in the face of scarce resources. This conception is well presented in Lionel Robbins' famous definition of economics: "the science which studies human behavior as a relationship between ends and scarce means which have alternative uses" (1948, p. 16). Since the scarcity of means available for achieving organizational purposes is an inevitable part of administrative life, the economic process in turn becomes an integral part of the administrative process.

A similar interweaving is found with respect to political and administrative processes. In the more narrow sense, the political process is one of getting control of the machinery of the state through elections or any other means. Most of these means require some form of organization. Since any such organization must be administered, administration necessarily enters the political process. From a broader point of view, politics can be regarded as the general process of mobilizing, maintaining and using influence or power. In this sense politics enters into the life of all organizations, and thereby into the very essence of the administrative process.

Accordingly, the serious student of administration faces a formidable task. He must penetrate the terminological jungle developed in these many other fields. He must keep abreast not only of the growing flood of administrative literature, but also of a still greater flow of thought and research in many other fields. Moreover, to adapt conceptions from other disciplines to the needs of administration, he must sometimes enter boldly into these other domains and himself formulate hypotheses, conceptions, and theories which he cannot always obtain ready-made from those who are less aware of the needs in administrative thought.

c. *The administrative processes.* While administration as a whole may be seen as a "disciplinary process" in its own right, it too is sliced up into processes such as Fayol's "elements" or Gulick's POSDCORB. The maturation of administrative thought brings with it an increasing, rather than a decreasing, number of administrative processes. Thus, as indicated in the fifth basic proposition, modern administrative thought seems to distinguish among at least three levels of administrative processes. None of these replaces the others. Each represents different cross-sections of, or supplementary ways of looking at, the same multidimensional reality. The fact that some analyses conceive of administration in terms of one of these processes alone merely attests to the importance of specialized intellectual labor. It need not constitute an explicit—and cannot constitute an acceptable—rejection of the relevance of other processes.[8]

At a high level of generality we find the processes of decision-making and communication. The analysis of these processes may be relevant to administration even when there is no explicit recognition of any differences between administrative and nonadministrative decision-making and communication.

At a more specific level we find such processes as planning, activating, and evaluating.[9] Each of these, it may be noted, involves decision-making and communication. More important, each is part of a "seamless web" with three aspects: planning, activating, and evaluating. Frequently, these aspects of behavior take place simultaneously. When there is a time difference, there is no fixed sequence; any one may be followed by either or both of the others. Moreover, most larger (or molar) behavior units tend to be composed of smaller (or molecular) behavior units of the same type.[10] The planning aspect itself involves (a) making a plan for plan-

8. Thus, although Simon has preferred to concentrate upon the analysis of the process of decision-making and choice, he has never claimed that all aspects of administration must be subsumed under decision-making. In *Models of Man* (p. viii) for example, he refers to the dual mechanisms of influence and choice.

9. "Planning" is here used in the sense of "developing organizational purpose-fulness." Hence, it relates to all the categories of organizational purpose. "Activating" refers to all forms of initiating action. It therefore includes in a broader context "control" (in the sense of directing action), Fayol's "command," Gulick's "direction," and Simon's "mechanism of influence." The concepts of "activating" and "evaluating" represent a separate handling of two ideas often lumped together in the idea of "control" (in the sense of checking up on action and where needed, initiating corrective action). When these fundamental processes of planning, activating and evaluating are applied to the purpose of organizational survival or growth, we have the process traditionally described as "organizing." Their application to an organization's operations yields "coordinating."

10. In somewhat different terms (and at the level of individual instead of

ning, (b) activating the people and mental processes needed to develop the plan and (c) evaluating the plan that has been developed.

Finally, at a much more specialized level, we find a growing number of technical processes. These include production management, accounting, budgeting and finance, operations research, personnel management, and marketing. Some of these fields, particularly accounting, have developed into mature professions. Others are moving toward some degree of professional status. With the passage of time, old techniques in these fields are constantly being refurbished. The fields themselves are constantly being subdivided; it is already impossible for any one accountant to achieve significant expertise in all of accounting's many subdivisions. In addition, new techniques are constantly being devised. All of these constitute additional administrative processes which both contribute to and are based upon the processes of decision-making and communication and of planning, activating and evaluating.

These administrative processes are the central concern of administrative rationality. Accordingly, decision-making, communicating, planning, activating, and evaluating are discussed in "Rationality: Administrative Processes" (Chapt. 29). Although adequate attention to the administrative tools goes beyond the scope of this book, the managerial aspects of using such tools are discussed at many points. Thus the discussion of service specifications in Chapter 23 is related to job classification, merit rating and program budgeting. The discussion of costs in Chapter 24 and "mobilization logic" and "use logic" in Chapter 26 is related to budgeting and accounting.

5. COOPERATION, CONFLICT, POWER

The idea of cooperation is implicit in the entire set of propositions. An organization, as Barnard has pointed out, is a form of cooperative system. An accepted pattern of purposes is both an antecedent and a consequence of cooperation among the members of an organization. The maintenance of cooperation, it is generally agreed, is a major task of the administrator.

The modern recognition of the importance of cooperation developed largely as part of the "human relations" revolt against mechanistic models of administration. With certain conspicuous exceptions, such as Follett,

---

organizational behavior) this method of analyzing behavior is presented in G. A. Miller, Eugene Galanter, and K. H. Pribram (1960), particularly in Chapt. 2, "The Unit of Analysis," p. 21-39. The "molar-molecular" terminology was developed by Tolman (1951).

this often led to a neglect of conflict and power (or influence). Indeed, both of these ideas have long been sources of discomfort to many people. Like sex under the Victorians, they have often been regarded as subjects that, while obviously important, are not to be openly discussed in polite society.

The modern tendency in administrative thought is to accept conflict as an inevitable concomitant of cooperative action in organizations. Hence the third proposition states that the formulation and achievement of an organization's purpose pattern are "blocked by conflicts, obstacles or changing circumstances within the organization or in the relations between the organization and its environment." Indeed, any "accepted pattern of purposes" is itself embedded in a broader setting of divergent purposes. The accepted pattern itself always contains an element of open or latent conflict among its various elements. While conflict may weaken or destroy the cooperation required for organizational action, some forms and degrees of conflict may unify an organization and strengthen cooperation among its members.

Another aspect of the emerging consensus in administrative thought is a more frank and open approach to power (or influence). A distinctive characteristic of any organization is that it enables people to develop the power to do things together that they could not do so well, or at all, separately. This power is needed to cope with blockage and conflicts and achieve results despite them. Thus a distinctive characteristic of administrative action is the effort to influence—or activate—people and groups in the organization and the organization's environment. In whichever direction it may be exercised, it is now recognized that power should be distinguished from authority and that varying relationships may exist between authority and responsibility. Hence the proposition referring to "the development, maintenance and use of power, or influence, with varying degrees of authority and responsibility" by both organizations and their administrators.

To understand the dynamics of any organization, it is not enough to know its accepted purpose pattern. It is also essential to know something about its internal and external conflicts and the distribution of power within it. These are referred to when people talk about the "private politics" of a corporation, association, university, or trade union. They become public politics only when they are brought more fully into the clear, as often happens in the case of government agencies and political parties.

These two themes of power and conflict are fundamental to all aspects of organizations and their administration. Accordingly, before entering into the detailed materials of Part IV and Part V, I shall develop each of them at greater length in "The Conflict-Cooperation Nexus" (Chapt. 11) and "The Power-Responsibility-Authority Triangle" (Chapt. 12).

c. *The Special and Unique Characteristics*

ANY DISCUSSION of the common characteristics of administration is apt to lead to the fallacious idea that administration is always the same and that differences are unimportant. On the other hand, single-minded attention to differences may lead to the equally fallacious denial of similarities. In modern administrative thought the tendency is to escape this dilemma by rejecting an either-or position. This means recognizing that two administrative situations may at one and the same time be *both* similar in some respects and different in others.

1. DANGER OF IGNORING DIFFERENCES

The danger of ignoring differences in administrative situations is dramatized by the mishaps of mobility. A successful Army officer becomes a business executive—and a flop. A successful business executive enters government service—and becomes a lost soul. A government official who has been successful in Washington or London is sent to Africa—and falls on his face. Or else, the individual stays in the same position, and the difference arises in his immediate environment. The able administrator of a small unit becomes unable to operate when he gets a new superior or when he himself is promoted to a higher administrative post. The founder of a small firm may be out of his depth when, as a result of his own achievements, it becomes a giant corporation. The brilliant organizer of revolution and war may, like Leon Trotsky, prove (and be pushed) out of place amid the more sober and less exciting tasks of consolidation and construction. Nor is administrative technology itself, for all its apparent impersonality, immune to the challenge of administrative differences. Methods of budgeting, recruitment and work simplification that are successful in one organization or country will often prove unworkable in another organization or country without adaptation or reconstruction.

Differences are also dramatized by the many misunderstandings that develop in interorganizational relationships. The chief of one section often deals with the chief of another section on the assumption that both sections operate in the same way. In dealing with other organizations administrators often assume a common language, or a common set of premises and values. This is an organizational variety of egocentrism; it is the fallacy of thinking that others are built in one's own image. It can lead to remarkable misunderstandings.

The importance of differences is accentuated by the fact that in a certain sense every organization—including those which are quite colorless as well as those with a highly developed sense of mission—has a unique personality of its own. To the outsider looking in, this quality may be lost. To him, everything may appear very similar to the administration of other organizations—just as most Chinese may look alike to a German or most Pakistanis may look alike to a Chinese. But when the outsider becomes an insider, when he passes through his period of groping and fumbling as a new initiate, when he "learns the ropes" and finds out "what makes things tick," when he in fact becomes a part of the spirit of the place, he will smile indulgently—and with some degree of justification—at the poor fool on the outside (be he professor, student or "practical man") who thinks he knows what administration in this place is all about.

On the other hand, the desire to feel that "we are different" is so great that actual differences are often vastly exaggerated. The need to regard one's self as different from others is one of the basic human needs, as discussed in more detail in "The Human Beings" (Chapt. 14). In organizations the satisfaction of this need is necessary in order to establish the identity of the group and provide the emotional basis for cooperation. Such satisfactions may be found either by being different or by seeing differences where they do not exist. I remember the government official of another country who tried to convince me that *his* government was different because, unlike the government of the United States of America, it was subject to influence by pressure groups. It took some time before his passion for difference was satisfied by finding more important—and more accurate—factors.

Similarly, the feeling that "they are different" may also be concretized in fallacious forms. This often happens when an American, for example, goes abroad as a technical adviser in a country just starting the industrialization process. The "culture shock" of finding certain differences in organizational activity in such a country may lead him to think that everything is different. He may see many differences that exist only in his imagination. He can compare what he sees only with his own image of his own country, which may be clouded by sheer ignorance and lack of self-knowledge. It is often easy for him to see the mote in a foreigner's eye without suspecting that the same kind of mote exists in his own eye. In any case, his standard of comparison will be his own limited field of experience.

2. BASES OF DIFFERENCES

A traditional approach to the differences in administration is based upon a simplistic differentiation which parallels the growth of special educational programs. This yields a taxonomy providing major distinctions among business, public, and military administration and minor distinctions among the administration of churches, schools, hospitals, libraries, welfare agencies, cooperatives, political parties, and others. As the basis for the division of labor in educational institutions, this has a lot to commend it, for it helps to focus attention on some of the special problems of administering these organizations.

But this "pigeonhole" form of classification does not go very far as an analytical tool for the study of differences. By itself, it provides no guidelines to the vast amount of differences among organizations in each category and at different places in any such organization. To be useful, it must be supplemented by additional methods of classifying various aspects of organizations and their administration. In other words it must be converted into a "depth" or "multifacet" classification. A multidimensional topology of this type would have to provide for the identification of differences in

- the characteristics not only of organizational membership and structure but also of environments and environmental relations;
- the purposes of organizations;
- the use of administrative processes; and
- the patterns of cooperation, conflict and power.

It should be immediately noted that these four categories are identical with those used in the previous section as the basis for identifying the most common characteristics of administration. The analysis of variety has not taken us away from, but has rather brought us back to, the unity of our subject matter. To put it another way, the basic propositions set forth in the first part of section B not only set forth the invariants of administration in all organizations. They also provide bases for discovering the variants. The variant factors are the constants themselves as they appear in different forms and patterns.

The special characteristics of any given group of organizations can usually be established without using facets at all of these four levels of analysis. It would never be necessary to use all facets at each of these levels even to identify the unique characteristics of administration in a given organization (or unit thereof) at a certain period of time in a given environment. How far one may want to go in using this instrument at any one time will depend upon the specific situation, the purpose of the analysis, and the availability of information. How far one may be able to go will depend also upon his skill in using the kind of concepts presented in the subsequent chapters.

D. *Key Terminological Problems*

To ROUND OUT our preliminary answer to "What is administration?" and prepare the ground for more detailed analysis of common, special and unique characteristics, it is essential to try to recognize the terminological ambiguities surrounding the terms "organization" and "administration." In so doing, I shall also present a consistent set of terminological preferences. Many of these may run counter to established usage in specific areas of administration in various countries. The reason is that much of present usage has developed within the confines of one or another specific area. My purpose is to produce a synthesis which, without ignoring the special characteristics of each field, can be fruitfully used in all of them.

1. *"ORGANIZATION" AND RELATED TERMS*

The term "organization" has thus far been used without any explicit definition. This gap must now be remedied. In addition, it is desirable to distinguish between "organization" and such closely related terms as "system," "bureaucracy," "institution," and "government."

A. *Organization.* In general usage the word "organization" has three different meanings:

i. The act of organizing—that is, of establishing an organization or changing its structure;
ii. Administration or management; or
iii. A certain kind of group—particularly a "formal organization."

For the first meaning, I think it more logical to use the participle "organizing." The second usage was developed by those who made the mistake of regarding organizing as the single or the major administrative process. It is already fading out; its demise should be accelerated. The third meaning—particularly in the sense of a "formal organization"—is the one used here.

But what kind of group is a formal organization? For our purposes, it is *not* a group in the sense of:

  i. an abstract category of thought, such as "blue-eyed people" or even all people who are presumed to have a common interest, let us say, in studying administration or lowering taxes;
 ii. a collection of individuals held together only by their common support for, and common attachment to, a religious, political, or intellectual leader;
iii. a "reference group"—that is, those people whose values an individual may refer to as he determines his own course of action;
 iv. any type of system; or
  v. any type of cooperation among people.

In positive terms, a formal organization may be regarded as a group or cooperative system, with the following characteristics:

  i. An accepted pattern of purposes (as already discussed)

 ii. A sense of identification or belonging

Both the directors and the workers of a telephone company regard themselves as part of an organization. This sense of identification is heightened by the felt distinction between "in-group" and "out-group." Despite their crucial importance to the organization, the people who merely talk on the telephone are "outsiders."

iii. Continuity of interaction

The members of an organization interact with each other with some minimum degree of regularity and continuity. Members leave an organization by falling below the required minimum—as when a factory worker does not appear on the job any more or when a union member stops paying dues.

 iv. Differentiation of function

The activities of members of organizations are based upon some minimum amount of formal differentiation of roles. In small organizations this differentiation may be rudimentary. In larger organizations it becomes elaborate.

  v. Conscious integration

The divided parts of an organization are held together not only by spontaneous cooperation but also by the conscious efforts of certain members responsible for bringing or holding them together. These, of course, are the administrators themselves, who bring people together for the formulation and achievement of an organization's purposes.

This definition necessarily involves the boundary-line problem of distinguishing between members and nonmembers or, in other terms, between "insiders" and "outsiders." The problem is peripheral in the case of organizations in which people work on a full-time basis. The employment relationship itself is a certificate of membership. It is acute, however, in the case of political and religious organizations, which invariably aim at the conscious integration of large numbers of people whose interaction may be irregular and discontinuous. Thus the person whose interaction with a political party may be expressed only on Election Day will usually be regarded as a "follower" of that party, a special form of "outsider," rather than as a member of the organization. A similar problem may also exist within an organization whenever a specific individual is assigned to part-time work in each of two subdivisions of the organization. Here, he is likely to be regarded as an outsider by both.

This discussion has already gone beyond mere terminology and has entered the sphere of organizational analysis. This analysis will be continued in the subsequent discussions of the formal and informal aspects of organizations (Chapts. 15, 16).

B. *System*. The term "system" is usually used to refer to "any set of interrelating elements." In this sense "system" may refer to

i. Any one of the concrete systems dealt with by general systems theorists from a solar system to the molecule and electron and from a cell to an organ, personality, small group, formal organization, political system, economic system, and social system;
ii. A system of rules or procedures influencing behavior; or
iii. A theoretical system bringing together various concepts and generalizations for the purpose of description, explanation, or prediction.

Any of these systems may be regarded as having boundaries (although these may be regions rather than lines) and as being either "open" or "closed."

Thus a formal organization is one type of system. Together with supplier, clients, and others beyond its boundaries, it may constitute a "cooperative system" in Barnard's sense. It may use various systems of rules and procedures. Its activities may presumably be explained by a theoretical system dealing with organizations and their administration.

C. *Bureaucracy*. In social science parlance, as distinguished from colloquial usage, the term "bureaucracy" is widely used to refer to certain aspects of complex formal organization. The most important of these aspects are the detailed subdivision of labor, hierarchical relationships, and general rules.

Some writers on the subject of bureaucracy, however, make the mistake of confusing bureaucracy with the entirety of certain formal organizations. This leads to an ignoring of certain important aspects of large-scale organizations—particularly the roles of nonbureaucrats. For larger organizations I find it desirable to make a threefold distinction between members of directorates, top executives, and bureaucrats.[11]

D. *Institution.* The term "institution" is used in at least two ways that are directly relevant to our discussion. It may refer to:

i. A certain type of organization—namely, one which is important in society, has lasted a long time or has a strong sense of identity and tradition—or a cluster of such organizations (such as governmental, educational, and religious institutions); or

ii. Certain practices or traditions, which may be observed within organizations or without respect to organizational boundaries (such as the institutions of dating, marriage, and divorce).

The idea of "institutionalizing" something may comprehend either of these meanings. To institutionalize a group of informal advisors means to bring them within the confines of a formal organization. To institutionalize certain practices means to regularize them or to embody them in formal procedures.

The "administration of institutions" clearly relates only to the first of these meanings; it is a category of general administration. The idea of "institution building"—for example, in the sense that the building of new institutions is important for underdeveloped countries—is also usually used to relate to institutions in the organizational sense. The use of more honorific terms in the name of an organization—such as institute, center, foundation or authority—is often resorted to as a way of helping create a public image of a strong, durable institution. The term "establishment" is often used to refer pejoratively to a cluster of such institutions or their bureaucracies.

E. *Government.* What is the difference between "administration" in the sense here conceived and "government"?

To answer this question we must recognize that the word "government" may be used for at least five different referents:

i. Certain high officials of a state or the state itself;

11. This distinction is already used in "The Dispersion of Power in Organizations" (Chapt. 3).

ii. Exercising authority over the people of a state—in the sense of "running the country" or "ruling";

iii. The cluster of public agencies which comprise a state apparatus, or a central group thereof;

iv. Directing the state apparatus; or

v. Directing any organization, an activity for which the Board of Governors of a university or a hospital may be responsible.

The last two of these meanings relate to the administrative activity undertaken at the highest levels of authority by the members of directorates. They can thus be regarded as an important part of administration. To escape these restrictions, I have used "governance" to refer to the administrative process at any level in any organization.

2. "ADMINISTRATION" AND RELATED TERMS

At an early point I stated my intention of using "administration" and "management" as synonyms. In addition to management, however, there are many other words that have often been used in a similar fashion. I shall therefore try to explain the problems in this area and my preferences with respect to each of them.

A. *Managers and executives.* Our first terminological problem is what to do with three pairs of words: administrator and administration, manager and management, and executive and execution.

With respect to the first two pairs, no consistent usage can be found. For some, "administration" refers to the activities of those at the higher level of responsibility and authority in an organization. In the British civil service, for example, the "administrative class" is composed of officials at the top of the bureaucratic hierarchy, while the "executive class" takes care of the lower "management" functions. In the field of business, this usage is often reversed. Thus Brech, a British writer in the business field, maintains that "administration" should be seen as merely a part of "management." He regards it as a "useful label" for certain "tools of management" (1953, p. 15-16).

Under these circumstances, I have found it desirable to drop the differentiation between the first two pairs of terms and use "administrator" and "manager" more or less interchangeably. By this usage either word may be used—with appropriate modification—to refer to any hierarchic level or any type of administrative or managerial activity.

Unlike "administration" and "management," the term "execution" is rarely used as a direct analogue of its paired member, "executive." It usually appears as a member of the pair "planning (or policy-making) and execution." Although I see no inherent objection to this use of the term, it should not be used too hastily to gloss over a large number of separable administrative processes.

As for "executive," I have arbitrarily used it as part of the term "top executive" for those officials who are immediately below the level of the board of directors of a corporation or the cabinet of a government and above the level of the bureaucrats. This is more in keeping with American business terminology than with British public administration terminology.

The term "executive" also has a special meaning in the field of government, as explained in the following paragraphs.

B. *Executive, legislative, and judicial.* One of the most time-honored distinctions in political science is the distinction between the executive, the legislature and the judiciary. This distinction was first made by Aristotle, was developed by Locke and many others, and was dramatized by Montesquieu in his theory of "the separation of powers." It has led to considerable debate concerning the desirability of alternative types of relationships between the various branches of government. It has also led to an increasing tendency to distinguish between certain processes or functions rather than between branches of government. This makes it easier to recognize that legislatures may legitimately engage in certain executive or judicial functions, courts in legislative and executive functions, and executive agencies in legislative and judicial functions.

However, the emphasis on executive processes, coupled with the interchangeability of "executive" and "administrative" has given rise to a number of ambiguities in the use of the term "administrative process" as applied to government.

The first ambiguity is that "administrative process" is sometimes used very broadly to refer to the totality of all activities in the executive branch of government. In this sense "administration" becomes equivalent to the work done by the executive branch of the government. Thus all employees in the executive branch become executive officials or administrators. The idea of administration as an activity of people in organizations responsible for getting work done by the organization vanishes in a fog of ambiguity.

The second difficulty derives from the use of "administrative process" in a much more narrow sense. It may refer to the operations of certain administrative tribunals as distinguished from other executive agencies (Landis, 1938); or the operations of any executive agencies which promulgate "administrative law," that is, general rules and regulations which have the full force of statutory law (Schwartz, 1958).

These two ambiguities contribute, in part, to an explanation of the phenomenon that many experts in public administration have found ample room for important and creative work without coming very near to many of the administrative or managerial problems of government agencies in the same sense that they are dealt with by writers on business administration. Be that as it may, it would seem more desirable to use words other than "administration" to refer to these other areas. There is nothing lost in referring to the executive branch, executive functions, executive tribunals, the laws establishing executive agencies, executive rule-making, the laws establishing procedures for executive rule-making, and the rules and regulations produced by executive agencies. With laws establishing "administration" and "administrative law" relieved of all these unnecessary burdens, it now becomes possible—without adding additional ambiguity—to recognize the existence of administrative activity in executive, legislative, and judicial agencies.

Terminological clarification along those lines will also make easier constructive use of the legislative-executive-judicial distinction outside the sphere of government. In the sense that it deals with the process of formal rule-making, the legislative process is one that takes place within all organizations, not merely in those organizations or units representing holders of formal authority. Executive action takes place in all organizations. Nor is the judicial process—in the sense of the adjudication of individual claims, complaints and appeals—limited to differentiated or publicly labeled judicial bodies. In industry, judicial functions are often carried on not only by individual administrators but also by management-labor committees and mediation or arbitration boards (*Brown*).

c. *Direction, supervision, and control.* The word "direction" has been widely used to refer to two different activities:

i. Administration at the higher levels, a meaning associated with the use of such terms as director, director-general, and board of directors; or

ii. The issuing of "directions," that is, orders and instructions, or even the orders and instructions themselves.

The word "supervision" has also been given two meanings:

i. Administration at the lower levels, a meaning closely associated with the fact that intermediate and lower officials are sometimes "supervisors"; and

ii. Certain limited types of administrative activity, particularly the process of "looking over" what has been done or controlling.

In my judgment both these terms are useful to help distinguish between various levels of administration. Thus I have used the term "directorates" to refer generically to government cabinets, executive committees of boards of directors and any other body which stands above the top executives and below the general assemblies and larger boards from which they derive their formal authority. I see no need for using "direction" as a synonym for orders.

Similarly, there is no need for "supervision" to refer to certain aspects of administrative activity. It is more convenient to use the term "supervisor" to refer to administrators (irrespective of the administrative activities they perform) at the intermediate and lower levels of organization.

The word "control" also has two meanings:

i. Administration in the restricted sense of domination, or power and authority, as when reference is made to those "in control"; and
ii. Supervision in the sense of checking up on what has been done and taking corrective action where necessary.

In the first of these two meanings the term is occasionally useful. The second of these meanings contains ideas which may also be expressed, as indicated earlier, by the two concepts of "activation" and "evaluation."

D. *Development administration.* The term "development administration" has recently been used to refer to various forms of public and private administration in countries engaged in ambitious programs of economic, social and political development. The need for this term has arisen through the inordinate attention in schools of public and business administration to staff services and specialized techniques, at the expense of administration that is "action-oriented" and "pointing to programmatic values." Apart from this, the term has the merit of suggesting the special problems of administration in organizations with dynamic programs of innovation that may upset traditional social processes (Weidner, 1962). Swerdlow illustrates this usage by using the term to refer to the administration of an urban renewal program in an American city or of economic development activities in an underdeveloped country (1963, p. ix, xiv).

Chapter 11

THE CONFLICT-COOPERATION NEXUS

I N EARLIER DECADES many writers on administration neglected the processes of human cooperation or conflict. Some, while ignoring cooperation, stressed certain aspects of conflict. Others, in the joy of discovering the glories of cooperation, ignored conflict.

One of the major advances of modern administrative thought has been an ever-widening recognition that conflict and cooperation are inextricably intertwined in the life of any organization. Administrative thought is thus beginning to catch up with the tacit knowledge of administrators, for whom the problems of obtaining cooperation and handling conflict have always been objects of daily attention and nocturnal soul-searching.

At any specific moment an administrator also may neglect one or the other. He may romanticize cooperation in an effort to escape the stress of conflict. In the heat of battle he may neglect opportunities for cooperation. On the wings of mechanistic models of behavior he may even try to flee the exigencies of both. All such efforts are futile. If they lead to anything at all, it is merely a new situation of combined conflict and cooperation.

The complexity of this conflict-cooperation nexus can be revealed only through a deeper exploration of human interests, organizational structure, organization-environment relations, and organizational purposes. These are the subjects of Parts IV and V.

As a prelude to this exploration, let us now look briefly at the phenomena of cooperation, conflict, and conflict resolution. By considering cooperation and conflict as two aspects of social action, or two sides of the same coin, we may achieve an analytical separation of processes that are inseparably connected in action. Conflict "resolution" may thus be seen as a shift in a conflict-cooperation pattern rather than an "end to conflict" or a "final solution."

A. *The Necessity of Cooperation*

To STATE that cooperation is a necessary aspect of any organization is almost tautological. As already pointed out in Chapter 10, an organization is one form of cooperative system. The difference between it and looser cooperative systems is that within an organization cooperation is based upon a sense of "belonging," continuity of interaction, differentiation of function, efforts at conscious coordination or integration, and an accepted pattern of purposes. As a result of these factors, cooperation within an organization is much deeper than in a cooperative system which is not highly structured enough to be regarded as an organization. It is this depth of cooperation which makes organization a vital source of social power.

The idea of cooperation is so much a part of our everyday life that we tend to view cooperative phenomena as self-evident. If two men work together to roll a boulder off a road, we quickly identify the observed behavior as cooperative. But the reason we are sure we are seeing cooperation is that we impute a common interest or purpose: the removal of the boulder. If we have reason to think that the only purpose of one of them is trying to humiliate the other by demonstrating that he is too weak to move the boulder by himself, we will withdraw our identification. If we note that they are trying to move the boulder in different directions, we will call it conflict instead. Hence the central element in cooperative action is some communality of interest or purpose.

With this definition in mind, let us now look at the various sources of cooperation and note that it may have negative as well as positive aspects.

1. SOURCES OF COOPERATION

At the outset it is worthwhile to distinguish between the various loci of cooperation. Within an organization there is cooperation between formally and informally established subdivisions and between individuals. In the latter category we include cooperation between superiors and subordinates and leaders and followers, as well as between peers, colleagues, and others. Moreover, there is always some degree or type of cooperation between an organization and its environment. A human organization cannot be a completely closed system. Various relationships must exist with clients, advisers, controllers, and opponents. Unless these relationships embody some minimum degree of cooperation, the organization will wither.

In a deeper sense, however, the forms of cooperation at any one of these loci vary in terms of the degree of *actual or perceived communality of interests*.

On the one hand, cooperation may be based on a sharing of interests. These interests may be immediate, as when the members of a work group try to complete an unpleasant task rapidly or when an external threat to an organization's existence creates a deep interest in survival. They may be longer-range, with considerable divergence of views as to the immediate steps leading toward their satisfaction. In either case, whenever these common interests are intensely felt and are "salient" in the lives of a sufficient number of people, they may lead to a widespread sense of organizational mission and dedication.

On the other hand, cooperation may stem from a mere avoidance of dissatisfaction. This is the lowest level of communality. It occurs in all those cases when the interest of some of the cooperating parties is merely to avoid the penalties of noncooperation. Here we find the "enforced cooperation" that takes place through the overt or implied use of punishments or threats. Often, this is the cooperation of routinized acceptance, consent, acquiescence or compliance. Yet, if the sanctions are a "clear and present danger" rather than an empty bluff, they may yield considerable vigor of cooperative action.

Between these two points on the spectrum, there lies the cooperation which is based upon different but converging interests. Here differing interests are brought together—usually through negotiation or bargaining—into a *quid pro quo* agreement. This is the kind of cooperation provided for by employment contracts, purchase contracts, lending and investing agreements, and "deals" or pacts between members of a coalition. On a temporary basis bargains of this type are apt to be unstable, to be overturned as soon as a new deal is negotiated. With the passage of time, however, they may congeal into shared interests whatever action is required to meet the terms of the bargain.

It would be a mistake to regard any one of these sources of cooperation as generally characteristic of one or another kind of organization. While shared interests may be spoken of more frequently in religious or political organizations, many members of such organizations cooperate largely because of the dissatisfactions that would result if they did not.

In armies, where the possibility of strong sanctions is obvious, there is considerable importance to be found in shared interests and *quid pro quo* bargains. For many people in employment organizations, the *quids* assured through the employment contract are rarely more than a partial basis of cooperation. The strongest foundation for cooperative activity in an organization is usually one which combines all three in generous proportions.

2. THE NEGATIVE SIDE OF COOPERATION

Since cooperation is a prerequisite of organization and the enlargement of cooperation an indispensable aspect of augmenting an organization's power, one is apt to regard it as an unmitigated good.

We are brought back to a more realistic viewpoint, however, by recalling such pejorative terms as "conspiracy," "collusion," "cabal," "plot," and "unholy alliance." All of these refer to cooperative efforts—often *sub rosa*—based upon interests or purposes which we do not favor. Thus, by virtue of its being oriented toward satisfying some interests, cooperation is often directed against other interests. Apart from the objects of cooperation and the parties to it, it is not an abstract value in itself. Thus, many ardent calls for increased cooperation often represent an effort to have people sacrifice legitimate interests. The cooperation of the Oysters with the Walrus, in Lewis Carroll's *Through the Looking-Glass,* soon led to their sliding down the Walrus' gullet. Nor did the Walrus' loudly expressed sympathy interfere with his eating more oysters than the Carpenter.

Another difficulty with cooperation lies in its possible association with stability and routinization. When cooperation is viewed in the negative sense of a mere absence of conflict, its extension is usually associated with an avoidance of change and the continuation of outmoded forms of action. In this sense a high level of cooperation may be a symptom of a low level of aspiration or effort. The extension of cooperation may mean adding to the organization's incapacity to act.

B. *The Inevitability of Conflict*

MANY OF THE earlier treatises on administration give the impression that administration is something smooth and easy. They suggest that tensions or disturbances develop because of administrative error or accident. Just follow sound principles and all will be well!

This approach to administration is associated with certain "smooth and easy" conceptions of social action in general. "There has always been a tendency in economics to gloss over interest conflicts" (Myrdal, 1954). Neoclassical economists in particular often jump from one extreme of seeing the market as an automatic adjustor of competing interests to the other extreme of failing to recognize the existence of competing interests. In sociology, as Coser has pointed out, some modern sociologists see conflict as a disease. With "the rise of bureaucratic structures requiring the services of social scientists in the task of administration," a sociologist often orients himself toward the provision of services to the higher administrators seeking formulas for harmony and prescriptions for avoiding conflicts (Coser, 1956, p. 29). Turning his back on sociological thought and research which identifies conflict as an integral part of social processes, he will often diagnose any kind of organizational conflict as pathological. He will prescribe therapy in the form of encouragement to this or that academic research or the hiring of this or that academic consultant.

Here also, as with power, there may be administrative reasons for the masking of conflict. In many situations of organizational conflict the bitterest enemies may follow the *Mahabhrata's* counsel to address an adversary "even more gently while delivering the deadly blow." Many administrators act on the principle that attention to basic conflicts exacerbates them and that the best remedy is to do nothing but pretend they do not exist. Social scientists at times have demonstrated the practicality of their wisdom by providing valuable aid in keeping up the pretense.

The practical administrator, however, usually takes conflict for granted. For him, conflict is neither incidental nor accidental. I have never yet found an experienced administrator who has been unwilling to accept the core of the following thought:

> Everything is very simple in administration, but the simplest thing is difficult. These difficulties accumulate and produce a friction of which no one can form a correct idea who has not seen administration.
> Friction is the only conception which in a fairly general way corresponds to what distinguishes real administration from administration on paper.
> This enormous friction which is not concentrated, as in mechanics, at a few points is, therefore, everywhere brought into contact with chance, and thus produces incidents quite impossible to foresee. . . .
> The knowledge of this friction is a chief part of that often boasted experience of administration which is required of a good administrator. . . . It is true that he is not the best administrator in whose mind this knowledge fills the largest space and who is most overawed by it . . . ; but an administrator must be aware of it that he may overcome it, where this is possible, and that he may not expect a degree of precision in his operations which just because of this friction is impossible.

This quotation is taken from Von Clausewitz's classic *On War* (Jolles trans., 1950, p. 53-55). For the purpose of highlighting the general relevance of Clausewitz's observations, I have taken the liberty of making two changes in his text: inserting "administration" in place of "war" and "administrator" in place of "general." One could just as well substitute "running a hospital" or "factory manager" or "division director."

"This enormous friction" is inherent in the use of power. If power takes the form of pressure, the result is resistance—or at least a struggle against inertia. If power takes the form of persuasion, it usually includes a good deal of bargaining.

1. LOCI OF CONFLICT

As with cooperation, here also we may start by distinguishing between the various loci of conflict.

One aspect of conflict is internal. In his classic study of social conflict, Simmel points out that conflict is the other side of the coin of cooperation. "A certain amount of discord, inner divergence and outer controversy is organically tied up with the very elements that ultimately hold the group together" (1955, p. 17-18). Individuals and groups within an organization never have identical interests. The differences in interests always produce some sort of conflict, overt, covert, or latent. The administrator, of course, must get people to cooperate in some fashion—in a wholehearted manner at best, and at the very least in such a way as not to interfere with others too much. But in either case the superior-subordinate relationship itself may be a source of conflict. Superordination is often resented by subordinates. The resentment may be all the greater when hidden under the mask of service acquiescence or tied up with an urge to be dominated.

The other part is external conflict. This fact is no less significant than the internal ones. Wherever there are objectives to be achieved, there are obstacles in the path. In part this may be merely the age-old story of Man against Nature. It is also the story of Man against Man, or group against group. In one case it may be a matter of merely passive resistance or friction. At times, however, it is a matter of head-on collision between two or more organizations. More frequently, it is competition, direct or indirect, for a larger share of scarce values, whether power, resources or social position (*Banfield*, 1951).

The line between external and internal conflicts, it should be noted, is not always clear. The internal struggles and tensions have an inevitable effect upon the kinds of conflict situations into which an organization moves, whether by steering or drift. The external conflicts in which it is engaged are inevitably reflected in the inner stresses of the organization. Both may be reflected in, and affect, the internal conflicts within any member of the organization. For an outsider, it is difficult to discuss this combination of internal and external conflicts, much of which is in the sphere of "organizational secrets." For an insider, privy though he may be to secrets, it is difficult to see these conflicts in perspective (just as it is probably impossible for one to serve as self-psychiatrist and objectively analyze his own internal conflicts). Yet no one can understand any organization very well until he achieves an awareness of its complex conflict pattern. Since the loci of cooperation are often the same points, this leads to the conflict-cooperation nexus as a whole.

2. SOURCES OF CONFLICT

Just as the sources of cooperation are found in actual or perceived communality of interests, the sources of conflict are found in some degree of actual or perceived divergence of interests.

At one extreme, conflict is rooted in a sharp incompatability—or head-on collision—of interests. Any satisfaction, or victory, for one side means dissatisfaction, or defeat, for the other. In game theory this limiting case is described as a "zero sum" game, that is, one in which the gains of one party in a two-party conflict plus the losses of the other party (a negative quantity) always add up to zero. In actual wars the conflict of interest need not be so extreme in order to evoke a considerable amount of antagonistic emotion and destructive action. Warfare itself can be "cold" as well as hot, repressed as well as open, psychological as well as military. Many conflicts within and among organizations often seem based upon a perceived incompatibility of interests and, even though physical destruction may not be resorted to, take on the characteristics of warfare.

At the other extreme, conflict may be rooted in interests that are different but not necessarily incompatible. Here, when conflict occurs, a large gain to one party may occur with little or no loss to others. Or else both may lose a little or gain a little at the same time. This is the conflict which may be found in rivalry and competition. It is found in the bargaining and negotiation situations which precede an agreed-upon exchange of services or goods. It is the irreducible minimum of conflict which is usually found among partners, colleagues, and members of any committee or unit within an organization.

Decision-making itself is a fundamental source of conflict, since it invariably involves conflicting considerations or pressures.[1] These conflicts are not particularly intense for the fortunate individual, unit, or organization which is faced with a choice between two goods, that is, two desirable forms of satisfaction. The choosing process becomes more painful, however, when—as is more often the case—the choice is between courses of action each one of which has many good aspects and many bad aspects. When the latter dominate attention, decision-making then becomes a search for the "lesser evil." Within organizations, decision-making conflicts are invariably enlivened by pressure for different solutions on the part of different individuals and groups in the organization or intervening in its activities from outside. These pressures, in turn, are internalized within the minds of various individual decision-makers and become the basis for the deep internal conflicts that characterize the life of many administrators.

Most conflicts are embedded in a multidimensional matrix of interests. They thus cannot be readily placed on a simple continuum from incompatible interests to different interests. Each conflict usually involves a complex set of interests, each one of which may be located at a different point on such a continuum. It can be properly identified only by a profile, or vector, of different points.

Such a conflict vector, moreover, is necessarily connected with a companion vector of points on various continua of shared interests. It is for this reason that Schelling has proposed that game theory should be extended to include common interest as well as total conflict games. He uses "bargaining game" and "mixed motive game" to refer to the "mixture of mutual dependence and conflict, of partnership and competition" (1960, p. 83-118). In using these terms he refers to the large proportion of conflict situations in which common and divergent interests are closely associated. Within organizations this relationship is fostered by procedures and rituals for the conduct of conflict on the part of cooperating individuals and groups. Similarly, the broader arena of conflicts between organizations and nations, opponents and bitter enemies often cooperate in the support of codes of competition and "civilized warfare."

3. NEGATIVE AND POSITIVE ASPECTS

The negative potentials of conflict are fairly obvious. Just as a deep enough internal conflict within the personality of an individual can destroy his ability to function, a deep enough internal conflict within

1. See "The Decision-Making Struggle" in "Rationality: Administrative Processes" (Chapt. 29).

any organization will result in some form of dissolution. In sharply split dyads, such as certain man-wife relationships, it may lead to separation, divorce, or murder. In more complex organizations, the results may range from insurrection and schism to the creeping paralysis of deadlock and disinterest. For those who want to destroy an organization or its effectiveness, there is probably no more efficient method than the promotion of internal conflict.

The destructive possibilities of external conflict are even more apparent. Overwhelming outside power can be used to effect domination or annihilation. For the weak, even weak competition may be disastrous. When combined with internal dissension, external assault may be irresistible—as attested by the wreckage of ancient empires and the liquidation of business corporations. The possibilities of mutual annihilation by the two largest power-blocs in the world stare us all in the face.

Modern administrative thought, however, recognizes the constructive potentialities inherent in conflict. This theme was presaged in Simmel's analysis of how group unity is enhanced by internal conflicts among those who share basic values and by external conflicts with out groups (1955, p. 17-20). It was first stated in an administrative framework by Follett's observations that "we can set conflict to work and make it *do* something for us." It is restated by Simon, Smithburg, and Thompson's discussion of organizational conflict "as an important means of securing domestic control" (1950, p. 311). It is vigorously illustrated by Schlesinger's fascinating account of the "controlled competition" deliberately promoted by President Franklin Roosevelt:

> One of his favorite techniques was to keep grants of authority incomplete, jurisdictions uncertain and charters overlapping. . . . Roosevelt liked the competitive approach to administration not just because it reserved the big decisions for the President but perhaps even more because it enabled him to test and develop the ability of his subordinates (p. 535-539).

Looking back on a longer period of Presidential technique, Neustadt restates the theme in his observation that "Government is energized by a productive tension among its working parts" (*Presidential Power*, p. 183). In studying certain organizations operating across national and cultural boundaries, Cleveland, Mangone and Adams describe a field office as "a consciously-created system of tensions" (1960, p. 153). In terms of more general relevance to any unit, Cleveland summarizes many years of public and private organizational experience by stating that a major task of every administrator is to create a "web of tensions." Only thus will creative energies be released and cooperation made something more than dull routine (1960, p. 8, 16).

c. *The Outcomes of Conflict Resolution*

THE TERM "conflict resolution"—like "problem-solving"—is subject to various interpretations. On the one hand, it tends to suggest a certain finality that is inconsistent with a process concept of organizational and administrative behavior. It also suggests a purely intellectual operation which, like the solution of a mathematical equation, can be confined to what one does in one's head, on a piece of paper, or through operation of a computer.

In the sense herein used, however, "conflict resolution" is used to refer to the ongoing process of making certain changes in the multifaceted conflict-cooperation nexus. In this sense, no resolution or solution need be final. It may, indeed, be merely a prelude to new and sharper conflicts. Moreover, it refers to all the myriad forms of action, not rational thought alone, by which conflicts are resolved.

The term "outcomes" is here used to divert attention from the myriad processes of conflict resolution and focus it instead upon certain crucial types of change that are the immediate results of such processes. Analytically, these may take the form of avoidance, deadlock, domination-defeat, compromise, and integration. Any actual outcome of conflict resolution is usually a combination of two or more of these outcome forms. It is made all the more complex by virtue of the fact that each of these forms raises confusing problems with respect to the difference between what has really happened and the symbols or perception of that reality. In any case, there is considerable support for Dubin's proposition that "resolutions of conflict in continuing group relations determine the direction of social change" (1957, p. 193). Such resolutions, as Coser points out, highlight factors that are not deducible from the conduct of conflict and must hence be studied separately (1961).

1. AVOIDANCE

Interest divergence among human beings and groups is so great that it is highly doubtful whether social intercourse would be even tolerable without many forms of avoidance. In fact, withdrawal from conflict seems to be one of man's most natural and traditional ways of coping with conflicting interests. Internal conflicts may be unconsciously repressed. Family conflicts may be avoided by having children sleep in separate rooms, by taboos on the discussion of delicate subjects or—as in some societies—by rules against husbands talking with mothers-in-law (Murdock, 1949). Within organizations interpersonal conflicts are avoided by people "keeping out of each other's hair," by developing codes of noninterference in another's "territory," by suppressing deeply-felt differences of opinion, and by postponing or evading decisions. In conflicts among nations avoidance is achieved through disengagement, a *cordon sanitaire,* isolationism or the division of disputed territory into spheres of exclusive influence.

If avoidance is carried to an ultimate extreme, it may indeed mean the end of conflict—as when family troubles lead to divorce, members leave an organization or the organization is dissolved. Under such circumstances the price of peace is disorganization.

Normally, there are limits on the extent and duration of avoidance. The repression of conflict at one point can easily lead to its violent bursting forth at another. Or else one or more parties to the conflict may see in disengagement an opportunity to strengthen his forces for a more violent return to the fray at a more opportune moment. Today's truce may be but a transient calm before tomorrow's *Sturm und Drang.*

2. DEADLOCK

Like avoidance, deadlock is such a negative state that it may be difficult to regard it as an outcome. As with the stalemate conclusion of a chess game, no side can win. But unlike chess the broader game of social conflict can often continue in a state of deadlock for long periods of time.

> The possibility of deadlock—or to use a closely related term, stasis—is inherent in the democratic process of peaceful group conflict. When few victories are ever complete, when power is widely dispersed among many veto groups, when every solution is a compromise that is objectionable to many, and when every settlement itself creates new problems, you have the makings of a stalemate (*Gross,* 1953, p. 26).

The negative aspect of deadlock is probably one of the reasons why peace is not always as attractive as the hatred of war might suggest it should be. A "no win" peace is never as appealing as a victory. It becomes more desirable only when the dangers of defeat make "no loss" seem more comfortable. "Peace through stalemate, based on a coincident recognition by each side of the opponent's strength, is at least preferable to peace through common exhaustion" (Hart, 1954, p. 370).

From the long-time perspective of protracted conflict, however, deadlock may have more positive aspects. It may keep an opponent's energies concentrated upon a certain front while one tries to advance on other fronts. It may provide a breathing space, with or without withdrawal, during which one mobilizes forces for renewed and more conclusive efforts.

3. VICTORY-DEFEAT

Victory by one party to a conflict (or defeat to others) is the neatest of all outcomes. The victor receives a clear-cut gain. The defeated suffers an unambiguous loss.

It is also a highly circumscribed form of outcome. Even in games and debates, where there are agreed-upon rules for keeping the score, a victory in one round may be quickly followed by defeat in the next, and vice versa. In more complex forms of conflict, the possibility of such change is still greater. Clear defeat may be transformed into a psychological victory by propagandistic success in calling it something else—as when President Nasser of Egypt embellished his political victory over the forces that had seized the Suez Canal by convincing Egyptian supporters that it was military superiority which forced the withdrawal of the invaders from the canal region. The very act of surrender, as Coser pointed out, may involve an "assertion of power" (1961). It may be used to establish conditions for subsequent gains. The anguish of defeat may, in fact, be a contribution to future victories by providing the unseasoned with an invaluable baptism of fire and by teaching lessons that could otherwise never be learned.

Above all, victory or defeat on one issue may be inextricably associated with defeat or victory on other issues. Under such circumstances, either one is merely one aspect of a compromise outcome.

4. COMPROMISE

A compromise occurs when each party to a conflict wins something and loses something. It may take place with respect to a single issue, or it may emerge as the aggregate of a set of specific victories and defeats on various issues. It is thus the most widespread outcome of conflict resolution.

It is also the form most beclouded by the symbolic and deceptive tactics of bargaining and negotiation. A skillful leader who wants one loaf of bread will usually ask for two and be willing to "compromise" by accepting half of his stated demand. If he accepts the one loaf, he may then be violently accused of betrayal or opportunism by supporters whose energies he mobilized by dramatic visions of greater gains. To offset such criticism, he may take the offensive with his supporters by understating the negative aspects of a compromise and hailing the positive aspects as a great and historic (albeit limited) victory. Similarly, during the process of negotiation he may have to provide opportunities for his opponents to justify their participation in the compromise by parallel (albeit logically irreconcilable) claims of a great and historic victory. Like the confidence man in a con game, he may have to "cool the mark" *(Goffman,* 1952) by saving the face and assuaging the feelings of any who regard themselves as injured by the compromise. No wonder that the conflicting interpretations of many compromises are themselves the seeds of renewed conflict!

The necessity of compromise is something that can never be learned painlessly. Nor is the learning process easy for those who have learned too well the ease with which a purely logical problem can be solved through the processes of deduction but have not learned the difference between such a problem and a genuine social conflict. For these, as with nonrealistic idealists, compromise is often seen as an unmitigated evil. If it is to be tolerated, the condition is often laid down that at least there be no compromise on matters of principle. But principles are usually the first things to be yielded, for the simple reason that they are so rarely a clean-cut expression of fundamental high-priority interests. Because they are sometimes willing to sacrifice principles which are not directly related to basic interests but are rather propagandistic devices for the extension of support, the most effective leaders in the social struggle often appear to be totally unprincipled men. In a world of sharp divisions and dispersed power, they may even have to yield on basic interests. It may be added that since interests and principles are always multiple and diverse, the safeguarding or serving of some invariably requires a yielding or even sacrifice of others.

At the same time, to laud compromise as a value in itself may lead to an eating away of moral values and the growth of a cynical "anything goes" attitude toward life. It also leads to a major role in organizations for those who are skillful in serving as brokers and "go-betweens."[2] These are people who usually care more about making a deal or keeping peace for its own sake than about making progress toward achieving substantive goals.

---

2. See discussion of "middlemen" in "People-in-Organizations: Informal Aspects" (Chapt. 16).

5. INTEGRATION

As Follett pointed out long ago, integration is a conflict outcome in accordance with which the interests of all sides have found a place without any side sacrificing anything. The process of working toward an integration involves getting behind the symbols that may hide the state of true affairs and bringing conflicts out into the open so that the underlying interests can be analyzed and re-examined. This is very close to the "working through" process developed by psychoanalysts. Its application to organizational conflict is well illustrated in the way in which the Tavistock consultants helped bring about an integration as an outcome to certain managerial conflicts in the Glacier plant *(Jaques)*.

Enthusiasm for integration should not lead one to believe that it is possible to resolve all or most conflicts in this manner. Although such a resolution is generally more desirable and although integration probably plays a much greater role than many cynics would think, there are undoubtedly many occasions when nothing is possible except some sequence or combination of avoidance, deadlock, victory-defeat, or compromise. An integration of any complex conflict, moreover, is a multisided operation that must usually include within it some elements of mere compromise.

One of the reasons for the difficulty of attaining integration as an outcome of conflict is that it always involves a broadening of the framework. It requires the conflicting parties to become involved in issues beyond the current agenda of attention. It takes into account the many and diverse interests of the combatants, apart from those which are the basis of contention. It is based upon an examination of new and hitherto unexamined courses of action. This requires on the part of at least some of the participants a broad perspective toward life and a varied acquaintance with the total environment. To get beyond the narrow confines of mere compromise, one must be able to analyze the wide range of people's interests and have a sense of what is and is not feasible in a complex environment. These are not common capacities.

The role of imagination and creativity must also be mentioned. Here we find an essential link between Follett's analysis of integration and Barnard's concept of "moral creativity." As Barnard points out, an executive should be able to invent a new moral basis for the solution of moral conflicts, instead of relying on compromise alone. Similar inventiveness is needed in resolving any other type of conflict.

In conclusion, let it be noted that the process of integrating divergent or conflicting interests is part and parcel of the process of developing an organization's power. The ultimate source of any organization's power lies in the power of human beings. It is integration that brings together the interests of members and nonmembers and makes it possible for an organization to achieve influence that individuals could not possibly attain separately. By this same token, it should be remembered that integration, like power, is also a sword that can cut in any direction. It can unite the forces of the devil as well as of the angels. Whether any specific integration is to be regarded as good or evil must, like any other outcome of conflict, be determined entirely by one's ethical premises.

Chapter 12

THE POWER-AUTHORITY-
RESPONSIBILITY TRIANGLE

O NE COULD EASILY JUSTIFY an entire book on power, authority, and responsibility, or even a separate book on each. These subjects are of considerable importance beyond the realm of organizations and their administration. Within this realm, as shown in Part II, their significance has been repeatedly recognized throughout the history of administrative thought.

The myths and taboos associated with the public discussion of power, however, have often led to an excessive emphasis upon authority and responsibility. This imbalance is being redressed by the modern tendency to deal with power, or influence, more frankly. It thus becomes easier to consider the interrelations among all three.

The consideration of these interrelations can be facilitated, in my judgment, by thinking of the three as separate sides of a triangle. Thus, changes on one side must always affect one or both of the other sides. In this context the terms are used as follows:

Power (or influence) = the affecting of situations by human action
Authority = the accepted right to engage in certain actions
Responsibility = the obligation to act in a certain way

The major task of this chapter is to go beyond these oversimplified, nominal definitions and to present a synthesis of more substantive ideas that, apart from many terminological differences, are part of the emerging consensus in modern thought. These ideas will prove indispensable as provisionally fixed starting points for the detailed analysis of people and purposes in the administrative process. They will therefore be interwoven into the texture of the following chapters and *pari passu* elaborated upon and refined.

A. *Power: Cause-Effect Relations*

TO GET RESULTS, as stated in one of the basic propositions (Chapt. 10), both organizations and their administrators develop, maintain and use power or influence. Any organization, from a ladies' club to an army, is a system through which people develop the power to do things that they could not do as well, or at all, by individual action. Any administrator is a person who is expected to exercise some kind of power in or on an organization.

Whether we refer to the power of organizations or their administrators, the concept may be used in the sense of either the *actual* or the *potential*. Actual (or kinetic) power is the production of certain results. Potential power is the capacity to bring about certain results. In either sense, the same idea—sometimes in more limited form—is referred to by "influence" (sometimes used only for weaker forms of power), "control" (sometimes reserved for stronger forms), "rule" or even "leadership." With all of these terms, reference is made to some cause-effect relation.[1]

---

1. The identification of power as a cause-effect relation is implicit in the common-sense view of a powerful organization or individual as one that "gets results" or "brings about action." It is explicitly stated by Simon and many other analysts of social power or influence, although some people try to deal with power without getting tangled in the dangerous web of philosophical controversy regarding causality. The difficulty of avoiding this web completely is suggested by the cause-effect relation inherent in all such definitions as the following:

¬ the production of intended effects (Russell, 1938, p. 35)
¬ making things happen, initiating change (Follett, "Power")
¬ affecting policies of other than the self (Lasswell and Kaplan, 1950, p. 71)
¬ the causation of behavior (Simon, 1957, p. 8)
¬ any process in which a person or group of persons or organizations of persons determines, i.e. intentionally affects what another person or organization will do (Tannenbaum, "Control in Organizations")
¬ the inducement of change (March, 1955)
¬ every action which compels certain action on others (Mannheim, 1948, p. 167)
¬ A's getting B to do what B would not otherwise do (paraphrased from Dahl, 1957)

In the broad sense herein used, the concept of power is by no means limited to the harshness of force and compulsion. As will be shown in the discussion of activation (Chapt. 29), the use of power takes the form of persuasion as well as pressure, of promoting self-activation as well as exercising external influence. It is always seen in the exercise of leadership.

1. THE MASKING AND UNMASKING OF POWER

The tremendous difficulties of measuring power often inhibit the use of the concept. Yet this inhibition is mild in comparison with the taboos of polite discourse. In public administration the idea of power-seeking and power-wielding by the public administrator interferes with the myth of the civil servant as a noble, neutral agent of the common will. Such words, it has often been felt, are used only by the violent critics of "power-mad government bureaucrats." They should not be used by the friends of public administration.

In business administration circles also, the public discussion of power has often been taboo. As Galbraith has pointed out, there is an unwritten "convention which outlaws ostensible pursuit of power and which leads to a constant search for euphemisms to disguise its possession" (1952, p. 28).[2] Recognition of the substantial power accumulated by business organizations clashes with the traditional model of a competitive economic system. It undermines the fiction that no entrepreneur has the power to fix the level of prices or the volume of production and that these decisions are made instead by the "impersonal forces" of the market. It also suggests the need for countervailing power in the form of labor organization or government regulation.

The taboo on the open recognition of power is all the more effective because, rather than being merely a restraint on intellectual speculation, it is itself a popular aid in the use of power. In many situations desired action can be better caused by concealment of power, by adroit manipulation and by what Liddell Hart calls "the strategy of the indirect approach" (1954).[3] The iron fist, after being encased in the velvet glove, is then

2. Despite Galbraith's limiting himself to the United States of America in the mid-twentieth century, the disguise of "ostensible pursuit" is hardly limited to one country or one period of history. It may be presumed, for example, that with women cosmetic disguise is minor in comparison with the disguise of their power over men.

3. Although Hart concentrates on the strategy of using military power, he maintains that his "idea of the indirect approach is closely related to all problems of the influence of mind upon mind—the most influential power in history.

hidden behind the back. The myths of ultimate authority and central omnipotence (discussed in Chapt. 3), while magnifying the power at certain spots, by the same token minimize the power at other spots. To the extent that administrators or bureaucrats are regarded as the obedient and powerless slaves of top executives, directorates, legislatures, or "the people," their power may be greatly enhanced. Any unmasking of the actual distribution of power may serve to reduce the power of those operating behind the mask.

On top of all this, any open discussion of power or influence may conflict with deeply treasured ideals and powerful inarticulate premises. The idea of elites with power is offensive to many people who believe in utopian patterns of quasi-anarchic democracy. The idea of control is resented by people who have been subjected to onerous controls and believe in more autonomy for everyone. The idea of influence is soiled in the eyes of those who have witnessed the outrageous misuse of influence. For all these reasons power, like sex under the victorians, has often been regarded as a subject not to be openly discussed but rather to be sought, thought about and used under the cover of darkness.

Nevertheless, the central role of power in administration has been brought to the fore by the seminal work of Follett, Key, Lasswell, and Long, and by the conceptual clarifications attempted by such recent analysts as Cartwright, Dahl, Dubin, March, Simon, and Tannenbaum. All of these commentators would probably accept Cartwright's comments on social psychology as applicable to other disciplines as well:

> Both early social psychology and modern society recognize the importance of power. If, however, we examine social psychology since the beginning of its scientific epoch, we search in vain for any concentrated attack on the problem. Surely this constitutes a weakness of modern social psychology. We can only conclude that twentieth century social psychologists have been "soft" on power. Direct investigation has been evaded in many ways. . . .
>
> But surely inability to deal with power within traditional theories does not mean that the problem should be ignored in the future. . . . The point may be stated differently: it is simply not possible to deal adequately with data which are clearly social psychological without getting involved with matters of power (1959, p. 2).

Similarly, it is now fairly widely agreed that it is simply not possible for administrators to administer without "getting involved with matters of power." Although a "concentrated attack on the problem" by empirical methods has not yet been launched, an indication of what might be

---

. . . The indirect approach is as fundamental to the realm of politics as to the realm of sex." p. 18-19.

expected is provided by Neustadt's pioneering analysis (1960) of administrative power-seeking by various Presidents of the United States—Harry S Truman, Dwight D. Eisenhower and, in the background, Franklin D. Roosevelt. Neustadt shows how they achieved varying degrees of personal power through ability in persuasion and in developing reputation and prestige among the "professionals" in their more immediate environment and among "publics" at large. By so doing, Neustadt has helped legitimate the analysis of the actions of administrators in "the development, maintenance and use of power." Case studies of top corporate executives have gone in the same direction—although writers on business administration have been less outspoken than those in public administration.

2. THE DIFFICULTIES IN ESTIMATING POWER

Although the growing literature on methods of measuring power[4] reveals many conceptual differences, these differences themselves stem from an ever broadening consensus on the importance of power in administration and other fields. They are also based upon widespread recognition that power is hard to measure (entirely apart from the complications introduced by taboos and masking) because of multiple causation, multiple effects, and the difficulty of tracing presumed results to specific causes.

A. *Multiple causes and effects.* The first difficulty is the large number of causal factors that always influence any action. Let us suppose that a unit chief tries to influence his superior to recommend a large budget increase for his unit. The unit chief uses various forms of direct or indirect influence. Some of these may be based upon the feedback information obtained from earlier attempts at influencing the same budgetary decision. At the same time his superior is also subjected to influences by other units, by advisers and by his superiors. He is also influenced by internal factors: his habits, interests, allegiances, and attitudes. Prominent among these internal influences may be his anticipations of what the unit chief may do in the future if the increase is or is not granted. Many of these influences, both external and internal, may stem from events that took place a long time ago: the past behavior of unit chiefs, his own experiences over the past ten years, or even occurrences during early childhood. If we go back far enough, we might even attribute the final

4. Among the most important recent papers on the subject are the following: Shapley and Shubik (1954); March (1955); Dahl (1957); Simon (1957, Part I); Tannenbaum (1962); Harsanyi (1962).

budget decision, at least in part, to the length of Cleopatra's nose.[5] Many influences, even the most recent, may be unnoticed and uncontrolled, to be taken for granted as parts of the situation, as contributing or conditioning factors or as "intervening variables." Those that are explicitly noticed—such as the superior's dislike for people in the unit or the adverse influence of his own superior—may prove both undesirable and uncontrollable. If we now turn from the unit chief to the organization as a whole and consider its power to get additional funds from a bank or legislature, we see the same situation. The causative power of the organization is also imbedded in a complex causation matrix that includes (a) various actions by the organization, (b) actions by others who may influence the financing agency, (c) internal influences, including habits, interests and anticipations within the bank or legislature, (d) the delayed or indirect influence of many actions in prior periods, and (e) unnoticed, uncontrolled, undesirable, or uncontrollable elements. The power wielder can probably never see all of these factors or appreciate the significance of all that he does see. This difficulty is enhanced by his need to concentrate upon those (the presumably "strategic" ones) that he can most readily manipulate.[6]

Resulting action is also multidimensional. Entirely apart from the budget decision itself, the effects of the budget dispute may include such things as (a) better morale in the unit because of the fight their chief put up, (b) deep animosities on the part of other units, (c) resentment on the part of the unit chief's superior which may contribute to retaliatory action at a later date. Similarly, the organization's effort to influence the financing agency may result in (a) better understanding of financial matters within the organization and (b) more external support in some quarters and more external opposition in others. In both cases, the effort

---

5. "All statesmanship, and all rational conduct of life, is based upon the method of the frivolous historical game, in which we discuss what the world would be if Cleopatra's nose had been half an inch longer" (Russell, 1950).

6. A noted physicist has described the problem of multiple causation as follows: "We do not have a simple event A causally connected with a simple event B, but the whole background of the system in which the events occur is included in the concept, and is a vital part of it" (Bridgman, 1946, p. 83). An anthropologist puts the problem this way: "It is the system as a whole which is involved in cause. To define the cause, one would have to define the whole system; one may not select out only certain factors" (Radcliffe-Brown, 1957, p. 42). One way of meeting the problem is to think not of causative factors but of "correlations" and "associations." While this approach may be helpful to researchers studying large arrays of events, the administrator must go further. He cannot dodge estimating the causative influence of specific acts, including acts of reciprocal influence.

to exercise power may result in delayed, unnoticed, unanticipated or undesired consequences. If the power wielder focuses entirely on a single intended result, he may lose sight of the whole matrix of significant consequences.

B. *Judging cause-effect relations.* As already indicated, the toughest problem in the estimation of power is establishing a relation between a particular causative factor and a presumed result. Let us suppose that the unit chief's superior does recommend the desired budget increase. Does this mean that causative influence must be attributed to any one or even the totality of the unit chief's efforts? Not at all! It is entirely possible that the same increase would have been recommended anyway. It is even possible that the unit chief's effort to influence the outcome may have in fact perilously endangered it, or may have even served to prevent a larger or a more enthusiastic recommendation.

These possibilities could be definitively determined if it were possible to know what would have happened if the unit chief had not tried to influence his superior's decision or had used different methods of attempted influence. To know this would require some way of isolating the unit chief's efforts at influence from the many other factors in the total causation matrix. In the laboratory of the scientist such knowledge may be obtained by a controlled experiment in which the results of introducing a specific variable are compared with the results obtained when everything is held constant except the same variable. When it is impossible to control all other variables (as in a biological laboratory), the experiment is repeated a large number of times, thus enabling a comparison of the "experimental group" results with "control group" results. In observing events outside of the scientist's laboratory, it is much more difficult to isolate variables, study large groups of comparable phenomena and establish control groups. Nevertheless, as Stouffer has pointed out, we can still keep in mind the model of a controlled experiment, even if in practice we may have to deviate from it ("Some Observations on Study Design"). Stouffer illustrates the controlled experiment model as follows:

	Before	*After*	*After — Before*
Experimental Group	x_1	x_2	$d = x_2 - x_1$
Control Group	x_1'	x_2'	$d' = x_2' - x_1'$

Here d symbolizes the results obtained with the factor which is being studied, d' the results without it. The difference between d and d' may be regarded as the measure of the power of the same factor.[7] Stouffer points out that in social science research, we often "have only one cell" instead of four and that "when this happens, we do not know much of anything. But we can still fill pages of social science journals with 'brilliant analysis' if we use plausible conjecture in supplying missing cells from our imagination." He advocates more careful research designs aimed at providing data on at least two or three, if not all of the four cells.[8]

Anyone trying to estimate the amount of social power also follows a similar procedure, implicitly or explicitly. Suppose we want to measure the power of an organization to make a certain kind of change in its environment—whether it be defeating an enemy, outdistancing a rival or influencing the behavior of clients. The essence of our analysis is a comparison between a presumed result (d) of a certain action and the presumed result if such an action had not been taken (d'). If we are starting from the present and estimating potential influence, we may have some data concerning x_1, but we shall have to use conjecture with respect

7. If one is interested in estimating future rather than past power, then both d and d' can be regarded as estimates of the probability that a given event will occur with and without the influence of a specific causative factor. In this case, as Dahl pointed out with a somewhat different set of symbols, no power relation exists if $d = d'$ and power is at a maximum if $d = 1$ and $d' = 0$ (1957, p. 205).

8. One of the limitations of Stouffer's model is that it does not directly suggest the multidimensional aspects of the phenomena to be described. Both the "before" and the "after" states of a system may be described more fully in terms of a vector. The transformation from an earlier to a later state (and to any subsequent state) may be expressed in terms of the operation upon an $n \times 1$ vector by an $n \times n$ "causation matrix." Similarly, the difference between the subsequent states may be expressed by the comparison between the appropriate system state vectors. Thus, let

C = causation matrix without action (or changed action) by given actor
A = causation matrix of action (or changed action) by given actor
P(A) = power of A
C' = C + A
O = vector describing state of system; 0_1 (0_t) before (after) serving as object of influence by C or C';
   0' after serving as object of influence by C'
Then,

$$C \cdot 0^1 = 0_t$$
$$C' \cdot 0_1 = 0'_t$$
$$P(A) = 0'_t - 0_t$$

This formulation directs attention to the interrelation between many causal elements and many aspects of the system influenced. It also allows for inclusion within the causal matrix of internal as well as external influences. As with Stouffer's model, however, it is based upon the oversimplifying assumption that the transformations are linear and that the elements in the system states are additive.

to x_2. If we are looking back at actual influence already exerted, we may have more data concerning x_2 and shall have to use more conjecture with respect to the past. To estimate x'_1 and x'_2, we shall have to draw upon experience or working generalizations concerning similar circumstances. The whole situation is more complicated whenever d is a series of events extending over a long period of time or whenever it is necessary to compare d not only with d' but with a series of alternative situations.

The difficulties in estimating power become still greater when one turns to the power of an administrator. Here the relevant measure is not—despite popular ideas to the contrary—the administrator's power to get individuals to do what they would not otherwise have done. The d, rather, is the power of the organization or unit (as measured by one or more aspects of its performance), while d' is what we presume its power would be without him. Thus an administrator who throws his weight around to force people to do many things they would not otherwise do may exercise much less administrative power than one who gets people to do what they wanted to do anyway. The touchstone is found in our estimate of how the organization would have performed without him— or, better yet, with another administrator.

3. SOURCES OF POWER

Increasing attention has also been given to the sources of power—or what Simon refers to as the "influence base." As he points out, "if we can measure the magnitude of the influence base, we can infer from this the magnitude of the influence. (E.g., if wealth is the principal influence base in a particular situation—the principal means for exercising influence—then in that situation we may measure influence indirectly by wealth.") (1957, p. 69.)

One of the many ways of analyzing the influence base is provided by the proposition that power is the product of the administration of resources: "The basic equation is $P = A \cdot R$" (Chapt. 2).[9] An organization poor in resources may compensate for this weakness by better administration. An organization with weak administration may be powerful by reason of vast resources. The most powerful organizations are those which are strong in both. The most powerful administrators are

9. In an earlier formulation (*Gross*, 1953, p. 142-150) I identified the sources of power as (1) wealth, (2) numbers of people, (3) organization and leadership, (4) strategic position, and (5) combinations. The first two may be included under the concept of resources; the next three relate to administration.

those who contribute to the building up of a group of administrators capable of mobilizing and administering a significant quantity and quality of resources.

The term "resources" here refers to both material and human wealth. Material resources include the capital provided by nature, man-developed facilities, machinery and goods, and financial claims against physical resources. Human resources are people and organizations. These human resources are indeed the most elementary sources of power. Material resources are sources of power only to the extent that people value them and have the desire and ability—by individual or group action—to exploit them. Even the world-shaking power of nuclear fission and fusion exists only because of the knowledge and abilities of people and organizations.

The term "administration," as already explained, is here used to refer to the process of governing or guiding an organization. Administrators play a major role in bringing material and human resources together into an organization. The use, maintenance, conservation, and development of these resources is guided in turn by administrators with varying degrees of authority and responsibility. Thus any source of administrative capacity may be appropriately regarded as a source of power. Authority, particularly the formal authority associated with official position, has long been regarded, and properly so, as a source of power. To this must be added responsibility. Above all, emphasis must be placed on the knowledge, abilities, and interests of administrators.

When we contemplate the various sources of power, it is clear that under certain circumstances their use in the present may quickly produce depletion in the future. A military commander with a small supply of ammunition must hold his fire until the most appropriate moment. If he scatters his shots quickly, the fighting power of his organization may be destroyed. In many circumstances, however, the use of power may build up the power base, just as an automobile battery is charged through use or a muscle is strengthened through exercise. Also it is a dangerous oversimplification to think that the power base of one organization or person necessarily depends upon a complementary weakness on the part of another organization or person. Such an approach derives from analogies with areas of all-out conflict; it ignores the significance of cooperative efforts. The best analogy for the power of an organization is provided by the grid of electric power stations. The more electrical energy that can be originated in each station, the greater the power potential of the grid as a whole. Similarly, the more power that can be exercised by every member of an organization, the greater the power potential of the organization as a whole. If some become stronger, this does not mean

that others automatically become weaker. In a well-administered organization it means that the organization as a whole is stronger (Tannenbaum,
1962; *Tannenbaum and Kahn,* 1958).

Above all, it is important to keep in mind Follett's observations on
power as reciprocal influence. The power of an administrator is very
much like love. The person who wants to be loved but is unwilling or
unable to love is bound to fail. One must "give" love in order to "get"
love. Similarly, one cannot develop his own power if he thinks only in
unilateral terms and is unwilling to give others an opportunity to influence him.[10] "The man who exercises control gives more of himself to the
organization. . . . While he controls more, he is not controlled less. . . .
Members in the effective union pay for the increased control which they
exercise (and for the effectiveness of their organization) not only in terms
of the greater effort that they put into union activities, but also by their
greater sensitivity and accession to controls within the union" (Tannenbaum, 1962, p. 244, 256-257). In this same sense, Likert (1961) describes
an organization as an "interaction influence system" and regards the most
effective organizations as those in which reciprocal influence by many
members leads to greater influence as a whole.

4. ENERGY AND INFORMATION

The growing recognition of the importance of power in administration has been accompanied by increasing attention to the relation of social
power to physical energy and information. From this point of view
an organization is often viewed as a system for energy conversion and
information processing.

Some disbursement of physical energy underlies all phenomena of
organizational and administrative power. People and groups are not one
side of a mind-matter dichotomy. Human life is a physical phenomenon.
Action taken by an individual or organization to influence people by
persuasion, even without any open or covert hint of physical force, involves significant energy disbursements. These may be measured in micro-
units by the electrical impulses in the nervous system or caloric consump-

10. This, of course, is much more than an analogy. Love itself is a form of
power, "an active power in man, a power which breaks through the walls which
separate man from his fellowmen, which unites him with others . . ." (Fromm,
1956, p. 20). One of the indices of maturity in administrative thought may be
regarded as the ability not only to recognize the role of power in organizations
(which may seem "tough") but to recognize love (which may appear "soft")
as a form of power.

tion or in macrounits by various measures of individual or organizational performance. Although the stage of careful measurement has not yet been reached, important steps have been taken toward studying people and groups as energy-converting systems.[11]

In studying the power used by people and organizations, inertia and resistance are often the first phenomena to be noticed. In discussing the "poverty of power," Merriam makes the following observation:

> There is nothing more surprising to the holders of power, or perhaps to their subjects, than the frailty of their commands in certain types of crisis. . . . When the order is given, obedience is reluctant, partial; resistance widens; and as penalties are made heavier, opposition becomes stronger. . . . These forms of resistance are understood almost as well by the ignorant as by the learned—indeed, sometimes more perfectly . . ." (1950, p. 150, 183).

Such observations suggest interesting analogies with Newton's three laws of motion. These might be restated to (1) deal with the importance of social inertia, (2) the magnitude of power in relation to inertia and mass, and (3) the inevitability of counteracting power or resistance. Another generalization concerning social power is suggested by Ohm's principle, according to which the electrical current in a circuit is inversely proportional to the resistance in the wire. As already indicated in the discussion of cybernetics (Chapt. 8), the concept of entropy stated in the second law of thermodynamics is often applied to organizations and social systems. This is often expressed as the tendency for an organization to run down for lack of energy available for specific purposes. In none of these cases, however, can one automatically transfer principles from one field to another. Although people and organizations are indeed physical systems, and as such subject to the laws of physics, they are special forms of physical systems (and from the cosmic viewpoint perhaps very exceptional cases). The general laws of physics, therefore, can provide only "starting point" ideas that must be considerably ad-

---

11. Neurologists, psychologists, psychiatrists, and psychoanalysts have long dealt with energy disbursements on the individual nervous system. Social psychologists have broadened this approach by such concepts as Lewin's "psychical field" (1935), and Cattell's "synergy" (1948). An anthropologist has formulated an energy "law" of cultural evolution: "Other factors remaining constant, culture evolves as the amount of energy harnessed per capita per year is increased, or as the efficiency of the instrumental means of putting the energy to work is increased" (Leslie White, 1949, p. 368-369). A political scientist has traced many connections between the growth of high-energy technology and the increased power of governments (Cottrell, 1955).

justed and combined with other concepts in order to be applicable to human organizations.[12]

One of the bridges between physical systems and human organizations is provided by emerging theories on information transfer and processing. Even when power takes the form of violence (as with warfare or the harsher forms of disciplinary action), its effective application depends upon a considerable amount of information processing to develop the required physical energy and direct its use. A little violence becomes much more influential when information on its actual use and possible future use is widely transmitted. If we remove from consideration the direct contact of mass upon mass which is provided by violence, we find that the use of any other form of power is dependent upon the transmission and receipt of information. As Dorsey has perceptively pointed out, the energy potential of a human organization or social system depends upon its success in the processing of complex information ("An Information Energy Model"). In Deutsch's terms the transmission of information "can produce sometimes very large changes at the point of arrival . . . but these changes need in no way be proportionate to the amount of energy that carried the signal, much as the force of a gun shot need not be proportionate to the amount of pressure needed to set off the trigger (1963, p. 146).

Further exploration of the relation between information and energy may go far toward revealing some of the mysteries of social power. Unlike physical goods, the movement of more information from one place to another does not imply that there is less information at the place of origin. The only necessary losses are the information lost and the energy expended in the transmission process. But the previous supply of information, instead of merely being divided and redistributed, is now larger. Where one person had an idea, now a group of people have similar ideas. While this enlargement of the total supply of information may reduce the monopolistic value that may have resulted from previous scarcity, it may also greatly enhance the value of the shared information. This is particularly true when the shared information serves to mobilize new sources of energy to be used in reciprocal and cooperative action.

12. An illustration of the difference is provided by the fact that the second law of thermodynamics applies only to closed systems. Yet human organizations and social systems are open systems. Obviously the "same law" cannot automatically apply.

B. *Authority and Power*

AUTHORITY usually receives much more attention than power, not only in the more traditional currents of administrative thought but also in the everyday language of organizational life. Authority is more conspicuous; the head of an organization or unit is a man with authority. His power may not be so clear. In any case to talk about it openly may be regarded as indelicate. It is more decorous to discuss it in the language of authority.

One of the major clarifications in modern administrative thought is the differentiation between authority and power. Despite disputes on related matters, there seems to be a widespread consensus that authority is a source or form of power, but that power (or influence) cannot be understood in terms of authority alone. The significance of this distinction is perhaps most sharply illustrated by Follett's observation that administrators can confer authority on others, but power "is not a pre-existing thing which can be handed out to someone. . . ."[13]

1. AUTHORITY AS ACCEPTED RIGHT

In my judgment, the best way to capitalize upon the existing consensus is to use "authority" as referring to an "accepted right."

This usage is consistent with the normal understanding that a person with certain authority has the right to engage in a certain action. A driver's license gives one the right to drive the vehicle; without it, he is unauthorized to do so. A traffic policeman is authorized—has the right to—stop the driver and vehicle with a motion of his hand. He also has the right to speak with his superior officer. He may even have the right —depending upon the nature of the police organization—to speak when not spoken to, to make suggestions, or to influence his superior in various ways. But, except under the most unusual of circumstances, he will not have the right to give orders. His superior enjoys this right. This is part of his administrative authority, which may be regarded as the right to exercise power over certain people for certain purposes through the use of orders and other forms of influence.

In legal terminology we may properly say that a person or organization *has* a certain type of authority. We may even regard such authority as *vested* in the person or organization. While this form of discourse has

13. See Chapt. 7, Section A-3.

its uses, it should not hide the fact that rights exist only because they are accepted by others. Hence, Barnard's dramatic statement that authority "does not reside in 'persons of authority' " but rather with the persons who accept such authority. Although Barnard refers specifically to subordinates who accept orders, his observation has wider validity. It applies not only to a superior's authority to give orders, but to a subordinate's right to make proposals. It applies to the authority of various "staff" officers and specialists to "intervene" in his business by requesting information and influencing his actions. In part, this "area of consent" or "zone of indifference" is determined by the general traditions and customs of an organization; in part, its boundaries are shaped by the individual relations that develop among people.

It is unduly confining, however, if we follow Barnard and Simon all the way and equate the acceptance of authority with the acceptance of any proposal made (or order given) by someone with authority. To do so suggests a dangerous return (at least in part) to the equation of authority with power or an equally dangerous equation of power with order-giving. An adviser's right to make proposals is not destroyed if his advice is sometimes accepted and, when accepted, modified. A superior's administrative authority is not negated if some of his suggestions to subordinates are not carried out (or even if his orders are somewhat changed, for better or worse, in the process of execution). The two elements come together only in the more extreme cases when the acceptance of a person's right to exercise administrative power is undermined by a demonstrated inability to use this right.

Let us now be more specific in pinning down the nature of authority in organizations. The authority of people in nonadministrative positions consists of rights to engage in certain actions which are required by their work or which neither violate the rules of the organization or impair the rights of others. The authority of administrators consists of the rights to engage in certain actions needed for the guidance of organizations or units thereof. These rights may be subdivided in various ways—such as rights to (a) receive, request, and transmit certain kinds of information, (b) make certain kinds of decisions, (c) initiate action through commands and other forms of activation, and (d) allot certain types of rewards and punishments. Some of these may be exclusively held, some may be shared jointly with others. All of them may be tied together in one bundle labelled "the right to exercise power in certain situations for the achievement of certain purposes." From this point of view administrative authority is like a hunting license. It legitimates, and sets certain limits upon, an administrator's search for power. It does not guarantee that he will find it.

2. AUTHORITY—LESS OR MORE THAN POWER

The crucial distinction between authority and power can best be understood by focusing on the two extreme cases of discrepancies between them

At one extreme, we find many situations in which people make little or no use of their rights. Those who enjoy accepted rights to speak or think freely may—through inertia, incapacity, or fear—neither speak nor think. Those who are authorized to drive cars or examine secret documents may do so only when the spirit moves them. In administrative posts within organizations this becomes more striking. Here we find many administrators who enjoy considerable authority but have little influence. Many of these make the mistake of equating formal or professional authority with influence. They fail to realize that significant power must be acquired through their own efforts in specific situations. Or else they limit their efforts in this direction to the acquisition of more formal authority, neglecting other sources of power. Among this group we find the "organizational figureheads" and "administrators in name only." They may be regarded as "reigning without ruling" or as having "abdicated" their tasks of leadership.

At the other extreme, we find situations in which power far exceeds authority. Some people in organizations exercise significant power over units—or perhaps even an entire organization—with little or no authority, or with authority acknowledged only by a minority in the organization. Many administrators exercise significant power far beyond the accepted borders of their authority. Among this group we find the *"eminences grises,"* the men with a "passion for anonymity," and the wirepullers behind the figureheads. As their power expands, protesting cries of usurpation are apt to be heard. Some among these will seek to legitimate their operations (and thereby strengthen their power base) by bolstering their authority. Over time, indeed, they may well succeed in achieving the accepted right to do what they have already been doing.[14]

Between these two extremes, some degree of authority is a necessary source of the power of administrators. Otherwise, their activities would be regarded as grossly "illegitimate." This is why the phrase "with varying degrees of authority" is an important part of the basic proposition dealing with administrators' power. The same proposition applies to the power of organizations as a whole. In order to get results, an organization must at least enjoy the right to exist and engage in a certain type of operations,

guished from mere "paper rights") are established in statutes and constitutions.

14. This is very close to the process whereby meaningful rights (as distin-

whether this right is formally stated in law or commonly taken for granted. The only exceptions to this rule are such "unauthorized organizations" as an organized group of criminals or an outlawed group of revolutionary conspirators. Yet even in these cases there is a good basis to assume that no such group can develop any significant power without some degree of at least tacit acceptance (if not active collaboration) from other individuals or groups in their own country or another country.

The use of the phrase "varying degrees of authority" may unwittingly suggest the possibility of a single element that can be precisely measured. Actually, any form of authority—and particularly administrative authority—is usually based upon a tangled web of unwritten and often unspoken understandings, precisely written statements that are relevant in only a minority of situations, and broad general statements that are subject to wide interpretation and interminable dispute. This tangled web is often perceived in different ways—and in the daily life of an organization even small differences in perception are important—by an administrator's subordinates, colleagues, superiors, and by external interveners in the organization's affairs.

3. SOURCES OF AUTHORITY

What are the sources of authority? What are the factors that lead people to accept the authority of administrators, particularly their special rights to engage in actions that are illegitimate for others to engage in?

One way to answer this question is to refer to custom or tradition. This answer will frequently be given in studies of the authority of a monarch in a feudal society or of fathers in a society with strong traditions of patriarchal family life. It may also be given with respect to any "boss" who has been around a long time. His authority is accepted now because it has "always" been accepted. The customs of the collectivity find their way into the habits of the members.

But reference to custom or habit merely pushes our inquiry further back into the past. We must now look for the earlier sources of the authority enjoyed by king, father, or boss. We must now ask what factors lead to the strengthening, weakening and changing of customs and habits with respect to authority.

Much of the accrued wisdom in this field (including the small portion supported by careful research) can be synthesized in the proposition that the sources of authority are to be found in (a) power itself, (b) social roles, and (c) the characteristics of the authority holders.

A. *Power.* The inclusion of power as a source of authority may seem to complicate matters, particularly since I have already referred to authority as a source of power. Yet the reciprocal relation between the two is an essential part of the power-authority-responsibility triangle. Difficulties arise only if one fails to keep in mind the definitions given above and falls back upon other usages which identify the two or make one a special case of the other.

The successful exercise of unauthorized power is itself a factor making for legitimacy; with the passage of enough time *de facto* may become *de jure*. It is in this sense that we must concede, whether we like it or not, that Might has often made Right. The process is more swift, as well as more acceptable, when authority is established through the softer forms of power.

A more subtle relation between the two occurs in the case of the authorized use of power. The usage of rights prevents the erosion that stems from nonusage; it contributes to the consolidation of rights. The legitimate use of rewards and punishments, finally, is an established method of preventing the erosion stemming from internal disaffection; it contributes to the maintenance of acceptance.

B. *Social role.* The most obvious form of authority in organizations is that which is embodied in the social role played by an individual or unit. A role as a whole consists of prescriptive expectations concerning future types of behavior. These expectations may be formulated in terms of authority and responsibility—that is, of actions that the role player has the right to engage in and of obligations to act in a certain way. Formal authority stems initially from those aspects of roles which are created by those who already have the authority to subdivide labor at lower levels. The act of formal subdivision creates patterns of formal authority, some manifest and some implied. These patterns are continually changed by subsequent "delegations" of authority and responsibility and by the steady accumulation of general rules and specific orders and requests.

The acceptance of formal authority within an organization is to a large extent grounded in the obvious need for a differentiation of rights. Just as the child learns to accept the authority of his parents, adults learn to accept the need for higher levels of authority in organizations. The complexities of organizational action make it essential for every member to accept a differentiation of rights. In fact, every organization member soon comes to rely upon the authority of others. Such reliance is an essential condition for the functioning of an organization.

Because it is essential, the acceptance of authority cannot be left to chance. It is bolstered by meaningful symbols—from uniforms and seals and crowns to titles, remuneration, and the material perquisites of office. The care taken in fitting such symbols accurately to an authority holder's position in a hierarchy will usually take precedence over efforts to delineate precisely what he is authorized or unauthorized to do. Similarly, elaborate rituals are used to enhance support for the higher levels of authority and concretize the legitimate transfer of authority to lower levels. But social roles—and the authority that comes with them—are not limited to those that are formally created within organizations. People may derive authority from their position in informal groups—as dealt with more explicitly in "People-in-Organizations: Informal Aspects" (Chapt. 16). They may derive authority from the "social position" to which they were born or which they have attained through personal achievement. To some extent such authority may carry over from general social relations to specific situations within organizations or from one type of organization to another. Thus the authority often enjoyed by an upper-class aristocrat or wealthy businessman in philanthropic or political organizations. Still another form of positional authority may be found in unusual situations. In times of crisis there will often be immediate acceptance of a person's right to take actions that would otherwise be regarded as entirely illegitimate. This may include breaking ordinary rules of behavior, the seizure or creation of a position of authority or even the removal of an incompetent authority holder—all of which is justified only by the critical nature of the situation. After the crisis has passed, as so dramatically illustrated by *The Caine Mutiny*, the situation may then be reviewed to determine whether or not the shift in the authority structure was justified.

c. *Characteristics of authority holders.* Another source of authority may be found in the personal characteristics of authority holders, apart from (or in addition to) their power and the formal or informal social roles they may occupy. Thus people of special or outstanding ability are customarily granted rights denied to others. People may win authority by acquiring special forms of knowledge. They may win it by the values they espouse or symbolize.

At one extreme these characteristics are combined in various ways to provide an authority base for gods. Divinity—and the divine right by which men have often ruled—is usually expressed in some combination of omnipotence, omniscience, and goodness. Midway between the gods and men are those supermen whose charisma—or gift of spiritual power— marks them as some form of hero, wise man, or saint. Further along on the continuum toward ordinary people we find the more bureaucratized charisma of those people who are not supermen but who are nevertheless superior because of some specialized form of ability, knowledge, or values. Here we find those administrators who have succeeded in adding personal authority to the authority accruing to them from the social role they occupy.

These considerations also apply to a unit or an organization as a whole. Thus a budget division, apart from the authority associated with its formal and informal functions, will enjoy more authority if it is perceived as able, knowledgeable, and well intentioned. The authority of a government agency will be similarly enhanced by widely perceived characteristics that win it admiration and respect.

To the three sources already listed, one might readily add consent. In the modern world, authority holders customarily justify their authority on the ground that it stems from clearly documented acts of consent by those over whom authority may be wielded. Thus, as discussed in "The Dispersion of Authority in Organizations" (Chapt. 3), "ultimate authority" is found in stockholders of corporations, members of associations and electorates of nations. Formal authority at lower levels is strengthened by being derived from their acts of consent. But elections, plebiscites, and other means of formally recording consent are merely one way of winning generalized acceptance of rights under conditions when some are ready to accept and others are not. Acceptance of authority is rarely unanimous, particularly in a bureaucratic organization. There is a sense in which one might say that holders of formal authority are continually engaged in a campaign to win more extended acceptance of their authority from subordinates, colleagues, and superiors. Every operation in which they engage might be regarded as one in which a silent and unofficial form of voting takes place. The larger their majority, the greater the chances will usually be that minority opponents—except for those who find special advantage in the position of a hold-out minority opposition—will go along with the majority.

4. AUTHORITY NOT AUTHORITARIANISM

Studies of authoritarianism (such as Adorno *et al.*, *The Authoritarian Personality*) often seem to suggest that authoritarianism is rooted in a reliance on authority as opposed to reason, or force as opposed to persuasion. They have often led democratically-minded students of administration to regard authority as an antidemocratic phenomenon.

The consideration of this problem leads us back once again to the failure to distinguish between authority and power. When authoritarianism is studied as a brutal style of riding roughshod over others, the concept refers to a form of power. The authoritarian personality is characterized by the urge to dominate others and vent aggressions upon them.

Or else, it leads us to the identification of a particular form of authority structure. In the authoritarian family, organization or state, we find a concentration of authority. Although the opponents of authoritarianism may orate against authority as a whole, what they really want is more authority for themselves—either by themselves replacing the present authority holders or by distributing authority somewhat more widely. As Rokeach has perceptively pointed out (1961, p. 234) "there is really nothing so ugly about authority." The ugliness arises in objectionable distributions and uses of authority.

Authoritarianism, moreover, can be fruitfully approached in terms of Rokeach's structural (rather than substantive) distinction between the open and the closed mind (1960). The authoritarian person has a "closed mind" approach to authority. In accepting the views of people with authority, he closes his mind to the cognitive correctness or consistency of what they are saying. In dealing with those subject to his own authority, he expects his position to be accepted apart from their rational consideration of it. In either case, the rewards and the punishments that accompany higher authority are expected to be decisive.[15]

The more open one's orientation to authority, the more attention will be paid both to information of a substantive nature and to information about the authority source itself. "The person has freedom to choose or not to choose to be influenced in a direction desired by the source, depending on his own assessment of both sets of information" (Rokeach, 1961, p. 235).

Thus, as Rokeach points out, a person may adhere to an ideology democratic in content, but his mode of adherence may be authoritarian.[16] This clearly applies to persons with administrative authority. We may here add, however, that a person may also adhere to an ideology undemocratic in content, while his mode of adherence may be nonauthoritarian.

c. *Responsibility and Power*

THE CONCEPT of responsibility presents fewer initial difficulties than that of authority, since the terminological confusion with power does not exist. Moreover, there seems to be a common core of agreement that the term refers to some sort of obligation or duty. This usage may be concretized in the definition of responsibility as the *obligation to act in a certain way.*

15. This is surprisingly close to the Simon concept of authority in general.
16. A delightful illustration is provided by Phyllis McGinley's poem about "the angry man" for whom intolerance is "a state no tolerant man can tolerate."

The difficulties begin when, going further into the nature of responsibility, we analyze its relation to both power and authority. Here we find that—with certain conspicuous exceptions, such as Follett and Barnard—administrative theorists have given only passing attention to the subject. Too much of the literature of administration has dealt with authority. Power is now receiving greater attention. For a better understanding of the power-authority-responsibility triangle, much greater attention is needed to the third side.

There seems to be an emerging consensus, however, that responsibility is an obligation that has two dimensions. One dimension may be expressed as responsibility *for*, the other as responsibility *to* (Friedrich, 1941, p. 189). My analysis starts with this distinction.

1. RESPONSIBILITY FOR

Responsibility *for* is the obligation of a person, unit, or organization to perform certain services. These services may be referred to as duties, functions, or even responsibilities. Whether they are formally or informally prescribed, whether they are written in job descriptions and statements of function or simply taken for granted, they are an integral part of a person's or group's social role.

Since the concept of responsibility refers to all the activities in which a person, unit, or organization may engage, it is extremely broad in scope. A full statement of responsibilities will always be much more comprehensive than a statement of authority, which by its very nature is usually limited to a few specific types of actions that would otherwise be unauthorized. This, in itself, often tends to detract attention from *responsibility for*. Lists of functions, duties, and responsibilities tend to become hit-or-miss and over-long.

With respect to administrative responsibility (as distinguished from other kinds of responsibility) there are two special complications. First, while it is easy to define administrative responsibility in general as the responsibility for actions that help in the governance or guidance of organizations, it is much harder to spell out just what kinds of *specific* actions an administrator is responsible for. To do this requires the application to a specific situation of a general set of highly developed ideas concerning the actions to be expected from administrators. In many organizations very few people, including administrators themselves, have explicit and readily communicable ideas as to what the administrators at various levels are really supposed to do.

Second, there is a certain sense in which administrators are responsible not only for what they themselves do but for what others, particularly subordinates, do. They are responsible for getting things done by others. This brings us back to the question that arose in the discussion of the administrator's power—how to make the great jump between an administrator's contribution to an organization's activities and the performance of the organization. It is a jump that the administrator can himself make only by the exercise of power.

2. RESPONSIBILITY TO

An obligation is a social relation. It necessarily involves both an obliger (the person with responsibility) and an obligee or obligees (those to whom he is responsible). The latter, in turn, may be internalized in the form of conscience or personal values (in Freudian terms, superego). A person is responsible *for* certain actions *to* others and/or himself.

Thus a person in a simple nonadministrative position in an organization, in addition to being responsible for certain kinds of manual or mental services, is responsible for performing these services in a way which responds to the expectations of administrative superiors. He may be *held accountable* by all of them.

The difficulties inherent in this many-sided relationship become greater in the case of administrative responsibility. The administrator is usually responsible for a greater variety of actions and to a larger number of people and groups, including his subordinates as well as a possible host of interveners and controllers at higher levels of authority or outside the organization. As Barnard has pointed out, the predicament of the higher executive is that he will usually be responsible to conflicting interests and conflicting codes of behavior. Hence Barnard's emphasis upon moral creativity as an essential of responsible executive behavior.

Here again there is a complication. *Responsibility to* is essentially a two-dimensional concept. It may be thought of in terms of two vectors moving in opposite directions. The responsibility vector moving from obliger to obligee is a *sense of responsibility*. It is the human response to the human needs or desires of others, something that cannot be wholly imposed from without (Fromm, *The Art of Loving*, p. 28). The responsibility vector moving from obligee to obliger, on the other hand, is *holding someone responsible or accountable*. It is inevitably associated with checkup, supervision, control, and punishment. A certain amount of motion in this direction is undoubtedly necessary to prevent a sense of responsibility from being diverted or corroded. Too much action in this direction can often readily undermine a sense of responsibility and seriously impair the activities that a person or group is responsible for. That this often happens in organizations is probably due to the attraction of the *holding responsible* approach for those who use it as a way of giving expression to pent-up aggressions and getting rid of their own sense of guilt by pinning the blame upon others. "Whose fault is it?" is a "question that seems to obsess the Western world" and lead to denials, counteraccusations and an emotional atmosphere of doubt and despair (Gragg, 1964).

3. IRRESPONSIBLE AND RESPONSIBLE USES OF POWER

As political philosophers have warned for centuries, great power may be associated with an extremely low degree of responsibility. The power-wielder may frustrate the expectations of most people in order to serve the interests of a few. He may violate the deepest moral expectations of everyone. He may achieve only the lowest of his self-expectations. Those who might want to hold him responsible might be unable to do so or even afraid to make the effort. This is the element of truth in Lord Acton's oft-quoted quip: "Power tends to corrupt, and absolute power corrupts absolutely."

A great amount of power may also be associated with a high degree of responsibility. If we expect people to discharge their responsibility for great and difficult undertakings, we must expect them to acquire and use a large amount of power. A decline in power may make it impossible to act responsibly. Increments in power may lead to more responsibility. It is in this sense that power may ennoble as well as corrupt. This is the element of truth in Woodrow Wilson's seldom-quoted remarks concerning the public administrator: "The greater his power the less likely he is to abuse it, the more is he nerved and sobered and elevated by it. The less his power, the more safely obscure and unnoticed does he feel his position to be, and the more readily does he relapse into remissness" (1887, p. 197-222). Hence government, for Wilson, should be come "a straightforward thing of simple method, single unstinted power, and clear responsibility" (1885, p. 332-333).

But we need not concern ourselves with absolutes in either power or responsibility. Absolute power is a myth. Power is always limited. It is bounded at its very base by the quantitative and qualitative limits of the various sources of power. It is held in check by the operations of competitors or opponents, the concessions that must be made to the opposition of those who are subject to it, and the inevitable frictions which accompany its use.

The "clear responsibility" of the Wilsonian dream, the situation in which the public executive commits himself to the discharge of precisely stated responsibilities representing the undivided expectations of a ma-

jority of the people—this is no less a myth. In a complex society responsibility is always blurred by the divergent and shifting expectations and
interests of many different people and groups. Nor is it possible in complex organizations for obligees to hold obligers responsible through major
reliance on direct sanctions.

Power, therefore, is a sword that can cut in any direction. Its use
involves inescapable risks. It may frustrate the expectations of those who
have legitimatized it. It may lead to the undoing of the power-wielders
themselves.

On the other hand, power is indispensable to the attainment of desirable purposes. Without power, idealism by itself is a recipe for futility.
Only through power can high and significant goals be achieved. It is
in this sense that Follett says that "more power, not division of power,
should always be our aim; more power for the best possible furtherance
of that activity, whatever it may be, to which we are giving our life."

To this, I might add a less poetic but extremely practical note: The
responsible use of power is one of the most effective ways to strengthen
power. As already pointed out, one of the great sources of power lies in
the motives, values, and allegiances of people and groups. Power users
can develop power only by responding to such factors. As a practical
matter, therefore, the administrator develops a special pattern of responsiveness. The more wisdom is exercised in doing this the greater the
resulting power base.

The other side of the coin is revealed in the case of the administrator
who fails to use the "license" given him by his position of formal authority.
His abdication is itself a failure to discharge his responsibilities. It may
be compensated for only by the action of someone else, hidden in the
wings, who usurps power in order to see that the organization discharges
its responsibilities.

D. *Authority and Responsibility*

ONE OF THE OLDEST MAXIMS of administration deals with the relation between authority and responsibility. Among writers on the subject this
has been stated in many ways:

> Authority is not to be conceived of apart from responsibility (Fayol,
> 1949, p. 22).
> At all levels authority and responsibility should be coterminous and
> coequal (Urwick, 1943, p. 46).

In each responsibility is inherent an equivalent authority (Brown, 1947, p. 39).

Parity must exist between authority and responsibility (Koontz and O'Donnell, 1955, p. 296).

In everyday organizational life the maxim tends to be stated as a means of complaining about a lack of "parity" or justifying efforts to increase either authority or responsibility. The widest complaints seem to come from administrators who feel that they have not been given enough formal authority. For them the maxim may become a justification of a drive toward enlarged authority (and perhaps greater power) or of a decline in their feeling of responsibility.

On the other hand, those in higher positions of relative authority often complain that people in lower positions do not use their authority responsibly. Like Fayol, they feel that there is a tendency for people in an organization to seek authority and dodge responsibility. Like members of elected legislatures, they complain about the irresponsibility of the bureaucrats.

In addition to being rooted in the personal needs of people at various levels, the parity maxim expresses the inevitable connection between rights and obligations. One of the oldest and most deeply rooted human concepts is that the exercise of rights carries with it certain obligations and that those with obligations to perform must be allowed to do what may be required for such performance.

The prescriptive limitations of the maxim have been repeatedly pointed out in modern administrative thought. Simon, Smithburg, and Thompson have shown that in the interdependence of modern organizations no administrator can be given in advance, as a matter of right, all the resources, clearances, and other forms of cooperation that are needed for him to discharge his responsibilities (1950, p. 215-216). The inevitable administrative subdivision of authority is too great. Because of this, people can be expected to feel responsible for inquiring into problems that they themselves are not authorized to deal with (Newman, 1951, p. 176). They can be encouraged to feel responsible for making their contributions toward many larger accomplishments that are far beyond the individual authority of any of them (Follett). To these limitations may be added the observation that a goodly portion of administrative activity consists of involvement in "polyarchic relations" (Chapt. 15, D). In these, responsibility is usually high and authority rather low. As pointed out in previous sections, moreover, both authority and responsibility are extremely complex concepts that do not lend themselves readily to over-all "parity comparisons." It is more feasible to deal with specific and identifiable increments or decrements. These are dynamic factors in the life of organizations and their administrators. While they tend to move in the same direction, they also tend to do so at different rates, with a change in one contributing to a change in the other. Thus more authority may eventually result in more responsibility. More responsibility may lead to more authority. A decline in one may lead to a decline in the other.

But the connection is never one between these two factors alone. Both of them are always related in some way to the power base. The appropriate framework for appraising their interrelations is the power-authority-responsibility triangle.

Chapter 13

SOME EXPLODING FALLACIES

ONE OF THE ACHIEVEMENTS of administrative thought in recent decades has been the demolition of many administrative fallacies that were previously widely accepted. Although they may still have some advocates, these fallacies are at least no longer actively purveyed by the majority of thinkers, writers and teachers in the field.

In this chapter I shall discuss the following fallacies of this type:

> The manager is the man on top.
> Authority and power flow down from the top.
> Efficiency is the sole goal of administration.
> Technical skill equals good administration.
> Rank-and-file members of an organization should be
>   free from outside pressures.
> Administrators should execute policy, not make it.
> In good administration things run smoothly and easily.
> Evading formal rules violates administrative theory.
> The principles of administration provide the answers
>   to administrative problems.

By limiting myself to this area, I am thereby foregoing—or rather postponing until the next chapter—the pleasure of attacking "popular" fallacies. The delineation of these well-exploded fallacies is a form of stocktaking. It summarizes the extent to which the emerging consensus in administrative thought has contributed to the "unlearning process." It is a way of telling ourselves that the work of the pioneers in administrative thought, the developers of specific aspects and the contributors from other disciplines has not been in vain. It is a way of saying: "We've made a little progress."

The purpose of looking back, therefore, is merely to consolidate our intellectual resources in preparation for new intellectual disputes far beyond any area of consensus conceivable in the immediate future. It is to prepare ourselves for dealing with other fallacies that are more subtle and more dangerous.

We shall see a common pattern. We shall see that most of these are fallacies in which a part is mistaken for the whole. They are similar to such propositions as "A triangle is something with one side" or—at a higher level of sophistication—"A triangle is something with two sides." In every case, as we shall see, there have been understandable reasons why people failed to see, or preferred to close their eyes to, the existence of three sides. The reasons, however, are not to be accepted as justifications. Nor can the kernel of truth in each of them be tolerated as a basis of administrative instruction—any more than we would tolerate a geometry teacher telling his class that a triangle has two sides.

A. *The Manager Is the Man on Top*

THIS IS THE FALLACY of thinking that a manager or administrator can be adequately symbolized by the figure of a man standing at the top of a pyramid. Whether the pyramid represents a small unit or a vast conglomeration of units, the task of the manager is simply to guide or direct the activities of his "lower level" subordinates.

One root of this fallacy is "organization chart psychology": taking too seriously charts designed to spell out certain aspects of the division of labor and hierarchical subordination. The still deeper roots are found in the fact that "on top" symbolizes domination. The idea is thus extremely appealing to those with a strong urge to dominate or to be dominated.

Yet any man who gets to the top will be confronted with three sets of facts.

The first is that he will always find somebody "on top" of him. This may be his immediate hierarchical superior, a governing board, a control body of some sort, or all of these together. If he should be a prime minister, a president, or a chairman of a board of directors, these will be the representatives of his organized constituencies. No matter what his level, the manager may well spend much more time looking up than looking down.

Second, he will find that he is hemmed in and pressured on all sides. He must concern himself with colleagues and associates within the organization. These are people without whose cooperation he cannot perform his tasks; yet instead of being merely passive cooperators they in turn are often trying to get him to do things they want him to do. And further, the manager must deal with a large array of outsiders whom he must activate or resist.

Third, he finds that he is subjected to a constant bombardment from below. The people whom he is supposed to direct are constantly making requests that he must deal with, sending messages that he must study, and in many subtle ways trying to direct him.

Thus he finds that instead of being on top he is "the man in the middle," a term once reserved for the lowest level administrators or foremen (those in the midway position between the nonadministrators and the higher ranks of administration). He is not at the apex of a triangle, but at the center of a confused and whirling vortex of centripetal forces. To the extent that he puts substantial energy into his job, he not only is buffeted; he buffets. He is the center from which centrifugal forces also emerge and impinge upon other "men in the middle" inside and outside of his organization.

B. *Authority and Power Flow Down from the Top*

THIS IS THE IDEA that likens administrative authority and power to a water tank on the roof of a building. Once the plumbing has been properly installed, the administrator opens and closes the spigots in order to send the proper amounts of authority and power to the proper places.

Like the man-on-top fallacy, this one also is encouraged by overemphasis on organization charts. It is concretized in job descriptions which concentrate on hierarchical relationships instead of specifying the actual services to be performed.

This fallacy also appeals to those who feel a psychological need for an enlarged image of their own power, a need which probably varies directly with the degree of an administrator's internal feelings of weakness and insecurity.

The first defect in this conception, as Mary Follet pointed out long ago, is that many positions carry with them their own authority. Once the work to be done within an organization has been subdivided, a significant amount of formal authority has already been conferred. The director of a hospital does not give authority to a surgeon; the position of surgeon already contains authority. If the director gives more or less authority, he is expanding or contracting the position itself. This is an architectural change, not a mere matter of turning the water off or on at the spigot.

Second, it is not possible to delegate power beyond that small portion of power which is embodied in formal authority. The formal authority is merely a license an administrator can use in mobilizing the power he needs to do his job. He must prove himself by his own actions, and in so doing, he will need support from superiors. But such support is never indefinitely given, at least never in the necessary quantities; it must be won.

c. *Efficiency Is the Sole Goal of Administration*

THIS IS THE BELIEF that the one goal of administration, and the sole criterion by which administrative performance may be judged, is some relationship between input and output. One also comes perilously close to this fallacy when he states, with Gulick, that efficiency is "axiom number one on the value scale of administration" and then proceeds to ignore all other axioms.

The efficiency fallacy is rooted in the neutralistic "safe and sane" conception of administration. It is imbedded in the desire to find hard, objective facts that can be precisely measured, rather than in the acceptance of slippery intangibles. Above all, it has served as a point of unity between those people who, while disagreeing about other things, may find a common meeting ground in the goal of efficiency.

Few fallacies in administrative thought have been more repeatedly exposed.

First of all, apart from efficiency itself, there is the whole range of other major categories of organizational purpose. Among the goals of every organization, in addition to efficiency, are (1) the satisfaction of various interests, both external and internal, (2) the production of goods or services, (3) investing in the organization's viability, (4) mobilizing resources, (5) conforming with certain organizational codes, and (6) using the most rational techniques, both substantive and administrative, that can be developed. Any one of these purposes, or any combination, may under certain circumstances be more important to an organization than efficiency.

Second, upon more careful examination, the efficiency goal often declines in importance. It is relevant only to the extent that an objective scarcity of resources exists and that the members of an organization perceive this scarcity. It is measurable in precise terms only when it is possible to count units of both output and input. Here the great paradox of efficiency is that while efficiency is determined by the internal operations of an organization, it is precisely in the production of intermediate services within an organization that it is extremely difficult to find units of output that can be precisely counted. This is the reason why Simon reluctantly came to the conclusion that the efficiency criterion is applicable "largely to rather low level decisions."[1]

D. *Technical Skill Equals Good Administration*

THIS IS THE BELIEF that because a person reaches an acknowledged level of achievement in some technical field, he is therefore *ipso facto* qualified as an administrator.

This fallacy represents the phenomenon of "prestige transferance." People may believe that because a person is an outstanding theatrical performer, he is therefore uniquely qualified as a commentator on politics or a judge of the quality of cigarettes.

The fallacy is also rooted in the natural desire of every technician to have a superior who, by virtue of being a technician in the same field, will really understand him. It is grounded in the technician's equally natural desire to obtain the prestige and other emoluments associated with higher administrative posts without deserting his particular specialty.

If this fallacy has been given less attention in administrative writings than the previous fallacy of efficiency, it has been far more frequently exploded in administrative life itself. Almost every organization can show one or more examples of a good technician who has become a wretched administrator, an unhappy man, and a lost expert. Although technical skill is by no means a necessary obstacle to administrative success (and in some cases may in fact represent a partial prerequisite), it is by no means a sufficient condition. When the skilled technician becomes a good administrator, it is because he has learned certain additional skills not directly included within the area of his previous specialty.

The life of this fallacy, unfortunately, has been prolonged by schools of business and public administration where undue emphasis has been placed upon technical skills in such fields as methods analysis and production engineering, accounting and budgeting, and personnel manage-

1. See discussion in section D-2 of "The Pioneers: New Beginnings" (Chapt. 7).

ment. In their justified enthusiasm for these important techniques, teachers have often tended to confuse these technical aids to administration with administration itself. The student has sometimes been allowed to graduate with the well-nourished illusion that his certified proficiency in one of these fields already qualifies him as an administrator. In contrast, the better schools channel the necessary enthusiasm for technique into an awareness of the problems of using techniques and technicians and of the place of each technique in the broader processes of administration.

E. *Rank-and-File Members of an Organization Should Be Free From Outside Pressures*

WHILE THE PREVIOUS FALLACIES can be stated interchangeably in terms of either "is" or "should be," this fallacy is invariably stated in terms of "should be" only. The reason is simple: Any flat statement that the rank-and-file members of organizations *are* free from outside pressures would represent a preposterous contradiction of readily observable facts. For the same reason, the "freedom from pressure" standard is usually applied only to the middle and lower levels of government organizations. Here it is used to voice resentment against "undue" pressure by outside politicians and outside pressure groups. Although historically rooted in the public service, this fallacy has also grown up in many private organizations whose top executives and directorates presume to arrogate to themselves the exclusive right of contact with outside forces.

The Achilles heel of this fallacy is that in a world where no organization can survive as an island unto itself, outside pressures make themselves felt throughout an organization. This is more or less obvious in a democratic society. It is less obvious, though just as true, in any dictatorship. No members of an organization can be, or should be, completely insulated from direct or indirect outside pressures.

Protective devices and procedures designed to cope with undesired pressures are, of course, essential. But any effort to handle the problem of protection by the complete denial of contact will, by itself, serve to weaken the defenses of an organization's members. The most delinquent children are sometimes those raised by over-strict parents. Like young girls in an environment of libidinous males, the rank-and-file members of an organization cannot learn to protect themselves unless they have contact with outside pressures. Only thus it is possible to learn the arts of passing the buck, postponing the issue, entrenched resistance, and —where this is required—justified acquiescence.

F. *Administrators Should Execute Policy,*
    Not Make It

THIS FALLACY is based on the narrow conception of administration as the mere effectuation of purposes determined by others. It was inherent in Taylor's sharp division between planning and execution and Goodnow's policy-administration dichotomy. In the field of the business corporation, this fallacy presents policy-making as the exclusive responsibility of boards of directors. In public administration this exclusive responsibility is regarded as the province of legislatures, chiefs of state, and cabinet members.

As with the belief in efficiency as the sole goal of administration, this fallacy is also rooted in the search for security. If administrators do not make policy, then they might be given full tenure of office irrespective of what changes in policy might be determined by the higher wielders of formal authority. They are also privileged to live on a tight little island of hard and objective fact instead of having to venture forth on the tempest-ridden sea of conflicting values.

The fatal defect in this belief is simply that the making and execution of policy are inseparately intertwined. Genuine policy—as distinguished from meaningless generalizations—comes into being through the activities of an entire organization. Purposes are given meaning and content by the people who cooperate in carrying them out. Purpose emanates from an entire organization in interaction with its environment. Those highest officials who may be vested with the formal authority for "policy formulation" often do little more than (a) legitimate the policies developed at the lower levels of the hierarchy, (b) make slight adjustments in some of the proposals submitted to them, or (c) make occasional choices between submitted alternatives. A large part of the work of people below the higher levels consists of preparing such policy proposals and interpreting them once they have been formally endorsed.

G. *In Good Administration*
    Things Run Smoothly and Easily

THIS FALLACY represents an administrative version of Utopia. It provides a vision of some glowing future in which purposes are unambiguously defined, the right people are always in the right places, and the organization moves forward without friction and in accordance with preordained procedures.

This fallacy is a form of escapism from the world of reality. It is a child-like fantasy indulged in by adults. At times it may serve as an ideal to guide people in the introduction of improvements. More frequently, it is a substitute for effective change, a standard which leads to organizational defeatism.

This fallacy has frequently been propagated—and probably will always continue to be—by a certain type of academic mind which delights in the inculcation of principles of action which have little or no connection with the realities of human action. The explanation of this phenomenon may perhaps be found in the attractiveness of Academia for people who are afraid of the harshness of the nonacademic world. But why is it that many students accept this fallacy so readily? Certainly this conception of organizational behavior does not conform with their own experiences in the family and the school, the two organizations with which they have had most contact. Is their readiness to accept the ideal of organizational Utopia itself a form of retreat from frustrations in family life and in school?

So long as motor vehicles are used, some people will always get hurt. Indeed, some will always get hurt badly. This is more reason, not less reason, to take action designed to reduce the accident rate.

The same is true in administration. Some people will always get hurt— and some very badly. This is why action is necessary to reduce the uncertainties, the friction and the tensions, the humiliations and the frustrations of administrative life. But no amount of well-intentioned action will ever eliminate them completely. To think that it will may indeed make it harder to reduce their incidence and easier for people to end up in the slough of disillusionment.

H. *Evading Formal Rules Violates Theoretical Principles*

THIS IS A MORE ESOTERIC FALLACY than the previous one. It consists of the belief so often voiced by practical administrators that whenever they break or evade the formal rules of an organization, they are thereby violating theoretical principles of administration. In its most virulent form it consists of the belief that by so doing they are also proving the impossibility of establishing theoretical administrative principles.

This fallacy has two roots. The first is the proliferation of premature, unjustified, and ill-formulated administrative principles. This has led to a rather unsophisticated revolt against the very idea of administrative theory or administrative principles, a revolt joined in by many academicians as well as practical administrators. Disdaining the extreme of blind acceptance of theoretical nonsense, the rebels have jumped to the other extreme of theoretical nihilism.

The second is the very wide-spread urge to break organizational rules. The existence of this urge is what accounts for a large amount of the informal relationships and procedures which always grow up along side formal structures and regulations. It also accounts for the inevitable degree of deviation which seems to be an indispensable prerequisite of any significant degree of conformity. The error, of course, enters in only when someone who sets himself the goal of breaking a theoretical rule thinks he has automatically done so when he succeeds in breaking an organizational rule. Very probably all that he has done is to deviate from some fallacious idea that has already been exposed. Modern administrative thought itself recognizes the limitations of formal organizational structure and the role played by informal operations. It is oriented more and more toward including, among other things, generalizations concerning people who break rules in organizations. Thus, the man who violates a procedural rule of his organization may well be operating in strict conformity with a theoretical law. He is not even an exception to the rule; his violation demonstrates his conformity.

1. *Principles of Administration Provide the Answers to Administrative Problems*

THIS CONSISTS of the belief that well-defined theoretical principles can by themselves—without the application of either skill or values—provide the answer to administrative problems.

As with the previous fallacy, this also has been rooted in the pretentious and premature work of earlier decades. It is also used by the "theoretical nihilists" who endeavor to prove the impossibility of administrative theory by assigning it an impossible function.

Today, however, among those acquainted with the current trends of modern administrative thought, there is wide-spread acceptance of these cogent ideas presented by Simon and his colleagues (1950, p. 20-21):

(1) Practical rules simply do not exist which can be applied in an automatic or mechanical fashion to actual organizational problems. . . .

(2) At the present stage of knowledge, administrative theory is of far

more practical use in diagnosing situations than prescribing suitable courses of action. . . .

(3) The practice of administration involves skills—skills that have become thoroughly incorporated in the administrator's personality—rather than mere intellectual knowledge. . . .

(4) Practical recommendations for organization action always depend upon the values of a person making the recommendations. . . .

Today it is generally recognized that valid principles of administration must themselves deal with the limitations of both theory and theoreticians in an administrative environment. It must deal with the components of organizational action other than theory and knowledge. From this point of view principles of administration are tools that administrators can use in finding answers to administrative problems.

Part IV

THE PEOPLE

Chapter 14

THE HUMAN BEINGS

T HE BEHAVIOR OF PEOPLE, as stated in Chapter 10, is at the very heart of the administrative process. The study of administration depends upon, or is a part of, nothing less than the study of man. The acceptance of this idea is a prerequisite for any serious study of people in organizations and their guidance by administrators. The study of organizational purposes must start with an understanding of the purposeful behavior of human beings.

One way to achieve such an understanding is to flee the world of ordered, systematic thought and research and turn to art and literature. In the works of Shakespeare, Goethe, Dostoevski, and the countless unnamed authors of the Bible, the *Mahabhrata* and other national epics, we can undoubtedly find genuine insights into the nature of man. Here there stretches out before our eyes the vast spectrum of the human comedy.

Yet at one small spot on this spectrum we find a whirling cloud in which psychologists, psychiatrists, psychoanalysts, sociologists, anthropologists, and physiologists use different languages to express divergent views on the spectrum as a whole. And at a small spot behind this welter of words we can find something approaching consensus on a few fundamental propositions concerning the nature of man. Among these are the following:

1. The purposeful behavior of human beings is motivated by a multiplicity of interests.
2. Human beings are always part of some specific group environment.
3. Conflict is an inevitable part of human nature.
4. Human beings are unique personalities.
5. A large part of human behavior is irrational or nonrational.

In selecting these propositions I have not chosen all those ideas which students of psychology might agree upon or regard as most important. I have selected those which, in disposing of certain popular fallacies concerning human behavior, are particularly useful in the foundation of a general theory of administration. In elaborating upon them, moreover, I have found it necessary to do a certain amount of adaptation and remodelling. This may remove some of them from the area of consensus. Yet in my judgment it brings them closer to the insights of art and literature and the wisdom of experienced administrators. It moves them more fully into the area of immediate relevance to administrative practice and theory.

A. *The Multiplicity of Individual Interests*

THE PROPOSITION that "the purposeful behavior of human beings is motivated by a multiplicity of interests" stands in direct opposition to various fallacies of single motivation. It conflicts with any theory that focuses on economic gain, sex, or something else as *the* sole or determining object of human desire and that subordinates or ignores all other objects. A single motivation theory is acceptable only if one maintains a sharp distinction between real human beings and the economist's "economic man" or the "sex-driven man" appearing in popular misconceptions of Freud. It becomes dangerous only when one forgets this distinction and tries to force the variability of human behavior into the procrustean bed of a single-factor explanation.

As an easy alternative to single motivation theory, we can readily prepare long lists of instincts, urges, drives, interests, needs, and desires. Yet by so doing we would jump from the frying pan of oversimplification into the fire of utter confusion.

A more ordered, but still flexible, approach is provided by dividing human interests or needs into the four broad categories of survival, commergence[1] (or belonging), differentiation and self-development. This

1. For further explanation of this term, see page 324.

is merely a way of saying that people are interested in surviving, in being "a part" of something else, of being somewhat "apart" from others, and in developing their full potentialities.

To this extremely simple statement might be added the additional point that many actions satisfy all these interests at once, albeit in different proportions. Thus a person's work may provide him with the economic prerequisites of survival, the satisfaction of working with certain people, a certain amount of prestige, and an opportunity for developing his creative abilities. If you ask him today what his purpose is, he may answer that it is "to finish ABC, which is supposed to be completed by the end of the week." ABC may be an assembly job, a memorandum or an investigation. Whatever it is, if it is a goal to which he orients himself with a large amount of dedicated energy, we may be sure that in doing so he is probably motivated by a varied set of mutually-reinforcing personal interests.

The relation between various interests, however, is extremely complex. The motive power of any one interest may be greatly affected by the extent to which others are gratified or frustrated. Activities seen as relating to one type of interest may in fact serve as a substitute for action to meet another interest.

Above all, there is reason to suspect the operation of a certain hierarchy of interests. When survival interests are satisfied and there is a reasonable basis for confidence in their continued satisfaction, they are no longer powerful motivators. Commergence and differentiation interests may now become much more important. With greater faith in their continued satisfaction, the higher interests in self-development may emerge more fully. At this level a high degree of satisfaction is rarely possible, and so these higher interests may continue as powerful motivators. It is in this sense that A. H. Maslow holds that psychological health, instead of being the absence of disease, is essentially the gratification of ever-higher needs (1954, Chapts. 4, 5, and 8).

The following four categories of survival, commergence, differentiation, and self-development are an adaptation of Maslow's analysis.

1. SURVIVAL: PHYSIOLOGY, SAFETY, ACTIVITY

In order to survive, a person must provide a minimum degree of satisfaction for certain basic physiological interests.

Among the most obvious are the interests in food, drink, sleep, and sex. Less clear, but often directly reflected in the appetites, are the needs of the blood stream for certain proportions of water, salt, and sugar and the needs of the body for various minerals, hormones, and vitamins.

Closer to the safety needs are the physiological needs for protection against weather, injury, and disease, needs which are met through various forms of housing, clothing, and medical care.

Survival also requires protection against physical attack by animals or other human beings. These interests are usually met through weapons, the designation of special security forces, resistance to attack, and, on many occasions, preventive action designed to wipe out sources of potential aggression.

Other safety needs are related to the dangers of interference with the arrangements people have worked out to meet their physiological needs. Instability and unpredictability are threats to all orderly arrangements. Unemployment is a direct threat to the satisfaction of the needs for food, shelter, clothing, and medical care. Hence the deep-rooted human interest in economic security.

When a person perceives serious threats to the satisfaction of certain survival interests, these interests may become the most important things in life. Man does indeed not live by bread alone. But as Maslow maintains, the qualification of "Unless he has no bread" must be added.

> For the man who is extremely and dangerously hungry, no other interests exist but food. He dreams food, he remembers food, he thinks about food, he emotes only about food, he perceives only food, and he wants only food. The more subtle determinants that ordinarily fuse with the physiological drives in organizing even feeding, drinking, or sexual behavior, may now be so completely overwhelmed as to allow us to speak at this time (but only at this time) of pure hunger drive and behavior, with the one unqualified aim of relief (*Ibid.*, p. 82).

Similar statements can be made about other extreme deprivations or threats. This is why in time of great crisis—war, famine, pestilence and mass depression—the motivations of people tend to become more simple, similar, and predictable.

In periods of purely personal crisis, the frustration of survival interests other than food and sleep may lead to puzzling substitution phenomena. Thus serious threats to economic security may lead to a preoccupation with sex. The thwarting of sexual gratification may result in a preoccupation with food. When the young infant sees recurring threats to his very survival, the result may be a compulsive-obsessive neurosis during all his adult days. Drawing upon a wealth of psychiatric data, Maslow describes such cases as follows:

> Compulsive-obsessives try frantically to order and stabilize the world so that no unmanageable, unexpected or unfamiliar dangers will ever appear. They hedge themselves about with all sorts of ceremonials, rules and formulas so that every possible contingency may be provided for and

so that no new contingencies may appear. . . . If, through no fault of their own, something unexpected does occur, they go into a panic reaction. . . . The healthy taste for the novel or the unknown is missing or at a minimum in the average neurotic (*Ibid.*, p. 89).

One of the most elemental of all interests is the interest in continuing to live. "The only certainty that men have is that they must die. And yet," as Ferrero has pointed out, "they all live, until the arrival of death, as though they were immortal. . . . They fight against death until the very last moment" (1942, p. 311). Despite progress in extending life, this fight can be only temporarily successful. No matter how much people may deceive themselves, insecurity on this point is unavoidable. This explains the popularity of various substitute measures—from sexual reproduction and the construction of monuments to the religious belief in life after death.

Another elemental need is activity for its own sake. The human organism is not designed for complete idleness. Either body or mind, and usually both, must reach some minimum level of activity. Under special conditions induced by drugs, hypnosis, or perhaps extremely low temperatures, it may be possible to maintain human life for long periods with little or no activity. But under usual conditions, inactivity means decay, disintegration, and death. People simply must do *something*.

As one succeeds in meeting his physiological, safety, and activity interests, he attains a certain feeling of relief. But this relief may well be associated with emptiness. What seemed so important before attained is no longer of much importance. Although he may still take action to meet recurring survival needs and to strengthen his confidence in their continued gratification, they are no longer powerful motivators. Mere life and activity for their own sake alone seems useless.

We can thus appreciate the problem faced by all political parties which have developed their strength by action designed to meet people's interests in economic security. When people are no longer worried about economic insecurity, the old slogans and appeals lose much of their former magic. This is one of the reasons for the decline of the British Labor Party subsequent to its successes with its full employment program after World War II. It is one of the reasons why, after the economic reforms of the Roosevelt New Deal in the United States of America, the Democratic Party has never been able to get back to its peak of previous popular support. It is why a trade union which succeeds in achieving economic security for its members often needs the compulsion of a "check-off system" in order to keep its members in the union. It is why employers' efforts to motivate workers by economic rewards alone may often end in utter failure.

Problems such as these are at the root of the widespread question "After X, what?" Depending upon how the X is filled in, this question takes many forms. Among these are: "After peace . . . or security . . . or affluence . . . what?" Each of these questions implies that there are and must be some other purposes in life than merely satisfying basic survival interests

2. COMMERGENCE: BELONGING, CONFORMITY, AFFECTION

According to Maslow, once survival needs are fairly well gratified, "there will emerge the love and affection and belonging needs, and the whole cycle already described will repeat itself with this new center." "Submergence" would be an excellent word to express the common element of becoming a part of something larger than one's self rather than remaining a thing apart. However, since this word carries overtones of "submerged" in the sense of "exploited" or "drowned," "commergence" is used instead. Although a new word, it vividly expresses the ideas of closeness, togetherness, and identification.

The interest in belonging to some group or groups is very closely associated with safety needs. Few people are strong enough to stand against attack without support from others. But belonging and togetherness have value in themselves, apart from their clear contribution to security. People obtain gratification from merely being a member of a family, a work group, a nationality group, a political party. They obtain more direct satisfactions from belonging to someone or some group that will meet their needs "to be nursed, supported, sustained, surrounded, protected, loved, advised, guided, indulged, forgiven, consoled" (Murray et al., 1938, p. 182).

The usual price of belonging to some group is conformity with its accepted codes on patterns of behavior. In minor things, this means following the fad and the fashion with respect to clothes, demeanor, and speech—a phenomenon adults can best understand when viewing the behavior of children and adolescents. In more important matters, it means conforming with the customs and mores concerning sex, treatment of children and parents, communication methods, and the balancing of conflicting interests. The need for conformity, heightened by the normal processes of acculturation, is often so great that deviations from accepted codes will often lead to bitter self-punishment through an overwhelming sense of guilt. As the Freudians have demonstrated, this punishment may be at its deadliest when the sense of guilt is pushed into the preconscious and the unconscious mental processes.

Commergence can also mean affection, an emotional sense of attachment. A person's needs for affection can be at least partly met through the simple process of day-to-day interaction with a colleague—even a rival—at the place of work or in the office. In this sense commergence is a positive relief from loneliness. It should not, however, be confused with love; the word "love" is taken in vain more than the name of any deity. It is often said of an administrator that "he is in love with his organization." This often refers to the affection felt by one who is incapable of loving.

Like any other interests, commergence interests may be met in extreme ways. Belonging may be carried to the point of denying individuality. This is the horror envisioned in the literature of antiorganizational revolt.

Conformity may become utter submissiveness to authority or complete dependence on others. Affection may become a form of escape from the harshness of changing society. This is the defeatist picture presented by Matthew Arnold in "Dover Beach," in which the poet sees nothing but love as worth living for in a world of lost faith and armed might.

But as Erich Fromm has pointed out, the cry "Ah, love let us be true to one another" is, in this context, merely an effort to find "a refuge from an unbearable sense of loneliness . . . an alliance of two against the world . . . this egoism *à deux* is mistaken for love and intimacy" (1956, p. 88). In a more extreme form commergence becomes a mystic identification with the universe, a psychological release from the bonds of individual human existence (as with the negative aspects of the Indian *nirvana* and *moksha*), a complete joining with the world of nature through death and disintegration.

As a person achieves the satisfaction of commergence interests, he feels that he has arrived. He can now sink his roots. But so can a tree. This is usually not enough for a man or woman.

Thus here too we hear the question "After X, what?" Is belonging enough? Are togetherness and affection our highest goals?

3. DIFFERENTIATION: STATUS, RESPECT, POWER

The differentiation interests often appear to be merely the other side of the coin from commergence. The need to be the same as others is closely allied with the need to be at least a little different.

Yet differentiation tends to follow, rather than accompany, identification. One can usually afford to be different only when one already belongs. The obvious exception to this principle is the case of the ingrained outsider, the "isolate" or the rejected person who compensates for his apartness by conspicuous deviation.

The essence of all systems of status is that by ranking people in various orders they provide a clear system of differentiation. They meet the individual's need not only to have some place in the world, but a special place. Their effectiveness is based, among other things, on the fact that status differentiation can usually be depended upon irrespective of what a person might do. Except for the people at the very bottom of the totem pole, this assures at least a bare minimum of deference and perhaps some prestige along with it.

Respect is another matter. It is not given so readily, nor can it be automatically maintained. Genuine self-respect is probably harder to achieve and maintain than the respect of others. In either form, respect depends upon perceived performance or acknowledged status.

The sharpest form of differentiation is found in the wielding of personal power. The mover and the shaker clearly separates himself from the moved and the shaken, the dominator from the dominated, the aggressor from his victim. Economic, government, political, and religious organizations include many people—usually their most active members—whose needs for survival, belonging, status, and respect are well gratified. It is hard to explain their behavior except in terms of their deep-seated needs for more power and more secure power.

A person's interest in power may be expressed in many forms. For all those who yearn to shape great events, there are probably far more who feel an equally deep need to dominate just a few other people. In the case of a parent, it may be a need to dominate a helpless child—or an equally helpless mate. Or it may take the more positive form of nurturance needs, the needs "to give sympathy and gratify the needs of a helpless other: an infant or another that is weak, disabled, tired, inexperienced, infirm, defeated, humiliated, lonely, defected, sick, mentally confused. To assist another in danger. To feed, help, support, console, protect, comfort, nurse, heal" (Murray *et al.*, 1938, p. 182).

In any of their forms the differentiation interests are closely associated with the emergence of the ego and the sense of personal identity. As Maslow points out, these needs (which he prefers to call "esteem needs"), relatively neglected by Freud, were stressed by Adler and his followers and have since won widespread recognition among both psychoanalysts and clinical psychologists. There is general acknowledgment today that the "thwarting of these needs produces feelings of insecurity, of weakness and of helplessness. These feelings in turn give rise to either basic discouragement or else compensatory or neurotic trends." On the other hand, the satisfaction of these needs may lead to "feelings of self-confidence, worth, strength, capability and adequacy..." (1954, p. 90-91).

As a person achieves a certain level of satisfaction of his differentiation interests, he experiences a sense of elation interwoven with feelings of superiority. Yet this too pales. He may seek to restore the lost elation by straining for ever larger amounts of status, respect and power. If he succeeds, his victory may be counterbalanced by actions which, while necessary to make him stand more apart from others, have the indirect effect of making him less a part of anything else and even jeopardizing his personal survival. And the personal fruits of such a victory will be unquestionably diminished by the inexorable operation of the law of diminishing returns. He will be caught on the endless wheel of seeking more and more from life and, in fact, getting less and less.

So once again, we confront the question "After X, what?" What does it matter if we gain status, respect, and power and lose our souls in the effort?

4. SELF-DEVELOPMENT: LEARNING, CREATIVITY, LOVE

For many centuries mankind has been groping toward a common answer to this fundamental question. Philosophers, religious leaders, and poets have used different words to stress a common theme. In modern times the words themselves have sometimes tended to converge. For Erich Fromm, the highest goal in a world of sanity is man's freedom "to be himself, to be productive, to be fully awake" and to "respond to the world with our senses in a meaningful, skilled, productive, active and shared way" (1955, p. 347, 355). For Karen Horney, the goal is "spontaneity of feeling, an awareness and aliveness of feeling . . .the striving for wholeheartedness" in a context of mutual sharing and understanding (1955, p. 241-242). For Hans Selye, the endocrinologist, "man's ultimate aim is to express himself as fully as possible, according to his own lights" (1956, p. 299). Kurt Goldstein, the biologist and psychologist, finds the unifying concept needed to explain the diversity of human behavior in "the tendency of the organism to actualize itself. . . . The organism has definite potentialities and because it has them it has the need to actualize or realize them. The fulfillment of these needs represents the self-actualization of the organism" (1930, p. 203-204). Using Goldstein's term, Maslow elaborates the same theme in the following manner:

It [self-actualization] refers to a man's desire for self-fulfillment, namely to the tendency for him to become actualized in what he is potentially. This tendency might be phrased as the desire to become more and more what one is, to become everything that one is capable of becoming.

The specific form that these needs will take will of course vary greatly from one person to another. In one individual it may take the form of the desire to be an ideal mother, in another it may be expressed athletically, and in still another it may be expressed in painting pictures or in inventions (1954, p. 91-92).

The clear emergence of these needs, according to Maslow, depends upon prior satisfaction of the physiological, safety, belonging, and esteem needs. In fact, the steady gratification of these needs during one's early formative years can go a long way toward freeing a person from over-concentration on these needs in his later years. He can thus become more of an autonomous, self-actualizing person. In time of crisis he is also more capable of withstanding the frustration of any needs.

The difficulty with the term "self-actualization" is that it carries with it certain overtones of predestination, as though the self-actualizing person is working out some predetermined pattern. This same connotation attaches itself to the terms "self-fulfillment" and "self-realization." Another connotation is that self-actualization, self-fulfillment, or self-realization necessarily lead to some final state in which they have at last been achieved. In my judgment, "self-development" is a more adaptable term. Its use helps emphasize that at this point we are discussing action, never completely predetermined, to meet needs that can never be completely fulfilled. It helps stress the role of individual will and effort, as contrasted with an automatic process. It suggests an important relation between self-development and national development.

No matter which term is used, this basic idea has many facets. One of these is the interest in learning. Maslow divides this area into two parts. At a somewhat lower level he identifies the desire to know, as may be expressed in simple curiosity. At a somewhat higher level he finds that "after we know, we are impelled to know more and more minutely and microscopically on the one hand, and on the other, more and more extensively in the direction of a world philosophy, theology, etc. The facts that we acquire, if they are isolated or atomistic, inevitably get theorized about, and either analyzed or organized or both. This process has been phrased by some as the search for meaning. We shall then postulate a desire to understand, to systematize, or organize, to analyze, to look for revelations and meaning, to construct a system of values" (*Ibid.*, p. 96-97). At either level, knowing or understanding, learning is a process of growth, a process through which one becomes something more than one was before.

Another facet is the interest in self-expression. Actions to meet this need are often closely intertwined with actions of commergence, differentiation, or both. Yet in freer and more spontaneous forms these actions transcend the lower interests. The boy whistling in the fields, the girl singing to herself, the novelist or sculptor who really does not care what people think of his work—these are all meeting their needs for self-expression.

Self-development also involves the interest in creativity. Learning and self-expression are themselves creative activities. But the higher forms of creativity get somewhat beyond the self-involvement of both of these. Nor should creativity be thought of as something limited to the rarified atmosphere of the artist, the scientist and the intellectual. It can be much more humble. There can be creative shoemakers and carpenters—and creative foremen, division heads, top executives, and members of directorates. Maslow expresses this as follows:

> The creativeness of the self-actualized man seems rather to be kin to the naive and universal creativeness of unspoiled children. It seems to be more a fundamental characteristic of common human nature—a potentiality given to all human beings at birth. Most human beings lose this as they become enculturated, but some few individuals seem either to retain this fresh and naive, direct way of looking at life, or if they have lost it, as most people do, they later in life recover it. . . .
>
> If there were no choking-off forces, we might expect that every human being would show this special type of creativeness (*Ibid.*, p. 223-224).

While self-developing activity is rooted in actions that may serve to satisfy all one's interests, its most essential characteristic is that it enables one to transcend his interests. It is in this sense that self-development is on the borderline between motivated behavior and those forms of highly spontaneous behavior that lie beyond motivation. This, of course, is the essential characteristic of anything that can be called an ultimate aim. As an ultimate, it is purposeless. "The mystic experience, the experience of awe, of delight, of wonder, of mystery, and of admiration are all subjectively rich experiences that beat their way in upon the organism, flooding it as music does. These too are end experiences, ultimate rather than instrumental . . ." (*Ibid.*, p. 300). In this sense self-development is very close to the positive aspects of *nirvana* or *moksha;* it is a release from one's lower needs and a uniting with all mankind.

I doubt whether self-development can ever proceed very far if strictly ego-centered. True self-development involves an enlargement or broadening of the ego, an extension of the self so that it covers much more than self, a fusion or integration between the ego and others. In Selye's words, it involves a process which parallels the historic evolution of the single cell into intercellular altruism, the evolution of egotism into interpersonal altruism (1956, p. 282-283). This is self-development on behalf of interests broader than one's self.

At this level, self-development becomes a form of love. By "love"

I am not referring to the many things that masquerade under this much-abused term—not to sexual titillation, the accommodating exchange of favors and conveniences, the neurotic desire to dominate or be dominated, the idolatrous worshipping of a false image on a pedestal, and not the sentimental phantasies and daydreams so widely peddled by the cinema, radio and television, magazine "love" stories, and popular "love" songs. I am referring rather to love in the sense so brilliantly set forth by Erich Fromm (1956). This is love in the sense of a sustained activity of uniting with others. It may appear in the form of brotherly love, parental love, erotic love, self-love (quite different from selfishness), or the love of God in the sense that "God" is a symbol of all that is wonderful and beautiful in man and nature. It involves "the active concern for the life and growth of that which we love." It involves a responsibility for the psychic needs of others, a responsibility based upon knowledge. Above all, it means giving of one's self, loving rather than merely being loved. The giving and the receiving are inextricably interrelated. Neither the mother who wants only to give nor the beautiful girl who wants only to get is really capable of loving or being loved. If an exchange relationship is involved, this is not the exchange with which economists are accustomed to deal. Scarcity does not appear in the same form as in the market place. While love is a game involving many elements of conflict and tension, it is also one in which both sides may win at the same time. The more one gives, the more one may have left. The more one gets, the more the other may have. In its more physiological aspects, scarcity appears much sooner; sexual appetites may in most cases be quickly relieved. But love is far more than sex. In its fullest form it involves a deep mutuality and intertwining of human interests. (*Ibid.*, Chapt. 2, p. 7-82.)

The struggle for survival may wreck others. The pursuit of commergence and differentiation may prevent others from attaining similar ends. The pursuit of self-development in the sense of learning, creativity and love has none of these indirect results. In its more modest forms it is noninjurious to others. At its best it helps others meet their own needs.

While flouting the principles of economic scarcity, self-development interests also seem to transcend the otherwise inexorable law of diminishing returns. Here there is no easy satiation. One can never learn very much, let alone enough. One can never attain an ideal peak of creative achievement. There can never be enough love or too much love. Full satisfaction of these needs is simply unattainable. The process of pursuing the satisfaction of these as distinguished from other needs may thus be the most truly satisfying thing in life.

5. THE ROLE OF ECONOMIC GAIN

From the previous discussion one might get the false impression that since personal economic gain does not appear in any of the major headings, it has no role to play in the motivation of human beings. It is therefore desirable to correct such an impression by suggesting the specific nature of economic motivation.

First of all, some form of economic gain—particularly in an exchange economy—is a prerequisite for meeting man's survival needs. Food, drink, shelter, clothing, education: all these are dependent upon money. To a certain extent, the stability of sexual gratifications, even those associated with family life, is based upon money as well. Except in the case of those with accumulated economic means, full-time activity in any organization is therefore associated with some form of economic compensation.

Second, economic rewards are often recognized symbols of one's place in life. They may serve as a measure of the extent to which one has met the needs for both commergence and differentiation. Particularly in rapidly expanding market economies, they become general indicators of status, respect and power.

Third, in addition to being a measure of power, money is a direct source of power. It is an instrument of direct control over anything that money will buy. This is a power source of no small significance particularly since money can also indirectly enable one to get the things money cannot buy. Hence the phenomenon of many private business men who are "hell-bent" for enlarging their personal power but who justify their actions publicly only in terms of the pursuit of money.

Finally, as one of the most flexible instruments ever invented, money may also serve as a partial instrument in satisfying self-development interests and as a partial measure of progress in this direction. Many highly creative and self-expressive activities may take the form of the invention of new accounting devices or even of monetary manipulation. In the business world many of the most creative and even altruistic urges to develop new products, new technologies and new departures in basic science, are intertwined with—or disguised by—monetary calculations and rationalizations.

B. *The Individual-in-the-Group*

IN DISCUSSING COMMERGENCE needs I have already indicated the strength of the motives which impel individuals to participate in various groups.

It might also be added that in a world where isolated individuals can rarely cope with even their physiological needs, some minimum degree of participation is a stark necessity.

Yet even these observations understate the fact that no individual is "an island unto himself." Through no decision of his own, man is born into a family group. He grows up as a member of various groups and from time to time makes his own decisions about attachments to or affiliations with other groups. It may thus be confidently stated that "Human beings are always part of some specific group environment."

This proposition stands in opposition to the "Robinson Crusoe" theory of economic behavior or the Great Man theory of historical explanation. At their worst, these theories purport to explain human behavior in terms of pure individualism. At their best, they regard all other factors as "exogenous" or as part of a *ceteris paribus* to be examined by someone else; they then proceed to concentrate upon a thin and artificial segment of human behavior.

At this point it is pertinent to discuss groups in general, with special emphasis upon the relationships between the individual and groups. All of these relationships are equally pertinent to those groups which we call organizations.

1. MULTIPLE GROUP ATTACHMENT

Every individual is attached in some way or other to a number of groups. The most direct form of attachment is to a single membership group. But since most membership groups are composed of subgroups, many of them concentric, this form of attachment itself involves multiple membership. Thus in the family a young boy may belong both to the family as a whole and to the smaller group of children or young people. A post office clerk belongs not only to his unit, section, and division, but also to the postal service as a whole and to the civil service as a whole. A trade union member may belong not only to his local union and to a national union, but also to general labor federation and an international labor movement. This form of multiple membership is a direct function of the complex structure of groups and organizations.

The second form of multiple membership consists of membership in a multiplicity of groups. Rarely is any one individual wholly absorbed in the activities of any one organization and its subordinate parts. To the extent that this may be true, as with the housewife who lives only in and for her family or the executive who lives only in and for the organization, we are dealing with pathological cases. It is extremely rare that a healthy human being can find sufficient satisfaction for all his needs through one group alone. The only clear exception is the infant, whose early needs are met solely within the family. But the very process of acculturation by the family leads to the emergence of needs that can be met only outside the family. Thus the child joins one or more educational institutions. As an adult, his livelihood depends upon membership in some work group. During this process of growth he becomes a member of various play or study groups and may join one or another religious, neighborhood, political, national, or professional groups. This form of multiple membership results from the breadth of human needs as contrasted with the more narrow purposes of most groups and organizations.

Finally, one may be strongly attached to the values and objectives of a certain group without actually being a member. Among social psychologists such a group is usually called a "reference group." Thus many people may be followers or "fellow travellers" of a professional organization, a trade union or a political party without wanting to become a member. A reference group may also be one whose objectives are passionately accepted as a way of demonstrating his qualifications for future acceptance into membership. Thus the top executive group of a corporation may be a powerful reference group for an aspiring junior executive. For many people, however, the most influential reference groups are those who sit on certain pinnacles of prestige to which they themselves cannot realistically aspire.

2. THE INDIVIDUAL'S SOCIAL ROLE

As well defined by the Hartleys a "social role consists of the behaviors expected of individuals occupying certain positions in specific groups" (1952, p. 516). This is one of the most important concepts not only in social psychology but in social science as a whole.

It is these mutual expectations concerning the behavior of others—and, of course, conformance with them—that make it possible for the members of a group to achieve the necessary minimum of cooperation. Without such expectations group action would collapse under the weight of over-frequent experimentation and unpredictability.

When groups become more complex as a result of size, technology, and environmental pressures, social roles themselves become more complex. The reason is the growing interdependence of behavior between the members of the group, an interdependence which may require an elaborate meshing of individual roles. In the more firmly established organizations an effort is often made to define social roles through formal job definitions, an effort often thwarted by inadequate techniques of service definition and a neglect of essential interrelationships within an organization. In any case there are limits on the extent to which human expectations can be adequately expressed in writing, even if one should assume a static situation. The expectations that underlie any social role include the expectations of many different people, including not only associates and subordinates, but also different people at higher levels of responsibility. There are always bound to be certain conflicting expectations which cannot be quickly resolved except at considerable cost or certain expectations that one person will compensate for the deficiencies, physical or mental, of another. People prefer to leave expectations of this type ambiguous or unwritten, even though this may require a little time for a newcomer to learn his role.[2]

Over any significant period of time, moreover, the situation is never static. With new problems, products, personalities and technologies, new behaviors become essential. New expectations emerge. Old roles are shaken up. Moreover, the old structure of roles is always being shaken up by the new distribution of skills. Youngsters come along who know many things their elders never learned. The old timers must adapt, give way or fight a defensive action on behalf of their time-hallowed past behavior patterns. For the youngsters also the process may also be painful. The more they advance and the higher they go, the more they must abandon previous roles and learn the requirements of new ones, and the more they are in danger of rapidly becoming "oldsters."

At the same time, social role is never defined exclusively by others. Each individual himself contributes something to it. More forceful and creative personalities may through successful performance in flexible situations establish the major outlines of their own social role. Even in rigid situations the timid soul will contribute something to the role he enacts—much as even the mediocre actor of Hamlet's part will contribute something not specified either in Shakespeare's lines or the director's instructions.

The entire situation is complicated by unavoidable defects in the communication of expectations. Superior officers, for example, may take it for granted that a subordinate knows what is expected of him, thereby neglecting to explain. Or else explanation, when given, may be unclear. If clear, it may be misunderstood or misinterpreted.

3. THE INDIVIDUAL'S SOCIAL STATUS

The concept of status has already appeared in our discussion of the hierarchy of individual needs. Status is a concept fundamentally based

2. This subject is discussed in more detail in "Operating Goals" and "General Functions" in "Output: Operations and Functions" (Chapt. 23).

upon a group orientation. It exists in the eyes of others. One's own conception of status is mainly a reflection, whether clear or distorted, of the views of others.

In part, status has larger determinants than one's social role. A person's status may be ascribed to him because of attributes which are mainly unrelated to his personal performance—such as birth, family connections, race, sex, size, beauty, or age. In some societies, as emphasized in Parsons' list of cultural pattern variables, ascription is far more important than achievement (1951, p. 154).

In the era of the administrative revolution, however, increasing attention is given to achievement. Status is determined more and more by skill, knowledge, education, wealth, and power. In particular, it is determined by one's social role. Subject to only few exceptions, the hierarchy of social roles established within any group is the status system of the group. In organizations, as pointed out by Barnard, status is based both upon trade or occupation and upon formal positions of responsibility and authority, and is reinforced by various symbols and insignia (1948, p. 207-244).

But status is rarely limited to a single group; there is usually some carryover among roles in various organizations. The successful businessman and the political leader will often enjoy higher status in a fraternal organization, and occupy higher roles, than the unsuccessful businessman or the lowly political hack. Of course, status incongruence may occur—as when a person of higher education occupies a lower-skilled position or a person of some favored race or religion performs a social role usually assigned to members of a supposedly "inferior" race or religion (*Adams*). This is usually a source of dissatisfaction and anxiety to the persons involved, a factor that may in fact impel them into the leadership of powerful movements as a way of attaining the personal positions to which they see themselves as entitled. If the situation is reversed—as it may well be when someone succeeds in climbing beyond the status ascribed to him—the dissatisfaction will be felt by those who object to the shaking of established expectations by the "new arrivers."

4. DEGREES OF GROUP IDENTIFICATION AND LOYALTY

An inescapable consequence of multiple group attachment is differing degrees of identification with different groups and with the social roles one assumes within them. This is merely another way of saying that multiple loyalty is inevitable. Often, when one must make a choice between two different sets of expectations, multiple loyalty is transformed into divided loyalty.

In the family, multiplicity of identification is indicated by the extent to which a child identifies himself with the family's children, the parents, the grandparents or the family as a whole. In a large organization, a person faces a choice between his immediate work group and the many larger units of which the work group is a part. The natural tendency seems to be that the most deep-seated attachments develop within those groups whose members have the most frequent personal interactions. Homans formulates this tendency in his hypothesis that "the more frequently persons interact with one another when no one of them originates interaction with much greater frequency than the others, the greater is their liking for one another and their feeling of ease in one another's presence" (1950, p. 243). This tendency is reinforced when people share common backgrounds and similar social values.

Identification, moreover, is a reciprocal relationship. Rejection by other members of the group will place a person in the position of an "isolate" or a "deviant." Acceptance must be earned through ascribed attributes or performance in accordance with the norms of the group.

No matter what the degree of actual or potential acceptance, one's degree of identification and loyalty to any group is also affected by one's level of aspiration. The person who orients himself toward higher status will usually identify himself somewhat less with his immediate work group. He will usually show greater loyalty to those reference groups whose judgments may affect his future roles.

The nature of certain roles—particularly administrative roles—is also a factor. The typical manager belongs to a number of overlapping subgroups: his immediate subordinates, his immediate superiors and his immediate colleagues. If he identifies too closely with any one of these groups, he runs the risk of injuring his relationships with the others. Hence every manager is usually a "man in the middle," a person of necessarily divided loyalties and allegiances. Moreover, to the extent that an administrator sees his role as that of continuing initiation and thereby establishes a one-way interaction pattern, the degree to which he may be accepted within any one group will be small. This is one of the reasons why many people find loneliness and isolation in positions of administrative leadership.

The diversity of personal attachments and loyalties is compounded by one's membership in entirely different groups. Just as one must achieve some working balance between one's attachments to various parts of a given group, one must also achieve some working balance between attachments to family, work place, political party, and national or religious group, to mention but a few. At the very least, these various groups compete for time and attention. Often, they demand different forms of behavior. Thus one's attitude toward various candidates for appointment to a vacant position will vary with the degree of one's loyalty to family, friends, political party or the perceived needs of one or another part of the organization. In policy decisions affecting large groups of people, the pressure of competing loyalties may be still stronger.

c. *The Individual's Conflicts*

ONE OF THE POPULAR FALLACIES concerning human nature is the concept of the Adjusted Man, the myth of the well-oiled personality who is perfectly adjusted to his environment and has risen above all inner conflicts. This is the individualistic version of the fallacy that in good administration things run smoothly and easily. It leads to unrealizable goals concerning personal behavior and unrealistic diagnoses of personal problems.

Conflict is an inherent part of an individual's life. One cannot rise above conflict. One can merely respond to it in varying ways. Hence the proposition that "Conflict is an inevitable part of human nature."

This is not to say that individual conflict in the abstract is either good or bad. Here too, as with organizational conflict, there is a double potential. Conflict can be destructive of human happiness and even of personality itself. Or it may motivate one to higher and higher levels of need gratification. In either case it is impossible to understand a person very well without learning something about his conflicts and reactions to them.

1. THE NATURE OF AN INDIVIDUAL'S CONFLICTS

As with organizations, individual conflict can be internal or external. Internal conflicts are derived, first and foremost, from the multiplicity of human purposes, social roles, and group attachments. It is only natural for people to want to do things which, if objectively compatible, are rendered conflicting by the shortage of time or which, if time is available, are inherently conflicting.

External conflicts develop as an individual's desires or actions are impeded by some natural obstacle, by one or more other individuals or by one or more groups. The very process of acculturation is one of conflict and tension between the individual and those who expect his behavior to conform to their desires. Many external conflicts, particularly those relating to multiple group attachments and multiple social roles, are internalized. They thus reappear in the form of sharply conflicting purposes and values. These are often the sharpest and most disturbing of all inner conflicts.

Apart from their source, an individual's conflicts vary in terms both of degree and of the interests to which they relate. A low degree conflict is that of a simple choice between alternative means—as when a woman chooses which dress to wear to a party. A more complex conflict arises in choosing among escorts. If there is an abundance of alternatives to choose from, the situation may be confusing but the conflict will not be intense. The conflict rises in degree if, in a society where the customs forbid it, she seriously considers having sexual relationships without marriage. The conflict becomes still more serious if two suitors or lovers decide to fight to the death for her hand. In every case a certain kind of action is impeded or frustrated. In the lower degree cases, the conflict can be settled by small modifications and shiftings. The highest degree cases are head-on collisions of the all-or-none variety in a situation characterized by a scarcity of alternatives.

Equally important as a determinant of intensity is the level of interests which are involved. Here it may be stated that the lower the interests on the hierarchy of individual motivation the more disturbing a conflict may be to an individual and the deeper the emotions that may be aroused. Thus a low degree conflict relating to one's physical survival is usually far more upsetting than one relating with respect to commergence, differentiation or self-development. It takes a very intense evocation of higher needs to lead one to the sacrifice of survival through martyrdom or suicide. The truly self-developing person, paradoxically, is the one most capable of standing up under the strain of acute frustration or giving up power, position and life itself on behalf of something larger than himself.

2. "NORMAL" RESOLUTIONS OF INDIVIDUAL CONFLICT

There is nothing that is more of a routine and every-day part of an individual's life than the way he handles his conflicts. Even unusual and unprecedented conflicts are usually handled in a "normal"—in the sense of healthy—manner.

Unfortunately, this aspect of normal behavior has been obscured by the lack of attention given to normal people by experimental psychologists and the inescapable emphasis of clinical psychologists on pathological cases. This overemphasis on the pathological handling of conflict is only partly counterbalanced by the tendency of the psychiatrist or psychoanalyst to go to the other extreme and find that everyone in the world (including the doctor) is neurotic. In discussing "normal" solutions to individual conflict, we are therefore venturing somewhat further into the area of hypothetical and the unverified than is necessary in the subsequent section.

Any such discussion, however, must be preceded by a qualification concerning the words "resolution" or "solution." Their use implies no aura of finality whatsoever. Every resolution or solution itself creates or leads to new conflicts. In fact, one of the most instructive ways of evaluating and ranking solutions is in terms of the character of the new conflicts emanating from them.

The first element in the normal reaction to conflict is delay. This is inherent in the very blockage which is the essence of conflict. This delay may involve a long period of time, while the parties to the conflict survey the terrain and search for solutions. At times, it may appear to be—or may actually be—interminable. Or else the delay may be momentary, while the tracks are cleared for some sort of action. In either case, the period of delay usually involves the piling up of additional conflicts related to the solution of the original conflict.

The second element is tension, or stress. This results both from the actual delay and from the anxieties involved in the prospect of further frustration. It inevitably carries with it a certain amount of painfulness. On the other hand, unless too acute, the tension itself usually stimulates a higher level of mental and physical energy and feelings of excitement which may be regarded as highly pleasurable. People who have become accustomed to working at high tension find it extremely difficult, therefore, to adjust to situations in which no serious conflicts need be faced.

The final element is some sort of resolution. Here as already outlined in section C of "The Conflict-Cooperation Nexus" (Chapt. 11), the pattern is extremely variable. It may include almost any conceivable combination of avoidance, deadlock, victory (or defeat), compromise and integration. Not only organizational conflicts but also the inner conflicts of individuals, it should be noted, can be resolved through integration. Here there is a reevaluation of personal interests, a systematic examination of the objective situation and the development of "the possibility of something better than either of two given alternatives," the possibility of both interests being met and neither frustrated. This is very close to a description of what is done in the best of modern psychotherapy.

Unfortunately, there is little or no research evidence which would indicate the extent to which the normal solutions to individual conflict are distributed among the categories of avoidance, deadlock, domination, compromise and integration. The tendency among practical people and cynics is to regard integration solutions as exceptional. My own hypothesis is that without underestimating the amount of pure compromise, one can regard integration of conflict as a normal part of the behavior of healthy people. The difficulty with psychotherapy is that the rituals of organized medicine and exaggerated analogies with physical disease have often prevented psychiatrists and psychoanalysts from giving enough attention to the inner conflicts arising from a complex and rapidly changing environment (Szasz, 1961).

No matter what the nature of the resolution, it is perfectly normal for people to react emotionally to conflict situations and to seek methods of expressing their emotion. These emotions may be expressed in acts of open aggression or hostility. They may be repressed and find their outlet in other areas through sublimation (the use of a substitute activity to gratify a frustrated motive), compensation (success in one area to make up for self-esteem lost in another area), displacement (the disguising of an uncomfortable goal by the use of a more acceptable one), or projection (the disguising of a source of conflict by attributing one's own motives to others). While these forms of reaction to conflict were initially discovered and dissected in the area of pathology, they are probably just as important to normal as to abnormal life. It is hard to conceive how people could handle their conflicts without the defense mechanisms which they provide.

3. "ABNORMAL" RESOLUTIONS OF INDIVIDUAL CONFLICT

Having reversed the usual process by first discussing normal conflict solution, I shall now return to the field of more usual concern to the psychologist: abnormal and pathological solutions to conflicts.

This is far more than an academic concern to the study of administration. There are at least some small bits or aspects of the abnormal or pathological in every individual. There are much more than small bits or aspects of neurotic behavior in most organizations. In some organizations examples may even be found of psychotic behavior.

Neurosis or psychoneurosis may be roughly defined as "a personality disorder, less severe than a psychosis, in which a person is unusually anxious, miserable, troublesome, or incapacitated in his work and relations with other people" (Morgan, 1956, p. 640). Whether we use this or another definition, the line between normality and neurosis is not easy to draw.

To some small degree, the distinction may be found in the nature of an individual's conflicts. Neurosis usually develops in connection with high-degree conflicts which frustrate the usual satisfactions of the most elemental needs for survival, commergence, and differentiation.

To a greater degree the distinction is found in the nature of individual behavior in reaction to conflicts. In neurotic behavior the normal reactions of hostility and aggression are expressed in a more extreme fashion. Or else, if repressed, sublimation, compensation, displacement, or projection are carried to greater lengths. In addition, more specifically neurotic forms of behavior may develop. These include fixation and compulsion, compliance and helplessness, withdrawal and isolation, sadism and masochism, hysteria, and highly idealized self images combined with deep-seated feelings of inferiority. In almost all cases the individual suffers acute and painful anxiety, although this may be interspersed with brief periods of joy and relief. In many cases, the neurosis is expressed in ailments of the digestive, nervous or respiratory systems and other types of psychosomatic disorders.

Finally, the neurotic reaction involves a lack of awareness concerning the underlying conflict or conflicts. The fatal process of repression, disguise, displacement, and false idealization is carried so far that the individual is even more removed from an adequate perception of reality than the ordinary limited human being. This is why many therapists emphasize "bringing the patient to a thorough understanding of his conflicts—their general effect on his personality and their specific responsibility for his symptoms" (Horney, 1955, p. 241-242).

In contrast with neurosis, psychosis may be defined as "a mental or personality disorder, more severe than a psychoneurosis, characterized by a bizarre, unrealistic behavior that is often so incompetent and dangerous that the person must be given custodial care" (Morgan, 1956, p. 640).

Here the flight from reality is more far-reaching. It takes the individual into an inner world of self-delusion. It removes him from contact with others through the normal devices and symbols of communication. It may lead to extremely severe states of depression, to delusions or hallucinations, or to one or another form of schizophrenia: simple, paranoid, catatonic, or hebephrenic.

It would be utopian to believe that the reaction of individual members of an organization to the conflict inherent in organizational and administrative activity is always to find normal solutions. On the one hand, organizational conflict often provides the final straw that moves a person across the border between normality and neurosis. On the other hand, certain forms of high organizational performance are often the result of obsessive and compulsive behavior. Organizational activity— and perhaps administrative activity in particular—often provides opportunities for people to channel and harness their neurotic impulses. The cost of such self-administered therapy can be measured only by the sacrifice of other aspects of organizational performance and the negative impact on the lives of other members of the organization. The fact that both of these costs may be substantial does not imply that they are not frequently incurred.

It is much less frequent for the psychotic person to function within an organization—at least at the lower levels. It seems that one can survive within an organization despite paranoia or schizophrenia only if one occupies an extremely high position in the directorate of a rapidly expanding organization—as with Hitler, Mussolini, and Stalin. By many relevant criteria such people, who if not fully psychotic were at least on the border between psychosis and neurosis, have proved effective organization leaders. In the case of the state organization in Germany, Italy, or Russia, the results of such leadership are to be measured in bloodshed and murder. In simpler organizations the results may appear in the debasement, humiliation and frustration of colleagues and underlings.

D. *The Individuality of Personality*

THE BELIEF in personality types or stereotypes is perhaps the most widespread of all popular fallacies concerning human nature. For many centuries people have made the grievous error of thinking that they have discovered the most important thing about someone else when they have identified his color, race, national origin, or religion. More pretentious but no less fallacious efforts have been made to establish personality types on the basis of astrology, phrenology, physiognomy, morphology, and endocrinology. Similar tendencies have been encouraged by specialists who, having developed scientific methods of measuring a few human traits, have unscientifically presented them as so-called "personality tests." Many people who should know better still paint crude pictures of a world peopled by introverts, other-directed people, executive types, and other stereotypes.

Although the study of human personality is a field in which divergence and disagreement are rampant, there is one point upon which most serious researchers and students are agreed: that the human personality is much more than any single trait or cluster of traits. Almost every theory of personality uses words like organization, system, structure and pattern to express the wholeness of human personality. When seen in their wholeness, rather than in terms of a few special aspects, it is then clear that human beings are unique personalities.

1. UNIQUENESS

The first determinant of personality is inherited characteristics. These are transmitted through the genes within the chromosomes. Biological investigation indicates that there are between 20,000 to 42,000 gene locations in the chromosomes. The theoretical number of possibilities in the offspring of any two people is more than twice as many. It may thus be concluded, as one biologist has put it, that "all human beings who have ever lived . . . have not scratched the surface of possible gene combinations in Homo sapiens" (LaBarre, 1954, p. 97).

Environmental factors are even more varied. In conjunction with hereditary factors, they produce a biological organism which is itself unique. Recent biochemical research has demonstrated tremendous variability among individuals with respect to almost every aspect of the structure and chemical composition of the human body. This undermines the old demarcation between the normal and the abnormal:

> If we consider the possibility that among the numerous measurable attributes that human beings possess there may be many which are not mathematically correlated, we are confronted with an idea which is opposed to the basic dichotomy of normal and abnormal. If 0.95 of the population is normal with respect to one measurable item, only 0.902 (0.95^2) would be normal with respect to two measurable items and 0.60 (0.95^{10}) and 0.0059 (0.95^{100}), respectively, would be normal with regard to 10 and 100 uncorrelated items.
>
> The existence in every human being of a vast array of attributes which are potentially measurable (whether by present methods or not), and probably often uncorrelated mathematically, makes quite tenable the hypothesis that practically every human being is a deviate in some respects (Roger Williams, 1956, p. 2-3).

Psychological variation, itself greatly affected by biological variation, is probably still greater. Every person grows up in a unique situation. His development is affected not only by the general cultural environment but also by the specific treatment he receives from parents, other family members, teachers, playmates, and other associates. In response to these environmental situations he develops various skills and abilities. He acquires certain attitudes and interests. He weaves himself into an intricate web of interpersonal relations and group affiliations. He develops a unique pattern of need satisfaction and need frustration.

This infinite variability does not imply that classification is impossible. On the contrary, classification of some sort is essential to any scientific effort to understand human personality. A large part of psychological research and analysis is based upon one of three classification systems. One emphasizes the stimulus aspect of personality—that is, how a person affects others. The second emphasizes the response aspect—that is, the pattern of response to defined stimuli. The third emphasizes the "inner organization of emotions, values and beliefs which determine a person's superficial responses (gestures and the like) and in turn determine his effectiveness with other people" (Stagner, 1960). Yet no classification system is scientifically valid if it purports to express the totality of any person's personality by identifying him as one or another type. The utility of classification systems, rather, is that, like the Bertillon system of fingerprinting classification, they provide a method of coping with the individual's uniqueness.

2. THE MANY FACES OF INDIVIDUALS

The preceding discussion is based on the oversimplified assumption that personality is a phenomenon that can be objectively observed. The full complexity of personality is understood only when we remember that personality, unlike such a simple matter as fingerprints, appears as something different to different observers.

Every man and woman has many different faces. To illustrate this simple fact of life, there is no need to use extreme cases of split personality. We need merely remember that the result of multiple group affiliation is multiple roles. This is why Mr. A is A_1 in the eyes of his subordinate and A_2 in the eyes of his superior. Nor does he appear as the identical Mr. A to both associates and clients. Likewise, he is not seen as the same person by his wife, his parents and his children. Appearance, moreover, should not be too quickly contrasted with reality. Mr. A appears different to different people not only because of their peculiar way of looking at him but also because he acts differently toward each of them. His multiple roles produce a multisided personality.

One of Mr. A's most significant faces is his own self-image. If this self-image is too dramatically at variance with the faces seen by others, Mr. A will probably be confined to a mental institution. But even the person who runs a mental health institution or commits others to it has a self-image quite different from the faces perceived by others. This too is a part of reality, and an extremely influential one at that. Even the most carefully observant psychologist, psychiatrist, or psychoanalyst may himself perceive only part of the series A_1, A_2 . . . . A_n. How can he confidently conclude that one of these, or one set of these, is correct and the others wrong?

But even if pinned down at a specific point in time, the personality is bound to change. While this process may be theoretically confined within certain limits, Mr. A of today is never the same as Mr. A of ten years ago. Under the impact of accumulated development, learning, and aging, each face inevitably changes its features.

E. *Normal Irrationality*

EVEN MORE MISLEADING and dangerous than the fallacies of the Economic Man, the Robinson Crusoe Man, the Adjusted Man and the Stereotype is the idea that people are—or could sometime become—creatures who always act rationally. This is the fallacy of the Rational Man. From this point of view, irrationality is the province of the uneducated, who must be taught, the unintelligent, who lack reasoning ability, and the abnormal, who should be cured.

This fallacy has had the great historic value of serving as a myth to justify the authority—if not to suggest the infallibility—of rulers and administrators. But the more successful rulers have known better. They have usually acted on the assumption that most other people are at least partly irrational. They have often succeeded in perceiving the irrationality of fellow rulers, rivals and—at times—themselves.

It is indeed true that neurotic and psychotic behavior is irrational and that the uneducated can never reach high levels of rationality. But normality and education do not imply strictly rational and logical behavior. There are many entirely normal forms of nonlogical behavior and educated irrationality. Hence the proposition that "a large part of human behavior is irrational or nonrational."

The nature of human rationality is discussed at greater length in Chapter 28. There a major distinction is made between the characteristics of rational action and the processes of calculation designed to help achieve rational action. Rational action is discussed in terms of three dimensions: desirability, feasibility, and consistency. A high degree of rationality in one of these dimensions, it is shown, may often be associated with a low degree of rationality on one or both of the others. Also, rational action, as measured by any dimension, is limited by environmental blocks, by individual and organizational limits on learning and by the self-imposed boundaries which are usually a prerequisite for scientific and technological analysis.

To these limits we must add those which bear upon the processes of calculation themselves. As pointed out in Simon's discussion of "bounded rationality," the human calculator usually suffers from imperfect information, limited computational ability and the lack of a complete and consistent preference ordering. We must add Barnard's profound observation concerning the possible irrelevance of rational techniques to certain materials that "cannot bear the weight of ponderous logic." We should recall his contention that in many situations the logical statement of a problem may change the situation that is being analyzed and thus render the formulation inaccurate. Thus rationality itself, in the more narrow sense, may turn out to be an irrational form of behavior.

Finally, both rational action and rational calculation are dependent upon three aspects of behavior which may lead to irrationality as well. First of all, emotions and feelings are the wellsprings of the very considerable energy needed for rational calculation. As Maslow has pointed out, there are few people more driven by the white heat of emotion than the scientist intent on finding an objective solution. Much of human action—rational, irrational and nonrational—is affected by love, hatred, resentment, anger, envy, and fear. Even when action is most fully premeditated, these emotions may determine more than anything else the nature of the information perceived, the computation system used and the purposes emphasized or sacrificed. Second, there is the area of automatic action. In part, particularly in the very young, this is based upon inherited instincts. In large part, it is the result of habit or imitation. In either case, premeditation and calculation are either absent or peripheral. Automatic action on many routine problems is essential to allow people to concentrate attention on those which are of a less routine nature. Third, there is the great area of unconscious and preconscious calculation. This area stands midway between automatic and premeditated action and often succeeds in dominating both. One need not accept Freud's special version of how the subconscious operates in order to recognize its tremendous importance. The subconscious may serve as a receptacle for conflicts which might otherwise obstruct rational calculation. Subconscious thought processes may themselves be capable of operating more rapidly and more successfully than their conscious counterparts.

Chapter 15

PEOPLE-IN-ORGANIZATIONS: FORMAL ASPECTS

*I*N THE PREVIOUS CHAPTER we looked at people apart from their roles in any specific organization. We saw that every person is a unique personality motivated by many interests, attached to many groups, affected by internal conflicts and acting nonrationally as well as rationally.

In this chapter we shall look at organizations. We shall focus upon their general characteristics and certain formal aspects of organizational structure.

In so doing, we cannot avoid using many terms that seem to take us very far from human beings. The word "structure," in particular, suggests something nonhuman and impersonal. One reason for this is that people often think of organizational structure in terms of the structure of buildings. This has given an architectural or engineering flavor to much of human thought, at both the common-sense and theoretical levels, about organizational structure.

But the relationships in human organizations are quite different from those among the parts of a building. They have meaning only in terms of the expectations and actions of human beings. When we talk about organizational structure, we refer to some pattern which joins the parts of an organization to the purposes of the organization as a whole. Any such pattern consists of some combination of roles for units and members and the relations established among them by hierarchy, polyarchy, and codes of behavior. These roles, relations, and codes have both their formal and informal aspects, sometimes referred to as the "formal structure" and the "informal structure." The difference between them is that the former are—and the latter are not—prescribed by the holders of formal authority.

While the informal aspects of organizational structure are more intimately related to the personality of individual members, this chapter will demonstrate that it would be a great mistake to regard the formal aspects as lacking in human qualities. They too are forms of human behavior. Instead of being fixed and unchanging like the walls and girders of a building, they are modified by a continual series of official changes. They are often embodied in oral decisions and requests; they can never be fully set forth in writing. Like their promulgators, they can never be free from internal inconsistencies and conflicts. As with all prescriptions for human behavior, they are never complied with completely.

The informal aspects of structures, particularly informal roles, are discussed in the next chapter. The broad subject of organizational codes, both formal and informal, is reserved for Chapter 27.

A. *An Overview*

BEFORE EXAMINING the internal structure of organizations, let us step back and take an overview of their general characteristics. In so doing, we shall see that entirely apart from its structure, every organization can be described in terms of output purposes, legal status, membership basis, production technology, and certain dimensions of size and time. The first three of these characteristics are often stated, at least partially, in formal charters—constitutions, by-laws, regulations, declarations of principle, agreements, contracts, covenants, and articles of incorporation or federation. All of them may have an important influence upon formal and informal structure.

Those characteristics which flow from an organization's immediate and general environment are discussed in Chapters 17 and 18.

1. OUTPUT ROLES

From the viewpoint of a society, polity or economy, the division of labor among organizations is made on the basis of—or evidenced by—the services or goods produced. The apostle's words, "By their fruits ye shall know them" (Matthew, 7:20), provide the most general basis for the identification and classification of organizations. The most obvious difference among political parties, churches, trade associations, fraternal societies, wholesalers, and railroads is that they provide different kinds of services for different clienteles. The most obvious difference among agricultural, mining, manufacturing, and construction organizations is that they produce different kinds of goods. (All of these organizations will be found in the census classifications of economic "sectors" or "activities," both of which are based upon distinctions among the major products produced.) Similarly, it is the output objectives of an organization more than anything else which define its distinctive role in society.

The fact that an organization is known by its output does not necessarily imply that its output is readily known. Some organizations are not quite sure what their fruits shall or should be. Few organizations produce just a single product. As explained in Chapter 22, their fruits may take the form of a highly variegated "output mix." As shown in Chapter 23, many services, particularly intangible ones, are extremely hard to identify.

Far easier to pin down is another important aspect of an organization's output—the basis on which its "fruits" are made available to clients. The term "business" or "firm" is usually reserved for an organization that sells its products to its clients. The sales revenue thus received is a major, if not the only, source of external revenue. (In the case of a bank, interest payments can be regarded as the cash payment for credit services.) This direct financial nexus between organization and clients makes it possible to place a monetary value upon output. The organization can thereby make a profitability calculation, which is the only generally feasible way of calculating output and input in the same units of measurement. In this sense, many government organizations, cooperatives, fee-charging hospitals, and schools—no matter how little profit they seek or attain—are business organizations.

On the other hand, there are those organizations (we might call them "nonbusiness") which transmit their goods or services to clients on some basis other than sales. The income of such organizations is obtained from government funds or nongovernment contributions. Although some or all of it may come from the clients of an organization, the route is circuitous rather than direct. Here we find legislatures, courts, armies, and governmental regulatory bodies—except in the borderline cases of mercenary troops and bribery.

Paradoxically enough, we must also include in the nonbusiness category most internal units in any business organization. Although they may be interested in contributing to the profit position of the organization as a whole (and this certainly distinguishes them from the units of a nonbusiness organization), there is no way of calculating a profit or a loss for themselves. The only clear exceptions are certain large subdivisions of those extremely large business organizations which have set up pricing systems for internal transactions. Another possible exception is in the case of some systems of piecework and incentive wages. Here the workers' position may be comparable to that of subcontractors who are directly paid for services rendered. Both internal pricing and piecework contracting, however, may exist within nonbusiness organizations.

2. *LEGAL STATUS*

The differentiation among organizations on the basis of legal status is a dangerous undertaking. Legalistic formulations have a hypnotic power. If one gazes upon them for a long enough time, one may end up being hypnotized into confusing form with substance and fiction with fact. Many a brilliant scholar has been carried off in a cloud of legalism, never to be heard of again in the world of reality.

Yet the legal aspects of organizations are themselves a part of reality. While they never reveal the whole story, they are always part of the story.

A. *Governmental or nongovernmental.* The most important legal distinction is that which may be used in placing all organizations somewhere on a continuum from governmental to nongovernmental. At one extreme, there are those clusters of organizations called "states" that exercise certain kinds of legitimate authority, or sovereignty, over all the people in a given geographical area. Each such cluster as a whole may back up this authority by using physical force of some sort, such force to be exercised by specialized organizations. National, as distinguished from local, states may also use such force or violence outside their geographical area.

At the other extreme, there are separate and clustered organizations that do not participate in any way in the sovereignty of states. Although they may try to extend their influence throughout the area of any state, their formal authority is limited to their members alone. Except for protective operations of a minor nature, they may not legitimately establish police forces or armed services.

In the middle stand a host of quasi-governmental organizations. These include (a) regional and international organizations formed by governments, but far from being federated governments, (b) mixed agencies formed by governmental and nongovernmental organizations, (c) government-established agencies that are instructed to operate as private bodies, (d) privately established agencies upon whom governmental authority is bestowed, and (e) those political parties that install—or try to install—their members in positions of power within governmental organizations.

B. *Corporate or noncorporate status.* In the sense that it may be thought of as having a personality of its own, every organization may be regarded as a corporate entity. In a legal sense, however, the corporate form allows an organization to enjoy certain rights that would otherwise have been denied it. The earliest of such rights was the right to hold property in perpetuity, apart from the death of the "natural persons" owning or controlling the organization. Among business organizations, the most important of such rights has become the freedom of stockholders from liability for the debts of the corporation. These and related "escape provisions" have enabled nongovernment organizations to mobilize and maintain larger aggregations of assets than would be technically possible through individual proprietorships, partnerships or nonincorporated syndicates, trusts or associations.

Among government organizations the corporate form has also served as an escape device. Here it has allowed government agencies to escape budgetary, accounting and personnel controls imposed upon "regular" government agencies, as well as formally sanctioned intervention by high state officials and legislative bodies.

There is a tremendous variety of corporate forms. Nongovernment corporations are set up in accordance with general laws in different states and countries and specific laws relating to certain types of enterprises such as banks, insurance companies and utilities. They may be stock or nonstock corporations. They may be mutual or cooperative corporations. Government corporations are usually created under individual laws. The diversity of these laws and the forms established under them is so great that many decades ago a skilled analyst observed that "the government corporation as a concept—as a definite and specialized form of administrative organization—is rapidly ceasing to exist" (Pritchett, 1941). Since then, with the development of more extensive controls over government agencies and consequently of still more varied patterns of escaping them, the diversity has become still greater. Moreover, the corporate form has become one of the major instruments for establishing private-public enterprise and blurring the line between government and nongovernment organizations. To the uninitiated, therefore, corporate law—both private and public—is indeed a jungle. Yet from this jungle have emerged forms of social innovation that have helped determine the nature and pace of the administrative and technological revolutions. As demonstrated by Sigmund Timberg's discussion of corporations as an instrument for international governmental cooperation on specific projects (1952), many new and striking innovations may still be expected in this sphere.[1]

3. BASES FOR MEMBERSHIP

The boundary lines of organizations, like those of some countries, are not always clear. Some people manage to stand astride them, with one foot on each side. Some shift back and forth from one side to another. Sometimes the boundary is a strip of "no man's land" peopled by those who belong neither here nor there.

Nonetheless, boundaries there must be. These are determined by the nature of membership and the conditions of entry and exit.

A. *Employment or affiliation.* There are two general bases for membership. The first is employment, which may be full-time or part-time, permanent or temporary, paid or unpaid. Business and government organizations are mainly composed of full-time paid employees for whom membership in the employing organization is a major part of their life.

The second is some act of affiliation or participation, as with associations, unions, professional societies, political parties, or churches. The members of these organizations might be called "affiliates," to distinguish them from the employed staff. In some organizations the higher officials may be both employees and affiliates. In others, the employees are excluded from genuine membership and are regarded as mere "staff," "personnel," or "bureaucracy." In either case participation by the majority of "affiliates" is apt to be casual, sporadic and tangential to their deeper interests. The "activists" are generally limited to a few cliques that run things, their rivals and the employees. In the case of some political parties and churches, the term "member" is vaguely used to apply both to the "organization" or "hierarchy" and to large, unstructured groups of followers or adherents.

A special and more limited form of membership is provided by those cases, such as schools, hospitals, and jails, in which a service organization and its primary clientele are joined together in a structured community. Students, patients, and inmates are rarely directly involved in the production of educational, health, and custodial services; they are rather

1. In another penetrating article (1946) Timberg breaks down the so-called "corporate fiction" into seventeen component fictions. Among these are the fictions that a corporation is governed by a "single group purpose," a "single group will" or a "single group." Nonetheless, he believes that corporations "should be regarded as not only the carriers of their own private interests, but instrumentalities for effectuating social and economic interests which the national and international community regard as paramount."

the direct recipients. Yet they are much closer to the organizations producing these services than are the roomers in a hotel or apartment house. They may be regarded as client-members.

A distinction must also be made between individual and group membership. This is particularly important in associations and federations in which the nature of affiliation determines the location of ultimate authority among members. Many large associations are based entirely upon individual membership, with groups of members engaging in separate or local activities. Federations tend to be based upon group membership. Some organizations have a dual basis of participation, with separate voting privileges for both groups and individuals.

B. *Entry.* At one extreme, some affiliation organizations are wide open in the sense that anyone can join them by unilateral action on his own part. This may range from signing a piece of paper to making a dues payment. In some cases minor prerequisites may be required—such as a given occupational background or a recommendation by another member.

In all employment organizations, however, and in many associations entry is conditional. The new member must agree to accept certain obligations. Sometimes the prerequisites for entry are many and difficult. Organizations with an eye to the future tend to realize that a series of entry decisions will eventually determine the entire future composition of the organization. This leads to a series of openly stated entrance standards relating to ability, experience, and education. It may also mean equally stringent prerequisites—although harder to detect from the outside—with respect to sex, color, religion, age, special background, physical attributes, and personal compatibility. To offset some of these barriers, entry may be policed by government regulatory agencies. Additional barriers may be established by trade association blacklists and by trade union insistence on the hiring only of people who are already union members (the closed shop) or are willing to join the union (union shop).

At the other extreme, there are various organizations which people are forced to enter against their will and not allowed to leave. This includes large parts of many armies, organizations operating with "forced labor," some "closed shop" trade unions, and some political parties and trade associations. It also includes a large part of the "client members" of compulsory school systems, hospitals, and jails. If we want to regard families as organizations, we must keep in mind that although family entry through marriage may be voluntary, one's entry through birth is always involuntary.

c. *Exit.* In most organizations people have the right to leave when they so desire. Only in compulsory schools and such "closed institutions" as conscript armies, jails, mental hospitals, and concentration camps are people compelled to remain against their will.

Apart from compulsion, many barriers are erected to prevent exits and maintain membership. The most obvious are contractual obligations to serve for a given period of time. More widespread are the many benefits such as pension plans, stock options, tenure, and seniority rights, any of which may be wholly or partially lost by leaving.

Still stronger barriers such as tenure and permanent status may be erected against an organization's effort to require members to leave. Even where these rights are not enjoyed, separation and expulsion actions are costly and nasty affairs. It is often easier to transfer a person to another unit in an organization or "kick him upstairs." In the case of the occupants of highest political office, removal may be impossible without a costly election campaign, a public program of vilification, impeachment proceedings, or the more violent extremes of coup d'etat or revolution.

4. PRODUCTION TECHNOLOGY

As already indicated in Chapter 2, the development of modern organization is intimately connected with the rising level of technology. Modern technology calls for more subdivision of labor, more hierarchy and larger organizations. It substitutes machinery and electrical energy for manual labor. It promotes the proliferation of white collar workers, technicians and professional people. It tends to convert the work of organizations into intellectual rather than physical operations.

In the early days of "scientific management" there was a tendency to see administration mainly as a problem in engineering. Then the human relations school countered with the motto "People are not machines." Now there is ever-increasing realization that people in organizations, while not machines, are very directly affected by the nature of the production processes they use, including machines. As stated by one of the researchers in the field, it is becoming increasingly clear that "The technology of the plant—the way jobs are distributed and flow into one another and the nature of the division of labor—molds the type of work groups that evolve within the plant . . . the technological structure of the organization, in turn, exerts a major influence on the source of motivation and morale, the work group. This is the reason for the statement that the field of personnel relations has come the full circle to the point where engineering considerations are once again crucial" (Sayles, 1958, p. 4). The Tavistock analysts look at industrial organizations as "sociotechnical systems" (*Trist et al.*, p. 196).

Thus, on an assembly line, a welder may have no direct contact with anyone in the plant except the man on his right and the man on his left, plus an occasional systems expert or quality controller who looks over his shoulder. In a small file room, six people may work closely together as members of a tightly knit group. In another situation workers may belong to a much larger department and may be divided into a number of smaller, informal groups working in competition one with the other. In many schools the accepted processes of education dictate that individual teachers work as lone wolves. Their main responsibility is "giving" a number of courses and for this purpose they need have no contact (except for somnolent faculty meetings) with their colleagues. These alternative patterns of production affect the extent of cooperation among individuals and units. They thus create many of the special problems of motivation and morale that are faced by administrators.

In a larger sense the production processes also determine the distribution of attention among material assets, people and ideas. There is a major difference between organizations in "primary industries," where attention must continually be focused on natural resources, and "secondary industries" with their attention focused on processed materials. There is a still greater difference between these and the "tertiary industries," dealing with services, particularly those services centering around relations between people and groups. In all of these sectors, there are major differences between the more "labor intensive" organizations and the more "capital intensive" ones with their problems of "hard goods" technology and long-range planning of expensive fixed investment.

Perhaps even more important is the rate at which new methods and processes are introduced. Technological change of any significance whatsoever is a threat, real or imagined, to the power or security of someone, often of many people in the organization. In its more obvious aspects, any technological change which enables the production of similar output with less labor threatens to reduce employment. But even where such an effect can be counterbalanced by expanded production or by transfers to other work, the change itself threatens established positions and expertise. It renders obsolete the accrued capital of knowledge in the hands and minds of those who operated in accordance with the previous processes. It may even suggest that the people responsible for the previous processes are inferior individuals, as compared with the wiser souls who promote the new processes. Furthermore, it may turn upside down the old world of established relationships and lead to a complete reorganization of work groups, tasks, responsibilities, and individual status. Similarly, rapidly changing technology is guaranteed to destroy organizational lethargy and routine. It places a higher premium upon administrators who are capable of adjusting quickly to new situations and of

WHICH IS BIGGEST?

	U.S. Dept. of Defense[a]	American Telephone and Telegraph[b]	CIO-AFL[c]	United Nations[d]
Members				
Employees	3.5 million civil & military	40,000 in central holding company	600 in national office	37,600 (including all U.N. programs and specialized agencies)
		729,000 in holding company and subsidiaries		
Affiliates (non-employed members)	476,000 in about 6,000 local national guard units	25 subsidiaries	132 unions 62,353 locals	110 member nations
		(over 2 million stockholders)[e]	15 million union members	(over 2 billion people)[e]
Material Assets		$24.6 billion		
Expenditures	$51 billion	$8.7 billion gross expenses	n.a.	$550 million
Output		$100 billion gross revenues		
Spatial Distribution	International, with operations in outer space	National, with foreign offices and operations in outer space	National, with foreign offices	International

a. United States Budget for fiscal year 1964. National Guard data from Encyclopaedia Britannica.
b. American Telephone and Telegraph *Annual Report* for 1961.
c. *Statistical Abstract of United States of America*, 1960. Table 298.
d. United Nations documents.
e. Included for background purposes, although they are "holders of ultimate authority" rather than members of the organization.

getting people to accept new rules and procedures to take the place of those that must be discarded.

5. SIZE

The size of an organization may be measured in five dimensions: (i) Number of members, with attention wherever appropriate to distinctions between employed, affiliate, client and individual-or-group membership; (ii) Material assets, such as land, buildings, equipment, machinery, inventories, credits, and cash. Often the most relevant measure is the quantity of a single type of strategic asset—such as hospital beds, classrooms, freight cars, or airplanes; (iii) Actual or budgeted expenditures. With government agencies and the internal units of all (including business) organizations, expenditures are widely used as a measure of output; (iv) Quantity of output. Monetary measures are possible only with business-type organizations. In other cases the quantity of different types of output cannot be directly aggregated; (v) Spatial distribution of members, assets, expenditures, or output.

Although a major increase in any one dimension may imply increases in some of the others, there is no necessary relationship between any two dimensions. This point is developed further in the discussion of organizational growth, particularly in "The law of disproportionality," in Chapter 25.

In considering the size of all organizations as a whole, or even of any large group of organizations, the most useful dimension is the number of members. First of all, the assets acquired, expenditures made and output produced by an organization are more measures of organizational action than of the organization. When we count members, we are coming closest to the organization itself, which essentially consists of the interactions among its members.

Second, membership size is the only dimension for which data are generally obtainable. Comparable data on the value of assets and output can usually be obtained only for business organizations; when obtained they are subject to serious problems of interpretation. Expenditure data for national labor federations are often kept secret. Spatial distribution cannot readily be quantified in comparable terms. This problem of comparability is illustrated in the table "Which Is Biggest?" Membership data provide the easiest basis for comparing the four giants: the United States Department of Defense, the American Telephone and Telegraph Corporation, the CIO-AF of L and the United Nations.

Once we go beyond employment figures, however, there are problems of comparability in membership data. By the number of affiliates, the CIO-AF of L, with its 15 million members, is certainly bigger than the United Nations. By the number of people represented, the United Nations is larger. By the number of people employed the United States Department of Defense is the largest of them all—and probably the largest single organization outside of the U.S.S.R. and China.

Despite these limitations, membership data provide a useful way of measuring the distribution of organizations by size groups. Thus an interesting comparison may be made between business, Federal Government and labor organizations in the U.S.A.:

PERCENTAGE DISTRIBUTION OF ORGANIZATIONS

Membership Size Group	Business, 1956[a]	Federal Government Agencies, 1960[b]	Trade Unions, 1958[c]
Under 1,000	99.0	41.5	7.5
1,000-10,000	.9	27.9	27.5
10,000-1,000,000	.1	29.7	64.0
Over 1,000,000	.0	1.9	1.0
Total	100.0	100.0	100.0

a. *Statistical Abstract of United States of America*, 1960. Table 625. Includes military employees and Coast Guard.
b. *Ibid.*, Table 502. Federal agencies only. Excludes Central Intelligence Agency and legislative and judicial branches. Executive Office of President regarded as one agency.
c. *Ibid.* Table 299.

Thus we see that while most business organizations have less than 1,000 employees, less than half of the Federal Government agencies fall in this group. (We may be sure that the proportion in this smallest category would rise considerably, if state and local government agencies were also included.) In contrast, almost two-thirds of the trade unions are in the 10,000 to one million category. By emphasizing the number of organizations, however, this table understates the importance of the larger organizations. A major shift to the higher categories is obtained by distributing the total number of members by the size of the organizations to which they belong:

PERCENTAGE DISTRIBUTION OF ORGANIZATION MEMBERSHIP

Membership Size Group	Business, 1956	Federal Government Agencies, 1960	Trade Unions, 1958
Under 1,000	65.0	.2	.1
1,000-10,000	17.6	1.0	1.3
10,000-1,000,000	17.4	25.0	85.0
Over 1,000,000	.0	74.0	13.6
Total	100.0	100.0	100.0

Sources: Same as in previous table.

If the available membership data on associations were compiled by government statistical agencies, it would be more appropriate to include trade unions together with other associations and to make a formal distinction between affiliates and employees, with an indication of the ratio of the one to another.

The effect of variations in group size has long been a subject of attention by social scientists. Thus Simmel stressed the difference between two-person and three-person groups. In a group of two "the social structure here rests immediately on the one and on the other of the two, and the secession of either would destroy the whole. . . . As soon, however, as there is an association of three, a group continues to exist even in case one of the members drops out." When a third member is added, he may combine with one of the others, become a mediator between them or follow a policy of divide and conquer (1950, p. 123, p. 145-169). It might be added that the third member may also become a "semioutsider" or a "sleeping partner."

As the small group becomes somewhat larger, cases of communication, attitudes of intimate sympathy and close identification may be lost. Smaller subgroups and factions are likely to develop. Leadership skills become a much greater factor in the creation of unity.[2]

As organizations become still larger, many relations become less personal (*Medalia*). There is even more specialization of function and more reliance on formal authority, rules and "antagonistic cooperation" (*Arensberg and MacGregor; Ellsworth*). With continued growth the organization faces increasingly serious problems of internal communication (*Burling et al.*), morale (*Worthy*), and absenteeism (*Covner*). These problems are heightened by geographical spread (*Kaufman*) and absentee ownership (*Warner and Low*). By the time it becomes a really large organization it loses much of the flexibility it enjoyed in earlier days. "Large organizations with different purposes seem to resemble each other more than small organizations with different purposes do. It is not too fanciful to think of a single organizational type toward which all giant organizations tend. An army, an industrial enterprise, a newspaper, a philanthropy, and a university all resemble each other, or, more exactly, they all approach a common type. Their small group prototypes, by contrast, do not resemble each other . . ." (Caplow).

In looking at large organizations, however, we must keep in mind Barnard's well-founded observation that nowhere in the world "can there be found a large organization that is not composed of small units"

2. This question has frequently been explored by the psychologists of group dynamics, but with more attention to discussion groups than to work groups. See particularly Hare (1953).

(1938, p. 110). Thus, many administrators within a very large organization are men and women responsible for the activities of small units. The differences between these units and "independent" organizations of similar size is merely that the former are part of a larger organization instead of merely some loose cooperative system. Without much more research on the matter, the implications of this difference are not so clear. Many small organizations—from bootblack stands and cigar stores to junk dealers and bricklaying firms—are probably as specialized as any "fractionated" unit in an industrial or government giant. Many small units in a large organization probably enjoy freedoms of action and initiative rarely approximated by the small entrepreneur. In any case, as already discussed in Chapter 3 and as elaborated upon in Chapters 16 and 25, the growth of organizations is followed by an inevitable dispersion of power. The deliberate cultivation and promotion of this dispersion may, indeed, be the result of conscious administrative action (*Kaufman; Chandler; Dill*).

6. TIME

There are also important time dimensions of any organization and its operations. Among these are the continuity, duration, and pace of its operations. Organizational age will be discussed in Chapter 25 in the context of survival or liquidation.

A. *Operational continuity.* Some organizations are involved in "continuous process" operations. Their members work—or must be ready to work—"around the clock." Among these are steel, chemical, and cement plants with ovens and other facilities that need day and night attention. In the case of hospitals, hotels, police forces, and armies it is the clients who need continuous attention or protection. In contrast with those that operate during the daytime only, these organizations require a high degree of scheduling and internal control. This degree is still higher for those that are expected to be ready for unexpected emergencies.

From a longer range viewpoint the activities of any organization fluctuate over a period of time. These fluctuations are sometimes violent. In agriculture these fluctuations are determined to a considerable extent by the cycle of the seasons and the biological attributes of specific crops. It is this assumed certainty of the agricultural production cycle which has throughout the centuries given rise to a certain common psychology among people involved directly in the cultivation of land. Both the cycle of the seasons and the inevitability of certain "acts of God" are taken for granted. It is only when modern technology enters the picture and disrupts the traditional cycle that new attitudes are developed and a new agricultural psychology comes into being. For military organizations these fluctuations are both more violent—since they involve a change from peace or "cold" war to "hot" war—and more unpredictable. Except for cases of clear aggression, no one is ever sure when war will break out. Thus military organizations spend most of their time getting ready for emergencies which may never materialize—or at least will not do so in any predictable manner.

B. *Operational duration.* Although the printing of a daily newspaper is a very quick operation, the production of printing presses takes much longer. The construction of a new building to house both the printing presses and the whole staff of the newspaper will take still longer. The newspaper announcement of the opening of a giant new dam or of the discovery of a new use for atomic energy will usually be the culmination of work which started many years ago.

The most obvious implication of a long drawn-out production process is the necessity for long-range advance planning. A little less obvious is the human problem which arises whenever people are expected to work hard on behalf of goals whose realization is far distinct in the future.

For military organizations the largest of all question marks is the assumption that should be made concerning the duration of "the next war." To plan for a long, drawn-out battle of attrition is one thing. To plan for participation in one tremendous holocaust which may last only a few days—or even a few hours—is something else entirely. The latter assumption wrecks all previous concepts of defense and attack, build-up, and mobilization. Under this assumption, the management of mass murder becomes a matter of split-second decisions made by an unbelievably small number of people whose identity cannot be fully determined in advance.

C. *Pace.* There is a great difference between the administration of a slow and leisurely operation and the administration of one which moves forward at a breakneck pace. In the former case more things can be done in accordance with rules and routine. Less conflicts will usually arise. Those which do can be mediated more readily. In the latter case, even in large and presumably inflexible organizations, routine will be swept aside in order to cope with crises. People will step on each other's toes and, when this happens, both sides will shout more wildly. The energies of both the managers and the managed will be drained. And yet—and this is one of the great glories of administration in times of crisis—both sides may get deep satisfaction from seeing that things are really accomplished and this sense of satisfaction may itself develop new resources of personal energy. This is why the fast-paced operation will usually attract people of more outstanding abilities and more audacious minds.

In military organizations there is an extremely sharp contrast between the leisurely pace of peacetime and the rapid pace of war. Officers best suited for one of these periods may be ill suited for the other. This is illustrated by the famous statement of a quartermaster-general (which probably appears in the lore of all armies): "My office was running splendidly until the war disrupted it." Efforts to maintain continuous "combat readiness" without the imminence of combat may easily become routinized and illusory.

B. *Roles and Functions*

As WE LOOK INSIDE an organization, we find that its components or building blocks are its various units (or groups of members) and individual members. More specifically, the building blocks are the behavior expected of them and used as a standard to judge their performance. This is equivalent to the concept of social role presented in the previous chapter with respect to individuals and at the beginning of this chapter with respect to organizations as a whole. Here we concentrate on the social roles occupied by units and individuals. These are often referred to by the terms "function," "mission," "job," "task" or "duty"—used in either the singular or plural. The terms "position" and "office" are reserved for the social role occupied by individuals.[3]

1. OUTPUT, FUNCTIONS, WORK FLOW

The principle "By their fruits ye shall know them" is as applicable to the units of an organization as to an organization as a whole. The difference is that the role or function of a unit consists of intermediate rather than end products. Many units commonly have names which refer to the nature of their output such as personnel division, inspection section, tool-building shop, and legal department. If a unit's name is not fully descriptive (as with "the Administrative Office") this is often because it produces a varied output mix that cannot be aptly designated by one or two words. In any event a unit's output mix—and thereby its function in the organization—can be understood only by looking at the specific services it is expected to render.

3. A more detailed analysis of roles and functions, together with the extremely important distinction between operating goals and general functions, is presented in Chapter 23.

The only other bases of functional subdivision among units are location (as with field offices) and time (as with night shifts). Yet both location and time are subordinate to product. Any locational or temporal classification is superimposed upon product classification. A field office is an organization which is located in a certain place in order to produce certain products at that place. A night shift, day shift, or holiday shift produces certain products at a given place in time.

Proper attention to the importance of product classification as the basis of internal organization has been thwarted by the popular, but misleading, distinction between products, functions (in the sense of certain types of processes), and clients as different bases for organization. Actually, a "functional" or "process organization"—such as an engineering department or an electrolytic process division—is one which produces a specific type of service. A "client" organization—such as a ladies' dresses section of a department store or an adult education division of a university—is one which supplies certain products to specific categories of clients. In each case the use of terms relating to function, process and client is justified only to the extent that it aids in identifying the services or goods produced by a unit or in distinguishing between intermediate and final products.[4]

The output principle applies to individual roles also. The basis of every position or office is the bundle of services for which the occupant is responsible. The nature of these services is revealed both in the formal subdivision of labor among various positions and incurrent delegations and redelegations of responsibility. Many aspects of formal roles, apart from those that may be confidential or secret, can be only partly understood by outsiders or by organizations' members who do not interact frequently with the incumbents. Written job descriptions, as pointed out

---

4. In his classic "Note on the Theory of Organization" Gulick first suggested that a worker can be placed in a unit on the basis of one of these four considerations: the major *purpose* he is serving, the *process* he is using, the *persons* or *things* dealt with, or the *place* where he renders his service (1937, p. 15). Many other writers have taken up the same classification system. Business administration writers have often narrowed down the extremely broad term "purpose" to "product," and have broadened "process" to include professional functions, technical processes or the use of certain types of equipment. Simon has vigorously criticized the purpose-process-clientele-place differentiation by claiming that the only difference between purpose and process is that the former is at a higher level in the "means—and hierarchy" and that clientele and place "are really not separate from purpose, but a part of it" (1947, p. 28-33). Here he comes very close to recognizing the important distinction between final and intermediate products, but less close to the necessity of basing organizational classification squarely upon product classification or to the crucial distinction between output purposes and other organizational purposes.

in Chapter 23, tend to be out-of-date or to center on titles, financial rewards and the perquisites of office (which may range from a rug on the floor to a beautiful secretary). The loving care often given to the meticulous delineation of these matters is due in large part to their important contribution toward meeting the survival, commergence, differentiation, and even self-development needs of an organization's members.

Separate expectations concerning the output performance of units and individuals, in turn, are linked together by more general expectations concerning the "work flows" through which the various intermediate products contribute to the end products of the organization as a whole. A work flow that centers around the movement of raw materials (with or without processing) or identifiable documents (such as applications and purchase orders) can readily be visualized by administrators. It can be scientifically analyzed by production engineers.

Work flows centering around information and influence are harder to pin down. In large organizations they tend to be more significant. In organizations whose end products are intangible services they are "the works." Under such circumstances the work flow basis of unit and position functions may be rather vague. This vagueness is still greater in new and growing organizations, in which the end products themselves are unclear or changing (*Simon*, 1953; *Orzack*). With technological improvements in production processes the relation between established functions and actual work flow is often destroyed. At the same time new functions may be established whose relation to work flow and end product may be highly uncertain and sharply questioned within the organization. In any case, the total work flow in any complex organization is extremely difficult to understand. This difficulty is enhanced whenever organization charts, which are easy to prepare, serve to detract attention from work flow, which is almost impossible to chart or visualize in its entirety.[5]

2. FUNCTION COMBINATIONS

The output mix (or general functions) of any unit or position may be regarded as a combination or "bundle" of smaller, separable functions. With greater specialization, the processes of "cellular fission" usually lead to a large number and variety of positions and smaller units. This, in turn, leads to more complex patterns of combining positions and smaller

5. Many of the difficulties in developing techniques for the analysis of total work flow are shown in Chapple and Sayles (1961), which is based on the principle that "the technology or flow of work is the major criterion for designing the structure" of organizations.

units into larger units. Thus at both the highest and lowest levels of an organization administrators are continually faced with the question "How to combine functions?" Except for the first days of an entirely new organization, this question usually arises in the form of "Where to place a new function?" and "How to change the existing combination pattern?" Thus the search for any answer—even one calling for a drastic reorganization—is inevitably affected by the existing combination pattern. The answer itself is usually formulated—or justified—in terms of one or more of the following technical considerations:[6]

A. *Jointly produced output.* Positions or units performing dissimilar functions may be combined to cooperate in producing a similar set of intermediate products. Many of the largest units are based on this consideration. The "composite work group" provides a way of doing this with the smallest units (*Rice, 1958; Herbst*).

B. *Similar activities.* This consideration leads to the grouping together of specialists whose services may contribute to the production of a variety of dissimilar subsequent products—as with central units of lawyers or typists.

C. *Most use.* "The reception desk may be made a part of the purchasing department, sales department, or personnel department, depending upon which has the most callers and relies most frequently upon the receptionist to provide initial information and advice" (Newman, 1951, p. 137).

D. *Attention.* A new activity may be assigned to the administrator who will give it the desired form of attention—whether this means support, control or suppression. This may mean a "clean break" from its point of origin (Koontz and O'Donnell, 1955, p. 129-130).

E. *Independent check.* Care is often taken not to assign "policing" activities such as inspection, auditing, and investigations to those who are being "policed."

F. *Competition.* The development of similar combinations may provide "deadly parallels" whereby the performance of each may be judged competitively. The detachment of a subordinate unit may revitalize its former "parent" by providing stronger competition for budgetary allocations.

G. *Coordination.* The combination of dissimilar units may be necessary to keep competition within bounds and obtain more cooperation or better integration of divergent policies.

---

6. This list is derived, in part, from the acute observations embodied in Newman's "factors in grouping activities" (1951, p. 131-144) and Koontz and O'Donnell's "principles of association" (1955, p. 122-135).

H. *Costs.* Some combinations—particularly highly specialized similar activities—are conspicuously costly if a small volume of operations leads to idle time. This can be overcome by a broadening of the bundle. Costs resulting from red tape, inflexibility and personal aggrievement are harder to take into account.

The fact that these considerations may sharply conflict gives but a small indication of the difficulty of combining functions. Many changes in the fission-fusion pattern within an organization are far more than technical matters. They always have a direct bearing upon the personal satisfactions of the incumbents of positions and the members of units. They may have an important effect upon the distribution of power and status within the organization and upon relations with external groups. Whether so conceived or not, they may turn out to be ways of reshaping the objectives of the organization as a whole (*Simon*, 1953).

At the level of individual positions another consideration is the degree of monotony that may be created by narrow bundles of highly similar activities. This may result in a loss of work satisfactions and output (*Katz et al.*, 1950). This situation may be remedied through "job enlargement" (*Mann and Hoffman*, 1960; *Walker and Guest*, 1952). The broadening process usually requires more attention to training. Any more significant enlargement of the bundles also requires considerable freedom by incumbents in "switching" from one line of activity to another, or considerable looseness in the identification of activities. This freedom and looseness are greatest at the higher levels of administrative authority. Here also we frequently find "job enlargement" in the form of "multiple hat assignments," as when a person is assigned to two different positions or is given special ad hoc assignments in addition to his "regular" position.

3. SPECIALIST-ADMINISTRATOR COMBINATIONS

A built-in role conflict of increasingly serious proportions is often found in the combination of administrative and nonadministrative activities. The resulting mixture or compound is relatively stable when the nonadministrative or technical work involves no great difficulties and no great amount of personal commitment. But when such work is of a high order of technical complexity and can be properly performed only by the continuing investment of intellectual energy, a serious conflict may emerge.

The role conflict of the specialist-as-administrator often becomes particularly acute as he advances in his career and enters positions with increasing administrative responsibility.

In the first phase of a specialist's career, he has little or no administrative responsibility. In order to obtain more professional responsibility he must improve his professional ability. In the case of the "pusher," responsibility may grow more rapidly than ability. In the case of the "timid soul," ability may grow more rapidly than responsibility. But by and large the two elements move upward together at not too dissimilar rates.

In the second phase professional responsibility and ability both become greater, with the possibility that the latter may grow more slowly. This possibility is linked with the fact that at this phase the first major increment of administrative responsibility may enter the picture.

At this phase two aspects of the specialist-administrator role conflict may begin to emerge. First, it may become difficult to adjust to the addition of administrative responsibility, a responsibility for which the specialist has not been prepared, and perhaps not even warned about in the course of his professional training. If adjustment is slow, people will say that "he doesn't understand people" or "doesn't know how to get along with people." Second, administrative and specialist professional responsibilities compete for time and attention. "These administrative burdens," the specialist will complain, "keep me from getting down to work."

At the third stage the administrative burden rises sharply again. Professional responsibilities may increase also—but not necessarily. It may be increasingly possible to rely on the expertise of subordinates. It now becomes much more difficult to "keep abreast of things" in one's professional field. The conflicting time pressures now become more serious. The administrator may feel that he is being torn to pieces. Many years of training, his professional loyalties and ambitions, his intellectual predilections, all push him toward a continuation of the professional career which he has so arduously built up in his younger years. Yet in most cases this can be done only at the cost of sacrificing leisure, health, family life or administrative performance. The problem of coordinating the work of other specialists pulls him away from his own specialty. Moreover, organizational necessities, the peculiar structure of the ladder of advancement and his managerial ambitions impel him up the rocky road of administrative power and responsibility. For him personally this may produce an inner conflict with serious implications. For the organization it may mean—although not always—that a good scientist, doctor, or economist has been sacrificed to obtain a bad, a mediocre or an unhappy administrator.

At the fourth stage the chief engineer becomes a general manager, the doctor becomes a hospital administrator or head of the health department, the nursing supervisor becomes chief of nursing services, the dean becomes a university president, a field commander becomes a chief of staff. For all of these people, the increment to administrative responsibility is the largest in their careers. Their professional responsibilities inevitably decline—although the great variety of organizational, production, and staffing patterns make it impossible to generalize as to how steep this decline may be. At the time of this great "jump" no immediate loss of professional ability is involved. Yet now it becomes impossible for such people to give adequate attention to professional literature, conferences, writing, or research. Their "inside" work increasingly involves relations with other managers rather than specialists. In addition, there is an increasing preoccupation with "external" relations.

At either the third or fourth stage the conflict may be resolved by victory for the administrator in the individual's personality and withdrawal by the specialist. There may be deep regrets concerning the outcome; there may be elaborate pretenses that he is still an outstanding professional. Yet the die has been cast. Now that he is a full-fledged administrator, he will never go back to his "first love." His present love is a jealous mistress demanding all his devotion and attention.

Various efforts have been made to handle the problems of specialist-administrator role conflicts. One line of action has been to establish specialist roles which are as high in rank and prestige as, or even higher than, those of top administrative roles. No matter how much further action may be carried along this line, however, it could not appreciably affect the growing magnitude of the problem. In a technological age top administrative roles are more and more defined in terms of a compound of administrative and specialist responsibilities. Where this is not true, a specialist background—if not outstanding achievement—often enters as an informal prerequisite in connection with the prestige aspects of a position and the confidence which people must have in its incumbent.

Another line of action is found in educational programs—whether at pre-, mid-, or top career stages—designed to help specialists in the difficult process of learning to carry administrative responsibilities. Although these may be of great benefit to the organizations in which specialist-administrators play an important role, this does not mean that they will necessarily ease the acute personal conflicts of the individuals involved. The person who is pulled in two directions by a strong horse and a weak one is not necessarily better off if the weak one is strengthened.

4. INTERLOCKING FUNCTIONS

The combination of functions into bundles, however, is not as significant as the combination of actual activities into the work flows of an organization. This requires many points of interlocking action among both people and units. The very nature of the interlock will make it seem that functions are being duplicated. Thus the functions of a machinist will include certain services with respect to the care and maintenance of the machinery and tools he uses. But a special maintenance man may also be responsible for similar services. The line between their respective responsibilities can never be drawn so rigorously as to avoid an area of apparent overlapping. At a somewhat higher level there is a similar area of ambiguity and potential conflict, in the respective responsibilities of the foreman and the head of the maintenance department. This area may become still larger when we consider the respective roles of procurement, engineering, accounting and economic analysis personnel in determining when to replace old machinery with new. In one sense we can say that each deals with the same problem. In another it is clear that each deals with a different aspect of the same problem. Both of these viewpoints are correct. From the point of view of the organization as a whole it is clear that the various aspects are so inextricably interrelated that there are few places where one's responsibility clearly ends and the other's begins. The interlocking of functions requires some form of "overlapping" or apparent "duplication."

This is even more obvious in giant business organizations, large government departments and in the structure of government as a whole. Here one will even find scattered throughout the system people with the responsibility of considering similar aspects of problems, albeit from different viewpoints. Thus many units of the same systems will have their own analysts of the current economic outlook, their own Latin-American experts, their own nuclear fission scientists. Some of these may not only provide similar services; they may even compete for identical clients. Whether or not this is wasteful cannot be automatically deduced from evidence on overlapping or duplication. As one writer has put it, men would be pretty badly off if their shirt tails were not long enough to overlap with the top of their trousers. Nor does this observation sanction their reaching to one's ankles. It merely means that one cannot reach judgments about wastefulness without a careful analysis of the specific circumstances and alternatives. It also serves as a warning against the naïve aspiration—so often and so futilely voiced by alleged experts on administration and organization—for an organizational structure that will provide a crystal-clear picture of everyone's function and once and for all eliminate all duplications, overlappings and ambiguities. As a conspicuous case of an "oversell," this aproach may help "clinch the deal" in getting approval for a job analysis survey. It will also help those administrators who need expert assistance in "taking off" into a flight from reality.

C. *Hierarchy: Superiors and Subordinates*

HIERARCHY is the most conspicuous part of the formal structure of any organization. As such, it has frequently been falsely identified with the totality of formal structure. Still worse, the adjustment of hierarchic relationships has been falsely identified with the totality of the administrative process. This overemphasis is probably rooted in the psychological importance to many people of domination-submission relations and in a natural tendency to interpret organizational phenomena in terms of childhood experiences with superior parental authority.

In the field of administrative thought this overemphasis has led to a preoccupation with abstract prescriptive or normative principles on the "should be" side of the subject. Relatively little intensive research has been done on the "is" and "has been" of hierarchical relations.

1. THE ESSENCE OF HIERARCHY

The essence of hierarchy is the distinction between the role of "superior" (or "superordinate") and "subordinate." The person or group in the superior role is expected to exercise authority over the subordinate. The subordinate, in turn, is expected to accept the authority of his superior and be responsible to him.

We usually regard an organization as hierarchic, however, only when the superior-subordinate relation is carried further by making the first subordinate the superior of another subordinate. As an organization becomes more hierarchic, the number of subordinates who are also superiors becomes larger. We thus find authority and responsibility "flow" in an unbroken line from higher levels of authority to the lowliest subordinate. This line (traditionally called the "chain of command") may be referred to as the "line of authority." The various points on this line in different organizations are illustrated on page 371.

A large proportion of hierarchic relations are between a superior person or unit and a number of subordinates. The number of such subordinates may be referred to as the "span of authority" (the more traditional and limited term being "span of control"). The wider this span the more the lines of authority may branch out. The total number of people subordinate to the highest authority in the organization may be increased by widening the span, lengthening the line, or both.

Hierarchic level, it should be noted, does not by itself determine the grade or status of all positions or the personal rank of all incumbents. At each level we usually find a considerable range of positions and rank.

LINES OF AUTHORITY

Army	Government	Business	Catholic Church
Commander-in-Chief	Chief of State	Board Chairman	Pope Bishop
Army commander	Minister (or Secretary)	President	Priest
Corps commander	Service director	Vice-president	
Division commander	Office director	General manager	
Regimental commander	Bureau director	Production manager	
Battalion commander	Division director	General foreman	
Company commander	Section chief	Foreman	
Platoon leader	Unit chief	Group leader	
Squad leader	Group leader		
Private			

Thus a top administrator's direct personal assistant or secretary may have a much lower grade or rank than an administrator three or four levels below him on the line of authority.

In most cultures the concepts of "higher" and "lower"—and such related terms as "level," "top," "middle," "bottom," "above," "over," "under," and "below"—seem to be an ingrained part of man's perception of superior-subordinate relations. Historically, this has been explained by going back to the days of more primitive battle, when the military superiority of horsemen over footsoldiers was associated with their reaching a greater height. Divinity—particularly in the case of monotheism—is often thought of in connection with the heavens above. Man's superiority over woman may be symbolized by over- under- positions of sexual embrace. A more mundane explanation can be found in the frequent correlation, quickly learned by every infant, between height and strength.

Superior hierarchic authority is never absolute. At the lower levels it is always confined to a certain area of operations and limited by superior authority. At the peak of an organization it is always limited to the purposes of the organization, as well as being subjected to various external controls. Even in *The Leviathan*, where he proposed "absolute" monarchy as the ideal form of government, Hobbes placed reservations on the monarch's use of his "undivided sovereignty." Even in the Catholic Church, where the doctrine of "papal infallibility" has reigned since its formal proclamation in 1870, the Pope is infallible only on matters of faith and morals and not on administrative matters. Nor does the Pope have unquestioned authority to draw the dividing line between the "theological" and the "administrative."

Hierarchic centralization of authority, paradoxically, depends for its very existence upon a certain amount of decentralization. The centralizing effects of the line of authority are achieved mainly by grants of formal authority from those at the higher to those at the lower positions on the line. These grants may be spelled out, or be implicit in the formal positions that people occupy (Follett's "authority of the position"). Or they may take the form of current and accumulated delegations of specific authority from their superiors.

Moreover, higher authority is further limited by one of the great unwritten "laws" of formal hierarchy—namely, that the lines of authority serve as the formal channels of communication. The superior is expected to communicate with the "two downers" (and "three downers" and so on) through the formal line of authority, not directly. Although he preserves a residual or ultimate authority through his right to review the activities of his inferiors, he gives up—or at least substantially modifies—his right to exercise this authority through direct relationships at lower levels.

No organization can hold together without some pattern of hierarchy. In the words of Shakespeare's Ulysses (*Troilus and Cressida*, Act I, Scene 3), as he bewails the breakdown of hierarchic authority in the Grecian Army sprawled outside the walls of Troy:

> The heavens themselves, the planets and this centre,
> Observe degree, priority and place,
> Insisture, course, proportion, season, form,
> Office and custom in all line or order . . .
>
> Take but degree away, untune that string,
> And, hark, what discord follows!

The higher positions in any hierarchy provide a unifying symbolism of tremendous significance. Whether their legitimate occupants are revered, feared, loved, cursed, or sneered at (and all of this may occur together), they symbolize the purposes and values of the collectivity. They provide places where important decisions may be made or legitimated and where internal conflicts may be authoritatively settled. The entire hierarchic structure provides a foundation for confidence in the ability of an organization and its members to get things done. The lines of authority are the backbone of the internal communication system. They also serve as possible ladders for internal advancement, thus strengthening the identification of upward-aspiring individuals with the organization as a whole. Thus one need not regard hierarchy as the totality of organizational structure to agree with Ulysses that discord would follow should we "untune that string."

2. THE INVERTED PYRAMID

Hierarchic structure has been traditionally described in terms of a simple pyramid. This is based upon the idea that as we move from the higher to the lower levels of authority we find more and more people.

But this idea does not apply to the highest levels of formal authority. Here a comprehensive picture of hierarchic relations demands that we place an inverted pyramid on top of the traditional pyramid. This concept, implicitly set forth in Chapter 3, must now be presented more fully. In graphic terms it can be dramatized by the following illustration.

THE UPPER PYRAMID OF FORMAL AUTHORITY

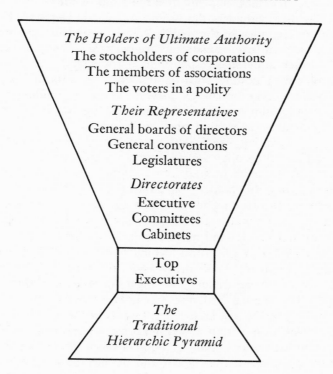

The Holders of Ultimate Authority
The stockholders of corporations
The members of associations
The voters in a polity

Their Representatives
General boards of directors
General conventions
Legislatures

Directorates
Executive
Committees
Cabinets

Top
Executives

*The
Traditional
Hierarchic Pyramid*

At the highest level we find *the holders of ultimate authority*. For corporations these are the stockholders, for associations the total membership, and for a political community the voters. These may include hundreds, thousands, or even many millions of people. In organizations composed of other organizations—such as trade associations, general federations of labor, loose cartels, and weak federations of states—the holders of ultimate authority are the member organizations or states.

At the next subordinate level we find *the representatives of the holders of ultimate authority,* as they operate in legislatures, conventions, in general boards of directors. This group is much smaller, ranging from a dozen or two dozen people to a maximum of a few hundred.

Still lower on this inverted pyramid we find the *directorates.* These are the small executive committees, central committees, and cabinets. They usually range in size from two or three people to a maximum of one or two dozen.

Below the directorates are the *top executives.* From the viewpoint of the traditional pyramid they are the "men at the top." But no matter how firmly their feet may be planted on the peaks of the bottom pyramid, they carry on their shoulders the weight of the top pyramid. From this viewpoint they are "men in the middle." The lower-level administrators, in turn, have an even larger superstructure over their head, although they may have smaller individual responsibilities for supporting it. In either case the problem of dealing with higher levels of authority is often so onerous that little time or energy may be left for attending to subordinates. The only administrators who have no superstructure over their heads are the owner-operators of small enterprises.

There are interesting size variations. In some organizations—particularly the smallest—there may be no upper pyramid at all. In others all three levels may be concentrated into a small directorate. In a family-owned corporation the holders of ultimate authority may indeed be fewer in number than the members of the directorate—in which case we once again have a pyramid-type structure resting on its base rather than its apex. With universities and hospitals, likewise, there may be but two levels: a large board of governors, which holds the ultimate authority, and a smaller directorate. With many associations, the inverted pyramid at the top of the structure may be gigantic in comparison with the relatively small pyramidal structure of employed staff.

This general set of hierarchic relations is rendered more complex by multiple roles. In government organizations a minister standing at the top of the bureaucratic pyramid, together with his director general, may also be a member of the cabinet and the elected legislature, as well as a voter. In corporations stock ownership may be distributed in various ways among directorates, top executives and throughout the lower levels down to the workers. In a producer's cooperative the workers and bureaucrats as a whole are the owners, holders at ultimate authority. In associations and political parties built on the basis of "democratic centralism" the holders of formal authority are various groups of subordinates who elect their representatives and entrust them with formal authority.

3. MORE THAN PYRAMIDS

As we descend to a lower level of formal authority, however, we often find much larger numbers of people. This brings us back to the traditional hierarchic pyramid.

The tremendous potential of the pyramidal form for bringing large numbers of subordinates under central authority is suggested by establishing a model pyramid with nine levels of administrators and six subordinates for every person in the pyramid. This yields the following pattern:

```
                1
                6
              3  6
            2  1  6
          1, 2 9  6
          7, 7    7 6
         4 6,  6  5 6
        2 7 9,    9 3 6
      1,  6 8 0,  2 1 6
      ─────────────────
      2,  0 1 6,  1 3 9
```

A pattern of this kind would enable one top executive (or seven, if we include his immediate subordinates) to exercise formal authority over 2,016,139 people. A tenth level would bring the total to 12,097,435—and an eleventh to 72,585,211! Although with varying numbers of subordinates the arithmetic would also vary, this diagram suggests that organizations of huge size can be established hierarchically without more than eight to ten levels. This probably explains why I have found very few organizations with 10—and none with more than 12—hierarchic levels (as contrasted with the much greater number of levels often found on salary scales). Unfortunately, there has as yet been no systematic statistical research in this field.

If we look carefully at a large set of pyramidal hierarchies, we shall find a number of standard variations. The "fat" ones have wider—and the "thin" ones—narrower spans of authority. The "tall" ones have longer —and the "short" ones smaller—lines of authority. There is a tendency for the fat ones to be shorter and the thin ones to be taller. Within each pyramid we shall find major variations in the span of authority from one level and one unit to another. We shall find many short lines of authority that connect only two or three levels, with many fewer lines running from the very top to the very bottom. In fact, we shall find that the over-all pyramid is a cluster of smaller pyramids of varying sizes and shapes.

If we look still more closely, we shall find that factors such as these often destroy the pyramidal shape entirely. This is particularly true whenever there is a decline in the percentage of unskilled employees' positions at the lowest level and a proliferation of skilled and semiskilled positions at the middle. In his study of the U.S. armed forces (1960, p. 65-67), Janowitz has illustrated this change in the following tables:

Pyramid *Army Enlisted Personnel, 1935*		*Octagon* *Air Force Bomb Squadron,* *Post-Korea*	
	%		%
Master sergeant	.8	Master sergeant	7.0
First sergeant	.9	Technical sergeant	10.3
Technical sergeant	1.3	Staff sergeant	15.2
Staff sergeant	3.6	Airman first class	24.4
Sergeant	9.4	Airman second class	28.1
Corporal	9.0	Airman third class	13.5
Private first class	25.4	Basic airman	1.5
Private	49.5		
Total	100.0	Total	100.0

His data on the officer corps show the same kind of change in the higher ranks:

OFFICER CORPS, 1920-50, HIERARCHY OF RANKS

	Army		*Air-Force*		*Navy*	
	1920	1950	1950		1920	1950
	%	%	%		%	%
General	.4	.8	.5	Admiral	1.3	.8
Colonel	4.1	9.4	4.3	Captain	4.4	6.8
Lt. Col.	4.7	11.5	10.0	Commander	7.6	10.9
Major	14.9	20.7	17.8	Lt. Cmdr.	14.4	18.3
Captain	35.9	34.9	34.6	Lieutenant	32.8	28.8
First Lt.	32.6	13.9	26.4	Lt. (j.g.)	16.6	24.0
Second Lt.	7.4	8.8	6.5	Ensign	22.9	10.4
Total	100.0	100.0	100.0	Total	100.0	100.0

Janowitz's perceptive analysis of these trends is as follows:

This parallels the changing pattern of civilian social structure, where the upper middle class proliferates because of the expansion of new professional and skill groups. In part, this represents an effort to raise the status and income of the soldier. In part, it represents a tendency of organizations to grow internally. Basically, this expansion of the middle strata of ranks—officers and enlisted men—is a typical manifestation of organizations which have grown more complex.[7]

Similar data for other kinds of organizations would unquestionably reveal many hierarchic patterns far closer to octagons, pentagons or other shapes than to traditional pyramids.

4. THE LAW OF MULTIPLE HIERARCHY

The traditional hierarchic model is based upon the simplistic assumption that every subordinate has only one direct superior. This assumption is an excellent projection of the make-believe world that subordinates often concoct for themselves in an effort to escape the complexities of organizational life. It is rationalized by analogy with parental authority and the higher levels of authority. If one father, why not one boss? If one board of directors, one cabinet or one president, why not just one superior?

But just as the lines of authority may converge in their upward flow toward one spot at the top we usually find that in their downward flow two or more lines of authority—not just one—converge upon one subordinate. This is frequently, although not always, based upon a distinction between different kinds of authority. In the Federal Government of the U.S.A. and some other presidential systems the President is subject to the authority of, and responsible to, both the holders of formal authority (the voters) and to the legislature. Many subordinate officials of corporations and government agencies are subject to certain forms of authority formally exercised by committees of boards of directors and legislatures. In universities a department head may be directly subordinate to one dean and on other matters to another dean or to the rector, vice president or president.

This phenomenon of multiple subordination is even more widespread at the levels below the top executives. Here we find that various members of an organization may have "functional," "technical," or "professional" authority over other members who are subordinate to them only on certain types of problems or with respect to the enforcement of certain rules. Typical cases are found in the authority of budget, auditing and control personnel over everyone in an organization and of "staff" specialists over administrators in the "line" or the "field." In such cases we find many members of an organization who are subject to the authority of

7. It should be kept in mind that Janowitz's figures do not deal directly with hierarchic levels of organization. Many people with lower rank occupy subordinate positions in units at high levels in the military organization.

people of lower rank or grade, or at lower hierarchic levels. This is very close to what Simmel described as "the expediently distributed alternation of superordination and subordination" (1950, p. 286-291). Thus in one type of situation A may have direct authority over B and B over C, with X having no direct relation with any of them. But with varying situations the formally prescribed patterns may vary as follows:

Situation 1   *Situation 2*   *Situation 3*   *Situation 4*

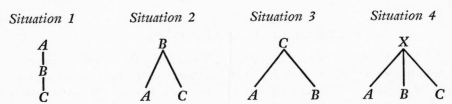

These shifting patterns are essential to operations under interlocking functions.

Another form of multiple hierarchy is found in appeal, grievance and suggestion systems, all of which are explicitly designed to provide additional lines of communication and authority. The very purpose of appeals systems is to allow subordinates to go over the heads of their superiors (*Evan*). Union-management grievance systems subject administrators at many levels to new "masters." Suggestions systems sidetrack them by providing additional channels of upward communication (Redfield, p. 140-158).

A special form of multiple hierarchy is found whenever groups of people belonging to different "classes" work together within the same organization. In most civil service systems there are various categories of civil servants, many of whom work together within a given organization. Military organizations usually have special career systems of their own; and in many military organizations civil servants work together with military officers. In the U.S. State Department various categories of civil servants work side by side with Foreign Service Officers, Foreign Service Reserve Officers, and Foreign Service Staff employees. In overseas establishments "alien clerks" are added to this heterogeneous mixture. Many of these special classes of employees are subject to the authority not only of their immediate hierarchic superiors but also of those who are formally responsible for the administration of the civil service and career systems.

Hence there is good basis for the Macmahon-Millett-Ogden finding, based upon their 1935-1941 analysis of the U.S. Works Progress Administration (1941, p. 266), that:

> The theory of hierarchic decentralization should openly proclaim that
> lines of authority in the organization are frequently dual or even multiple,

that the reaction of technology on administration is apt to increase the proportion of situations in which such conditions exist, and that the arrangement of structure and the training of personnel must provide for nicely divided loyalties.

The Macmahon-Millett-Ogden study, however, concentrated upon the dualistic distinction between "administrative authority" and "technical authority." More intensive studies of modern organizations would reveal more refined distinctions. They would probably also reveal that a large proportion of intra-organizational disputes result from divided loyalties and revolve—at least technically—around the boundaries between one form of authority and another.

Although the modern growth of specialization is a major factor in promoting a more complex interweaving of various types of authority, it should not be thought that multiple hierarchy—like Taylor's "functional foremanship"—is a recent invention that has grown up with the expansion of modern staff services. The formal hierarchies of ancient India, as described by Kautilya, and of the Byzantine Empire included special internal espionage or control systems directed by top rulers but operating at various levels. As far back as the twelfth and thirteenth century A.D. the formal structure of the Catholic Church provided for a separate hierarchy of papal legates—either a cardinal or a nuncio—who were authorized to by-pass the bishop and intervene in certain aspects of the affairs of both diocese and parish. The famous general staff system of the Prussians was based upon the concept of a "dual command function."[8] In each of these, the additional centers of authority served to strengthen central authority against the decentralizing tendencies inherent in large-scale organizations.

D. *Polyarchy: Coordinates*

EVEN WITH fully developed roles and rules, hierarchy itself is never enough to hold an organization together. It is essentially feudal in nature—albeit without fiefs and hereditary position. It deals with "vertical"

---

8. ". . . Scharnhorst began to bring into existence that peculiar Prussian device, the system of a command function jointly performed by the commander and the chief of staff. . . . The chief of the staff officers of a command was more than a coordinating subordinate; his status has been described with considerable accuracy as being that of 'junior partner' to the commander. Although the ultimate decision remained that of the commander, the chief of staff still shared in the results. Should a situation arise in which a commander disregarded the recommendations of the chief of staff, the latter . . . could insist on making his opinions a matter of record" (*Hittle*, 1949, p. 61).

relations alone, as with the line of authority from lord to vassal and sub-vassal. With the growth of specialization and economic interdependence, feudalism breaks down; horizontal and crisscrossing relations develop. In modern organizations such relations—which may be called "polyarchic" —fill in the otherwise bare and gaunt structure of formal hierarchy and round out a formal structure of much greater capacity and flexibility.

If hierarchy is a relationship between superior and subordinate, poly-archy may be defined as a coordinate relationship of responsibility. This does not mean that any two coordinates in this sense are at the same hierarchic level or of the same rank or grade. It merely means that their relationship is not one of superior-to-subordinate or that it takes place outside the sphere of their superior-to-subordinate relationship. Although polyarchy includes nonauthoritative relations among organizations, it will here be used only with reference to such relations within organizations.[9]

1. SHARED RESPONSIBILITY

One form of polyarchy is *shared responsibility*. This occurs when-ever coordinates share the responsibility for the same tasks or services. It is the fundamental relation between the members of any collegial body —whether it be a large assembly, such as a legislature or convention, or a smaller body such as a committee, board, council, commission, or panel.

The most conspicuous use of shared responsibility is in the upper pyramid of formal authority. Here the representatives of the holders of formal authority invariably interact on a polyarchic basis. The formal hierarchic elements in legislatures and conventions are limited mainly to the roles of those responsible for the scheduling of activities, the handling of committee work, and the internal direction of factions and parties. In the decisions of the legislature as a whole or of any of its committees all members have equal votes. The internal relationships are far more those of bargaining and power than those of formal authority. (Only in the relatively rare case of one-party systems with tight caucus control over all factions are internal relations on a formally hierarchic basis. Such a structure is far removed from the ordinary concept of a legis-lature.) Committees also play a major role. Their smaller size provides the basis for a division of labor within the legislature and other bodies representing the holders of ultimate authority. Appearing in the form of boards of directors, executive committees, cabinets, commissions,

9. This usage of "polyarchy" is not quite the same as that of Dahl and Lind-blom (1953), who concentrate on relations among organizations and regard hier-archy as "control of people by leaders" and polyarchy (or democracy) as "control of leaders by people."

councils and other collegial devices, they provide the typical organizational structure for directorates.

The most widespread use of committees, however, is at somewhat lower levels. Here they serve as one of the major methods of formally bringing together people from various points in the hierarchy. This is a representative function in many ways comparable to the representative functions of legislative assemblies. Although committee membership may be determined by hierarchical superiors, the representative pattern is crucial. When a problem cuts across the interests of many units in an organization, there is often no formal way to deal with it other than to establish a committee with representatives from each of these units. One alternative is to redefine the roles of these units so that the problem clearly belongs to one of them rather than to others; but this is a costly, time-consuming process of reorganization which may create more difficult situations with respect to other problems. Another alternative is to assign the problem in question to one unit in the regular hierarchy. But unless the roles of the other interested units are to be seriously impaired, these other units will usually have to be kept informed as to what is done or even asked for their advice. This, in turn, can often be done economically only by bringing representatives together in the form of a committee.

This representative function may be limited to one hierarchic level— as when a top executive sets up a "management committee" composed of his immediate subordinates. It may also span different levels in a hierarchy. Committees are often a formal instrumentality for enabling administrators to engage in systematic two-way communication with "two down'ers" and "three down'ers" without blatantly violating the hierarchic authority of intervening superiors.

Committees also play a major role in the adjudicatory processes within organizations. They provide a customary structural form for "internal courts" dealing with appeals, grievances and the application of stringent sanctions. They are used for the purposes of obtaining collective judgments on the qualifications of individuals considered for recruitment or promotion to important posts, on individual and group performance and on the merits and demerits of proposed courses of action. They provide an organizational framework for internal negotiation and for the reconciliation—and sometimes concealment—of the divergent views and interests. They are instrumentalities for mobilizing the power needed to obtain organizational action and for delaying, sidetracking or stopping organizational action.

For all these reasons large organizations are invariably given to the practice of establishing tremendous numbers of committees. These may

be temporary or permanent, staffed or unstaffed, authorized to make decisions or only to offer advice and proposals. Their role may be narrow
or broad, carefully defined or subject to the interpretation and initiative
of committee members. They may be composed of the organization's
members only, nonmembers only, or both.

Although all these committees, even the temporary ones, are part
of the formal organizational structure, few organizations keep central
records on the number, type and role of all their committees. Nor is the
committee structure usually shown in formal organization charts. When
occasional checks are made on the full use of committees, the results
often produce a profound shock and sense of embarrassment. In any large
government department, for example, it will usually be revealed that
formal action has been taken to establish hundreds of committees. Many
higher officials will be found to have formal membership in dozens of
different committees.

One factor in the proliferation of committees is "committeeitis." Thus
"let's set up a committee" becomes an automatic panacea for dealing
with—or dodging—complex problems without exploiting the possibilities
of using the existing hierarchic structure or without trying to integrate
a new committee with it. Another factor is the anticommittee bias of
"management experts" whose concept of formal structure is limited to
simplistic models of formal hierarchy. If they give insufficient attention
to the structural role of committees, their advice on organization and
reorganization lacks realism. A new organization chart may be formally
accepted within an organization and then just as formally negated by the
decisions on the committee structure.

Trade unions may also provide an important—albeit sometimes un-
recognized—part of an organization's formal structure. This is particularly
true of union officers, union committees and management-union committees whose operations are based upon a formal agreement between
the union and the organization. These individuals and committees will
operate at various points in an organization's hierarchy but they are not
subject to the hierarchic authority of the organization. Rather, they
provide formalized opportunities for hierarchic subordinates to escape
subordination and negotiate—directly or indirectly—with their erstwhile
superiors on a formally equal basis. Although they may be closely linked
with external labor bodies, they are also an integral part of the organization's structure. In fact, the union's internal structure and its tie-in with
various levels of management will always have a major effect upon the
distribution of authority and responsibility among administrative positions.

2. DISPERSED RESPONSIBILITY

Another form of intraorganizational polyarchy occurs among coordinates with *dispersed responsibility*. People responsible for different tasks or services are expected to attain certain common objectives by a process of mutual cooperation and adjustment.

The simplest case of dispersed responsibility is that of the relations between the different members of a single work group. A more complex case is that of the relations between the various administrators subject to the direct authority of an hierarchic superior. A still more complex case is the long series of coordinate relations that take place as materials or information in the production process weave their intricate path back and forth across unit boundaries.

Many of these relations are prescribed by those with formal authority. General rules sometimes include minute requirements for polyarchic relations. The most formalized example is provided by the rules governing an organization's budget-making process, which establish the framework for formalized bargaining among coordinates for their respective shares of scarce inputs. To the extent that they depart from hierarchic lines, clearance, consultation and "touch base" (or "keep them informed") procedures also deal with polyarchic relations. Production schedules set forth detailed work flow patterns among people and units with little regard to hierarchic levels. More important, polyarchic relations may be officially expected without any, or many, specific steps being formally prescribed. Role specifications often deal directly with cooperation and negotiation. Incumbents are selected in terms of their estimated ability to "get along" with coordinates. Coordinate subordinates are often instructed, or expected, "to work things out yourselves."

The extent of polyarchic relations in organizations is suggested by Landsberger's pioneering work in applying the Bales interaction analysis to the horizontal and vertical relations of production planning, production and sales personnel (1961). A simplified version of his findings in two plants follows.

PER CENT OF HORIZONTAL INTERACTIONS ORIGINATED

	Plant A	Plant B
Production planning and control	32	40
Production	17	41
Sales liaison	62	62

The horizontal interactions of sales liaison people are greater because "their job is mediating between the field sales force and the factory." A similar study has shown that "the purchasing agent's internal relationships (as opposed to his external relations with salesmen) are almost entirely lateral; they are with other functional departments of about the same rank in the organizational hierarchy—departments such as production scheduling, quality control, engineering, and the like" (*Straus*). These lateral relations are probably far more significant wherever mechanization reduces the need for supervision (*Simpson*) or, as in many government agencies, multitudinous clearances are essential to operations.[10]

To a certain extent, intraorganizational polyarchy of this type thrives only when covered by a hierarchic "umbrella." Higher hierarchic authority can be depended upon to legitimate agreements that would otherwise be unviable. It can be appealed to for the settlement of conflicts that would otherwise be irreconcilable. All this makes it much easier for coordinates to work things out among themselves on the basis of reciprocity, negotiation, bargaining, and mutual adjustment. Reciprocally, hierarchy depends upon polyarchy. The holders of superior authority can have time and energy for mediation, arbitration and legitimation on some matters only if a much larger amount of matters are handled through polyarchic relations alone.

In the actual processes of interaction polyarchic and hierarchic relations are closely blended. Hierarchic channels may be used as an instrument of polyarchic relations. Polyarchic relations may be used as channels of "fanning out" the orders of hierarchical superiors. In the full web of interrelations the distinctions between the two kinds of relations often fade away. This is particularly true when major attention is focused on the work to be done and the authority—in Follett's language—of each position. A suggestive hint as to how these interrelations might be analyzed has been provided by Stinchcombe's use of input-output matrices. Since a command or a bit of advice may travel through both hierarchic and polyarchic lines of communication, an input-output matrix may help indicate the nature of the tremendous variety of interrelations that take place through a complex communication net.[11]

10. In an overgenerous effort to explain Weber's neglect of this aspect of bureaucratic operations, Landsberger suggests that there may have been less "horizontal work flow" at the time when Weber wrote. Without getting into the question of how to measure "more" or "less," it seems more reasonable merely to assume that Weber simply did not see the horizontal relations that took place.

11. Stinchcombe (1961). A simpler technique is used in Weiss and Jacobson, (1955). It may be expected that much more refined techniques will eventually be developed. While Weiss and Katz use a simple matrix showing first-order relations, Stinchcombe attempts a "squared matrix" in order to show second-order relations also. It should be possible to go still further and, by applying an adapted form of the mathematical techniques used in input-output analyses for economies, deal with the sum of all internal relations and with external relations also.

E. *Centralization with Decentralization*

FEW ASPECTS of formal structure are more important than the pattern through which responsibility and authority are dispersed throughout an organization.

Few aspects are more difficult to pin down. Neither centralization nor decentralization are absolutes. An extreme of either one would destroy any organization. Not only do the two always appear together; they complement each other. The arteries of decentralization bring the life-blood of responsibility and authority to the various members, while the veins bring it back to the center. The decentralization of some functions is impossible without the centralization of others, and vice versa.

Nor can the nature of a centralization-decentralization pattern be detected by observing merely one aspect of formal structure. Role prescriptions and combinations are basic to the pattern. Hierarchy and codes of behavior, although they may appear to be centralizing forces only, are also techniques of decentralization. Polyarchy, despite its decentralizing aspects, is also an instrument of centralization.

To make it more difficult, centralization and decentralization must be thought of in terms of three dimensions: namely, the distribution of responsibility and authority by (i) vertical levels, (ii) horizontal levels and (iii) geographical location. The first of these is often thought of in terms of the extent of "delegation" of responsibility and authority. If this term is to be used, it must be kept in mind that delegation may be embodied in both the prescription of the function and in current requests by superior authority. Horizontal dispersion is affected to a large extent by the way in which functions are divided and combined. Thus the centralization of files, secretarial services, or purchasing takes certain functions away from certain spots and places them at others, but without necessarily raising them to a higher level of authority. The third is far more than a simple matter of geography. Dispersion in space affects the nature and reliability of communication systems, thereby forcing certain forms of decentralized action and centralized control.

The extent of decentralization at any one point can be appraised only with reference to specific functions. Unit heads may have more responsibility with respect to handling subordinates than in their dealings with outsiders, more responsibility in personnel than in financial matters, more leeway with current expenditures than with capital expenditures. The extent of decentralization with respect to any of these functions can be measured by (i) the type and number of decisions that can be made, (ii) the significance of these decisions in terms of their effect on costs, output and the number of people whose interests are affected, and (iii) the extent of freedom from review, reporting and consultation relations with superiors and others.[12] The extent of decentralization at any part of an organization cannot be regarded as an automatic indicator of the general pattern throughout the organization. Many divisions which have won a considerable degree of freedom from superior and horizontal control are run by "authority-hoarding" administrators who do their best to deny a similar degree of freedom to subordinate units. The administrators of tightly controlled subordinate units may react against what they regard as overcentralization by extensive delegation to subordinates of the small authority they enjoy.

Some of the factors making for centralization at the higher levels of an organization are obvious. A certain amount of centralization is essential to maintain a common pattern of accepted purposes, to coordinate many activities that may otherwise serve to defeat each other, and to provide a general framework for decentralized action. It is needed to prevent or counteract external efforts to weaken or destroy the organization through divisive action. It is needed to deal with external controllers—and in fact, may be demanded by them in order to see that control is effective. The larger an organization, the more important (and the more difficult) it is to develop central policies and controls that can hold it together. Less obvious, and much harder to pin down, is the drive of many top executives for larger amounts of personal authority as a means of satisfying their needs for status and respect. This factor may sometimes be associated with—and may often help to promote—a complementary interest of subordinates in escaping personal responsibility.

On the other side of the coin, the most objective factor in favor of decentralization is the advantage to be gained from the division and specialization of labor. So long as it is human beings instead of machines whose labor is divided and whose activities are specialized, some amount of responsibility and authority must inhere in both positions and units. Larger amounts may prevent or alleviate delays and congestion at higher levels and can lead to decisions that are not only swifter but more in tune with the facts of specific situations. They may lead to greater satisfaction and morale on the job, encourage initiative and ingenuity and

12. For purposes of job evaluation in connection with salary schedules, Jaques has attempted to measure responsibility in terms of the maximum time span during which an individual is expected to exercise discretion on his own account until his use of discretion is subjected to review (1956). Yet this method abstracts itself from the complex nature of interactions between the reviewer and the reviewed. The time spans used by Jaques seem to be imputed or "shadow" quantities rather than the results of direct observation.

promote the fuller development of individual capacities. The larger an organization and the more complex its operations, the more significant these advantages of decentralization (*Baker and France*). Yet these considerations must also be seen in the light of personal interests and motivations. Some people at lower levels are "authority hoarders" who favor centralization for the same reasons that would-be despots at the top favor centralization. Others, as already suggested, fear decentralization because they lack the self-confidence in their ability to assume more responsibility or authority.

One of the many paradoxes of this subject is the fact that higher levels of competence must usually be reached before there can be more decentralization, while more decentralization is usually required in order to bring about the needed increase in the level of competence. Because of this "vicious circle" administrators always have an easy justification for not extending decentralization. When extensions are made, a price is usually paid in the form of inevitable errors and mistakes. This price can be kept within bounds only by "recentralization" or by new central functions—in the fields of training, communication, policy-making, or control—to buttress up the extension of decentralization. Another paradox appears in periods of emergency. At such times there are certain matters that can only be handled on the basis of far-reaching decentralization. When immediate action is needed, subordinates are usually not expected to wait until they get orders or clearance from superiors. Yet for other actions—and the ultimate case is the decision to unleash atomic missiles in response to a presumed attack—there is good reason to "pass the buck" to the top executive. Still another paradox appears in the conflicting effects of modern technology. More effective systems of automation and of information processing tend to promote and facilitate more centralization. The constant development of new skills, technologies and professions tends to promote and require more decentralization. One of the results of these built-in paradoxes is a continuous shifting back and forth in the pattern of centralization and decentralization. Not only are decentralizing measures usually accompanied by their centralizing supplements; but, in addition, they usually create problems that are solved by new measures of centralization with their decentralizing supplements.

Chapter 16

PEOPLE-IN-ORGANIZATIONS:
INFORMAL ASPECTS

SINCE THE PREVIOUS CHAPTER was limited to the more formal aspects of organizations, it could not possibly deal with the totality of organizational structure.

To obtain a total picture of any organization, we must also consider the informal structure. This is found in *those aspects of structure which, while not prescribed by formal authority, supplement or modify the formal structure.*

We shall initiate our probe of informal structure by noting the inevitability, as well as the variety, of informal roles, relationships, and rules.

We shall then set forth a large number of informal role facets—some general in nature, others applying only to administrators—that can be found in almost every organization. This will provide us with some rather vivid illustrations of the intertwining of individual personality with organizational role.

Finally, we shall chart the actual structure of internal power as manifested on various issues. This will bring us directly into such crucial matters as the dispersion of power within organizations and the nature of "organizational democracy."

388

A. *The Inevitability of Informal Structure*

MUCH OF THE INTUITIVE WISDOM of experienced administrators stems from their awareness of informal structure. Their "tacit knowledge" of their organization tells them that formal structure is merely the part of the iceberg that appears above the water. It often makes them inherently—although not necessarily coherently—skeptical of reorganization proposals that deal with the formal structure alone.

A coherent explanation of informal structure requires a recognition that roles, hierarchy, polyarchy, and codes each have their informal aura or penumbra *(Bakke)*. They may develop in fields untouched by formal structure, thereby supplementing or extending it. Or else they may combat, or even replace, the formal structure. In either case, they may subsequently become formalized.

As far as roles are concerned, the formal division of labor into units is only the starting point for group formation within the organization. Within any formally established unit informal subdivisions will usually come into being. Others will cut across divisional lines. Still others will cut across the organization's outer boundaries and include nonmembers. Such groups may be united on the basis of working relations with the organization, friendship cliques, specialist or professional skills, "old school ties," political party affiliations, national origin, religion, and other shared interests *(Argyris, 1954, 1959; Bloom; Burling et al.; Cumming and Cumming)*.

Administrators at all levels, furthermore, will often associate themselves with one or more informal groups of "buddies" from inside or outside the organization. As with the "kitchen cabinets" of many Presidents of the United States, these may be far more influential than the more visible and formally established cabinets and "executive committees" *(Gross, p. 100-101)*. Their informal status makes it easier for their members to avoid publicity and attack and for their organizers to reorganize, replace or abolish them.

Similarly, the formally established position is only a starting point for the total role played by any incumbent. It is invariably overlaid by a series of less authoritative—although not necessarily less powerful—expectations. As a result of conflicting elements in the incumbent's personality and in the expectations of others, these may produce deep role conflicts. Some of these informal aspects may be minor or ephemeral. Others may become the dominant elements in the total role. Still others may become widespread and deeply felt expectations that are passed on from one generation to another. It is in this sense that we say that the various "strong" Presidents of the United States "enlarged the concept of the Presidency." After the example of the two Roosevelts, of Wilson, and of Truman, no American President—not even an Eisenhower—could be as passive as Buchanan or Coolidge.

The relationship between total role and individual personality is so close that it would be a misleading question to ask whether personality is a determinant or a resultant of total role. It is usually both. The total role of any President is unquestionably affected both by his own personality and that of various predecessors. On the other hand, there is a genuine basis for the common saying that "the office makes the man." When Thomas à Becket, King Henry II's Chancellor, was made Archbishop of Canterbury, he suddenly became a strong defender of the Church against the King. When a more or less ordinary man like Truman becomes President, he often becomes extraordinary. But in either case it is only because the expectations surrounding the new office awaken or develop potentialities formerly hidden in the depth of the incumbent's personality.

Because of this intertwining with personality, informal roles are extremely varied. The next two sections of this chapter are devoted to an identification of some of the elements underlying this variety.

Hierarchy also has its informal aspects. Informal patterns of authority —considerably affected by the presence of informal groups—emerge in every organization. People with no formal administrative roles will often achieve and exercise informal administrative authority *(Belknap; Grusky; Horstall and Arensburg; Stanton and Schwartz; Strauss and Sayles; Zaleznik,* 1956). These are the so-called "informal leaders," who at times may sit at the apex of elaborate informal hierarchies. People with formal authority will sometimes fail to exercise it; these are the "in name only" administrators or leaders *(James D. Thompson).* Others may exercise power far beyond the authority granted them. These are the people who are attacked by their opponents as "empire builders" or "usurpers of authority," and praised by their admirers as men who "enlarged the conception of the office."

Moreover, the formal lines of authority can never carry the entire burden of serving as channels of internal communication. They are therefore supplemented by an intricate network of informal communication channels *(Blau,* 1956, 1959; *Gardner; Whyte).* This network provides an important role for the informal groups referred to above. It also includes what is usually referred to as "the grapevine." An equally important part of the communication network is found in the various formal devices mainly, or ostensibly, established for other purposes.

"Suggestion box" systems encourage the free flow of innovating ideas around—or through—the barriers established by hierarchic superiors. Grievance committees, appeals procedures and "open door" policies by top executives are designed to allow complaints to move upward without being scotched by hierarchic superiors. House organs, general announcements, and general meetings are official devices for sending communications downward, and allowing a few to come up, without using the hierarchic channels.

Polyarchy is a natural hotbed of informal relations and practices. Whether based on disparate or shared authority, polyarchic relations are by their very nature extremely difficult to formalize. Since hierarchic relations may often produce serious interpersonal strain and since they often rely for their effectiveness upon an overuse of scarce sanctions, both superiors and subordinates often enter into a silent conspiracy transforming formally hierarchic into actually polyarchic relations. Thus a large department in a hospital, although formally headed by a famous doctor, may in fact be headed by a loose informal partnership composed of himself and the head nurse or a triumvirate which also includes a resident physician. The "boss," as already indicated, may share authority with an informal "kitchen cabinet." An "advisory committee" may give orders instead of advice. On the other hand, formally polyarchic relations are sometimes informally transformed into rigid hierarchy. The best example is the committee of "equals" thoroughly dominated by its chairman.

Informal rules and rituals are also an important part of any organization's codes of behavior. In many areas informal codes seem to precede formal ones—just as historically the common law seems to precede statutory law. But much of the common law of the organization defies codification and some of it—particularly in units with an *esprit de corps* of their own—defies the formal rules of the organization as a whole. In fact, formalization itself often seems to have the direct effect of promoting informal systems of action *(Babchuk; Belknap; Dalton, 1950, 1955, 1959; Lombard; Page; Weiss).* Together with informal roles and groups, these may be referred to as an "informal culture" *(Argyris, 1959, 1960; Dunham and Weinberg; Levinson et al.; Sykes; Turner; Zaleznik, 1958).*

One way of looking at formal structure is to note that formal roles, hierarchy, polyarchy and codes deal mainly with authority and responsibility. In contrast, the informal aspects of organization are more closely related to power. Only by looking at these informal aspects as well can we complete the authority-responsibility-power triangle and see an organization as a system of power.

We can now understand why many formal reorganizations seem to have little effect. They deal mainly with formal authority and responsibility and much less with the realities of power. Any potential effect upon the distribution of power may indeed be counterbalanced or negated by unsought or unnoticed changes in the informal structure. *Le plus ca change, le plus c'est la meme chose.*

We can also understand why it is that when we look at formal structure alone many organizations seem never or rarely to change. Thus one eminent commentator on the Federal Government of the United States has observed that "Except for the increase in size, the form of American Government is not very different today from that of Washington's first administration" (Blaisdell, 1948, p. ix). Insofar as one chooses to close one's eyes to the revolutionary changes in the informal structure since the days of Washington, this observation has some justification. But from a broader viewpoint we might point out that this is a case of *le plus ca parait la meme chose, le plus ca change.*

With the "discovery" of informal structure by some of the modern pioneers and researchers in the field of administration, some people have responded with the prescriptive principle that rational administrators should recognize informal aspects in order to eliminate them. If informal lines of communication exist, they should be used by administrators. When informal leaders develop, they should be appointed to positions of formal authority. Where informal rules are acceptable, they should be institutionalized. The "discrepancy," it is urged, can thereby be eliminated.

Yet unfortunately for this point of view the acts of elimination may themselves bring new informal aspects into being. New informal channels of communication, new informal leaders and new informal rules—these are the inevitable result of any effort to eradicate the informal aspects of organizational structure.

B. *Informal Role Facets: General*

AN INFORMAL ROLE is not merely *any* pattern of actual behavior; it is a pattern appearing in people's expectations. Nor are these expectations oriented merely toward what people *will* or *might* do; they are expectations concerning what people *should* do. As with formal roles, they are more a basis of evaluation than prediction. But informal role expectations are not limited to the authoritative statements of those with formal authority for the division of labor. They are therefore more varied in nature and more changeable. Although they are often a greater source of role conflict, they may also be much closer to actual behavior.

None of the role facets discussed below are total roles. If we call someone technique-oriented, the purpose is to identify one aspect of his total role rather than establish a stereotype. Nor does the use of pairs and triads mean that we are always talking about dichotomies or trichotomies. A person may be expected to serve as Nay-Sayer in some situations and Yea-Sayer in others.

1. THE TASK-ORIENTED, TECHNIQUE-ORIENTED, AND PEOPLE-ORIENTED

The Task-Oriented see their role as "getting the job done." They see the job to be done in terms of "output" and its uses by specified clients within or outside the organization. They want to be relied upon as people who "deliver the goods."

The Technique-Oriented see themselves as masters of procedure and method. With control officials, this may evidence itself in a ritualistic conformity with regulations. With specialists and professionals working in rapidly developing fields, it may sanction sacrifice of the organization's demands on the altar of professional pride or personal intellectual gratification. In either case the formal output goals are displaced. It is largely among the Technique-Oriented that we may find the "trained incapacity," "professional deformation," and "occupation psychosis" excoriated, respectively, by Veblen, Warnotte, and Dewey.

The People-Oriented, on the other hand, may play the role of patron saint and good samaritan to people in need. In the federal enforcement agency studied by Blau, "some officials lost sight of the generic objective of raising the standard of living of American workers in the course of dealing with particular underpaid (or unemployed) individuals. They were so concerned with the plight of the employees with whom they had contact that helping these specific persons became the major goal of their investigations and the main source of their work satisfaction. Thus one agent . . . said: 'You spread a little sunshine in this job. That's what I like' " *(Blau,* 1955, p. 191-192). Sunshine spreaders are also found in private organizations and in strictly managerial positions as well.

2. NAY-SAYERS AND YEA-SAYERS

Every organization needs Nay-Sayers. Unacceptable requests must be turned down. Yes Men must be counterbalanced. Utopian plans and proposals must be exploded. Role deviation must be countered. This may require not only a thick skin but also a high dexterity in the arts of saying "No" despite pressures to force a "Yes." More frequently, it may accentuate the "negative personality" of control or review officers who, irrespective of what the conditions may be, find deep pleasure in actions of reduction, rejection, and refusal. In the field of advice the Nay-Sayers can usually be depended upon to find weak points in any proposal and—when it is clear that their warnings will not be heeded—to magnify them with Cassandra-like prophecies of imminent doom.

The role of Yea-Sayer is always needed to balance the Nay-Sayers. In his simplest form the Yea-Sayer may be merely a "Yes Man" who sneezes when higher authority takes snuff. The more constructive Yea-Sayer is the one who, even though doubting whether a difficult job can really be done, will himself help to do it. He supports—or even originates —the proposals that are attacked by the Nay-Sayers and helps circumvent their opposition.

3. RULE-ENFORCERS, RULE-EVADERS, AND RULE-BLINKERS

In part, the Rule-Enforcers are Technique-Oriented Nay-Sayers. But they are also something more. They are "people of the book." The guidance found in the rule book takes precedence over the wishes or protestations of superiors, subordinates, colleagues, or outsiders. Where the book is not clear, their inner voice reveals the true meaning. Where neither is clear, they follow the unwritten rule: "When in doubt, don't."

Although the Rule-Enforcers conform more closely to the bureaucratic stereotype, many of the most successful bureaucrats are rule evaders. These are the "operators," the people who know how to get things done "irrespective." They are often adept at "riding the rules" and slipping through loopholes. They may be even more adept at evading or breaking the rules completely—and just as completely covering up their tracks. Some of the most successful Rule-Evaders for certain purposes are the very people who, for other purposes, are among the more conspicuous Rule-Enforcers.

The Rule-Blinkers are a still further departure from the bureaucratic stereotype. They are not against the rules; they just do not take them very seriously. In some cases they favor a general "indulgency pattern" as in the case of Gouldner's gypsum factory where the foremen were expected to close their eyes to infractions of the rules against workers' taking materials home for household repairs (*Gouldner*, 1954, p. 45-56). In other cases, eyeclosing is regarded as part of their role as an effective superior. "The toleration of illicit practices," reports Blau, "actually enhances the controlling powers of superiors, paradoxical as it may seem. By voluntarily relinquishing some of his prerogatives, the supervisor creates social obligation . . . the supervisor surrendered some of his immediate power in exchange for greater ultimate power" (1955, p. 169).

4. *THE INVOLVED AND THE DETACHED*

The Involved are those who are fully immersed in their work and the activities of the organization. In part, this is a matter of energy and dedication. It is also a matter of ego-involvement at the expense of other interests or as a substitute for less valued interests. Among manual workers, the Involved are often regarded as rate-busters and may have to pay the consequences. Among clerical and secretarial workers they include the many people who, having little else to go home to, take their work-time worries or pleasures home with them. The specialists and administrators among the Involved work long overtime hours and when they go home take along not only their worries but their work also.

Among the Detached, some are merely Slackers who "go along for the ride." They too may sometime be expected to pay the consequences. Others work in an energetic and devoted fashion, but are expected to "call it quits" at the end of regular hours. Thus in the federal regulatory agency studied by Blau "the practice of working overtime without compensation, to which some officials resorted who had trouble meeting the production quota, was generally disapproved. . . . This censure of working overtime can be considered a functional equivalent of restriction of output among manual workers which was compatible with the professional orientation of these white-collar workers" (1955, p. 146-147). As Blau suggests, the role of Detached can often best be assumed by the more skillful people who perform superior work with less effort than others.

At the higher administrative levels, where greater involvement and dedication is more customarily found, there is less approval or disapproval attached to one or the other. Here the difference is manifested less in the amount of energy actually expended than in the degree of psychological immersion. For the Involved a crisis in the organization is a personal crisis and an organizational defeat a personal defeat. Under similar circumstances the Detached can look at things from afar and have a good laugh at his own or the organization's expense. This role is facilitated by other interests and involvements. Like the "good executive" whom Clarence Randall contrasts with the "self-appointed overworked executive," the Detached often "spends a great deal of time with people who know nothing whatever about his business and who are not particularly impressed with his responsibilities. Many of them do not even know what he does, and care less. This helps him keep his own importance in perspective" (1959, p. 128).

5. REGULARS, DEVIANTS, AND ISOLATES

The role of Regular is defined by his relationship with his group. He accepts the values of others in the group and is accepted by them. He is "in." If the work of the group requires collective action, he is a Team Player. If the group is successful, it's "we did it." Many Regulars in a unit, however, may be Deviants from the point of view of the larger organization.

The Deviant's role departs from the values of the group or larger organization. Like Len, in Zaleznik's study of a factory group, the Deviant is not able to work out a comfortable relationship with other members of the group. He glories in his role as a "maverick." Essentially a lonely person, he is seen as a threat to the group. Or else, indeed, he may be created by the group itself as a scapegoat upon whom the aggressive feelings of its more disturbed members may be vented *(Zaleznik,* 1956, p. 80-91).

The Isolate is the true Lone Wolf. Standing further from the group than the Deviant, he is more an infidel than a heretic. Like Axel in the same Zaleznik study, he may be technically able, but socially incapable, of playing a highly differentiated leadership role. He therefore settles on "aloofness as a way of differentiating himself from the group." Because of his distance, he may be much less of a threat to the group than the Deviant *(Ibid.,* p. 91-95).

Many administrators try to play the role of Regular by becoming People-Oriented with respect to their subordinates or by organizing a "management team." Such efforts can be only partly successful. By the very nature of their "in-between" positions and divided loyalties administrators are always deviants in some of their group attachments. At the highest levels of power the administrator is always, at least in part, an isolate. After all the collective consultation has been engaged in, all the experts been heard, all the maneuvers been explored, the time comes when in the privacy of his heart and in the light of his own inner torments, he must make his own decision. This is what is referred to when people describe the "terrible isolation" of the American Presidency.

6. NEWCOMERS AND OLDTIMERS

The Newcomer to an organization is in some ways like a newborn infant. It is assumed that he knows little and must be taken care of by others. In some organizations he is expected to be "seen but not heard" for a considerable period of time. This situation may be formalized by novitiates, apprenticeships, and trial periods.

A particularly difficult Newcomer role is that of Successor. President Truman's job during his first year in office was unquestionably rendered more difficult by his unenviable role as successor to Franklin D. Roosevelt. In the case of lesser men, the passage of time may indeed brighten the predecessor's halo. Thus the new manager of Gouldner's gypsum factory suffered in comparison with the "Rebecca myth" that grew up around the memory of the man he succeeded *(Gouldner*, p. 79-83).

The Oldtimers, having been "around" a long time, "know the ropes" in a way that no Newcomer can possibly hope to learn them. They will often resolutely prevent any Newcomer from moving too fast unless he first pays them the attention and obeisance which they feel they have earned. By tacit agreement they may often see to it that "Newcomers" of five or ten years ago still feel like strangers, particularly when they are seen as potential threats to the Oldtimers.

More positively, the Oldtimers often achieve power far beyond what might easily be inferred from their formal positions. In organizations with a high degree of turnover unusual disparities may thus be created. In the state hospital studied by Belknap, the "hard core of senior attendants"—people at the bottom of the hierarchic totem pole—had the lowest turnover rate. Belknap reports that "The informal organization of the wards is maintained and transmitted in its essentials by a core of about 18% of the attendants" *(Belknap*, 1956). Other hospital studies report on cases where the organizational continuity has been provided by, and major power concentrated in, the hard core of nurses, nonprofessional administrative personnel, or even the chronically-ill patients *(Caudill*, 1958; *Cumming and Cumming)*.

7. CLIMBERS AND STICKERS

The Climbers are expected to "get ahead." They are chosen not merely because of their assumed ability to handle their present positions, but because of their potentials. One or more paths of advancement are already laid out. Both their perspectives and their loyalties, therefore, will usually include the larger organization rather than the immediate work group.

The role of the Stickers is to "stay put." They are supposed to be satisfied with life and their position in it. The Stickers tend to cluster at the lowest levels of a hierarchy and at the top of various "career ladders." Unskilled, menial and low-status positions are filled by people who are expected to "know their place." Their mobility is blocked not only by the lack of opportunity but by their own lack of education, ability or experience. On the other hand, those who have already moved far have few places left to go. The top specialists may indeed seek to become top executives or even members of directorates. But when they have "arrived," the only mobility left is lateral and their basic role is one of survival. Since there is never enough "room at the top" for all who regard themselves as capable of filling the top roles, this often brings them into direct collision with those who are still Climbers. Some of the greatest tensions within organizations—and indeed in societies as a whole—stem from role conflicts between those who see themselves as Climbers and others who expect them to "stay put."

8. THE COSMOPOLITANS AND LOCALS

The Cosmopolitans in an organization are those who see themselves as members of a broader professional, cultural or political community. Within the organization, as Gouldner points out in his study of a college community, they may have the greatest prestige and may indeed become temporary "empire builders." But they are not committed to their local empires. They are Climbers interested in larger worlds to conquer (*Gouldner*, 1957; *Bennis et al.*, 1957; *Carlson*).

The Locals are less mobile. They are more rooted in the local community. They are more intimately wedded to the organization, where they probably reach comfortable middle-level positions. If they are still interested in climbing, they want to do it there. Since a larger number of them are Oldtimers, they are a force to be reckoned with. They are usually the most skillful both as Rule-Enforcers and Rule-Evaders.

c. *Informal Role Facets: Administrative*

As ALREADY INDICATED, each of the role facets discussed above may relate to either by administrators or nonadministrators. We now come to roles that are more exclusively administrative or managerial in nature.

Almost any of these roles, however, may be assumed by people with no formal administrative position. When this happens it is merely another example of the extremely important role of informal leader, already referred to in the discussion of informal hierarchy in Section A of this chapter.

1. GENERALISTS: GENTLEMEN, MIDDLEMEN, INTEGRATORS

The role of generalist is a complex role rooted in various combinations of attitude, ability, and knowledge. The Gentlemen Generalists are those who are expected to demonstrate unswerving loyalty to the values of their class or caste. They are expected to conduct themselves like gentlemen among their peers and maintain the loyalty and respect of their inferiors. Their knowledge is supposed to derive from an education in matters regarded as important by the upper classes. It is usually founded upon early training in the revered classics of an earlier period, supplemented by "school of experience" knowledge concerning the problems faced by higher elites. Examples are the Confucian scholar-administrators, the earlier British and Indian Civil Services, educated Kings and Princes, and the crown princes of various business dynasties.

The Middlemen are the "uncommitted persons" who are expected to "make the deals" inside the organization. Apart from their concern with their own self-preservation and self-advancement, they are expected to place highest value upon organizational survival and growth. They are looked to for the ability to get things done through persuasion, negotiation and compromise without too much discrimination as to just what those "things" may be. They are expected to be experts in their knowledge of the organization's formal and informal structure.

The Integrators are the true generalists. They are expected to see the woods as well as the trees and to be motivated by interests broader than their own or even of their own organization. They are looked to for skills not only in communication and compromise but in the constructive integration of divergent interests. They are expected to understand the organization's broad environment as well as, or even more than, its internal workings. They are expected to know enough about relevant techniques to enable them to understand, evaluate, and coordinate the activities of many specialists and professionals.

2. BUILDERS AND CONSOLIDATORS

The Builders are those who are expected to establish new organizations, enlarge old ones, or initiate new programs. Difficulties stimulate them to greater efforts. In the earlier days of the administrative revolution the Builders were rugged individualists, robber barons, economic royalists, or flaming revolutionaries like Garibaldi, Mazzini, Lenin, and Trotsky. In the midtwentieth century they are more cultivated, operate on a larger scale and are propably more numerous. They are the innovating entrepreneurs and institution builders in the private sectors, in national governments and in international agencies. But when a great period of ebullient growth draws to an end, their part is finished. They may then be a heavy burden on the organization or else—like Trotsky—be pushed aside by a Consolidator.

The Consolidators are expected to "clean up the mess" left behind by great Builders. They are more adept at the arts of maintenance, routine, and slow and deliberate, rather than daring, growth. Many stereotypes of the Good Administrator have been built in the image of the Consolidators, with little attention to the less orderly Builders.

3. THINKERS AND DOERS

The Thinkers are traditionally expected to think of things for others to do. This is characteristically the role of specialists, experts and staff advisers. The Doers, in contrast, are those with the dread responsibility of translating thought into action. Their own thought deals more with "how" than "what" and with narrower aspects of "how." They pick up where the Thinkers leave off.

Some administrators perform both roles at the same time. In addition to being Doers, they are also responsible for originating major courses of action. But this is a rarity. Most administrators rely on others for original as well as detailed thinking. This combination is most successful when the Doer takes on the challenging task of integrating the detailed, original thought of large numbers of specialists.

4. GRANDSTAND PLAYERS AND
BEHIND-THE-SCENE OPERATORS

The Grandstand Players are expected to play a conspicuously public role. They see themselves as "carrying the ball" on a huge field as thousands cheer them for their brilliance or courage. Whether Team Players or Lone Wolves, they thrive on publicity.

In exchange for the personal gratifications that may be involved, the Grandstand Players are often Expendables. They are expected to man difficult positions under sharp attack. Like soldiers before a battle, they think they may live forever. But after they have absorbed enough punishment of this type, their usefulness may be over. They may then be unceremoniously dropped, or else kicked upstairs.

The Behind-the-Scene Operators thrive on getting things done. By passing the ball to the Grandstand Players, they manage to be non-conspicuous. Here we find the *eminences grises*, the assistants "with a passion for anonymity" and the "faceless men." Occupying the more sheltered positions, they walk out on few limbs. They are willing to sacrifice publicity and public esteem for security. These are the Non-expendables of administration.

5. AUTHORITARIANS, LAISSEZ-FAIRES, AND DEMOCRATS

The Authoritarians are expected to dominate situations. The more genuine Authoritarians do this by detailed instructions to their sub-ordinates and close supervision over them. To achieve more through domination they may—like the "Leader" in the New England factory studied by Argyris—deal with subordinates separately, erect barriers between them and do everything possible "to prevent the barriers from being destroyed or overcome" *(Argyris,* 1953, p. 43-46). The same "divide and conquer" strategy may be applied to employees' efforts at self-organization through trade unions. The more superficial authoritarians are less interested in actual power and more concerned with defer-ence and the ceremonial recognition of their authority.

The Laissez-Faires are those who substantially withdraw from the use of their formal authority. They neither dominate subordinates directly nor try to influence them indirectly. Their permissiveness is not neces-sarily rooted in disinterest. It may stem from preoccupation with superiors, external affairs or other internal matters.

The Democrats are expected to encourage initiative by their sub-ordinates, participation in decision-making, and a more "free and easy" pattern of interpersonal communication than is possible with Authoritar-ians. They see themselves as sources of help and advice rather than a constant stream of orders. Thus the head of field engineering in one of the two electronic manufacturing companies studied by Barnes is quoted as follows: "I've tried to set up relations with the supervisors under me so that they can talk with me. For example, I don't try to make the technical decisions . . . but I do like to have them come up and use me as a sounding board . . . I'll make suggestions to them and sometimes I can help them from my own experience. Sometimes, too, I can refer Supervisor B and his project engineers to others in the company whom I know to be doing related work" *(Barnes,* p. 93-97).

Most administrators are all three together. Which of the three facets is predominant will, of course, be affected by the administrator's own personality needs. It will be affected by the personalities of his sub-ordinates, who may, as the case may be, crave domination or autonomy.

It will also vary from one situation to another. Times of crisis may require a leader to play a more dominant role on some matters and a laissez-faire role on others. As subordinates develop their capacities for more independent action, the democratic role is more in order. After spectacular success in pulling his plant "out of the red" and putting it firmly "in the black," the authoritarian leader described by Argyris shifted to a more democratic role *(Argyris,* 1953, p. 104).

6. IMPERSONALS, PERSONALS, AND CHARISMATICS

The Impersonals are close to the roles assigned by Weber to bureaucrats as a whole. They are not expected to reveal emotions or be conspicuously irrational. They are expected to think in terms of abstract categories of people rather than individuals. Many of them are Rule-Enforcers and Involved.

The Personals act more obviously like human beings. They demonstrate their interest in individuals. They show their enthusiasm or "blow their top" more readily. They may be either Authoritarian or Democratic.

The Charismatics are the inspirational leaders. As described by Weber, they have some indefinable "gift of grace." But Weber was wrong in thinking that the charismatic role has no place in large modern bureaucracies. Wartime inevitably produces charismatic leaders both in home-front organizations and in armies themselves, probably the most bureaucratic of all organizations. Even in less eventful times the Builders and the Grandstand Players often assume the Charismatic role. Yet those who succeed in doing this are not ordinary human beings. In fact, their extraordinary capacity invariably makes them somewhat inhuman. They can relate themselves intimately with people in general, even humanity as a whole, but not so readily with individuals.

7. THE FAMILY SUBSTITUTES

From time immemorial the heads of organizations have tended to assume the role of Father, Mother, or Sibling Substitute to their subordinates. In modern organizations, where old-fashioned "paternalism" is supposed to be on the wane, this tendency is nonetheless strong. It may also lead to the role of Husband or Wife Substitute. Members may find the outlet for their libidinous energies not only in deep intrapersonal relationships (or spiritual fusion with the Body Corporate) but in the comfort of a dependable relation with someone in higher authority. The paternal (or maternal) role is evidenced less by the harshness of disciplinary action, the sweetness of personal favors, or the security of social security measures. It is found mainly in the provision of emotional support, confidence and backing.

D. *The Power Structure*

WHO ARE THE PEOPLE who make the important decisions? Where are the centers of motive power within an organization?

If one tries to answer such questions by looking at the formal structure alone, it is hard to respond without using one of the myths of ultimate authority or central omnipotence. Although their scientific and normative validity may be "shattered," as suggested in Chapter 3, their active propagation and widespread acceptance is probably an inevitable byproduct of the process of building and strengthening formal structure

Should one look only at various aspects of informal structure, however, the first impression may be one of chaos and confusion. One may quickly conclude that "no one decides anything" or even that "nothing is ever decided." This conclusion could be supported not only by the general principles of process and multiple causality but also by the observed interdependence of organizational roles.

The only way to bring order back into the picture is to focus it directly on the structure of internal power. This requires an examination of how people-in-an-organization are divided on various matters and how the power is distributed on various sides of the dividing lines. It also leads to a consideration of what is meant by "organizational democracy."

1. THE DISPERSION OF POWER

If we return to the "double pyramid of formal authority" (as set forth in section C-2 of Chapter 15), we may now ask what changes are needed in it to provide a general model for the distribution of organizational power.

Some of these changes have already been spelled out in Chapter 3. There we say that as an organization becomes larger and more powerful, there is a sharp decline in the importance of the two top strata of the inverted pyramid: the holders of ultimate authority and their representatives. The more important areas of power become the directorates, the top executives and the bureaucrats. When employees of the organization organize into trade unions, a fourth center of power comes into being. We saw that, contrary to the "iron law of oligarchy," there can be no one all-powerful controlling group.

As we proceed further with this analysis, we then see that it is hardly possible to recreate the so-called "iron law" within any of these four centers. When the holders of ultimate authority are members of an organization, they are divided both formally and informally. When not members, they may be organized only through some representative system. Representative bodies are invariably arenas for the exercise of dispersed power. When this is not so, it is because power is exerted over them by directorates. At the level of the directorates, indeed, also of the top executives, there is a greater possibility of highly concentrated power for limited periods of time. Yet this is invariably counterbalanced by power centers at other parts of the organization. Among the bureaucrats the dispersion of power reaches its highest point. Here it is created by the very processes of formal specialization and delegation and augmented by the proliferation of informal groups, leaders, and lines of communication.

To all this must be added the pattern of external influences upon the organization. As pointed out in the following chapter, there is no sharp dividing line between power exercised from within and power exercised from outside. External power often operates through the members of an organization. Some of the strongest groups within an organization are those that operate on the basis of alliances and coalitions with outside groups.

As thus far discussed, however, these various areas or centers of power are merely unrelated sets of elements. They are rarely, if ever, arrayed on the field of interorganizational conflict in accordance with the pattern suggested by the double pyramid of formal organization.

To visualize the actual dispersion of power within an organization, we must start with a specific issue or cluster of issues. This may be a major appointment (and intraorganizational appointments are major matters for internal conflict and power plays, even within a so-called "merit system"), the issuance of a new regulation, or the installation of a new method of operation. Around this issue we then see an array of "forces," each one of which is a coalition of people or groups from different places in the organizational structure.

In the particular case here illustrated three of the four coalitions are headed by top executives. C_1, in contrast, is headed by two people at the next higher level of authority. They, in turn, are backed up by one bureaucrat, three holders of ultimate authority, and one from the trade union. From the vector's size, used to symbolize its effective power, it can be seen that C_1 is considerably stronger than C_3, which is composed of merely one top executive and one directorate member. C_2 has the same kind of top leadership as C_3 but also enjoys a certain amount of support from all other levels. C_4, likewise, draws support from all centers of power, but has more widespread and more tightly organized support among the bureaucrats. It is the strongest group on *this* issue.

A more careful analysis would require a number of refiinements. The most important is the addition of outside individuals or groups to the various coalitions. Each element symbolized, moreover, might refer to an entire subset rather than a specific individual. Above all, the specific power of any given subset or individual would also have to be indicated. This would vary in terms of the leadership, composition and structure of each coalition and the specific nature of the issue at hand.

To analyze the total distribution of power within an organization, we must cover all issues or at least a fairly representative set of issues.

THE DISPERSION OF ORGANIZATIONAL POWER
ON A SPECIFIC ISSUE

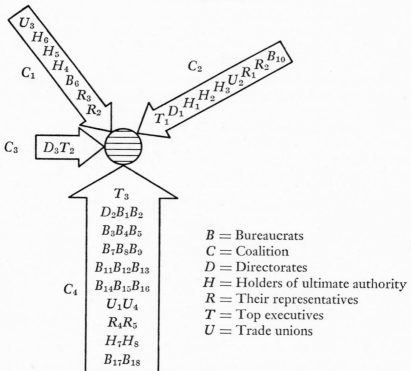

B = Bureaucrats
C = Coalition
D = Directorates
H = Holders of ultimate authority
R = Their representatives
T = Top executives
U = Trade unions

We must then rank these various issues in terms of their importance. Although this itself is a difficult and complex undertaking, it is what an experienced manager does on a rough-and-ready basis as he "learns the ropes" in an organization.

A number of hypotheses may now be set forth as to what analyses of this type may show.

First of all, on the most important issues—those that involve larger numbers of people and are hotly contested—the largest power will usually lie with a coalition of the C_4 type with substantial external support. Second, on issues involving two or more groups of the C_4 type, the amount of power on any one side will be decisively affected by relative leadership abilities displayed in each group. Third, on the issues that involve less people and are not contested, an extremely large amount of power will often be found in the hands of single individuals, pairs or small groups. Finally, there will be a general tendency for larger amounts of power to be exercised by people in higher positions of formal authority—most particularly from the directorates downward. In part, this is because formal authority is itself a source of power. One of the many reasons for this is that formal authority provides the authority holder with an excellent basis for the leadership of nonformal groups and coalitions. Another reason is that the prerequisites and awards that come with formal authority are themselves rewards and incentives that attract those people most capable of mobilizing power.

2. ORGANIZATIONAL DEMOCRACY

If central omnipotence is a myth, if actual power is always dispersed within an organization, then perhaps no organization can be run dictatorially. Perhaps every organization might be regarded as democratic.

Neither of these conclusions is warranted, however. There *is* validity in the distinction between dictatorial and democratic. Some organizations *are* unquestionably more dictatorial and others more democratic.

But the distinction has little merit if based upon voting, representation systems, and the other formalistic paraphernalia of democracy in political systems. These forms are applicable to organizations as a whole only when ultimate authority is in the hands of all members. Even when this is so, as with associations, cooperatives and collectives, the effect on the distribution of actual power within an organization is questionable.

A more fundamental approach to intraorganizational democracy is one which measures democracy in terms of *the members' participation in decisions concerning their own activities and the activities of the organization as a whole.* As Follett pointed out many years ago, participative democracy is much more meaningful than mere consent or acquiescence. Her judgment can be buttressed today by what we have learned concerning the way in which the heads of organizations and states have obtained consent or acquiescence by threats, propaganda, or manipulation. More positively her judgment can be supported by the fact that actual participation provides a greater opportunity for people to meet their needs for commergence, differentiation, and self-development. In fact, organizational democracy is one of the greatest factors in promoting the individual self-development of human beings. By participating in organizational decisions affecting his daily activities and those of many others, a person develops capacities that were hidden or stunted. He may not only meet his needs for belonging, status, and power; he may enjoy the endless satisfactions of intellectual or esthetic creation. In contrast, a person's entire self-development may be stultified, or even set back, if his organizational environment reduces him to acting as though he were a machine.

Participation, however, is a multifaceted concept. There can be no single measure of democracy in an organization—although for any particular purpose there may be value in concentrating upon a single facet alone. The three major facets can be identified by asking *who* participates, *how deeply*, and *on what?*

The most obvious participants are the administrators themselves and the "multiple oligarchies." In this sense the onward speed of specialization and the multiplication of administrative personnel is profoundly democratic. This democratic trend is carried still further when even the people at the lowest ranks or the lowest levels in the hierarchy—in Drucker's memorable words—are allowed or encouraged to participate in "the managerial vision." In the case of both administrators and nonadministrators the scope of participation is affected by the extent of internal conflict. Without the winds of conflict and the information borne upon them, many decisions are inevitably made in small and narrow circles. Mobility within the organization is another important factor in widening the circle of participants. With a greater proportion of Climbers to Stickers, there is a greater extent of interest in matters extending beyond one's individual position or unit.

The depth of anyone's participation is still harder to measure than the number of participants. At the one extreme, right at the edge of nonparticipation, is the mere sense of participation and the indirect or vicarious participation by one's elected, appointed or self-chosen representative. At the other extreme, there is the full participation in the form of direct and continuous activity at the work bench, desk or conference table. In some cases this may be isolated personal activity—as in the case of a worker repairing a special-purpose tool or a teacher in his classroom.

In others this may be personal participation in a group decision. The two may often be found together. Between the two extremes of a mere sense of participation and full participation, we find the more sporadic, illicit and fragmented participation of a group that is run by an authoritarian or dictatorial administrator. Here the actual participation of subordinates may still be great. The administrator may leave large elements of decision-making to his subordinates as he takes unto himself those which best satisfy his craving for self-expression and prestige. The subordinates may in fact retaliate through a long series of minor and scarcely visible decisions that are by and large beyond his control. But the extent of their participation will be impaired by the inhospitable atmosphere and the lack of a legitimate place for it in the organization as a whole.

The *on what* of participation must be understood within the general principle that *in organizations no one decides everything but every administrator—in fact, every member—may have an opportunity to help decide some things*. In a way this is similar to what happens in a democratic state at the time of a national election; every voter has a chance to help decide something. But there are a number of major differences. The voter in a national election makes a minor contribution to an occasional decision of great importance. The member of an organization makes a relatively larger contribution to a continuing series of decisions of lesser importance. The narrowness of organizational decision-making is compensated for by the multitude of decisions and the depth of participation in each. What is narrow from the viewpoint of the organization or of society as a whole, however, may be of transcendental importance to the individual. The decisions he helps to make in his organization may not shape the course of national policy or the future of the world but they may be much closer to matters directly affecting the largest number of waking hours in his own life. Moreover, the decisions in which he participates are inextricably intertwined with those of the High and the Mighty in the hierarchy of his organization. Their decisions are possible only because of large numbers of prior decisions by the Low and the Many in the same hierarchy. Moreover, whether they are carried out or reversed will depend upon the subsequent interpretation, reinterpretation and embellishment given them by the Low and the Many.

What is the relationship between intraorganizational democracy and strong leadership?

To answer this question, we must keep in mind that leadership strength has little relation to the brute, physical power expected of military leaders in the day of hand-to-hand battle. It has even less relationship to some of the characteristics often associated with allegedly powerful leaders: aggressiveness, an overbearing personality, stubbornness. Its only connection with force is the ability to draw upon vast reserves of personal energy.

Leadership strength in organizations comes from the use of personal energy to activate large numbers of people in achieving the goals of an organization. This strength can be measured only by such achievement, with due attention paid to the unavoidable obstacles and the physical resources available. Such achievement, in turn, is based to an important extent upon energetic participation by all the members of the organization. The strong leader, therefore, is often one who gains strength by promoting interorganizational democracy.

Chapter 17

THE IMMEDIATE ENVIRONMENT

*H*UMAN ORGANIZATIONS are "open" systems. They are rendered open by four phenomena that cut across organizational boundaries:

- entries and exits, which transform outsiders into members and members into insiders;
- multiple membership, which results in members' loyalties to outside groups;
- resource exchange, which involves the absorption of inputs in the production process and the delivery of output produced; and
- mutual or reciprocal influence on the part of both members and outsiders.

Some organizations go very far in limiting some of these interchanges. The most conspicuous examples are hospitals, jails, concentration camps, armies, ships or submarines at sea, monasteries, and communal settlements (Goffman, 1960). But the complete closure of any channel is improbable. The complete closure of all is impossible. No human organization is a closed system. The nature and extent of its "openness" is an important characteristic of all organizations.

The relations between organizations and the broad social environment are discussed in the next chapter. Here I shall concentrate upon the more immediate environment.

Any organization is usually surrounded by a complex array of people, units, organizations and opinions that interrelate with it on the basis of various roles. An oversimplified picture of this "encirclement" is provided by the following chart.

PUBLICS WITH OPINIONS

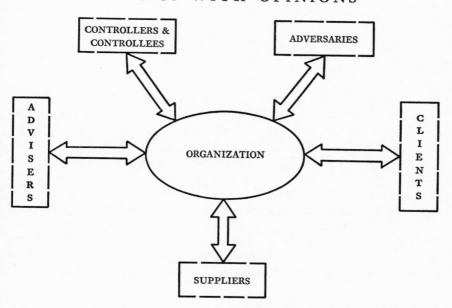

PUBLICS WITH OPINIONS

Any of these roles may be played by any type of organization, and many organizations play many of these roles at the same time. The less direct role of public opinion must also be recognized.

There is considerable variation in the visibility of the specific individuals and groups in these categories. Some of them, indeed, are well known to everyone in the organization; others are known to few organization members other than those who conduct dealings with them. Some operate in an open and above-board manner; others are behind-the-scenes operators. Many are still more intangible. Visibility, of course, is a relative matter. It depends upon the visual capacity of the seer as well as the characteristics of the seen.

But the mere identification of the various role facets, with their sub-facets, is not enough to indicate the texture of the organizational environment. I shall therefore identify some of these major strategies and the defensive or offensive strategies of the insiders. The external organizations and individuals playing these roles may be dispersed or clustered. Their interrelations with an organization may create a placid environment, a disturbed reactive environment, or a turbulent field (Emery and Trist, 1963). Their changing strategies of influence and intervention are a vital part of these various environments.

A. *The Clients*

THE CLIENTS of any organization or unit thereof are one of the most important elements in its immediate environment. Their importance derives from their role as *the receivers of the goods or services produced by the organization or unit.*

Here the word "clients" includes what is usually referred to by the word "consumers," but without the implication that consumption goods are exclusively involved rather than products used in production or investment. It also includes the idea of "customers," but without the implication that a direct monetary payment must necessarily be made. In this sense, the term cannot be used—as it has been by Gulick and Simon—to refer to the "people dealt with" by a government agency (who may indeed be the agency's adversaries) as distinguished from the "people served."

1. THE CLIENTELE NETWORK

To identify the clients of any organization, it is essential to recognize the chain of relations that may exist between the "direct" and the "ultimate" clients. The clients of a manufacturer include the consumer and the retailer as well as the wholesaler who buys all his goods. The clients of a trade school may include not only the students but also the future employers of the students. The clients of the man on one end of the assembly line are not only the workers at the lower end of the line but also the users of the final product.

The picture becomes more realistic if we think not merely of a clientele chain but of a "clientele network." The products produced by an individual, unit or organization usually fan out in many directions. The case of production for a single client is more the exception than the rule. Besides, the more varied the product mix, the more numerous the clients and the different types of clients. In fact, it is the differing needs of various clients that is a powerful factor in influencing the heterogeneity of an organization's "output mix."

2. THE INTERNAL CLIENTS

As already demonstrated, the clientele concept need not be limited, as it is in the terminology of marketing, to those who receive the products of an organization as a whole. The products of many units within an organization are produced to serve others within the organization rather than external clients directly. It is therefore helpful to use the concept of *internal clients*. This refers to those recipients of a unit's products who are external to the unit but within the organization as a whole. A full clientele network for any unit of an organization will start with such internal clients and then fan out into the organization's external clients.

Who are the various clients of the personnel department, the accountants, the purchasing officer, and the legal or economic adviser? Of the production gang and the man on the assembly line? Of this or that administrator?

From reading many official definitions of departmental functions and individual jobs, one gets the impression that the identification of clients is often subordinate to—or confused with—the identification of hierarchical relationships. A popular, but perverted, form of administrative philosophy holds that the job of subordinates is to serve their superiors. This might be justified psychologically, to a limited extent, on the ground that some superiors, perhaps the more immature, have a need for subservience.

But subservience by itself will not get goods or services produced, and under many circumstances it may interfere. Even to the extent that it might help, it would be a gross distortion to maintain that intermediate goods and services are produced at the lower levels of a hierarchy and move upward toward their consumers through the "chain of command" or the formal channels of communication. Any flow chart tracing the movement of intermediate products· is infinitely more complex. The clients of intermediate products can be properly identified only by focusing upon the specific processes of production within an organization. When we do this, we will see that, broadly speaking, the major clients of the accounting division, for example, may include at least three groups: (a) supervisors of production units; (b) the heads of all units; and (c) the top executives. As indicated in Simon's study of controllers' departments, different types of information may be produced for each set of these internal clients (*Centralization vs. Decentralization in Organizing the Controller's Department*).

3. THE LESS VISIBLE CLIENTS

For any organization which sells its products the identification of direct clients is an automatic byproduct of the commercial transaction. In the case of agricultural departments, public schools, social welfare agencies, and any other organizations which come into direct contact with specified groups of clients, the absence of an easily identifiable cash nexus is not serious.

For many other organizations, however, the identification of clients and their interests is far from easy. Who are the ultimate clients of the army, the tax collector, and the government agency regulating the price of electricity? It would be a ludicrous mistake to answer this question by referring to the enemy, taxpayers, or the electric company. The ultimate clients, rather, are the people whose lives are presumably defended by the army, the people whose interest in a relatively stable unit of currency is served by the tax collector, and those whose interests would be impaired by uncontrolled prices for electricity. In all of these cases the clients themselves are a relatively large, amorphous, unorganized, and unvocal group. They include many people who do not know they are being served, as well as many who are not yet born. Their specific interests are hard to discover. They may, indeed, be expressed and articulated by the very agencies involved in serving them.

A similar lack of visibility is found in many areas of business enterprise. A broadcasting agency or a newspaper publisher may never really understand its audience. Although various market research techniques may provide a good idea of the size of the audience, they will rarely provide any deep understanding of the interests of the various people composing it. Under such circumstances it is only natural that more attention be paid to organized and highly vocal interests of advertisers to whom time on the air waves and space in the newspaper may be sold.

The same problem also arises within all organizations, both public and private. Many units and individuals seem to lose sight of—or never sight in the first place—their internal clients. This is particularly true of units and individuals whose product is to gather information or supply information or advice. Although the formal justification for their existence is to meet the needs of others in the organization, these needs may lack definition and the "needers"—particularly in the case of new types of informational or advisory services—may be antagonistic. Thus the producers of these internal services are faced with the simultaneous tasks of market development and product development. If these tasks are not recognized, the producers of these services may soon become preoccupied with self-serving activities and lose contact with the rest of the organization. One of the sad paradoxes of organizational life is that this is exactly what often happens to specialists assigned the formidable task of helping to improve organizational performance.

4. THE NUMBER OF CLIENTS

As discussed in the next chapter, the number of buyers whom any seller confronts is an important part of the market situation. Thus the economist's terms "monopsony," "oligopsony," and "polypsony" can be used to refer, respectively, to situations where there is a single buyer, a few buyers, or many buyers.

These terms may also be applied to internal clients and to external clients with whom there is no cash nexus. Their relevance is based upon the relation between numbers and power. When an organization or unit confronts only one client, its freedom of action is usually thereby restricted. The single client may call the tune. From this point of view there is little difference whether the single client (or monopsonist) is a private corporation, a government agency, or another unit within a private corporation or government agency. When the number of clients is larger, the supplying group has more opportunities for initiative and manoeuver. Thus a filing or purchasing unit which serves many divisions within an organization has more opportunities for independence, and the unit serving one division has more reason to be subservient. To gain more independence it may seek more clients.

5. THE STABILITY OF CLIENT DEMAND

One of the most delicate and all-pervasive aspects of an organization's environment is the stability of demand for its output.

In some fields of activity, seasonal fluctuations bring about regular routines and procedures for expansion and contraction. This may include the payment of extra-high wage rates while work is available—as in many parts of the construction industry. It may require a careful division between the "fixed" labor force, whose members are maintained on the payroll, and the "temporary" workers, who are taken on and dropped as the occasion demands. Where trade unions are dominated by the former group, special pains will be taken to see to it that not too many of the temporary workers are allowed to enter their privileged circle. In the development of political campaign organizations, during the months preceding an election, efforts will always be made to mobilize the largest possible number of unpaid volunteers, working under the direction of the smallest possible number of regular staff members. Special forms of compensation—such as badges, buttons, public declarations, membership on important committees, or meetings with prestigious political leaders—must be devised as a means of compensating the volunteers. In all circumstances, however, the successful operation of highly seasonal activities requires the preservation of a stable core over a considerable period of time.

In some countries the fear of declining demand and the rising unemployment is one of the dominant factors of organizational life. This usually leads to the rather well publicized efforts of workers to seek job security through featherbedding, resistance to the introduction of more efficient methods, and the insistence upon the protection of workers' rights through strict seniority rules and hiring and firing procedures. Somewhat less publicized is the effect this has upon the efforts of managers to build indestructible empires capable of withstanding the assault of economic contraction and to obtain comfortable social security arrangements for themselves.

While national policy can go a long way toward preventing, or adjusting to, cyclical economic fluctuations in demand, and organizations can often develop their own adjustments to seasonal fluctuations, technological change still remains as a major unsettling factor. The development of motorized transport, for example, almost wiped out the market for cavalry units (except for occasional use in mountain areas or parades), stage coaches, and horsedrawn carriages. Mass production machinery has meant the destruction of many organization and suborganizations specializing in the application of handicraft skills. The data-procesing revolution in office work threatens the stability of countless thousands of organizations and suborganizations now engaged in older, and slower, techniques of gathering, analyzing, storing, and distributing data. With the rapid advances in both substantive and administrative disciplines, the threat of technological obsolescence hangs like the sword of Damocles over the head of any administrator who cannot adapt himself to change. A large part of the daily life in every organization consists of the activities of those who conceive of adaptation as the building of barriers to technological change and of those who dedicate themselves to smashing through, or sneaking around, such barriers.

B. *The Suppliers*

No ORGANIZATION can be entirely self-sufficient. It must obtain resources, assistance, or support from groups and individuals in its environment.

In part, the dependence of an organization or unit upon its suppliers, associates, and supporters is determined by the objective situation. The supply situation is much more difficult in a have-not country or in time of shortages produced by war or inflation. Assistance is not worth very much when it comes from people who lack capacity or understanding. Neither assistance nor support are easy to get from those who are uninterested or hostile.

Yet relations with suppliers, associates, and supporters are never fixed entities. Even in the worst of circumstances they are directly affected by the ingenuity and imagination of administrators. Even in the best of circumstances the availability of resources, assistance and support, and the terms on which it is obtained, will depend on the interrelations between the organization and the suppliers.

1. RESOURCE SUPPLIERS

We shall use the term "resource supplier" (instead of simply "supplier" as in more colloquial usage) to refer to those who supply an organization with goods, services, or money. This includes all those to whom the organization or unit is itself a client. For an organization as a whole the suppliers may include sellers of land, equipment, materials, and services, lessors of land and equipment, lenders, and investors. It also includes those who supply tax-supported or other nonsold services. For a unit the suppliers are the others in the same organization who provide it with intermediate products and with the resources (personnel, space, materials, equipment, and money) without which it cannot make its own contribution to the production process.

In its relations with resource suppliers, the organization itself becomes the client. Accordingly, the previous discussion on the number of clients is here applicable. When the organization is the only client, its position is much stronger *vis-à-vis* resource suppliers. When it is only one among many clients, its position becomes weaker. This is why governments often set up central purchasing agencies to handle supply operations for many government organizations. This is also why farm and business organizations often establish associations or cooperatives to handle central procurement functions.

2. ASSOCIATES

The associates are those outsiders who work together cooperatively in the production of a jointly-produced product. They may be suppliers or clients also. But in their capacity as associates they do more than merely deliver or receive products. They participate directly in the processing of the products they deliver or the production of the products they receive.

Thus both the suppliers of fuel for a space ship and the agency involved in space travel send its people to work together with the builders of the space ship. Among government agencies producing complex intangible services, this type of cooperation is necessarily so intimate that it is often hard to tell who is assisting whom. Production often becomes a symbiotic process of mutual assistance. This is also true of many relations between units in all organizations. A large amount of intermediate products— from major policy down to some of the more routine services involved in recruitment and costing—are jointly-produced products.

When jointly-produced products are not recognized as such, the necessity for cooperation between organizations or units and their environmental assisters is not recognized. Thus a personnel or accounting unit may think that it alone can produce the recruitment or costing services that are needed. Schools may operate on the assumption that education is merely the result of what teachers do, hospitals on the assumption that recovery from disease results merely from what is done by doctors and nurses. Yet in all of these cases the clients are also associated in the production process.

3. SUPPORTERS

The supporters provide the influence or encouragement which an organization or unit needs to handle all of its relations with its environment. In the world of business such support is often provided by large lenders, investors or clients. For government agencies it may come from friendly centers of power in legislatures or associations. An interesting example of the importance of support from hierarchical superiors is provided by the Bureau of Lands Management in the U.S. Department of the Interior. From a graft-ridden, bumbling organization in previous decades, this agency became a relatively honest and effective agency by 1950. Yet the able executive who guided much of the transformation process could never have succeeded if he had not enjoyed the active support of the Secretary of the Interior and the President of the United States (Clawson, 1959).[1] On the other hand, many newly-established units and many groups of advisers or technicians brought in from other

1. In a personal letter to the author on October 26, 1960, this executive made the following comment: "During the early reorganizing days in BLM, I had splendid support from 'Cap' Krug [Secretary of the Interior]. He understood organizational matters, had quick perception, would make up his mind, and stay hitched! I was able to make personnel changes, including separation of incompetent political appointees. I said then that guts in your boss was the most important ingredient in making organizational changes. . . ."

countries often find themselves wandering helplessly in a barren organizational desert. Those who once wanted them seem to have forgotten them. The idea that "nobody wants us" may destroy their vitality.

There is always a tendency for the resource suppliers, associates, and supporters of an organization to exploit its dependence upon them by assuming the role of controller also. In some cases, this effort at control may be limited to obtaining a favored position with respect to a narrow range of an organization's activities—as with the awarding of contracts. In other cases the price of support is total subordination. In almost every country there are examples of some government agencies that can be metaphorically described as "owned and operated" by a group of contractors or by a clique of legislators or politicians who provide it with essential support. In the business world the effort to obtain freedom from external suppliers is a major factor in "vertical integration." Governments move in the same direction when they nationalize major sources of supply. But in neither case does this necessarily eliminate dependence on suppliers; it merely brings external suppliers within the loose boundaries of an enlarged organization.

c. *The Advisers*

THE ROLES OF ADVISERS are very similar in certain respects to those of suppliers. Advice may be a resource even more valuable than equipment, manpower, materials or money. It may be regarded as an important form of assistance or support.

But there are also important differences. The adviser *as adviser* mainly helps a unit or organization use the resources it already has (although the advice to be sure may be oriented toward getting more of such resources). *As adviser* he does not provide assistance or support in carrying out the advice that has been given.

The relation between an organization and an external adviser or consultant is inherently difficult. If an adviser's help is not solicited, it will usually be resented as an unwanted intrusion. If an adviser's help is solicited, the purpose is not necessarily to obtain advice. Other motives may be to (a) enjoy the prestige of relations with "high-powered" advisers, (b) obtain a rubber-stamp approval of a course of action already decided upon, or (c) obtain resources that would otherwise not be available (as when foreign economic assistance is coupled with advice by the assisters). When a major motive is to obtain advice, the presumed superiority of the adviser is likely to be resented by some members of the organization. "His mere existence," Bryson has pointed out, "is a mild slur on the competence of the men he is dealing with, and to whom he is giving the benefit of his superior knowledge" (1951). In the case of the "foreign adviser," the slur cuts deeper, for his presumed superiority implies the inferiority of the entire host nation. This sense of inferiority may be alleviated in part by rejecting his ideas on the ground that "they won't work here."

Advisers respond to the inevitable tensions of the adviser-advisee relationship by assuming varying roles. One set of role facets is found on the continuum between information processors and action proposers, another on that between detachment and involvement.

1. INFORMATION PROCESSORS AND ACTION PROPOSERS

The information processors "play it safe." They use their special skills in assembling and analyzing relevant information. This often leads to forecasts concerning future situations. It may even include the delineation of alternative future courses of action, thus opening up before the members of the organization a range of choice they may not have otherwise considered.

An additional step is to identify the advantages and disadvantages of the alternative courses. But then the information processors draw the line. They regard the task of weighing these competing considerations as—in Max Weber's words—"no longer a possible task for science, but for the man of action. . . ."

This limited advisory role is very close to that of the informal organization role of the Technique-Oriented, as discussed in "People-in-Organizations: Informal Aspects" (Chapt. 16). It is often accompanied by a greater interest in the improvement of analytic techniques and the approval of professional peers than in the problems of the client organization.

The action proposers go further. Whether responding to their own personal needs for self-expression or to the demands of their clients, they submit specific proposals and recommendations. In support of this role, Johr and Singer use the concept "the obligation to advise." In their discussion of the work of economic advisers, they maintain that because of his superior training and his freedom to spend more time on specific problems, "the scientist is undoubtedly better equipped to perform the task of weighing and to reach a conclusion. . . . The social scientist has not merely the *right* to evaluate . . . it is also his *duty*. He should not, therefore, withdraw from the task of himself providing a solution to a problem of economic policy" (1955, p. 71-72).

The presentation of proposals carries with it certain other obligations that may involve the adviser still more deeply in the affairs of an organization. One is to bring general proposals down to more specific and actionable steps. Another is to present the detailed analyses upon which the proposals are based. Still another is to defend their proposals against inevitable criticism. This last point is a delicate issue. It implies a willingness to engage in open advocacy and contentious debate. Johr and Singer support such a willingness on the ground that withdrawal from controversy might leave the debate to those who are less qualified to marshal the evidence (*Ibid.*, p. 73). Moreover, such advocacy is often the best testimony as to the depth of conviction that lies behind advice. As Chairman of President Truman's Council of Economic Advisers, Edwin G. Nourse proved willing to engage in internal advocacy of his own proposals, but unwilling to advocate Truman's proposals before the Congressional Joint Committee on the Economic Report. Although he rationalized his position in terms of abstract statement concerning executive-congressional relations, the basic, and understandable, reason for his reluctance to appear as a public advocate of the President's proposals to Congress was that they were not consistent with his own convictions (*Nourse*).

The fact that the administrators of an organization may want specific proposals, of course, does not commit them to any course of action when those proposals are received. The filing cabinets of corporations and government agencies are filled with detailed proposals that have been solicited from outside advisers and then unceremoniously ignored. At the other extreme, an adviser's proposals may be promptly seized upon, misinterpreted, and carried into action. The most that any action proposer can reasonably demand is attention and consideration.

2. THE DETACHED AND THE INVOLVED

The presumed detachment of an external adviser is one of his greatest sources of strength. This strength emanates from the presumption that he does not (at least in the beginning) have any personal interest in the structure of power within the organization. This is the reason why members of units are often highly antagonistic to advisers who are external to their own units but members of the same organization. Similarly, members of organizations often prefer foreign advisers. "A prophet is not without honor—save in his own country." In either case, the external adviser's strength is greatest as long as it is perfectly clear that his affiliation with an organization is temporary. If he should be recruited as a permanent member, or even prove interested in an indefinite relationship with the organization, the "honeymoon" is over.

Yet the very detachment which makes the adviser strong during the honeymoon period is also a source of weakness. Unless he develops close working relations with some members of the organization, he will be friendless. He needs allies within the organization to help him assemble and interpret the simplest facts. He must get further involved in the organization in order to understand its power structure and "personality." As this process of involvement proceeds, he will often find that some of the most constructive solutions to the organization's problems have already been developed by people at lower levels who cannot obtain attention or encouragement from their superiors. Like a steam-generating plant's "economizer," which takes hot gas generated down in the boiler and brings it up where it can be used at higher levels, his greatest contribution may be to open blocked channels of communication within the organization and provide moral support for the creative forces for change already active within the organization.

Sometimes the organization itself prefers the detached role. This is particularly true in those many cases where administrators see a detached role for themselves. As Tilles has pointed out in his study of small manufacturing companies, "too often the relationship is viewed as either an opportunity to buy the 'right answer' or to have a high and expensive authority provide both the insightful diagnosis and the sure cure" (1961).

The more skillful administrators, however, see the activities of external advisers as something which they themselves must take active steps to manage. This invariably requires the temporary involvement of the outsiders in joint efforts to define the problem on which advice is being given and to seek feasible solutions. Thus even when he does not dictate the advice he receives (whether he wants to or not), the recipient may in fact become a coproducer of the advice he receives. Under these circumstances the adviser's detachment yields to involvement.

Over-involvement by outsiders is prevented or offset in a number of ways. If an external adviser or advisory organization advises a large number of organizations, there is less chance that it will go too far in its relations with any one of them. Moreover, an advisory organization can reap the benefit of both roles by sending in a team of advisers, some of whom identify with the organization and its problems while the others will remain dispassionately neutral. The organization, on its part, can decide to build up a special group of advisers for itself and limit the outsiders' role to that of selecting or training the inside group. The maturation of such a group is often the best terminal point in the relationship between the organization and its external adviser (Lippitt, Watson, and Westley, 1958).

Any organization's reaction to the way in which an adviser handles the problem of detachment and involvement is inevitably affected by the adviser's prestige. Whatever his behavior is, it will be more acceptable if he enjoys a high enough social status. Impressive titles are unquestionably a help. Thus many recipients of foreign aid will not accept experts who are anything less than full professors. This situation is recognized by the process of "upgrading" people before they are sent abroad as foreign experts. In the United States foreign aid program many universities have given temporary professorships to people whom they would not accept as full-time professors on their own campuses. An historic precedent for this form of upgrading is found in the case of Captain von Steuben, the Prussian officer who became General George Washington's principal military adviser during America's War of Independence against the British. Benjamin Franklin and other Americans in Paris at that time "realized full well that no matter what accomplishments Steuben possessed as a staff officer, he would never attract attention if he reported in as merely a Prussian ex-captain." In recommending him to Washington, therefore, Franklin gave him the exalted but entirely fictitious title of lieutenant-general. "As a supposed technician of high rank Steuben was able to accomplish much for the American Army that otherwise, coming from a humble captain, would probably never have been listened to" (*Hittle*).

In many cultures, moreover, in order to be respected, the foreign expert must be a person "who is relatively older, more deliberate, quiet, understanding and restrained. He is seen as wise rather than brilliant. He is not necessarily seen as quick thinking, outgoing and highly expressive. These are qualities associated with the young and, therefore, are not status qualities in these cultures" (Gore, 1961).

d. *The Controllers and Controllees*

EVERY ORGANIZATION or unit is subjected to the influence of one or more actual or would-be controllers.

The multiple nature of such controls over units of organizations has already been touched upon in the discussion of multiple hierarchy in "People-in-Organizations: Formal Aspects" (Chapt. 15). Here we need merely add that all controls over the units of organizations do not necessarily channel through hierarchic superiors. Many external control agencies, particularly government regulatory organizations, deal directly with the subordinate units of the bodies they try to control.

The relation between controller and controllee is far less ambivalent than that between adviser and advisee. By the same token it is fraught with even more tensions. Neither organizations nor units like to be controlled. They will usually resent even those control activities which they know are unavoidable or necessary. They will often engage in open or hidden resistance.

1. GOVERNMENTAL AND NONGOVERNMENTAL

As might be expected, most external control organizations are governmental or quasigovernmental. Some are established merely to control "lower" organs of government. Some have broad control functions over narrowly defined sectors—as with those which regulate a particular industry. Others have narrowly defined functions with respect to broad sectors of society.

In the heat of controversy that usually surrounds the activities of such control agencies, one often hears the contention that the unique characteristic of government agencies is the extent to which they are subjected to external control. In fact, it is this subordination to public control that often defines the "public" nature of an organization in the more democratic societies. On the other hand, it must be remembered that even in such societies the government corporation has been specifically devised to obtain freedom from certain public controls. Hence the British quip, also applicable to many other countries: "This country contains a large number of privately owned industries which are subject to stringent government control and a small number of publicly owned industries which are subject to no control whatsoever" (*The Economist*, February 3, 1962, p. 399). There is little basis, however, for either form of generalization. The number of control agencies and the stringency of controls to which an organization is subjected can rarely be deduced from its legal status.

Nor should we assume that all external control organizations are necessarily governmental. Lenders and investors often exercise supervisory authority over organizations to whom they provide financial assistance. Associations, federations, and cartels often wield authoritative controls over the activities of their members. Holding companies control various aspects of the operations of their subsidiaries.

In none of these situations, however, can the formal relationship be *ipso facto* regarded as the actual one. There is no empirical evidence to sustain the old adage that the acceptance of public financial aid necessarily brings with it public control. Many private organizations have for decades succeeded in obtaining direct or indirect government subsidies while being subjected to nothing but the pretext of public control. There are private industries which, although formally controlled by public regulatory bodies, have succeeded in turning the tables and controlling the regulators. The controllers may become mouthpieces of the controllees (*Devons*, p. 51). We may presume they have also been capable of achieving a similar relationship with private control bodies. The nature and extent of external control over an organization must be determined by direct observation rather than by jumping to immediate conclusions on the basis of its legal status. As a guide to such observations we may enlarge the above-quoted quip from *The Economist* by adding at the end: ". . . and a number of privately and publicly owned industries which control the agencies that are supposed to control them."

In an increasingly interdependent world these efforts to control other organizations, it should be noted, increasingly vault over national boundaries. The most obvious cases are those of organizations with branches in many countries—such as many large corporations, international associations, and cartels, the Catholic Church and the international communist movement—and national states which control colonial territories, trusteeships or "satellites." Equally important, but somewhat harder to pin down, are the operations of national states as they "intervene" in the operations of many organizations in many other countries. The nature of this foreign intervention has been forcefully revealed by Cleveland, Mangone and Adams.

> At State Department press conferences and in formal diplomatic statements today, there is still much talk about "noninterference in the internal affairs of other nations." But when one examines the true nature of contemporary American overseas operations, this ancient and honorable principle does not describe the present reality. . . .
> Any powerful nation today deeply affects the internal affairs of its many less powerful neighbors . . . (1960, p. 6-7).

Although the authors did not make the point, it might be added that as a result of this situation, the less powerful make increasing efforts themselves to control various aspects of the operations of their more powerful neighbors.

2. THE CONTROL NETWORK

As with clients, the external controllers of an organization vary in the immediacy of their contact with it. They are distributed throughout a complex set of control chains that can best be described as the "control network."

The immediate controllers are those in direct contact with an organization. A government regulatory body is an immediate controller when it issues a price order to specific groups of sellers. So is a budget agency when it impounds the funds of a subordinate spending unit. A holding company, similarly, exercises immediate control over its direct subsidiaries. Homeowners who appear before a city council to seek the reversal of a land use ordinance are attempting immediate control.

When a central bank endeavors to decelerate economic expansion in industry by imposing reserve requirements and other controls on banks, it is engaged in the immediate control of a relatively small number of banks and remote control of a much larger number of industrial enterprises. Similarly, the representatives of the holders of ultimate authority— whether a government legislature or an association's convention—can rarely, if ever, engage in immediate control of any formally subordinate organization or unit. If it operates through legislation or some other form of written rule, it will need an intermediary (or a series of intermediaries) to interpret the rule and confront the regulatee directly.

Immediacy and remoteness in this sense should not be confused with the specificity or generality of what the controller would like to see done or with the methods of influence that he uses. These important aspects of control are discussed in detail in the section on "activating" in "Rationality: Administrative Processes" (Chapt. 29). There is a connection, however, between these matters and the immediacy of control. Immediacy makes it easier to be more specific, while an effort to be very specific with remote control places a heavy burden on the communication system. Immediate control, moreover, even if "soft and sweet" methods of influence are used, is a more likely source of emotional tensions. The remote controllers are at least insulated from such shocks by their intermediaries.

To identify the major elements in any control network, it is not enough to look at the array of external controllers. Both immediate and remote control organizations frequently establish chains of control that penetrate the controllee organization.

Formal penetration is obtained by the official placement of members or representatives within the controllee organization in single positions. Both banks and government ministers will often appoint their representatives to serve on the board of directors of corporations they wish to control. Advisory committees are in widespread use as a vehicle for external bodies to make their views felt. A full-time liaison position may be established for the same purpose. Sometimes the controlling body will organize and staff a special control unit which will be formally accepted as a part of the controllee organization.

Informal penetration, which is probably more widespread, achieves the same purpose on an unofficial (and often *sub rosa*) basis. It is usually effected either by getting one's own people into strategic positions in the controllee organization or by winning the confidence or loyalty of people already there. Either approach is rendered easier when there is a common background of understanding and personal interest among members of the two organizations. At times the path may be greased by innocent favors or outright bribes.

The ubiquity of both formal and informal penetration stems from the ingenuity of the controllees as well as of the controllers. When some form of external penetration is inevitable, many organizations invite favored interveners at the expense of others. This may even go as far as opening the doors to a lesser enemy as protection against a more fearful enemy. Or else they may promote balanced penetration to play one group off against another. Penetration, moreover, may be merely a prelude to envelopment. Just as conquering armies have at times been enveloped and swallowed up in the course of time by the people they conquered, so the penetrators also may be converted into loyal members of the organization they were supposed to control. A classic example occurred in the U.S.A. during World War II when the Chairman of the War Production Board sent his chief aides into the military procurement agencies. Instead of serving as representatives of the central control agency, the "Nelson men" were soon won over by the agencies they had been sent to control.

E. *The Adversaries*

In ADDITION to the burdens of dealing with clients, suppliers, advisers, and controllers, every organization must also cope with external adversaries. These may take the form of competitors, rivals, opponents, or enemies.

Each of these adversary roles, it must be repeated, may be superimposed on most of the other roles already discussed. This is particularly true of control roles. Those adversaries whose activities are most to be reckoned with are those who engage in immediate or remote control activities.

1. COMPETITORS

Competitors are those who produce the same or similar products. Economic literature is rich in discussions of the effects of different types of competitive situations upon the activities of a firm. A large number of competitors can compel an organization to make greater efforts to meet the needs of its clients. Such competition may become unhealthy and destructive if it prevents the building of organizations large enough to benefit from modern technology or if it is conducted in a manner which leads to the destruction of assets. If the competitive challenge is reduced— as in oligopolistic or monopolistic situations—it is easier for a firm to use resources wastefully, restrict output, skimp on quality, impede technological advance, or develop one or another form of organizational arteriosclerosis.

Similar considerations apply both to government organizations and to the internal competitive situation within any organization, including business firms. Some degree of competition inevitably creeps into both fields. Here again the same considerations that are traditionally regarded as applicable to business enterprises are applicable here—albeit on a smaller scale. Complete monopoly makes for rigidity; a certain degree of competition may contribute to the vigor of administrative leadership. An oversupply of competitors may lead to wastefulness. Here too, just as in the case of a business firm, the competitive situation cannot be measured purely in terms of the number of other organizations producing identical products. Like business firms, suborganizations also try to achieve more monopolistic positions through "product differentiation" and "quality competition." To the extent that they can produce something a little different from, or better than, that which might be obtained elsewhere, their position is stronger. Here, too, the major competitive threat is the existence of substitutes—as when a top executive may turn to his budget and accounting staff, his economic advisers, his technicians or his line officials for basic services in connection with the charting of long-range policy.

2. RIVALS

Rivals are those who produce entirely different products but compete for resources, assistance or support. In this sense all producers of consumers' goods are rivals for larger shares of consumer spending. The sellers of housing and automobiles compete with the sellers of food and recreation services. When government raises taxes this is an act of rivalry with all organizations that might otherwise obtain the tax increment in the form of sales revenue.

In the government sector the most bitter and unending form of conflict is that surrounding the allocation of funds among and within the various government agencies. Every budgetary increment for any one organization or unit withdraws funds that might otherwise be available for all others. If total government expenditures are stable or declining, this rivalry becomes particularly intense. Subordinate units in an organization are usually rivals for the attention and support of their superiors.

3. OPPONENTS AND ENEMIES

Opponent roles are played by external individuals and organizations who, although not necessarily competitors or rivals, nevertheless impede the operations of an organization or unit. The more passive opponents are those whose cooperation is needed, who have nothing to lose by cooperation, but see no reason to cooperate. Their interference is mainly a matter of inertia or disinterest. The more active opponents are those who see a conflict of interest. Thus a manufacturing enterprise that tries to build a plant in a residential area may be vigorously opposed by homeowners and their representatives. In the same way we may regard sellers as the opponents of government agencies that impose maximum price regulations upon them. In this case, as in that of regulatory activities of government, the clients are not the people with whom the government agency is most in contact, but the buyers whose interests are served by price control. Only when the price regulations are designed to serve the sellers, as is often the case with minimum price controls, can the regulatees be regarded as the clients. Similarly, taxpayers are the natural opponents of tax collectors.

Enemies are opponents whose opposition carries them into the more bitter forms of conflict. They are often competitors and rivals. They may also be found among clients, suppliers, advisers, or controllers. Wherever they may be, they are not interested merely in blocking those operations to which they are opposed. For them the perceived conflict of interest is so great that they want to curtail or destroy the power of the unit, organization or nation which they oppose. For a unit of an organization the most deadly enemy may well be found in another unit. For an organization as a whole the most deadly enemy is the one whose representatives have penetrated the organization. Such enemies are particularly dangerous because of their knowledge of the organization's inner operations, their access to confidential information, and their ability to work under cover.

F. *Publics with Opinions*

EVERY ORGANIZATION is surrounded by some vague, circumambient phenomenon often referred to as "public opinion." In its broadest sense, public opinion might be regarded as the workings of the value system of a particular society. It may also be a very specific part of the organization's immediate environment—as when an organization enjoys high esteem for its competence or suffers disrepute for its incompetence.

Yet the term "public opinion" is both misleading and dangerous if used to refer to some mythical organic entity that comprises the entire society, or to some artificial average that purports to represent all opinions in the society or at least outside the organization. Different opinions are inevitably held by different people. Under most circumstances, except for a few broadly stated issues during a period of national crisis, there will always be less than complete consensus in opinion. There will usually be at least two different opinions on a single question, and often many more. There may be any one of a varying number of patterns of dispersion among these various opinions. Hence any meaningful discussion of public opinion must start with a recognition of diversity. It is in this sense that people often talk about the opinions not of the public as a whole but of specific "publics." Indeed, there is nothing unusual in the same organization's being regarded as competent by one public and incompetent by another.

As soon as we start to identify the publics whose opinions are of greatest importance to an organization, we immediately come to the external roles of clients, suppliers, advisers, controllers and opponents. The leaders of the organizations that play these roles, in fact, are the "opinion leaders" whose opinions are always of greatest concern to the administrators of an organization.

But this does not exhaust the possibilities. There are two other types of publics. The first are those groups and organizations who do not at the moment play any of these roles but who *might do so* at some time in the future. Most business organizations and many government agencies are continuously looking for new clients. In more complex and interdependent societies almost any group of any significance may some day be a source of assistance or support, a passive obstacle to the winning of assistance or support or a direct competitor, rival, adversary, or even enemy. The opinions of these groups, while insignificant today, may become a force to reckon with tomorrow.

Second, there are the opinions of individuals who do not now play any of these roles and who do not belong to those organizations who may play a relevant role in the future. Such opinions, indeed, are at the outer reaches of an organization's immediate environment. Yet they may some day become the views of clients and suppliers. This potentiality is more significant because of the ever-present possibility that even unorganized opinion reflects interests that can be transmuted into power by the activities of new and existing organizations and coalitions.

Because of the importance of these various publics with opinions, the administrators of organizations are invariably engaged in some form of activity designed to influence such opinions. This, in turn, presupposes certain beliefs concerning the structure of existing opinions. To help provide an informational basis for such beliefs administrators try to keep "their fingers on the pulse of events," "their ear to the ground," or their "eyes on the situation."

Whether they use fingers, ears, eyes, or all together, administrators cannot readily discern, let alone measure, the opinions of either organized or unorganized publics. The same opinion will be expressed and felt by different people with varying degrees of intensity and stability. Many opinions are latent and unexpressed. Many expressed opinions serve to hide a welter of conflicting interests, emotions, and tendencies. Most people have no opinion on most subjects. As the techniques of modern opinion sampling have matured, many surveys have helped administrators come to grips with these problems. But in so doing, they have tended to concentrate on unorganized individual opinion. General surveys, as V. O. Key has pointed out for opinions on governmental activities, "tell us almost nothing about the dynamic relations between the upper layer of activists and mass opinion. The missing piece of our puzzle is this elite element of the opinion system" (1961, p. 536).

But to survey the opinions of group leaders creates even greater complications. Opinions felt most deeply may be repressed or else disguised to serve current leadership strategy. The firmly stated opinion of an organization leader may hide considerable dispersion of opinion among the members of the organization. Because of the high costs that are usually involved, specific surveys prepared to meet the use of individual organizations are usually limited to present and potential clients—as with the "deep analysis" methods of the "motivation research" opinion analysts used by various business organizations (Ferber and Wales, 1958). In fact, a specific and continuing opinion survey geared to the elite structure of all the key groups in an organization's environment has probably never been attempted. Such a survey would probably require a greater amount of time from an organization's administrators than they could spare. It would certainly require a greater amount of cooperation from many external organizations than is consistent with the major roles they play.

The administrators of units are concerned with the opinions not only of publics outside the organization but also of other units, informal groups and individuals inside the organization. Here the same considerations apply that have already been discussed. Here, too, formal survey techniques may be used. Thus far, however, their use has been generally limited to across-the-board analyses of opinion and morale. Few efforts have been made to undertake pinpoint surveys with respect to internal clients, suppliers, advisers, or controllers. Even when survey techniques applicable to such refined analyses have been developed (as they inevitably will be), this will remain a field in which opinions are informally identified and measured by administrators themselves in their daily give-and-take with the various units and people within an organization.

Chapter 18

THE GENERAL ENVIRONMENT

*T*HE TASK OF THIS CHAPTER is to deal with the broad social environment of organizations. This requires a discussion of the characteristics of societies themselves. By "societies" we refer to the large aggregations of all people and groups living within a defined geographical area.

Every society is unique, thereby providing a distinctive environment for the organizations which operate within it. It has a unique historical past and unique potentials for the future. In the present it constitutes a unique aggregation of individual and group behavior. Sometimes a society is merely a combination of sharply differing subsocieties. Like organizations, moreover, societies are also "open" systems and also affected by their environmental relations. The specific nature of the influence is determined by immigration and emigration, multiple loyalties (if not membership), the exchange of goods and services, and mutual influence.

Yet all societies are also similar. They are similar in the sense that men and women throughout the world have certain biological and psychological attributes in common. These similarities have been accentuated by contact between societies, the growth of similar technologies and methods of organizations, the facing of similar or common problems. In a sense, albeit a very limited one, it is even possible to speak of the "society of man" as a whole.

Any society is extremely difficult to describe. For the observer from within, certain aspects are so much taken for granted that they are not perceived. The outside observer will often exaggerate the importance of certain aspects and miss others entirely. Those who try to observe many societies will usually fail to go deeply into any one of them.

A casual look at various societies can be provided by establishing a set of "ideal types" or stereotypes. But like the remarks of a tourist guide, these can merely serve as an impressionistic introduction. Unless immediately supplemented by measures of dispersion, such indicators of central tendency can be grotesquely misleading.

A more intimate approach can be found by reducing all societies to a number of factors or elements that appear in various forms and combinations in every society. This makes it possible to identify the general environment of organizations in any single society and to identify differences with any other society. One way to do this is to divide a society into an economy, a polity, a culture or any other subsystem which our conceptual tools enable us to construct. This approach has the advantage of conforming with the traditional division of labor in academic organizations. We are then faced with the task of interweaving the subsystems, a task often neglected by those whose interest in society as a whole is limited by their preoccupation with a particular set of conceptual tools.

In this context it is advantageous to take a broader approach which provides for this interweaving at the outset by trying to deal with the total social structure at a high level of generality. One way of doing this is to apply the concepts used in analyzing the structure of organizations. Thus the structure of a society can be regarded as a *pattern of interrelated group roles*. Here also roles, hierarchy, polyarchy and codes are a composite of both the formal and the informal.

But the concepts used in analyzing organizational structure cannot be automatically transferred from one level of systems analysis to another. In a society the major actors can best be viewed as groups and organizations rather than individuals and units. A society is much more diffuse and complex than an organization. There is less reason to get bogged down, in a preliminary view, in all the intricacies of hierarchy, polyarchy and codes. There is much more reason to get the total picture into focus by trying to discern a society's power structure and value structure.

Here, moreover, it is no longer possible to postpone the discussion of the resources available to organizations. These are ultimately those that may be found in the organization's general environment. For this reason our discussion of social structure will be prefaced by a discussion of the resource base.

A. *Resources*

ONE OF THE MOST SIGNIFICANT of all differences among various societies is found in the popular distinction between "haves" and "have-nots." The gap between them is properly regarded as a source of international tension. The basic reason is that either the scarcity or abundance of resources creates serious problems for organizations and their administrators. To appreciate the significance of these matters we must consider just what it is that the haves have and the have-nots do not.

1. OUTPUT

The easiest measure of the difference between "rich" and "poor" societies appears in estimates of their current output of goods and services. In one of the most impressive efforts in this direction Rosenstein-Rodan (1961) shows the following picture:

	Population, 1961		"Real" Gross National Product, in Dollars, 1961		
	Millions	Per Cent of World Total	Billions	Per Cent of World Total	Per Capita
Developed Countries					
Western Europe	261	8.7	385	22.0	1,472
Oceania	16	0.5	24	1.4	1,513
United States	185	6.2	515	29.4	2,790
Canada	18	0.6	38	2.1	2,048
Japan	95	3.2	58	3.3	613
South Africa	15	0.5	9	0.5	598
	590	19.7	1,029	58.7	
Communist Bloc					
Soviet Union	215	7.2	212	12.1	986
Eastern Europe	100	3.3	82	4.7	825
China	694	23.2	116	6.6	167
North Korea	9	0.3	2	0.1	211
North Vietnam	17	0.6	3	0.2	199
	1,035	34.6	415	23.7	

Underdeveloped
Countries

Africa	206	6.9	34	1.9	164
Asia	780	26.1	89	5.1	425
Latin America	210	7.0	120	6.8	154
Europe	67	2.2	34	1.9	501
Middle East	106	3.5	29	1.7	257
	1,369	45.7	306	17.5	
Total	2,994	100.0	1,750	100.0	

These estimates point up some striking disparities. The United States with only about 6 per cent of the world's population produces about 30 per cent of the world's 1961 output. Per capita GNP in the U.S.A. is 17 or 18 times larger than in Africa, Latin America, or China. The variations are also large within each of the three groupings. In the communist bloc over 70 per cent of the output was produced by two areas, Russia and Eastern Europe, accounting for only a third of the bloc's population. These differences become still more vivid when pinned down to such specific product categories as food, clothing, housing, health services, education, recreation and cultural activities. One of the most meaningful of all such specific measures is the consumption of energy from mineral fuels and waterpower (the major sources of energy other than musclepower and woodburning). In 1950, for example, per capita energy consumption in the U.S.A. was about 10 times the same figure for Japan, 20 times that of Yugoslavia, 30 times that of Turkey, 40 times that of Peru, 50 times that of Egypt and 60 times that of India (Woytinsky and Woytinsky, 1953, p. 941).

2. WEALTH

Behind these differences in current output lie other disparities in the stock of such man-developed capital as

- farms and livestock
- buildings, roads, bridges, dams, and harbors,
- energy-producing facilities that can supplant the musclepower of people and animals,
- machinery and tools that use such energy in agriculture, manufacturing, transportation, and communication, and
- supplies of consumers' and producers' goods held for future use.

Although it is fantastically difficult to estimate the aggregate quantity of such stocks in any society, we know that the variations are substantial.

The capital provided by nature, no easier to quantify, is also unevenly distributed. Some societies—conspicuous among them the U.S.A.—have been blessed with a large variety, great amount, and high quality of soil, animal life, forests, vegetation, minerals, rivers, and rainfall. Some societies are rich in many categories but lacking in others. Others may be generally poor, with a sprinkling of isolated riches such as oil or copper. Still others have relatively little of anything.

But people themselves are the most important of all resources. It is people who produce the current output of goods and services. It is people who create and renew the accumulated stock of facilities, machinery, and tools. It is people who find or neglect natural resources, develop and use them or—as the case may be—deplete them. Only the energy and imagination of people can compensate for the lack of nature-provided resources by trading with others and the discovery of substitutes.

In a sense, therefore, the potentially richest societies might be thought of as those with the most people. But among all societies, even the most populous, there are wide disparities in health and acquired abilities. A society cannot escape the "have-not" level if a large part of its people are illiterate, ill fed, and ridden by preventable diseases. It cannot reach the "have" level without a labor force that includes a large proportion of skilled workers, technicians, specialists, professionals, intellectuals, and administrators. It cannot remain at the "have" level without a continual enlargement in the quality and quantity of people in these categories. This seems to necessitate also the continual enlargement of urban areas, which have thus far proved the only way of assembling the resources and external economies needed by large-scale organizations.

3. SCARCITY AND ABUNDANCE

In an environment characterized by low levels of output, capital, or human resources, sharp limits are placed on what an organization or an administrator can hope to do. In a "have" society, except for times of war or serious inflation, an administrator can have a telephone call made to a supplier of necessary materials, parts, or equipment. He can turn to the labor market to get people of such-and-such skills. In a nonindustrialized economy, however, it may take many months to get the needed supplies. The supplier himself may be nonexistent and, if existent, he may have no telephone. The shortages of skilled people will be just as acute. In many cases, there will simply be no conception of what a certain skill is—office secretary or cost accountant. Nor will there be highly developed government agencies capable of providing needed statistics. Even if there already exists a substratum of essential services in the field of health, public utilities, policing and transportation, the experienced administrator or expert technician from an industrialized country will often find himself at an utter loss in such a poverty-stricken environment. Unable to obtain reliable local information, to find understanding people to work with, or even to find a competent secretary, he may be as useless as the English aristocrats stranded on a desert island in Barrie's *The Admirable Crichton*. Here the most useful fellow may instead be someone who, while only a minor underling in "more civilized" society, at least can do better when forced to live by his wits.

An environment of abundance may create as many special difficulties as an environment of scarcity. Abundance leads to free and easy ways that cannot readily be modified. The interdependence essential to the creation of abundance may also create an overdependence on established ways. It is in this sense that a rich society runs the risk of becoming "soft." An abundance of natural resources or man-made capital removes the pressure (Galbraith might say "the need") for economizing on their use and conserving them for the future. As Galbraith has observed, "Wealth is the relentless enemy of understanding" (*The Affluent Society*, p. 1). Overproduction of goods or services—whether "over" relative to effective demand or in more absolute terms, whether general or concentrated in a few fields—leads to a drastic shakeup among the producing organizations, including the possible liquidation of many of them. An oversupply of people relative to suitable employment opportunities leads to an erosion of human resources. But surplus people cannot be stocked, as can surplus goods. Nor can they, short of emigration, famine, or war, be readily liquidated. If the number of unemployed is large, many of them will inevitably be employed in organizations that could get along without them. If the number grows, many will gravitate toward organizations that aim to produce drastic changes in the social structure.

At lower levels of economic development, underemployment of human resources—particularly in agriculture—is a concomitant of scarcity in output and man-developed resources. In the "have" societies unemployment often appears cyclically together with an "overproduction" in current output relative to effective demand. As the level of abundance rises in "have" societies rapidly changing technology continuously brings new skills into being and renders old skills obsolescent. Under such circumstances administrators can never escape the simultaneous problems of manpower scarcity and manpower surplus.

B. *Social Organization*

As POINTED OUT in "The Rise of the Administered Society" (Chapt. 2), it is only through organization that people can convert resources into the power to do significant things. Increasing power has been provided by the administrative revolution which has brought—and is still bringing—with it more organization, larger organizations, more bureaucracy, and more administrators.

Although the onward sweep of the administrative revolution is universal and unidirectional, there are tremendous variations not only in its rate of motion but also in the emergence in each society of a unique array of organizations and organizational roles. Every organization is inescapably affected by this aspect of its environment.

1. FAMILIES

Although families are to be found in all societies, there is a tremendous variation not only in their internal structure but also in their relation to other organizations in society. This relation can be dramatized by thinking of various societies in terms of their place on this three point "family role" continuum:

A - - - - - - - - - - - - - - B - - - - - - - - - - - - - C

Families or extended families as *the* organizations	Families as important units in larger organizations and constellations	Families as peripheral to larger organizations

At the limiting extreme of A, families or extended family organizations are the only organizations in society. The family itself, through its various combinations and subdivisions, carries on all organized activities. At and around B, many other organizations are active in society—particularly governments, armies, and churches, but also certain producing and trading organizations. But one family, or a small set of families, becomes the dominant factor in most organizations. Thus we have governmental dynasties, hereditary priesthoods and patrimonial business enterprises. The wave of the administrative revolution usually carries a society from the vicinity of B toward the vicinity of C. The area of family domination contracts as monarchies topple over and surviving dynasties tend to become ceremonial figureheads. The dynasts themselves find that family members cannot be relied upon to carry on the monarch's business and often establish merit systems. In business enterprise family activity lingers longer. Here the family serves a triple function as a source of capital, a reservoir of manpower that can be trusted and a motivator to build up family fortunes. The family firm and the paternalistic enterprise are often the prime movers in building new, large enterprises. Where the family is not large enough to supply the necessary capital and manpower, it may be enlarged. In Japan, the house of Mitsui maintained its dominant position in industry by expanding to include "eleven families plus cousins." Slowly and painfully, however, the requirements for skilled manpower force a retreat from family domination and nepotism. Except for such last strongholds as very small scale enterprises, family farms, and a scattering of family corporations, holding companies and foundations, the role of the family in large-scale organization is now peripheral (Harbison and Myers, 1952). Nor does the family hold its own even as the major producer of the traditionally "familial" services. A not inconsiderable portion of child care, sexual activity, recreation, eating, and laundry may be transferred elsewhere. Energies previously absorbed by the family are thereby released, often to be concentrated on the operations of other organizations.

Nevertheless, even at this point on our continuum the family still has an important influence upon administration. The family is still the first place where the human being acquires his attitude toward authority, social mobility, and cultural values, attitudes that determine a large part of his subsequent behavior in other organizations.

2. GOVERNMENT

All organizations in any society can be distributed on a continuum ranging from governmental through mixed to nongovernmental. Colloquially, we use the term "socialist" to refer to any society with a larger proportion of governmental or mixed organizations. A more discerning use of this scale necessitates a frequency distribution based upon a general classification of products or—in national accounting terms—the sectors of origin of national income. By this approach we can see that the "mixed economy" of many societies derives not only from mixed organizations but also from varying frequencies of governmental organizations in different sectors. Thus in India the relatively small areas of industry, transportation, and communication are predominantly governmental and the extremely large area of agricultural production is overwhelmingly nongovernmental.

Any picture provided by such a frequency distribution, however, must be modified by more qualitative considerations concerning the influence of governmental upon nongovernmental organizations. By regulation, control, assistance, and less direct forms of influence government organizations can become a dominant factor in the activities of nongovernmental organizations. Thus in the U.S.A. a Federal government generally regarded as "nonsocialist" wields much greater influence than the "socialist" government of India over private agriculture.

At this point we may note the limited usefulness of the frequent efforts to appraise the role of government in terms of government expenditures as a percentage of gross national product. This measure is useful only to calculate marginal changes within a given society or to compare societies which differ little in basic structure. If we should compare the U.S.A. with the U.S.S.R., the difference would be rather small in comparison with the vast difference in the nature of producing organizations. The reason is that the largest expenditures in both societies are those of households and individual consumers.

3. BUYERS AND SELLERS

One of the differentiating characteristics of organizations, as pointed out in Chapter 15, is whether or not they sell their end products. Sellers, however, imply buyers. The term "market" refers to some pattern of relations between buyers and sellers.

An important aspect of every society is simply the extent of buying-selling relations. First of all, many organizations produce goods or services for their own members only. In many nonindustrialized societies this is true of a large portion of family-produced agricultural products. This principle of "production for use by the producers" in all societies also applies to "household services" in general, and many of the services of "self-serving" associations. Second, there are many kinds of nonsale transactions with external clients. In certain primitive societies—as with the Trobriand islanders of Western Melanesia described by Malinowski—products flow circularly from one group to another, thus constituting an unplanned system of reciprocity (1926, p. 40-41). As societies grow wealthier philanthropic organizations distribute charity or "patronage" as a means of helping the needy, promoting the arts and protecting their own members against more vigorous redistribution activities by government. Nonetheless, the growth of government, particularly in the era of the administrative revolution, invariably brings with it a large volume of nonsold services distributed largely on the basis of administrative judgment and client pressure. The large-scale redistribution activities of government are made possible through governmental power to appropriate wealth through its powers of taxation and money-creation.

But the growth of nonmarketed government services should not lead us to an exaggerated dichotomy between markets and governmental activity. Governmental action itself has always been an indispensable factor in the growth of markets. In the nineteenth century "the road to the free market was opened and kept open by an enormous increase in continuous, centrally organized and controlled interventionism. . . .

Administrators had to be constantly on watch to ensure the free work-ings of the system. Thus even those who wished most ardently to free the state from all unnecessary duties . . . could not but entrust the self-same state with the new powers, organs and instruments required for the establishment of *laissez-faire*. . . . *Laissez-faire* was planned . . ." (Karl Polanyi, 1957, p. 140-141).

Specifically, governments have

- established the monetary and banking systems without which markets cannot develop very far beyond primitive barter,
- actively promoted both internal and foreign trade,
- provided the indispensable governmental services which protected property rights and contracts and afforded acceptable means of media-tion for market disputes,
- regulated markets in order to protect not only buyers and sellers but other groups whose interests would be jeopardized by uncontrolled market conflict, and
- entered many markets as important buyers, particularly in periods of war-inflated government purchasing.

Moreover, twentieth-century socialism—despite ideological leanings toward a utopian era in which everything would be freely distributed —has unquestionably produced a larger expansion in the volume of products marketed by governmental organizations. The fact that most prices in the Soviet Union and other communist-bloc countries are determined by government agencies merely means that the pattern of price determination is different from that in the so-called "capitalist" countries. It should not lead us to ignore the fact that in the former societies markets are also seen as an indispensable vehicle for controlling the distribution of goods and services (Bornstein, 1962).

The tremendous variety of market systems has rarely been analyzed empirically in any society. Yet we can readily distinguish the more important variables. One set of variables is provided by the simple dis-tinctions between the number of buyers or sellers. Thus any market can be characterized by its position in one of the nine cells in the following buyer-seller matrix.

		SELLERS		
		One (o)	*Few (f)*	*Many (m)*
B	One (o)	o,o	o,f	o,m
U				
Y	Few (f)	f,o	f,f	f,m
E				
R	Many (m)	m,o	m,f	m,m
S				

Thus, an m,m market represents the traditional idea of many buyers and sellers. On the same row we find not only the traditional monopoly (m,o) but also the oligopoly with many buyers (m,f). In the same column we find the monopsony with many sellers (o,m) and the oligopsony with many sellers (f,m). At the opposite end of the diagonal we find the market (o,o) in which one buyer confronts one seller. Other variables relate to the homogeneity, heterogeneity or uniqueness of the products involved; the supply situation; the extent of cooperation or organization among sellers or buyers; the extent and nature of government control; the availability of information on costs, output, and related matters; and the ease of entering the market as either buyer or seller. An extremely perceptive effort to group these variables into a set of generally discernible market types is provided by Wiles in his typology of (i) primitive higglers, (ii) price takers, (iii) full cost chargers, (iv) discontinuous producers, and (v) marginal cost chargers (1961, p. 4-5). To apply these distinctions to an entire economy would necessitate interweaving them into the matrix of organizations classified both by output (economic sectors) and governmental status.

4. ASSOCIATIONS

Another important aspect of any society is the role played by associations—that is, by organizations whose major members, apart from employed staff, are affiliates rather than employees.

In an advanced industrial society like the U.S.A. the number and aggregate membership of such associations is extremely high. The table on page 444 shows the distribution of over 11,000 associations in 1959.

Although comparable data are not available for other countries, there is enough evidence to indicate a luxuriant outgrowth of organizations in all highly industrialized societies. According to Finer, "Britain is more 'organized' than even the U.S.A., for long thought to be the home of 'joiners' " (1958, p. 5). In less developed societies the roles of associations are often usually more limited. They are performed rather by what Almond calls "nonassociational" and "anomic" interest groups. The former are "kinship and lineage groups, ethnic, religious, status and class groups which articulate interests informally, and intermittently, through individuals, cliques, family and religious heads, and the like." The latter are "more or less spontaneous breakthroughs into the political system from the society, such as riots and demonstrations" (1960, p. 33-38).

By cutting across membership in families and employment organizations, associations contribute to the "multiple membership" dimension of any society. They supplement the market by providing many unsold services for their own members. By bringing together many buyers or sellers with common interests, they also provide a channel for participating in or otherwise influencing specific markets. They provide facilities whereby competing or interdependent organizations can exchange information, mediate their differences, or coordinate their policies—as with community chests and trade associations (*Litwak* and *Hilton*, 1962).

Associations also play a major role in the activities of national and local government agencies, executive, legislative, and judicial. They provide the specialized personnel and skills required to collect and assess information on governmental operations and to influence the choice of governmental personnel, the organization of government, and the nature of government decisions. But the flow of information and influence is not unidirectional. Government organizations, in turn, often use such associations as means of collecting essential information and of extending their control over larger sectors of society than they could reach if left to their own devices.

NATIONAL ASSOCIATIONS IN THE UNITED STATES, 1959[a]

Type	Number of Organizations
1. Trade, business and commercial	2,462
2. Agricultural, including commodity exchanges	377
3. Governmental, public administration, military and legal	191
4. Scientific, engineering and technical	332
5. Educational and cultural	671
6. Social welfare	274
7. Health and medical	526
8. Public affairs	224
9. Religious	527
10. Fraternal, foreign interest, nationality and ethnic	460
11. Horticultural	74
12. Veteran, heritary and patriotic	135
13. Hobby and avocational	213
14. Athletic and sports	183
15. General (not elsewhere classified)	118
16. Labor unions	230
17. Chambers of commerce (international, binational, national, state, local)	4,155
18. Greek, letter societies (social, professional, honorary)	330
Total	11,482

a. National Organizations of the U.S., Vol. I of *Encyclopedia of Associations*.

5. POLITICAL PARTIES

Political parties are associations whose major activity is the effort to place their members in key positions in government. In societies where elections are not conductd they do this through intrigues, deals, coups d'etat or revolutions. Where elections are held, they do this by nominating candidates and trying to get them the votes required for election. The victorious candidates are always expected to appoint to office (or help get appointed) other party members—although the growth of civil service systems narrows the number of such appointments.

In order to win elections, negotiate deals or provide the support for coups d'etat or revolutions, all parties and party leaders are interested to at least some minimum extent in government policies and programs. In "personalist" parties where party leaders themselves clearly symbolize the interests of certain groups in society, or where they are merely engagd in rivalry to serve identical groups, the program approach of parties will not be highly articulated. Where parties serve a wide variety of interests, party programs will largely be a jumble of contradictions or when the communication system in a society allows the people "down river" to hear what party leaders say "up the river" a mass of generalities. Where parties represent fewer interest groups in society, they may differ very little from an ordinary association. In such cases a party can afford to be highly "ideological." If an ideological party of this type wins seats in a legislature, it will then have to make programmatic compromises if it wants to be very influential in the legislative process. If it joins a coalition cabinet, it will compromise its programs through the normal process of coalition building and coalition operation.

Party "systems" are often distinguished on the basis of the number of political parties in a society: one, two, or many. This is an acceptable starting point as long as a number of qualifying factors are promptly introduced.

First of all, some parties are of little or no consequence. They may operate merely to get publicity for a few people. If they actually run candidates in elections, they may never get enough votes to elect their own candidates or influence the fate of other candidates. With only a few exceptions, this has been the situation with minor parties in national elections in the United States. Hence the logic of referring to the United States as having a "two-party system." Similarly, there are many areas of the U.S.A. where the second party has been of practically no significance—and in fact has sometimes been merely an appendage of *the* party. Hence the frequent reference in the U.S.A. to "single-party" districts, towns, or even States.

Second, even where there are two or more substantial parties, it may well be that one party is firmly seated in control of the government and that rivals have no chance to dislodge it. In India the Congress Party has consistently won an overwhelming majority of the national legislature and of most state governments. In Israel the Mapai Party, although generally winning only a plurality of seats, has always been the organizer and kingpin of coalition governments. Although opposition parties in both countries are free to organize and campaign, it is difficult to see how any single party or coalition of parties could undermine the one-party hegemony of either the Congress Party or the Mapai. The same can be said about Mexico's Party of Revolutionary Institutions.

Third, a multitude of factions may often be found in one-party and two-party systems. "Insofar as factions develop freely inside a single party," Duverger points out, "this becomes simply a framework which limits political rivalries without destroying them; prohibited outside the single party, pluralism is reborn inside the party, and there it can play the same part. Thus the internal divisions in the Democratic Party in the southern states of America, where it is for all practical purposes in the position of a single party, are such that the party is nearer to classical democracy than to Fascism, thanks to the system of the primaries; as far as they are concerned it is possible to transpose the fundamental distinction between bipartism and multi-partism. . . . It is therefore conceivable that a single-party system may coincide with some kind of political democracy" (1954, p. 278).

In the United States the Democratic Party has long been sharply divided between its more liberal (mainly Northern) and more conservative (mainly Southern) wings. The Republicans have also been divided—somewhat less on liberal-conservative lines, somewhat more on foreign policy issues. Moreover, the electoral system of the U.S.A. is so constituted as to orient the Presidency and most Governorships somewhat more toward the voters in the larger metropolitan areas, and to orient the Congress (even when the majority of seats are held by the same party whose candidate has won the Presidency) more toward the rural areas. From this point of view a full-fledged two-party system can hardly be said to exist. This situation is reflected in the frequent calls for a stronger two-party system—one in which "the parties are able to bring forth programs to which they commit themselves . . . and possess sufficient internal strength to carry out their programs" (Committee on Political Parties, 1950, p. 17-18).

In analyzing party systems in developing countries, Esman has distinguished five types: (1) conservative oligarchies (Iran, Ethiopia,

Northern Nigeria, Afghanistan, and Peru); (2) competitive interest-oriented parties (Philippines, Brazil, Greece, Chile, Malaya, and Jamaica); (3) authoritarian military reformers (Pakistan, Burma, South Korea, Thailand, and the Sudan); (4) dominant mass parties (Mexico, India, Egypt, Algeria, Puerto Rico, Tanganyika, Tunis, and Guinea); and (5) communist totalitarians (China, Soviet Union, and the communist countries of Eastern Europe). "The dominant mass party regimes," he finds, "appear to combine the advantages of purposeful leadership, a developmentally oriented doctrine, the capacity both to mobilize and to discipline widespread support and participation, and the ability to deploy a variety of action and communication instruments. For these reasons, this type of regime seems to be particularly relevant to the needs of transitional societies undergoing rapid and radical transformation" (1963).

c. *The Power Structure*

As WITH SINGLE ORGANIZATIONS, the total structure of a society emerges from the role interrelations provided by hierarchy, polyarchy and codes of behavior.

To rise above the details of these relationships and obtain a perspective on the system as a whole, it is essential to consider the distribution of power within it. Who are the people who make which decisions? Where are the centers of power?

For the leaders of any important organization within a society these are the kind of questions which, precisely because they are so important, are hard to ask. Some sort of answers to them—no matter how limited —are part of the "tacit knowledge" of skillful administrators. But when experienced administrators become involved in more extensive relations within their own society, they are likely to find their previous answers less relevant. If they attempt relations with other societies, they may lose their bearings completely.

In previous chapters we have attacked the myths of central omnipotence by analyzing the factors that bring about a dispersion of intra-organizational power. We shall now concentrate upon interorganizational power—the distribution of power in a society as a whole.

Here also we find an inevitable dispersion of power. This does not deny the existence of extremely significant differences in the pattern of dispersion. These variations will be discussed in the subsequent sections on democratic and dictatorial patterns and on stratification.

1. THE DISPERSION OF INTERORGANIZATIONAL POWER

The underlying factor in the dispersion of power within any society is pluralism of interests. No matter what the degree of concentrated formal authority may be, this underlying pluralism makes itself felt in actions that are not totally subordinate to the authority wielders. To the extent that these dispersed interests are expressed by groups, organizations, cliques and coalitions they are transformed into significant power centers.

To the naïve observer, the primitive tribe—with its tribal chief and strong traditions from the past—might appear an exception to this rule. The anthropologists, however, have revealed the deep conflicts that are an inseparable part of tribal existence. An indication of the dispersion of power in a small tribe of about 17,000 people in Northern Rhodesia is provided by Turner (1957, p. 89-90):

> Beneath all other conflicts in Ndembu society is the concealed opposition between men and women over descent and the economic system. Influenced by this basic opposition, but possessing their own autonomy, sets of struggles arise within the social structure: conflicts between persons and between groups who invoke different principles of residential affiliation to support and justify their own specific interests, political, jural and economic; struggles between persons and groups couched in terms of a common norm which each party claims the other has broken; and conflicts between persons, united by a single principle of descent and residence, for positions of authority determined by that principle.

When societies become larger and more complex, other patterns of power dispersion develop. In feudal societies, dispersion is written into the system by the distribution of fiefs and the relative lack of horizontal interaction. The effort to establish greater control by a monarch brings him into direct conflict with the aristocratic nobility. The dispersion pattern is made more complicated by the entry into the fray of organized churchmen, merchants, artisans, and occasional "anomic" groups of peasants. Under such circumstances a large state or empire can be brought into being only by coming to terms with diversity. This is one of the central factors that made it possible for the Romans to build a much larger and longer-lasting empire than the Athenians. They were willing to give Roman citizenship to the people of conquered territories. In fact, a large part of Roman law was based on the recognition of greatly disparate interests throughout the Empire. The Athenians were a tighter "in-group." They felt that the "polis" which they loved would be destroyed by extending Athenian citizenship to others (Kitto, 1951). Instead they relied on semiprofessional military force to keep their empire together and were soon destroyed by the more professional and specialized military forces that rolled down from Macedonia.

With the development of large bureaucratic organizations, the pattern of power dispersion changes but the dispersion continues. Bureaucracies tend to become competing or countervailing sources of power. In the military forces this competition develops among the different branches and field commands. In the civilian government it is found among the different branches and the various agencies within each branch. A still greater dispersion is usually found among buying and selling organizations. As these organizations become larger, we usually see many "concentrations" of power in various sectors. Under such circumstances the pattern becomes one of the dispersion of power among giants rather than pygmies. At the same time new power centers usually arise with the emergence of different kinds of associations and political parties and factions.

But what happens when the giants get together?

The simplest way to get together is polyarchic relations among different organizations. As pointed out in Chapter 15, polyarchy may take the form of either dispersed or shared responsibility. In the first case, we see the kind of dispersion that takes place among negotiators and bargainers. In the second case, we see the more integrated form of dispersion that takes place within any collegial body. In both cases, it is possible for larger and larger concentrations of power to emerge through coalitions—formal or informal, fleeting or enduring—of different groups. In fact, the power to get things done in collegial bodies comes into being only through some type of coalition. But it is hardly possible—without a hierarchic umbrella—for any coalition to bring together all the significant sources of power in a society. Even if it were possible, it must be remembered that a coalition—whether a "holy" or "unholy" alliance among "natural" or "strange" bedfellows—represents a special pattern of power dispersion: ". . . group power can be extended through combinations only at a discount. While these discounts will vary in size, even when they seem comparatively small, they are an integral part of the power structure of a society" (*Gross*, p. 148-150).

The more ambitious way to develop a centralized pattern is to bring polyarchic relations within a framework of hierarchic subordination. This can be attempted on a truly extensive scale only by an organization capable of making legitimate use of force and violence, namely a government. The most ambitious effort to centralize social power in government is the totalitarian effort to convert society into one big organization. Although some of the organizers of the French Revolution envisioned a society of this type, their vision died with them on the guillotine. More than a century later, inspired in part by the spectacle of ever-larger organization by business corporations, this vision was reborn in the ideologies of the Italian Fascists, the German Nazis, and the Russian and Chinese communists.

But despite the ideological trappings of modern totalitarianism, large-scale organization in society as a whole is very much the same as in a single corporation or government agency. The only difference is that a society is usually more diffuse. Thus in a totalitarian society the dispersion of intraorganizational power is automatically transformed into the law of the dispersion of interorganizational power.

In a totalitarian society this dispersion is rooted in the highly specialized role differentiation. Here, the growth of bureaucracy to greater proportions than in any other society means a vast increase in the number of small, specialized domains of knowledge and power. These dispersed power centers can be brought together in part by polyarchic relations and by codes of behavior. But still greater reliance is placed upon the "hierarchic umbrella." Hierarchy can mature, however, only with substantial delegations of authority, which themselves become a springboard for dispersed power. Moreover, more complex hierarchic forms produce ever greater ambiguities and conflicts concerning the divisions of authority. They increasingly provide for not merely dual but multiple hierarchy. Within each military and civilian organization in the U.S.S.R., for example, the pattern of divided authority is as complex as in any large business or government organization in the U.S.A. Each such agency, in addition, is subjected to the authority of various agents of the Communist Party, the secret police, the State Bank, the Ministry of Finance, and the Ministry of State Control. In turn, the formal determinations of the structure of the state-society invariably give rise to a tremendous amount of informal roles, hierarchies, codes of behavior, and polyarchy. Whether more of these supplement the formal structure or more of them counteract it is not relevant to this discussion. In either case, they undoubtedly contribute to the dispersion of power within the Soviet society.

2. DEMOCRATIC AND DICTATORIAL POWER PATTERNS

If we have established the existence of a pattern of dispersed power in any totalitarian society, the classic case of centralized power, we have effectively destroyed the idea of central omnipotence as it applies to a society as a whole.

But we may at the same time have created the false impression that if power is dispersed in both totalitarian and democratic societies, there is no real difference between the two. To eliminate such an impression and to refine our discussion of the social environment within which organizations operate, we shall therefore distinguish between the dictatorial and the democratic patterns of power dispersion.

As with single organizations, the democratic nature of a society can best be measured by asking the question: *Who participates how deeply in what?* In Chapter 16 we discussed this question in terms of organizational democracy and dictatorship. Here we shall discuss it also in terms of political, economic, social, and individual democracy. These are additional ways of dealing with the "what" of our central question.

Political democracy entails a wide and deep participation in the great decisions concerning the top personnel of government and the general direction of government policy. In elections a substantial portion of adults are given an opportunity to choose between candidates of opposing parties or factions. Between elections it is possible to effectuate changes in policy through pressure, propaganda and negotiation by various organizations. In part, the extent of these democratic processes may be appraised by the nature of the electoral system and the freedom to organize and campaign (traditionally referred to as the freedoms of assembly, religion, petition, speech and press). But democratic forms and freedoms can be ignored by the people or exploited by dictators. The more important measure is the actual extent to which people take advantage of these rights.

In addition to political democracy there are four other modes of widespread participation in the various activities of a society. In each of these the *what* is somewhat further from the great global questions of statesmanship and politics but much closer to the daily lives of people. *Organizational democracy*, as pointed out in the previous chapter, makes it possible for more members of the organization to participate more deeply on matters that affect their personal work and the activity of their organization. *Economic democracy* provides people with opportunities for useful, satisfying, and remunerative employment, including the educational facilities that make it possible to take advantage of such opportunities. *Social democracy* provides guarantees that political and economic rights shall not be impaired because of a person's color, race, caste, religion, national origin, or sex. This is the area of democracy often referred to by the term "civil rights." Finally, *individual democracy* provides the individual with what Mosca called "juridical defense" against injustice at the hands of those who are stronger. Here we find the codes of "civil liberties," "due process," and the specialized organizations whose role it is to enforce such codes.

The interrelations between these five pillars of democracy are intimate.

None of them can be strong if the others are extremely weak. In the absence of social democracy political democracy may indeed exist—but as the privileged way of life for only a segment of the population. With the sustained impairment of economic or individual democracy it will crumble into dust. With a low level of political democracy, in turn, organizational democracy can scarcely develop in more than a spotty manner.

Nevertheless, the development of these five forms of democracy is always uneven. Society A will push ahead faster on political and individual democracy, B on economic democracy, C on social democracy. Many of the disputes as to which of the three is more democratic stem from confusion as to which form of democracy is being discussed. There is no doubt but that many of the democratic societies which boast the loudest concerning the quality of their democracy are seriously backward in two or more of these fields. There is also no doubt but that important aspects of democracy in some of these fields have developed within the framework of dictatorial regimes. Still more aspects of democracy have often developed in aristocratic societies. Political and individual democracy, in fact, were propably first born in the struggles between monarchs and aristocrats. The nobility and the gentry may act democratically in conducting their relations with others at the same level in society. The effort to win allies from lower levels may mean a cautious and limited extension of these privileges. Such extension becomes still more meaningful when it is used by people at lower levels as a springboard for breaking down the social barriers.

So-called "absolute monarchies" are the oldest forms of dictatorship. Here the Emperor, King, God-King, Tyrant, or Despot often wields the arbitrary power to kill, jail, punish, or promote anyone in the country. But the "absoluteness" of this power is counterbalanced by the narrow area in which it can be exerted. This is well illustrated in Riggs' analysis of the Siamese monarchy, one of the most "absolute" in world history. The King of Siam spent most of his time on elaborate religious ceremonies and court rituals. If he had tried to devote himself to national problems and policies instead, he would have been acting like a man instead of a god, thereby undermining the divine basis of his authority.

> But even if he were to devote himself in this way to administrative tasks, he would lack the machinery, the communications net, for transmitting policy to the country, and carrying it out in day-to-day affairs. . . . Local magnates—ranging from high patriots to parochial strong men—ran affairs much as they pleased. All deferred in awe to the sacred power of the king, but one reason for their willingness to recognize the court was its willingness to leave local questions and rules alone, provided traditional dues and services to the crown were forthcoming (1961, p. 75-76).

The modern authoritarian dictatorship covers a wider area. Its essential aspect is the suppression of political democracy by eliminating the legal means for the peaceful replacement of the top personnel of government. Opposition parties are allowed to operate only if they do so as "straw men." Otherwise they are liquidated by killing or jailing opposition leaders or forcing them into foreign exile or underground operations. To prevent the growth of new opposition centers, freedom of organization, speech, and the press is prevented or curtailed. This also leads to unpredictable infringements of whatever individual democracy may have existed in the past. The past levels of social democracy may or may not be impaired. Depending on the specific circumstances the level of economic democracy may change slightly for the better or for the worse.

The totalitarian dictatorship is a "horse of another color." Its leaders are driven by messianic visions of tremendous personal and national achievement. They are not satisfied with the curtailment of political democracy. They strike at social democracy by using various minority groups as scapegoats. They tear up whatever individual democracy has existed by making the ruling party or faction the sole source to which an individual can turn for defense. Through vigorous programs of economic expansion they may eliminate unemployment but often at the price of curtailing individual choice of employment opportunities. Above all, they attack organizational democracy at its roots by trying to integrate all significant forms of human organization into the one big organization of the state. This means bringing all trade unions, professional and scientific associations, and religious, age, sex, cultural, national, communal, and recreational organizations under the umbrella of the government and party hierarchy. Not even the family is exempt from this drive. In the heyday of Nazi and Bolshevik fervor children were not only encouraged to leave their families; they were encouraged to denounce their parents. In the "brainwashing" operations in the "thought" reform colleges in Communist China, it is reported that in the final confession which every student must submit before being reborn as a member of the Chinese Communist Community the "central feature is the denunciation of the father, both as a symbol of the exploiting classes, and as an individual" (Lifton, 1960, p. 488). All such efforts are accompanied by a thorough mobilization of the press, radio, television, schools, and arts for the ceaseless reiteration of the dominant ideology, goals, and myths and for the diversion of attention from internal problems to external enemies. In turn, this entails a serious effort to block off communications with people in other societies.

There is no doubt that the leaders of a totalitarian society can mobilize a tremendous amount of power through such efforts. They can divert more resources from consumption to investment than either a democracy or an authoritarian dictatorship. They can do much better than either in concentrating investment in carefully selected sectors. To the extent that they are successful in their various projects they can win over a substantial portion of the population to their style of doing things. But these potentialities are not unmixed blessings. They also serve to nourish the intrigues, cabals, plots, and counterplots that are warp and woof of the coalition of elite groups and power centers. In this situation the often-discussed struggle for power revolving around the position of top man is far less important than it may seem. What importance the struggle has derives more from its relation to the deeper struggles among the political lieutenants whom Neumann calls the "forgotten men in most discussions of the totalitarian state" (1942, p. 73). These are the hundreds of people who are locked in bitter struggle for the number two, three, and four positions in the government, secret police, armed services, industry, and educational and cultural institutions.

On top of all this, power is diffused ever more widely by the essential elements of large-scale organization—the division of labor, hierarchy, polyarchy and the codes that are required to protect the increasing plurality of interests. Whatever success the one big organization has in its ventures depends more and more upon an ever-more refined specialization of labor and the development of large fragmented elites of specialists, professionals and scientists. Multiple oligarchy becomes still more multiple. The old coalitions and clusters become more complex and fluid. A proportionately smaller number of issues can be settled or dodged by the gas chamber, the firing squad, the mock trial, imprisonment, or banishment. As a new generation of experts arises to take the place of the "old men" who established the totalitarian state, the old myths tend to become ritualistic verbiage. The old methods of mass indoctrination lead to tedium, withdrawal, or open or suppressed rebellion. To retain power, the old-timers try to broaden their base by using the techniques of a Khrushchev or Tito instead of a Stalin. But in the face of the assault by the new generation, there is no way of restoring the old ways without a new ideology or the crisis situation of international war. The first is unlikely without the second. The second threatens the very existence of the state-society. Thus sustained peace holds forth the possibility of conversion to an authoritarian dictatorship and the slow emergence of varying degrees of political, organizational, economic, social and individual democracy. The regime may survive but only at the price of internal change.

3. STRATIFICATION

What effect does stratification have on the power structure of society? An extreme answer to this question is provided by Mosca's version of the myth of central omnipotence. In all societies, according to Mosca, "two classes appear—a class that rules and a class that is ruled. The first class, always the less numerous, performs all political functions, monopolizes power and enjoys the advantages that power brings . . . (1939, p. 50). Marx and Engels were more realistic. In dealing with earlier periods of history they recognized many classes in society. Although in dealing with the midnineteenth century they narrowed down to two great classes, the bourgeoisie and the proletariat, they recognized various substrata within each. Above all, their theory of class conflict recognized the existence of a certain amount of proletarian power (as distinguished from formal authority) rather than a complete monopoly of power by the bourgeoisie. A Marxian analysis of the class structure of any society is in fact a tool for discovering its power structure.

Any analysis of social strata, however, must use far more tools than those provided by old-fashioned or modernized Marxism. It must recognize all the determinants of social status other than economic roles. It must deal with the full range of strata in society and with mobility within classes and from one class to another. It must be able to cope with the special type of class system found in India's four great *varnas*, the thousands of *jatis* or subcastes which compose the *varnas*, and the "outcastes."

Above all, in analyzing social strata we must take pains to recognize the new-style stratification ushered in by the administrative revolution. This is a stratification based largely on position within the formal hierarchy of organizations, modified by a ranking of various organizations and occupations. A person's salary or other income attached to any position is particularly important. As a common measure applicable to all organizations, it provides a quick first approximation that can then be modified in the light of other considerations. With an increasing number of fine gradations and distinctions, the old lines between "proletariat," the "bourgeoisie," and "nobility" become meaningless. The term "middle class" becomes vestigial verbiage.

In considering the effect of stratification on the diffusion of power, the first consideration is the extent of mobility that is possible from one stratum to a higher one. If people are frozen to one lower stratum by a class or caste to which they have been born, this is the greatest of all limitations on social democracy. It usually means a low level of economic and organizational democracy. At the same time, within the limits of their frozen position, they may enjoy a certain amount of individual democracy. They may even play a role in political democracy.

Similarly, when there is a high degree of mobility, stratification serves as a contribution to organizational, economic and social democracy—without necessarily impinging upon political or individual democracy. It is not easy to climb a ladder with elastic or invisible rungs. The hierarchies of large-scale organization often provide ladders and rungs that can be depended upon—or at least provide a healthy challenge to people with ability, energy and ambition.

Nor should it be thought that the existence of a top stratum implies a major concentration of power at the top. In India, for example, the highest castes are of the Brahmin *varna*. Historically, the Brahmins have supplied India with most of its intellectuals and top priests. The second category, the Kshatriyas or warriors, comprised those castes which legitimated their status as traditional kings and lesser rulers. In India and in all other countries there are many areas of decision-making that are handled almost entirely by people in the lower strata, and where higher strata people would not be either willing or able to intrude. It might also be added that the peculiar pattern of power diffusion provided by the Indian style of caste system is entirely inconsistent with the power pattern of modern totalitarianism. Strange as it may sound, the caste system in India is a barrier to both democracy *and* totalitarianism.

In considering the relation of stratification to power, however, we must remember that no social stratum—no matter how tight and clear its boundaries may be—is equivalent to a center of power. At the most, it represents a power potential based on an underlying communality of interests. This potential is not automatically realized. It must be exploited by leaders and organizers. Moreover, the communality of interests may also be interwoven with—and usually is—all sorts of divergent or conflicting interests. These too may be exploited through organized effort. The most that a class will do is drift aimlessly, respond haphazardly to stimuli from various directions, or follow in the wake of one or more centers of organized action. In any of these cases, power is mobilized not by classes or more specialized strata but rather by organized groups—whether political parties, government agencies, business organizations, associations or, religious groups—or clusters and constellations of such groups. Hence for the purpose of understanding social change, the analysis of social strata provides us merely with the essential background for the analysis of the actual array of organizations.

D. *The Value Structure*

THE VALUE STRUCTURE of a society is *a patterned set of general attitudes concerning what is desirable or undesirable.* It expresss the way in which the basic human interests of survival, commergence, differentiation and self-development have emerged in that society. At a higher level of generality than specific purposes, it indicates how people behave in trying to satisfy these interests.

No organization can escape the value structure of the society in which it operates. It is not merely something that affects the organization through its relations with the external environment. It enters the organization through the values of its members and is thus moulding the very "personality" of the organization itself.

Nor can the members of any organization—whether government agency, corporation, or union—escape a serious "culture shock" when they enter into intimate relations with organizations in other societies. Apart from the simpler difficulties resulting from differences in language, food, and climate, they are bound to receive a cumulative series of "sudden jolts" resulting from differences in basic values (Cleveland, Mangone and Adams, 1960, p. 26-45). This may easily lead to an exaggerated conception as to the nature of these differences.

There is probably no aspect of any society more difficult to analyze than its value structure. The "cultural relativity" approach of sociologists and anthropologists has tended to overemphasize the differences among societies. As Kluckhohn has pointed out, too little research has yet been done on the universal values that stem from the physiological, psychological, and social similarities of people in all societies (in Parsons and Shils, 1951, p. 395). In any society, moreover, values vary considerably in intensity, durability, and extensiveness throughout a population. Value conflicts and sharp deviations from both proclaimed and accepted values are inescapable. Values are rooted in allegiances to particular organizations and organizational roles. They are deeply affected by a great variety of beliefs and disbeliefs, both religious and secular. It is small wonder, therefore, that studies of values often lead to long lists ranging from high metaphysical abstractions to specific preferences, prescriptions and prohibitions.

For the purposes of our study, we shall concentrate upon a small number of elements that enter every value structure and have an unmistakable effect on organizational activity. By emphasizing the varying forms in which they appear we hope to avoid the traps awaiting those who use ready-made stereotypes of "national character."

1. NATIONALISM AND LOCALISM

Nationalism is a conspicuous element in the value structure of many societies. It provides the "sense of identity" which is as important for a society as it is for an individual. By emphasizing common national interests or traits, it meets human needs for commergence. By emphasizing national pride, honor, and power, it meets human needs for differentiation.

The common element in all nationalism is the consciousness or display of differences. This is expressed in terms of not only a special cultural heritage but also an innate sense of national superiority. The sons of Israel were not the only "chosen people." The native tribes of North and South America looked down on the invaders from Europe. The Africans and Malayans felt themselves superior in many ways to the traders and settlers from India and China. The Indians and Chinese know they are superior to the North Americans with respect to "things that really matter." People in the U.S.A. tend to regard the "American way of life" as the best in the world, to be at least admired, if not copied, by others.

Beyond this common core there are many differences. One of these can be expressed by the continuum between the polar extremes of what Williams calls "totalistic" and "pluralistic" nationalism (1960, p. 456-460). The former is a "100 per cent" attitude of fanatical devotion to some vague national myths. Externally, it is expressed in isolationist or autarchic attempts to withdraw from the world or expansionist efforts to dominate it. Internally, it is expressed in discriminatory attitudes toward minority groups, thus impeding the development of organizational, social, and individual democracy. "Pluralistic" nationalism, on the other hand, emphasizes such specific values as democracy, religious freedom, or higher living standards. In a more quiet and less flamboyant way, it may be no less a source of national pride and honor. Either form of nationalism, in turn, may well lead to the adjustment of organizational purposes to take into account the "national interest."

Another difference lies in the extent of subnationalism within a society. In a country like India, with at least fourteen linguistic areas and separable cultural backgrounds, local loyalties are so great as to hold forth the constant threat of separatist movements. Under such circumstances national values may be little more than a thin veneer. In countries where important local and regional values are represented in the national power structure, separatism is unthinkable. In fact, the conflict among local values may be an integrating rather than a divisive force. Similarly, the binational loyalties of Japanese-Americans, Irish-American and Italian-Americans—when not carried to an extreme point—may strengthen instead of weaken national spirit in the U.S.A. Nor need nationalism itself necessarily be an impediment to supranational values. With the growth of the European community the Frenchmen who consider themselves Europeans do not necessarily give up being Frenchmen. Multiple membership and multiple loyalties are social phenomena capable of covering international groupings as well as the family, workplace, church, and club.

2. INDIVIDUAL AND GROUP INTEREST

Another variable is the extent to which the people of any society are oriented toward the satisfaction of individual or group interests. For Parsons, this is the "pattern variable" of "self orientation" versus "collectivity orientation," for Kluckhohn the "self-other" dichotomy, and for countless others the continuum from individualism, freedom, or autonomy, to conformity, standardization, and control. The importance of this variable to the administration of organizations is obvious. It affects the purpose patterns of organizations, the extent of cooperation that can be expected, and the usefulness of alternative administrative practices.

Yet there are few social values as misleading or as hotly debated as this one. In human society self interest and group interest are always intertwined; neither can exist in isolation from the other. The various patterns of intertwining are exceedingly complex. Their nature, moreover, is frequently beclouded by proclaimed values which serve to embroider more dominant values. The more dominant values, in turn, may be sharply conflicting. Thus along with individual personality, equality, and freedom Williams lists external conformity as a dominant value in the U.S.A. (1960, p. 450-454). Thus the "classic" values of American democracy have been expressed in the ideas of the dignity of the individual, "rugged individualism," opposition to tyranny, impatience with hierarchical authority. At the same time America has traditionally been a "nation of joiners." The most rugged individualists were organization builders. The most vehement opponents of governmental hierarchy either are at or aspire to the upper levels of nongovernment hierarchies. The devotees of the "sacredness of the human personality" may themselves be "cheerful robots" carefully conforming to the standards of their or-

In part, these contradictions can be resolved by distinguishing between the values placed on different groups. In one society the self may be more ganization or social stratum.

closely identified with families, in another with private groups or associations. In one society government may be seen as a far-away or hostile
entity, in another as an instrument for limited ends, in still another as
more completely linked with self interest.

In part, they can be resolved by focussing on specific kinds of behavior. In some societies the value of the individual is illustrated by laws
against suicide, while in others *hari-kari* or *suttee* may be permissible.
In some societies the importance of protecting all individuals against injustice leads to universalistic regulations tempered by nondiscriminatory
efforts at judicial equity proceedings. In other societies the approach is
more particularistic in the first instance, with justice considered more in
terms of each individual's social status.

Yet contradictions in this area cannot be avoided. Genuine conformity
to group interests may be associated with a large amount of individual
autonomy. It may, in fact, as Dalton has found, serve as protective color-
ation for covert "freewheeling" (*Dalton*, 1959). Or, as Williams has suggested, "the looser the package, the tighter the string—if the package is
to hold together at all" (1960, p. 453).

3. ACCEPTANCE vs. ACTIVISM

A more clearly dichotomous variable is found in the continuum from
acceptance to activism.

In some societies it seems natural and expedient to accept the world
as it is or events as they develop. Whatever is, is by that token acceptable.
Whatever happens would have happened anyway. The present order of
human relations cannot be changed, so why try? It is not given to man
to fathom the order in human nature. Anyone—other than a magician—
who thinks he can read the future is a madman. Anyone who tries to
do much to control it is a fool whom the gods will probably destroy.
In such societies high value is placed upon leisure, inactivity, contemplation, and mysticism. Activism is reserved for a privileged few who must
also make their obeisances to the unknown and the inscrutable.

In other societies, particularly those already hit by the ongoing wave
of the administrative revolution, we find what Parsons refers to as "instrumental activism" (1951, p. 180-200). Here, in contrast, we find widespread acceptance of the idea of human progress based on a more orderly,
predictable universe and on the power of human rationality as expressed
in science and technology. At times this idea of progress will be expressed in grandiose messianic visions of Heaven on earth, of a world
without poverty, despair, or unhappiness. At times it will be concretized
by what the economists call the "demonstration effect" of the benefits

that others have achieved through the more rational production and distribution of goods and services. This is the "revolution of rising expectations," expectations that are not limited to economics but are founded on the more general assumption that any aspect of the world can be changed by activism. Instead of thinking of the future in terms of the next few centuries, people tend to concentrate on four, five or six year plans. They divide up the future into scheduled activities. They develop and constantly refine conceptions of economy, efficiency and practicality. People are expected to "keep busy," "do something," and "get someplace in the world." In such societies the task of administering an organization is entirely different than in those where acceptance is still a dominant factor. Activity, speed, and technique become human values in their own right.

But here, too, although the differences are much greater than in the case of self and group interest, there are internal contradictions in every society. Where acceptance values have long been dominant, newer generations are bound to become activists and fight the older generations on this ground. Where activism has long been established, a growing number of people will start to wonder where they are really going.

4. THE "SPIRIT" AND MATERIALISM

In some societies the greatest values are placed on "things of the spirit." People and relations with them are deemed more important than goods or services. The mass of the people places great emphasis on ritual, custom, and ceremonies. The elite are interested in esthetic matters. The nonactivist elite are given over to a life of contemplation. Faith or mysticism are dominant elements of religion and philosophy.

In the more materialist society, material comforts—from the simplest necessities of life to the greatest of luxuries—rank at the top level of desirability. The hope of a higher level of consumption is the major motivator in economic growth. The promise of a higher level of consumption—apart from due attention to external threats—is the major promise of political leaders. "Conspicuous consumption" becomes a principle that shapes not only the dress, eating, housing, and locomotion of individuals and families, but also the buildings, furnishings and *décor* of corporations, associations, and government agencies. Nor is it limited to goods. Materialism also embraces the less tangible services provided by multitudinous adviser assistants or servants and by athletics, recreation, and entertainment. Tremendous energies are dedicated to the design, production and aggressive marketing of an increasing variety of all these material comforts.

This distinction has been used by Northrop (1946) in trying to define the difference between Eastern and Western civilizations. He finds the "highly ineffable and mystical quality of Oriental culture" rooted in concentrated attention "upon the nature of all things in their emotional and ethetic, purely empirical and positivist immediacy." Western civilization, in contrast, is oriented toward materialist conceptions of utility and economy. This leads to rational and nonmystical theory, science, and technology. The "reconciliation of the East and the West" can best be found, Northrop urges, by achieving a society which combines the orderly, scientific and systematic values of the West "with the compassion, the universal sensitivity to the beautiful, and the abiding equanimity and calm joy of the spirit which characterizes the sages and many of the humbler people of the Orient."

The two approaches, however, are in fact often combined under less impressive circumstances. Many of the "humble people of the Orient" have been thoroughly enslaved by the unavoidable, and ultramaterialistic, preoccupation with where, when, and how they and their children get their next meal. "Abiding equanimity" can be sharply disturbed by the intrusion of destitution and disease. The effort to introduce Western living standards and Western methods of attaining them has often led Easterners to a deeper and more thoroughgoing materialism than their most critical sages could possibly find and condemn in the West. On the other hand, many Westerners whose material appetites are easily satiated are mainly interested in things of the spirit. They may hide these interests behind the more publicly accepted façade of a drive for prestige, power or money. Behind this façade, freed from any concern with additional material comforts, they give themselves over to the life of learning, emotional and esthetic creativity and self-development.

5. COMMUNICATION

Other differences among societies are found in the varying values placed on alternative modes of communication. Organizational and administrative behavior in different cultures may be deeply affected by the balance between verbal and nonverbal communication, the pace of communication, the balance between honesty and deviousness, and the degree of indirection or directness. Hammond points out that indirection in communication is highly institutionalized in non-Western societies. In contrast, he finds (although without indicating that he has examined the American scene carefully enough) that it "is negatively sanctioned in American culture and must be relied upon covertly (1959). In his study of friction between Americans and Mexicans in Mexico, Fayerweather (1959, p. 25-27) reports that in Mexico indirection is used much more than in the United States as a means of avoiding tensions and conflicts. The formalities of etiquette, protocol, and organizational rituals, which differ extensively from country to country, are themselves often devices for channeling communication toward relief from tension and conflict. In some societies written communications also serve as a means of avoiding the possible tensions inherent in person-to-person relationships. In others they are often used as a mere convenience in facilitating person-to-person discussions, as with the case of discussion drafts. In still others this usage is rare; once it is written down a message acquires an aura of formal authority placing it beyond the realm of discussion.

But there is more to language than words alone. As Hall pointed out (1961), every culture has informal communication patterns. Some of these are found in the tone of voice or "superfix." Others are found in gestures, the contexts in which words are used, and even in the distance between two people who are talking with each other. The words alone express little more than the score of a Beethoven symphony. The specific culture of the society converts the formal notation into genuine music.

In all societies the basic network of communication is provided by face-to-face contacts. A major overlay is provided by the more impersonal communication networks of larger and more bureaucratic organizations. This overlay becomes deeper with the development of the administrative revolution. At the same time, a third layer comes into being with the development of the mass media organizations of the press, radio, television and cinema. This creates a complex communication system in which it is possible for increasingly large quantities of information to move with increasing speed through ever wider segments of the population. The very abundance of information enhances the role of interpreters and opinion leaders. Without them the top executives of large organizations—even more than ordinary people—would be helpless in the face of the growing information overload. This is an adaptation of "the two-step flow of communication" hypothesis set forth in Katz and Lazarsfeld (1955).